Penguin True Crime
The Dominici Affair

One of the best-known journalists in France, Jean Laborde
was legal correspondent on *France-Soir* for many years before
becoming legal correspondent for the mass-circulation daily
L'Aurore in 1964. Now retired from journalism, he lives in the
Pays Basque. He has also written numerous novels, many of
which have been made into films.

The Dominici Affair was a huge success in France and won
much praise. It was made into a film starring Jean Gabin in
the role of Gaston Dominici.

THE DOMINICI AFFAIR

Jean Laborde

Translated by Milton Waldman

PENGUIN BOOKS

It is a pleasure to acknowledge the help given me in the writing of this book by my friend and colleague Raymond Calame. – J.L.

PENGUIN BOOKS

Published by the Penguin Group
27 Wrights Lane, London W8 5TZ, England
Viking Penguin Inc., 40 West 23rd Street, New York, New York 10010, USA
Penguin Books Australia Ltd, Ringwood, Victoria, Australia
Penguin Books Canada Ltd, 2801 John Street, Markham, Ontario, Canada L3R 1B4
Penguin Books (NZ) Ltd, 182–190 Wairau Road, Auckland 10, New Zealand

Penguin Books Ltd, Registered Offices: Harmondsworth, Middlesex, England

First published in France 1972
This translation first published in Great Britain by William Collins Sons & Co. Ltd 1974
Published in Penguin Books 1989
10 9 8 7 6 5 4 3 2 1

Printed and bound in Great Britain by
Richard Clay Ltd, Bungay, Suffolk

Contents

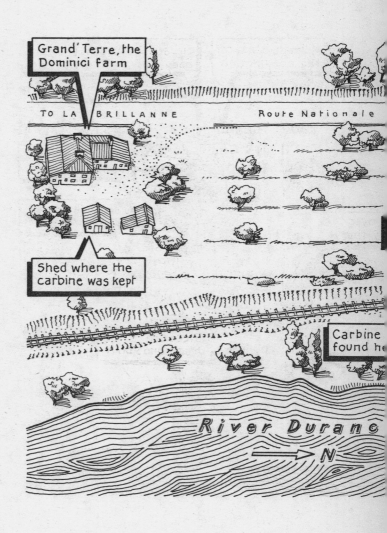

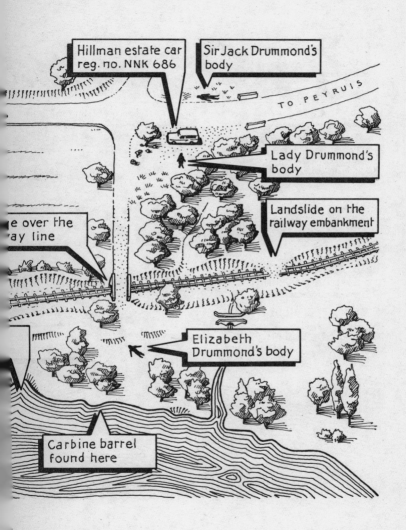

The Murders
August 5, 1952

1

Hands on hips, Faustin Roure, railway foreman at Lurs, a small village in southern France, contemplated the landslide on the river-bank at point 319,280 kilometres on the Marseilles–Digne line. The situation was serious but not catastrophic. The 8.0 a.m. express could pass, and that was the main thing. The amount of earth was considerable; about twelve cubic metres.

Gustave Dominici, son of the owner of the nearest farm, known as *La Grand'Terre*, had cleared the actual rails; mud now covered the track for a distance of only some four metres. Legally Gustave was responsible for the landslide: on the days immediately preceding he had watered his field above the railway line too liberally and was liable to a fine calculated on the number of minutes a train might be delayed. The previous evening an uneasy Gustave had come to see Roure at Peyruis, the nearest village, to report the incident. Faustin had promised to have a look in the morning.

On August 5, 1952 it was already very hot by 7.0 a.m. and the pale blue sky confirmed the onset of the dog days. The River Durance was very low; there had been a long spell of dry weather. A light mist, remnant of the evaporating dew, drifted above the mountain towards Ganagobie.

Faustin Roure decided to return in the afternoon with five or six workmen. It would take only a few minutes to remove the earth that still obstructed the traffic. The other essential was to cut away the broken branches of an acacia entangled in the telephone wires.

Faustin returned to the stony path which led to Route Nationale 96 at the side of which he had left his motor-cycle. At the bridge which crosses the railway he joined his assistant, Clovis Dominici, Gustave's brother, who seemed to be gazing at something on the bank of the River Durance.

'Have you seen it?' Clovis asked.

'Yes,' answered the foreman. 'It's not serious,' thinking Clovis was referring to the landslide. Clovis no longer lived at Grand'Terre. The eldest of the Dominici sons and now an employee of the State Railways, he lived at Peyruis. But the Dominicis – nine children, nineteen grandchildren – were a closely-knit family. Clovis often went to help his brother who worked the farm, while the father, the 'patriarch', 75-year-old Gaston, contented himself with taking his goats into the mountains.

But Clovis shook his head. 'Look,' he said, pointing to a spot halfway down to the Durance where, in the dry grass, lay the body of a child. 'She's dead,' he added.

Behind him Faustin Roure noticed Marcel Boyer, another railway linesman, a Dominici brother-in-law who had accompanied him. Faustin, on his motor-cycle, had overtaken them on their bicycles. They were on their way to work at the Lurs station. Faustin did not know that Clovis and Boyer had first stopped at Grand'Terre.

The three men started towards the body. 'She's dead,' Clovis repeated.

After a moment's silence they turned round and went up again towards the main road. No words passed between them. Faustin Roure didn't dare question Clovis about how he had discovered the body. Clovis was walking a little ahead, his shoulders hunched.

A few metres from the road Faustin stopped short at sight of a spectacle to which he had paid no attention on his arrival a quarter of an hour earlier. On the other side of the road, on a grassy spot separated from it by a ditch, stood a camp-bed; beneath it lay a body, with only the feet exposed. Faustin wondered if he was dreaming; it was there that he had shut off the engine of his motor-cycle, but he had noticed nothing out of the ordinary as he crossed the road to lean his motor-cycle against a tree. He had seen a car parked near a mulberry tree surrounded by a lot of clutter, but he hadn't paid particular attention to it; the campers had doubtless gone down to the Durance to bathe and wash up.

Faustin Roure now noted details which were to remain engraved on his memory. He noticed that the feet protruding from the bed wore sandals and grey socks. Six inches of the lower part of the leg were visible, 'but,' he stated later to Superintendent Chenevier, 'there was no flesh exposed.' An astonishingly clear recollection. But the circumstances themselves were exceptional. Every witness in this extraordinary affair would be called on to repeat his state-

12

ments so often that it became for each one a lesson as familiar and mechanical as the multiplication tables.

The three men then noticed the third body. It lay between the car and the river, two metres from, and parallel to the car and covered by a rug. 'It's a massacre!' Faustin exclaimed.

Clovis nodded agreement. Unlike the visual details, Faustin could never recall the few phrases they exchanged. He talked without thinking, terrified by what he was seeing.

He went to collect his motor-cycle, Clovis and Boyer their bicycles, and they started for Grand'Terre, but after several metres Clovis mounted his machine and hurried on ahead. Boyer followed him and when Faustin Roure arrived in the courtyard of the farm, the two were already there, forming a group with Gustave, his mother, Marie Dominici, his wife Yvette, a pretty brunette of twenty, and a fourth linesman, Roger Drac, whom a call of nature had delayed on his way.

'About one in the morning we heard shots,' Yvette was telling her brother-in-law Clovis at the moment Faustin Roure joined them.

'We thought they were poachers,' Gustave put in. Uneasy, Faustin Roure asked if they had notified the police.

'Gustave stopped a motor-cyclist on the road,' said Clovis, 'and asked him to go as quickly as possible to Oraison.' From this Faustin inferred that Gustave had already been over to the car. He decided that there was nothing more for him to do at Grand'Terre, nor for the three members of his crew; there was no shortage of work at the station. There were rails to be relaid and checked at several points. A triple murder was not his business once the police had been notified. In any event it was better to keep out of this sort of thing. The railway foreman had no inkling of the proportions the inquiry would assume.

'All right, lads,' he said, 'back to the job.' Marcel Boyer and Roger Drac at once obeyed. Clovis still lingered with his brother. Then he in turn mounted his bicycle. Faustin Roure decided to return to Peyruis; he had to warn the Inspector of Posts and Telegraphs of the danger from the broken branches of the acacia. He took the opportunity to pass by his own house and tell his wife that a crime had been committed at Grand'Terre.

Solidly seated in the sidecar of the motor-cycle driven by the gendarme Raymond Bouchier, police sergeant Louis Romanet

13

wondered what he was going to find at Grand'Terre. Shots, a corpse, that was all he knew. At 6.30 a.m., about half an hour earlier, the telephone had rung at the gendarmerie at Forcalquier. From the other end of the line came the voice of the sergeant at Oraison, the next town: 'Shots were fired during the night near the railway station at Lurs. A motor-cyclist has just informed us. It seems there's a dead body at the side of the Route Nationale.'

After notifying his superior, Louis Romanet at once set out in the police motor-cycle. He knew Lurs and Grand'Terre, and the owners, the Dominicis, who had lived there for twenty years. He had no thought of a murder. Doubtless a car accident. As to the shots, they were hardly surprising in a country where everyone, whether old enough for a licence or not, goes shooting game day and night – preferably night. It's not poaching; what lives and grows on the earth belongs to its inhabitants and there is always the excuse that the game was only vermin. Practically every night one heard shots, of which the targets might equally well be boar, badger or rabbit. It didn't occur to Louis Romanet to connect the shots and the corpse.

As they were approaching Lurs, a man on a motor-cycle coming from the opposite direction began gesturing excitedly. Romanet recognized him as Aimé Perrin, whose brother was married to a Dominici daughter. 'There's been a crime at Grand'Terre,' he shouted. 'I was coming to tell you.'

Louis Romanet indicated that he already knew.

'They were worried at your not arriving. It was Yvette who asked me to go to Forcalquier. She'd already left on her bicycle when I met her.'

'Who's the victim?' asked the sergeant.

'No one knows . . .'

The first thing that Louis Romanet saw was the parked car with a GB plate and the registration number NNK 686. It was an almond-green Hillman estate car. It had stopped by a triangle of gravel belonging to the Department of Roads and Bridges, on the left of the road facing in the direction of Marseilles. The two front doors were locked, while the rear door was merely shut with the key in the handle.

The interior was in indescribable disorder. The exterior bore no sign of a bullet. Romanet noticed, however, a shred of flesh caught in the rear bumper. He examined the car for fingerprints but found

14

none. With the gendarme Bouchier he took the first measurements. He also made an inventory of the objects scattered round the car: a camp-bed spread with some rugs; a beach bag, a towel, two seats probably from the car, a bottle, a child's white linen hat, a note-book, the writing in which 'seemed to be English', two five-franc coins.

The sergeant then studied the body nearest the car. It was that of a woman half-covered by a rug which concealed the upper part as far as the waist. Louis Romanet raised the rug. The head was face down, but he could see that it had turned blue and was spotted with blood.

He folded back the blanket and stood up. 'There's a man dead on the other side of the road,' Bouchier informed him at this point. 'He's lying under a camp-bed.'

The two men crossed the road and Romanet bent over the second corpse. It was that of a man dressed in a leather jacket, sky-blue pyjama trousers and a pair of unfastened sandals. He was slightly huddled up, his head towards La Brillanne, in the direction of Marseilles. His face was purple. Romanet took note of a wound in the chest which had probably been pierced by a bullet. He was about sixty years old, his hair thinning, his small moustache fair, according to the sergeant's first summary description.

The two returned to the Hillman and Romanet examined the body of the woman. Under one arm he could distinguish a large wound. He recorded her as being about forty, brown-haired, of fairly stout build. Romanet noted carefully the position of the victim in relation to the car: to the left of it and obliquely parallel – the detail was to be important – 5·25 metres from the back, 5·30 from the front; about midway, that is. The routine followed in the first moments of an investigation often turns out to be valueless. In this case it was to prove vital.

As he was getting to his feet after taking a measurement, Louis Romanet became aware of another presence; a tall, vigorous man with rugged features, dressed in brown trousers and a pullover, was standing behind him. Romanet knew him more or less – Gustave Dominici, the son of Grand'Terre's owner.

'What a night!' said Gustave.

'It certainly was.'

'We were very frightened.'

Romanet didn't take in the remark at once. What had Gustave Dominici meant? Had he seen, heard, did he know what had happened? The policeman followed the farmer's gesture in the direction of the Durance.

'There's a third one over there,' he said.

Romanet was staggered. The thing was turning into a massacre.

'A little girl,' Gustave went on.

They turned down the road. At the crossing Romanet noticed objects still strewn along the footpath, a beach cushion particularly. Then near by he found a ten-franc piece. Tramps, was his first thought; after the killing they had ransacked the car and made off with whatever objects of value they could carry.

The little girl looked about ten years old and wore light blue pyjamas. She lay on her back with arms outstretched in the form of a cross, her feet bare. Her head was a mass of blood. It had been crushed by a blunt instrument. The body was already cold, as were those of the two adults. Romanet presently measured the distance between the child's body and the Hillman – 77 metres.

'It's terrible,' said Gustave.

As they made their slow way back to the car, Romanet spotted a black notebook on the ground. The first page bore the inscription: 'Drummond, Jack Cecil, Director, born 12 January, 1891, at New Caster.'

Romanet realized that it had become a matter of urgency to inform his superiors and get the judicial preliminaries started. This was no ordinary affair. Three English people – tourists, no doubt – massacred in a corner of Provence! It would attract more than usual attention.

But before going to telephone, Romanet undertook a further search. If, as everything indicated, the murders had been committed by shooting, cartridges ought to be found, an essential element for the subsequent identification of the firearm – or arms. But the first object he discovered was an undischarged bullet at a distance of 6·40 metres from the car near an outlet for sprinkler water. Not far off Romanet collected an empty cartridge case, one therefore fired. The sergeant also found two other spent cartridges level with the woman's head.

'Looks like an American carbine,' was Romanet's immediate reaction.

He was equally interested in evidence of footprints at the edge of the riverbank. They went in both directions, to and from the child's body, and were made apparently by crêpe-soled shoes: three holes in the heel, five in the sole. The prints were quite clear, the soil being sandy, and showed no trace of cuts or wear. The measurements established their size. The policeman covered them with branches.

There were bloodstains too; Romanet and Bouchier detected some near an oak 6·50 metres behind the car and on the Route Nationale. They started at the sprinkler outlet in the direction of the man's body, decreasing in proportion as they approached it. They therefore enabled the victim's course to be followed as he fled from his assassin or assassins. There was no sign of a struggle around the car.

Louis Romanet decided that he had now enough facts to submit his report. Leaving Bouchier at the site, he made for the nearest telephone, that of a subscriber in Lurs, M. Silve. In a few words he brought the chief of the Forcalquier gendarmes up to date. Then he went to inform the mayor of Lurs at his office. 'I'm going to ask Dr Dragon to come along,' he added.

Meanwhile, Captain Albert, commanding the Forcalquier section, was doing the necessary telephoning to the public prosecutor at Digne and the judicial police, not forgetting officials of lesser importance whom the rules required him to alert: the justice of the peace at Peyruis and the field rangers at Lurs. The investigation of a French crime is a drama in which there is nothing niggardly about the cast of characters.

Louis Romanet was back. Bouchier made his report. There had been nothing untoward but the passers-by were beginning to stop and had to be continually moved on. As for Gustave, he was still hanging about. The sergeant turned to him and said, 'You will have to make a preliminary statement.'

Hands in his pockets, Gustave already had the absent-minded, constrained air with which he would confront all those who questioned him. He was a strapping fellow with curly black hair, prominent cheekbones, a gloomy expression, bronzed skin. 'I saw the English people last night for the first time — about half past eight, it must have been.'

'How did you know they were English?'

'By the car.'

'What were you doing outside at half past eight?'

'I was worried about the landslide. I wanted to see what condition it was in.'

Hands now on hips, Gustave answered without apparent reflection or embarrassment.

17

'They were going to bed, I think; they were in pyjamas. I even thought, hm, here are people who don't mind undressing in public. I passed close to them, and went on to the railway. Then I came home and went to sleep.'

'And the shots?'

Gustave parried the question. 'Round half past eleven there was something else. I heard a three-wheeler or a big motor-cycle behind the farm. It was carrying a man, a woman and a child. The man came into the courtyard and called out. But he spoke in a strange language and I didn't understand. He didn't persist. I fell asleep again and round one o'clock in the morning I heard five or six shots. They came from the Route Nationale, not far away, I think. The dogs barked for half an hour.'

'And you didn't try to see what was going on?'

'No,' answered Gustave simply.

'At what time did you discover the crime?'

'At half past five, when I got up.'

His first thought on awakening, he explained, had been to examine the state of the riverbank. He then went on to the railway line, taking the same route as the evening before. While passing close to the car he had noticed nothing out of the ordinary and had gone on to the landslide. It was from the top of the bank that he saw the little girl stretched out on the grass, her face all bloody.

'She looked dead,' he said. 'I thought she was the child of the campers.'

He had gone back to the road. It was then that he stopped a passing motor-cyclist, M. Jean-Marie Olivier, with the request to notify the police.

'When the shots were fired you didn't hear anyone cry for help or anything?'

'No, nothing.'

'Would you be able to recognize the motor-cyclist who came in the night?'

'No, it was too dark.'

'And the motor-cycle or motor-cycle and sidecar?'

'I didn't see them.'

So in those first few minutes of the inquiry spoke Gustave Dominici, whose name would soon become a household word, a man of whom the world would form an image, be privy to his ways and habits, every detail of his life. Grand'Terre, the place where he was born and which he had never left, the anonymous farm at which passing motorists were now beginning to cast a stealthy glance, was suddenly to become the focus of quite extraordinary interest. Yet, if Gustave is to be believed, the echoes of the terrible drama amounted to very little: a few shots to which he, no more than his wife or his father, paid any attention. As to the morning's discovery, it had happened by chance without Gustave showing much curiosity. He passed an abandoned car surrounded by great disorder. He discovered a little girl, dead or unconscious. Her parents were camped a mere 77 metres away – yet he remained stolidly detached. Why didn't he rush to the parents to see what had happened to them, inform them what had occurred if they did not already know?

But it was not Louis Romanet's business at the moment to subject this first statement to criticism. He finished the inventory of the car, finding a 5000 old franc note, a sum which in 1952 hardly corresponded to the needs of a foreign family travelling across France. It could be that robbery had been the motive for the crime and that the note had been overlooked by the murderer.

At 8.30 a.m. Dr Dragon arrived. He at once set to work. On the man's body he discovered two bullet wounds, one at the base of the left shoulder-blade, the other three centimetres above the right nipple. The woman had a wound below the left breast; the bullet had emerged above and behind the right breast, breaking the right humerus. The heart and lungs had been injured. A second shot had struck two centimetres from the base of the right shoulder-blade.

The child's wounds absorbed his attention. They were appalling. The skull had been literally bashed in by an instrument employed with great violence. The frontal region had been crushed as well as the right eye-socket. The mastoidal region had been equally mutilated.

While Dr Dragon was busy with his examination, an old man strolled tranquilly towards the scene of the crime, leaning on a gnarled stick, wearing velvet trousers and a dark blue striped shirt, a belt of some old material wound several times round his waist, a broad-brimmed hat on his head. With his stiff white moustache, his full face heavily creased over the cheekbones, his bushy eyebrows still black despite his age, he gave an impression of confidence and solidity. The gendarmes knew him well: Gaston Dominici, master of Grand'Terre.

'Well, Dad,' said one of them, 'quite some goings-on at your place last night.'

Gaston lightly shook his head. He had first learned the news, he said, from his daughter-in-law Yvette. He knew nothing about it. He had risen at 4.0, as on every morning, to herd his goats into the mountains, taking the direction away from the English people's camping site.

He approached the car and saw the body of the woman. A gendarme showed him that of Sir Jack Drummond. 'There's a third down there on the bank,' he said. 'A little girl.'

'Horrible!' said Gaston. Then with slow but still supple stride he turned towards the railway bridge. In a few minutes he was back. He declared later that he had suggested that 'you ought to cover the little one, the ants are beginning to crawl over her cheeks.'

A gendarme gave him a rug. The old man went down again to the railway. This time when he returned he stood at the edge of the road, watching the gendarmes take measurements and compiling their inventory. Gustave remained near the car, which seemed to fascinate him. There were now a great many people about. Gaston spoke with those he knew; a forester, M. Barrière, the village butcher who had paused while making his rounds. To all of them Gaston repeated that he knew nothing, any more than his son did. They had heard shots, it was true, but that was not an uncommon occurrence. The dogs had barked but that was no reason for getting out of bed.

At 9.30 a car brought the prosecutor from Digne, the examining magistrate, Roger Périès, and an officer of the gendarmerie. The public prosecutor's office was taking charge of the investigation. His back to the mulberry tree, smoking a pipe he had just lit, Gaston contemplated these lofty personages invading his property. He seemed completely untroubled.

Lurs, Grand'Terre, Peyruis, Ganagobie – what are they like, these places of Haute-Provence so soon to become familiar to every reader of newsprint?

First, Lurs. It is a village on a hilltop, the relic of a history going back to the Middle Ages and now reduced to a handful of survivors living in run-down houses that have long since lost anything of grandeur. Surrounding the village are vineyards and a pine wood bisected by a steep cliff; from there one can see Grand'Terre, which lies in the valley. There is little in common between the Dominicis and the people 'up there'. Moreover, at this period only stony paths gave access to Lurs. Only an important errand could take one there, or a fancy to watch from above the tumbling course of the Durance.

Opposite Lurs, on another hill, lies another village, or hamlet rather, Ganagobie. Originally a Franco-Roman settlement, it is now a dilapidated place, although the medieval abbey church and a cloister still stand intact amid the ruins of the abbey itself.

Of the former Benedictine community there now remains but a single hermit, Father Lorenzi, whose solitude was assailed for months by the prying and by journalists, convinced that the monk knew the truth about the drama 'down there', either through private confession or through divine revelation. If he did, it remains a mystery; Father Lorenzi, an amiable and smiling host, never imparted any information to anyone.

Then there is the partly disused railway station at Lurs, situated in the valley a few kilometres from Grand'Terre. The passenger trains no longer stopped there, only the freight trains. However, it was still in use at the time because of a coal mine up in the mountains. A cable line ended near by and the cars went back and forth over the six kilometres between Sigonce and Lurs. Above were the miners, below the linesmen. That was why the railway foreman, Faustin Roure, had at his disposal a crew larger than the traffic would normally justify. The nearest inhabited localities or hamlets, Oraison and La Brillanne, are at either end of the bridge over the Durance, while to the north lies Peyruis where Clovis, the son working for the railway, lived.

These are the names that recur most often. Round about swarmed Gaston's nine children, all except one settled in the immediate neighbourhood. Most of them were tillers of the soil like himself, closely linked to Grand'Terre, the cradle of their family, a few acres of earth squeezed between the Route Nationale and the railway, which for the father were the proof of his success.

But were these Dominicis really as unconcerned as they appeared at the outset? They were the first to express outrage. Moreover, they had the frank gaze of those who have nothing to hide. But was it merely a pose? Deep down, did they not feel anxiety about the confrontation awaiting them?

'That's Superintendent Sébeille coming along,' said a gendarme.

Old Gaston shook his head. The name meant little to him. He asked, 'Who is this Sébeille?'

'He's from the Marseilles Police Judiciaire,[1] he's said to be very good.'

That morning 45-year-old Edmond Sébeille had risen as on every morning at 7.0. He was alone in his flat in the rue du Docteur-Acquaviva in Marseilles, his wife and daughter of eighteen having left for their holiday in the house the Sébeilles owned in the Aveyron. The police officer expected to join them on August 14, the day his leave began. He made his coffee, smoked his first cigarette, then left to catch the 49 bus at 7.59 for the Bishop's Palace. It was in the old Bishop's Palace at Marseilles that the police had their headquarters, the regional branch of the Police Judiciaire especially, offshoot of the Sûreté Nationale, to which Sébeille belonged. It was a huge building reached by way of the Old Port, but overlooking the whole roadstead. The cathedral stood opposite.

At the beginning of August, the peak holiday period, the available force was at its minimum. Fortuitously, it seemed as if the usual crop of crooks was also taking it easy after a profitable season. There were few serious cases apart from the murder of an Arab which Sébeille's team was looking into. But the superintendent was not altogether easy. 'Just so long as nothing big turns up,' he put it to his colleague, Inspector Henri Ranchin. 'We're thin on the ground.'

It was about 9.0 a.m. Sébeille read his paper, arranged some documents, and was going over some reports when the internal telephone rang. Ranchin answered and almost at once handed the instrument to Sébeille. 'The boss – he wants to see you.' Sébeille took it. 'I've something for you,' he heard at the other end. 'Come along at once.'

It was the head of the department, M. Harzic, commanding the Ninth Brigade of the Mobile Police. Sébeille put on the jacket he had discarded and hurried to his chief's office. M. Harzic held out a service telegram. 'Three bodies,' Edmond Sébeille read, 'have been found today, August 5, 1952, at 6 a.m., within the Commune of Lurs, about 600 metres from the local railway station. Preliminary investigation points to a crime with robbery as motive . . .'

The message, in fact, contained several errors. It went on to say, for example, that the three victims had been shot, which was not true of the little girl. It stated that no indication of identity had been discovered.

[1] Police Judiciaire – formerly known as the PJ, corresponding to the English CID.

'Start right away,' said M. Harzic. 'You're the man for the job.'

He obviously had in mind a number of other Provençal cases Sébeille had solved; of fourteen crimes involving bloodshed, eight or nine had a rural background. Sébeille understood and spoke the Provençal dialect, an asset that had several times served him well.

His first difficulty was to gather a team together. It is virtually impossible to work on a murder single-handed. Evidence has to be gathered, witnesses examined, their statements verified, forensic checks made, a missing person perhaps traced, and most of it all but simultaneously. The police of the entire world are agreed upon at least one point: the first minutes of an official investigation are vital. Evidence can disappear, witnesses prepare their stories, the truth be destroyed without hope of resuscitation. Through no fault of his own, Sébeille lost precious time that morning of August 5.

Moreover, it was normally Nice that would have taken over; the Ninth Brigade had a detachment in the Alpes-Maritimes with authority in the Basses-Alpes. Sébeille mentioned this to M. Harzic, who replied, 'They haven't got anybody.'

Sébeille was little better off. He needed four or five men, not easy to round up with his present reduced force. It was noon before he and his assistants, Inspectors Henri Ranchin, Lucien Tardieu and Antoine Culioli, piled into the Citroën[1] driven by Inspector Girolami. First they had to cross the whole of Marseilles in order to fill up at an officially appointed filling station. It was only at 12.15 that Girolami was finally able to head for the Basses-Alpes. He hurled the car along like a stunt man in a film chase.

We'll never get to Lurs, thought Sébeille. We'll all be killed first.

Of medium build, dark-skinned, with black hair thinning at the temples, and a ready smile, Sébeille was an incessant smoker and a man of uncommon tenacity and patience, driven by a conscience and an unfaltering love of his profession inherited from his father, a former equally dedicated stalwart of the Marseilles police. Energetic and intuitive, he was perhaps inclined to be over-impulsive and to believe success certain at the faintest flicker of a light on the horizon. At times he confused hope with reality. A later profile of him would say that 'he began with the principle that reality must necessarily fall in line with his own preconceptions.' A severe judgment, maybe, though one based on the doubtful science of phrenology, but even if he fought this tendency – and we shall

[1] In French *la traction-avant*, but these were at the time all Citroëns, I believe. (*Tr. note*)

see that he tried – it pinpointed Edmond Sébeille's chief defect.

As the car ate up the miles, Sébeille drew on his perpetual cigarette-holder, which within a few months was to become as renowned as Maigret's pipe, and tried to concentrate on the triple crime. In reality his thoughts kept returning to an incident in his boyhood when, at Valensoles, some 20 kilometres from Lurs, a whole family – parents, two children and maidservant – had been murdered. On that occasion the murderers proved to be two voyeurs, and the man responsible for bringing them to justice was Edmond Sébeille's father. To Sébeille, it seemed a good omen.

At Lurs, meanwhile, the arrival of the police officers had been awaited with impatience. The prosecutor, M. Sabatier, the examining magistrate, Roger Périès, the gendarmes under their chief, Captain Albert, locally experienced, were all there as required. But the Police Judiciaire being the main instrument of justice, the examining magistrate and the machine proper were hamstrung so long as these officers were not on the spot to go through their own routine first. And at least three hours – the most valuable of all in this case – had already gone by.

As the hours passed, Gaston Dominici seemed to grow bolder. At first he seemed satisfied to look on, silent and impenetrable. At his side was his grandson, Roger Perrin, son of Germaine, whose husband worked the neighbouring farm of La Serre. He was an odd, flighty adolescent of sixteen, soon to have his own share of the lime-light, but at the moment enjoying himself hugely watching the gendarmes as they checked and measured everything possible and imaginable.

'Instead of gaping as if we're strange animals,' said one of them, 'you'd do better to help.'

The lad obeyed, taking the steel tape to the spots indicated by the gendarmes. But when he passed in front of his grandfather the old man grew angry. 'What are you doing there?' he growled.

'You can see.'

'It's not your job, drop it,' ordered Gaston.

The gendarmes stared at the old farmer: why this sudden irritability? But Gaston avoided their eyes, emphasizing with a brusque gesture the order he had given.

Often he returned to Grand'Terre by way of the orchard, greeting visitors who came along 'just to have a look'. There were of course the members of the family, sons and daughters, sons-in-law and daughters-in-law, but also friends and neighbours. To all Gaston told the same story: he had heard nothing except some shots which seemed to him nothing out of the ordinary. Boars often used the path which led from the road to the Durance and cut across his land. Country folk knew it and would lie in wait at the spot where the English people had camped.

All the visitors were offered either a small glass of *pastis* or of rough, dry white wine from the vineyard. Each time Gaston wiped his white moustache, then again inserted his pipe between his lips. Presently he sat down for a moment on a log of wood placed at the foot of a tree. Lively and rough-hewn, he was the mountain shepherd incarnate, shrewd and unruffled.

Nevertheless, Gaston Dominici was not in one of his serener moods. Going to Grand'Terre to wash the blood and dirt off his hands after his first examination of the victims, Dr Dragon was astounded at the way he was received. Gaston and he were about the same age, they knew each other well: the doctor sometimes came to Grand'Terre to treat one of its inhabitants.

'What are you after?' demanded the farmer.

The doctor was surprised by the snarl in his voice. 'I only want you to give me a little water,' he replied.

But Gaston remained seated, his gaze fixed without friendliness on the perplexed doctor. Beside him his wife stood motionless, rigid almost. 'Water, water,' Gaston echoed, still unmoving, sounding lost somehow, distracted.

Dr Dragon became impatient. 'It shouldn't be that difficult; some water, that's all I'm asking.'

Grudgingly Gaston at last fetched a dented bowl from the corner of the yard.

'This is the horses' bowl,' he said, 'and if I give it to you they'll smell blood and won't drink out of it any more.'

The doctor lost his temper. 'I didn't ask you for a bowl, only for water.'

'Over there.' Dropping the basin, Gaston indicated the farm pump.

While the doctor held out his hands, Gaston consented to pump. Puzzled, Dragon scrutinized the pink 75-year-old face. There was not a trace of feeling or even of irritation. What had caused that sudden outburst? The doctor was far from suspecting Gaston or indeed any of the inhabitants of Grand'Terre. He attributed Gaston's ill-temper to the invasion the crime had provoked and to the fact that by assisting the police he had aligned himself with the invading forces.

But although Gaston seemed fully restored, he did not speak or look at the doctor again, letting him depart without a word. The doctor left Grand'Terre, bemused.

The busiest man in the triangle of gravel, which was being increasingly invaded by sightseers, was undoubtedly Captain Albert. He would soon have to yield precedence to Superintendent Sébeille, so he was making the most of his time.

A bicycle leaning against the mulberry tree aroused his curiosity. 'Was it there this morning?' he asked Louis Romanet.

'No,' replied the sergeant.

The captain consulted the identity disc: Gustave Dominici. It struck him as odd that the young farmer should have used his bicycle to cross the 150 metres which separated Grand'Terre from the fatal plot of raised earth. He decided to release the squad's champion police dog, Wash. The animal made straight for the Durance, over the bridge, then along the railway. He stopped suddenly and within a few metres the gendarmes discovered a spectacle case. The animal then turned back in the direction of Grand'Terre, hesitated, circled several times, sniffed the air, turned his back on the farm, and set off for the lucerne field. It was impossible to interpret his movements. Plainly there was a strong scent that day, but he was unable to transmit its confused message to his owners. Wash grew discouraged. He sniffed the earth, his body trembling or becoming taut. Each moment the gendarmes hoped for a new lead, but in vain.

At 1.30 p.m. Edmond Sébeille arrived, guided by a police motorcyclist whom the Marseilles officers had met on the way. According to Sébeille, their reception was rather cool. Périès, the young magistrate with whom he was to collaborate for many long months, remarked in an icy voice, 'So here you are at last.'

Sébeille explained the reason for the delay. What a mess, he thought to himself, as he took in the mob and the general disorder.

His first task was to clear the ground. It was not easy. The crowd had come to see the show and meant to enjoy it to the end; clashes occurred constantly. Sébeille himself turned angrily on a photographer who was calmly taking pictures of the bodies. Each bystander automatically became an amateur detective. The official investigators began their work under the scrutiny of a throng which watched and commented upon their every move like a Greek chorus. But it was not a theatre. The dead were really dead, the guilty one really guilty.

Having obtained relative freedom of movement, the superintendent checked over the facts already gathered by the gendarmes. He had a sketch made of the area, then went over to Grand'Terre itself. He found a cluster of unprepossessing buildings, the walls fronting the road without windows; Grand'Terre firmly turned its back on passersby. It was reached by a driveway ending in an unpaved courtyard. A low narrow door facing the Durance led to the kitchen. Sébeille scanned the placing of the various windows. One of them looked north towards Peyruis and the site of the crime. The police officer asked who occupied the room. 'Gustave and his wife,' he was told.

Sébeille wanted to know if the triangle of gravel which had been the scene of the tragedy was clearly visible from this room. He found that the view was partly hidden by an orchard which extended from the farm to the path leading to the railway and by the projecting roof of a shed. In order to gain an unobstructed view it was necessary to go up a flight of stairs to an unused room above the young couple's. Gaston Dominici slept alone in a room whose windows faced south-east, that is, towards the Durance. It was Sébeille's first visit to Grand'Terre.

The superintendent next went to examine the Hillman. 'Has anything been touched?' he asked.

'No,' Captain Albert assured him.

Whether that was so is doubtful. Much later, during the reinvestigation by Superintendent Chenevier, a well-known journalist, Roger Lachat of the *Dauphiné Libéré*, writing to a Paris weekly which was publishing the opinions of a number of reporters from the capital, maintained that the only people who could sensibly discuss the affair were 'the special correspondents from the provinces who were quickly on the spot and, having seen the bodies, at once searched the Hillman and learned the identity of the Drummonds before the police, the gendarmes or the prosecutor's office'. If the journalists had indeed had such facilities at the very beginning, they were undoubtedly not the only ones.

Then the superintendent had his first break: Captain Albert handed him the four cartridges that had been discovered. Two had been discharged; they carried the inscription ALC. The two others were intact and on the bullets Sébeille deciphered WCC 43 and 44. The superintendent at once deduced that the weapon must be an automatic carbine whose operation had been imperfectly understood by the user. As a result he had needlessly reloaded the chamber after each shot as with an ordinary rifle. In reloading he had ejected an undischarged cartridge, which explained the presence of two of them on the ground. To Sébeille it was a glimmer of light; the error might one day identify the murderer.

The mobile laboratory busied itself with the fingerprints on the car. A man came up to Sébeille and introduced himself as Gustave Dominici.

'You'll probably find my prints,' he said, 'especially on the rear door. A gendarme couldn't get out because the lock stuck. I helped him.'

Sébeille thought the intervention 'odd'. Subsequently the gendarmes denied the incident; none of them had needed help from Gustave to get out of the Hillman, which they had entered for the purpose of making their inventory.

Photographs were being taken of the bloodstains, especially a big one near a cesspool a few metres from the car. It was a different matter with the footprints on the path. The photographer examined them at length, then made a face. 'Useless,' was his verdict.

The shred of flesh stuck to the rear bumper held Sébeille's attention for a moment. Like the gendarmes, he studied the papers found, the travellers' cheques, the car's travel documents, including that for the embarkation at Dover, reckoned up the money, including the 5000 old franc note in the child's pocket-book and the small change. It was indeed very little ready cash for a family of three.

Sébeille moved on to examine the bodies. On the man's he observed a place between the thumb and forefinger where the skin was torn off; he compared it with the shred on the rear bumper. He must have run away from the killer, knocked his hand against the bumper and injured it, Sébeille reflected. He went over to the body of the woman, where his observations coincided with those of the gendarmes. Then, with Inspector Ranchin, he descended the fifteen-metre bank where the child lay. The same thought came to both men simultaneously: she was caught by the murderer as she was running away terrified, and savagely slaughtered.

'She was barefoot,' noted Sébeille in his report. 'The soles, though clean, had been lightly indented by stones, though without any scratches.'

This detail should be remembered for it cropped up again and again during the investigation and the trial. Here the superintendent contradicted Dr Dragon who first examined the body and saw neither dust nor stone marks on the feet. To the police officer the inference was plain. The child herself had run the 77 metres which now separated her from the car where she had slept. She had not been carried, senseless or otherwise, into the gully to be finished off out of sight. She had collapsed on the spot where the murderer had caught up with her.

Not until 4.0 p.m. were the bodies transported in a van to the hospital at Forcalquier for the autopsy to be performed by Dr Nalin and Dr Girard. Sébeille remained a while longer to leave instructions for his inspectors. 'Look along the edge of the Durance,' he directed Ranchin, 'in case the killer got rid of his gun by throwing it in the water.'

Inspector Girolami was the one assigned to visit Grand'Terre. He found Gaston and exchanged a few words with him. On entering the courtyard the officer's eyes were drawn to a pair of trousers drying on a wire opposite the kitchen door. They were still very wet and therefore recently washed. The inspector was interested. 'Who does the washing for the farm?' he asked abruptly.

Gaston was surprised: what was the point of the question? Girolami merely repeated it.

'My eldest daughter,' the old man finally answered. 'She comes for the laundry every week and washes it at home.'

'How odd,' remarked Girolami thoughtfully.

'Why?'

'To bring the clothes back wet and dry them here.'

Gaston looked amused. He regarded the young officer with a smile and, as was his way when he found himself with people of another generation, at once addressed him with the familiar *tu*. But one couldn't take offence; there seemed to be nothing provocative about the old man; no defiance, no fear; not even the wish to assert the superiority which old age confers. On the contrary, he displayed a sort of fatherly friendliness that not even a police officer could resent.

'You're out of your mind,' he retorted. 'She brings them back dry and ironed.'

Girolami pointed to the trousers drying. 'And those?'

Gaston shrugged his shoulders. 'Ask Gustave.'

Girolami found Gustave near the triangle of earth, hands in pockets, waiting.

'Whose trousers are those drying in the courtyard?'

Gustave didn't seem to understand. The inspector patiently repeated his question. Gustave reflected. For hours, weeks, months, he would act like this with the police, seeming not to understand, delaying his replies, opposing the simplest questions with a stubborn silence.

'My father's, I expect,' he said finally.

'Are you sure?'

'I only wear blue trousers; it's my father who wears velvet ones.'

Obviously he had seen the trousers or how could he have specified their material? Girolami did not pursue the matter, nor mention that his father had been responsible for the suggestion that he see him, but went back to Sébeille who still had not left for the hospital at Forcalquier, and told him of his discovery. It didn't seem to excite Sébeille. 'Leave it for the moment,' he said, 'and get on with something else.'

Disappointed, Girolami obeyed. After all, he was only an 'inspector-chauffeur', the direction of the inquiry was not his business. Yet he was curious to know whom the trousers belonged to and why the Dominicis had varied their practice of entrusting the washing to the eldest daughter. Was it so urgent at that juncture to remove stains and spots? If so, why? The question remains unanswered.

'It's a detail that became hazy in my memory,' Sébeille wrote in his memoirs.

It is obvious that at the time he had not paid much attention to the young inspector. His excuse was the hundred-and-one things he had to think about while restoring order to an investigation that had got off to a bad start. At the moment when Girolami was talking with his chief, Sébeille was absorbed in an effort to fix every detail in his mind. When he returned to Grand'Terre in the evening the trousers had disappeared. No one gave them another thought.

Just as the police were getting into their car to set off for Forcalquier, a gendarme ran up to the superintendent and held out an object which Sébeille couldn't at first recognize. 'It was found under the little girl's head,' said the gendarme.

It was a bit of polished wood that the police at once identified: a fragment from a rifle butt. So the murderer, having shot the parents, had bludgeoned the child because the rifle's magazine had been emptied by his clumsiness in reloading it and had struck with such force that the butt had splintered. For Sébeille it was another piece of essential evidence; perhaps he would really have an easier job than he had expected on arriving at Lurs.

At Forcalquier the two doctors were well into their macabre task. Their tentative conclusions were as follows:

Sir Jack Drummond was fatally wounded by two bullets piercing his back. He was erect when hit by the first. The second struck him while bending slightly forward. His bladder was empty. His wife died as the result of three bullets entering her breast and left shoulder. She must have been lying down or with her chest slightly raised when she was wounded. Her assailant must first have been on her right, then behind her. There is no sign of sexual assault. The child has two very deep wounds on either side of the medio-frontal suture. The blows were delivered with extreme violence by a powerful person. There is reason to believe that the victim was lying on the ground when struck. There is no indication of sexual assault in her case either.

According to the medical report, the three victims had reached the same stage of *rigor mortis*. It could therefore be inferred that their deaths had been all but simultaneous, although in the case of the child the doctors did not exclude a certain interval of coma. They thus found themselves, without knowing it, in opposition to Dr Dragon, who that morning had found a considerable difference in rigor between parents and child. But he had not yet filed his report, so Dr Nalin and Dr Girard were still unaware of his conclusions.

But on his way back, Superintendent Sébeille was making a calculation: two bullets for the man, three for the woman, plus the mark of one flattened on the parapet; six fired in all. But only four cartridges had been found, of which two had not been fired. At least four were missing. What had become of them? Who had picked them up?

The Durance is a watercourse acclaimed by Provençal poets and hymned by lovers of Provence, but Inspector Ranchin felt no inclination to quote them. He bruised his feet on pebbles and floundered in grey water bearing all manner of refuse in its current. In shorts like his colleague Culioli, he explored the banks, sounded the eddies and backwaters in which the gun might have disappeared.

Eventually he came across the carcass of a sheep floating not far from a steep bank and being held back by other debris. It partly concealed a piece of wood which even at first sight was definitely not a fallen branch. Ranchin queasily detached the carcass. A rewarding move; it was indeed the stock of a broken gun. He flourished it triumphantly at Culioli; the other part of the carbine couldn't be far away.

They slowly ascended the bed of the stream, battling against the current which at that time of year was not as strong as usual. Some thirty metres along, midway in an arm of the river and submerged in the mud at a depth of sixty-five centimetres, they laid hands on the barrel of the carbine. They were then exactly level with the spot at which the little girl's body had been found. So, after attacking the child, the killer had immediately got rid of the incriminating weapon.

They came out of the water. Captain Albert saw them arrive, beaming. Ranchin attempted to join the two pieces. They fitted perfectly. One part of the stock was still attached to the barrel. The magazine was still in place, empty; there was no cartridge in the barrel. It was an American carbine bearing on the metal part the markings: US Carbine, cal. 30 KI, ROCK-OLA No. 1,702,864; and on the butt, two muzzles intertwined within a circle, surmounted by a rectangle in which were stamped the capital letters RMC. These letters were reproduced in the groove designed for the passage of the strap.

The weapon was in very poor condition, a circumstance the inspectors thought would favour them; it shouldn't be difficult to identify the owner of a carbine with such marked characteristics. In fact, it was patched up by means of an aluminium ring similar to those used to attach identity discs to bicycles. A screw and nut served to attach the barrel to the stock. In addition, a cable – like that used with a bicycle brake – was passed through the trigger guard, of which only one part remained, and fastened it to a hole in the ring.

It was beyond doubt a relic of the Liberation struggles. American troops had hunted down the Germans in this part of the Basses-Alpes. Afterwards a certain number of arms taken from dead soldiers or quite simply traded for money or food came to light. There was even talk of a whole truckload of rifles having been bought for a few handfuls of bread by peasants belonging to the Maquis. If the fact was never proven, it was nevertheless true that nearly every farm concealed a small arsenal of rifles and sub-machine-guns. It was now necessary to determine into whose hands that broken carbine from the Rock-Ola factory in Chicago had fallen to achieve a massacre in that remote Provençal countryside.

At 7.0 p.m. Superintendent Sébeille, back from Forcalquier, was greeted by an excited Ranchin. The inspector pointed to a nick in the butt into which the fragment found under the dead child's head fitted exactly. There was also the possibility of fingerprints, despite twelve hours in the water. Sébeille later declared that he at once passed the carbine to the experts at the Bureau of Identification but they had found no useful clue. He would later be reproached for not having continued with this verification. In any event it is not mentioned in the police reports for August 5.

The crowd round the police was still dense: spectators, but also reporters and the people from Grand'Terre. Sébeille showed the firearm to the latter. 'Have you ever seen this?' he inquired.

By way of reply he received nothing but sullen looks. He repeated his question. 'No, never,' answered the Dominicis.

But the superintendent's recovered confidence was not disturbed. 'The carbine will speak,' he said a little later. It was a formula he was to repeat several times, for it expressed his deep conviction.

The Rock-Ola and the cartridges were placed under seal for forwarding in due course to the director of the police laboratory at Marseilles, Professor Olivier. The journalists were beginning to press and Sébeille, a little more relaxed, gave them his first statement.

'In my opinion, if I may trust our inquiries so far, the victims were awakened by one or more persons prowling around the car. The little girl, who slept inside, cried out, and her parents, who were on the camp-beds outside, came to her help. The man who carried the gun then threatened Sir Jack Drummond, who tried to flee but was shot in the back. He collapsed near the rear bumper, which he tried to get hold of. Then he found the strength to cross the road, where he fell. Immediately afterwards the assailant fired at the wife, who was struck down on the spot. Then he dashed after the little girl who had blindly run away. He caught her on the bank of the Durance, and since he had no more ammunition he killed her by hitting her on the head with the rifle-butt.'

'So robbery was the motive?' was the gist of the immediate questions.

'Probably,' Sébeille replied. In fact, an investigation was opened against 'X' for murder and robbery. A warrant of inquiry was at once delivered to Sébeille and his team.

The day ended for Edmond Sébeille rather better than it had begun. He could now see what line the inquiry would take. In all probability the murderer did not live far from the site of the crime; one did not carry long distances a firearm in such poor condition. A hunter after game, a poacher, a motorist from a neighbouring village attracted by the sight of the camping ground could be the answer. But in that case, why had the child fled towards the Durance instead of running to the nearby farm where she might hope to find help? From the first, this question was to nag the superintendent continually.

Captain Albert came up while Sébeille was still brooding. 'An abandoned uniform of the Foreign Legion has been found in a thicket,' he told him.

The superintendent listened to the details supplied by the gendarmerie officer. They went against his own theories but no such clue could be ignored. After all, a deserter might well have broken into a farmhouse, stolen a carbine, used it for an act of violence, then fled after throwing it into the Durance. The Basses-Alpes offer a natural route for the fugitive whose only hope is to reach the Italian frontier, the traditional goal of prisoners on the run from the Toulon penitentiary. If the uniform belonged to the murderer of the Drummonds, he would soon be in the hands of the police; a telephone call to the office of the Legion would determine if there had been a recent desertion. A wanted man tagged with a description wouldn't have much chance of getting away. 'Do whatever is necessary,' Sébeille told Albert.

With slow steps Sébeille crossed the railway bridge. Night fell, lengthening the shadows and imparting a touch of freshness. The magistrates had left and Captain Albert was assigning his men to their duties. Only the inspectors remained, surrounded by a handful of journalists, others having gone looking for a telephone in order to phone in their first stories. Sébeille felt the need of a quiet moment's seclusion at the site, soaking himself in the atmosphere and etching on his memory the pictures it suggested.

He paused at the top of the slope down to the Durance. A few metres from there a little girl had perished from the blows of a killer maddened with fear that the child had seen and could identify him. To Sébeille it was clear: whatever the motive of the initial crime, the death of the child, and perhaps of her mother, had no other than the suppression of awkward witnesses.

He was about to rejoin his colleagues when he saw an old man following some fifteen goats coming towards him. He walked leaning on a stick, obviously more from habit than necessity. For the shepherd gave an impression of strength which his nearer approach confirmed. His shirt opened on a round muscular chest, tattoo marks stood out bold on his sunburnt skin: a naked woman on the torso, others on his forearms.

'Are you from around here, Grandad?' Sébeille greeted him.

The old man pointed at the farm with his raised stick. 'I'm the owner of Grand'Terre,' he said.

The tone of voice was unmistakable: pride in being able to declare himself master of this plot of land. He was very erect as he faced Sébeille, his look tranquil and good-natured, and there was something reassuring in his full moustache, silvered except for a brownish tinge caused by the short pipe he kept almost permanently in his mouth, in his snowy hair like worn felt, his easy gait.

'In that case you must know a few things,' remarked Sébeille.

Gaston Dominici pulled a face. 'Not much,' he replied.

'The shots, at least.'

'Vaguely, about one in the morning. I thought it was poachers shooting rabbits. I fell asleep again. About four I got up and went off with the goats.'

'And you saw nothing?'

The farmer shook his head. 'No, I left in the direction of Ganagobie, that's the other way. It was when I came back at about eight that my son Gustave told me what had happened.'

The two men went back up towards the road. 'It's very dry,' said Sébeille, indicating the orchard in which a few rows of vegetables also grew.

'Don't talk about it,' sighed Gaston.

They conversed partly in French, partly in Provençal, mingling reflections on the crime and on the drought, which had become worrying. They came to the place where the English family had camped. 'Ah!' exclaimed Gaston, 'they were blackguards who did this. If I get hold of them . . .'

He pointed with his stick at the mulberry tree. 'There,' he said, 'that's where the woman fell. She didn't suffer.'

He must have read surprise in the superintendent's eyes, but if it worried him, he didn't show it. He went on in a completely natural voice: 'I say that, but I'm only supposing. After what hit her!'

Did he know more? Should the occasion be seized to force him to explain? A careless observation, a slip of the tongue, can be put to profit. But to make a reticent witness talk requires the support of at least some tangible evidence in reserve with which to challenge, to press him. And at 7.30 p.m. on August 5, 1952, Edmond Sébeille had nothing. With what weapons could he attack a simple shepherd who reacted with genuine indignation?

Moreover, Gaston Dominici resumed, 'Did they give you the fragment of wood?'

'Yes.'

'It was I who found it under the child's head.' He said it almost boasting.

It was hardly the remark of a man who feared the truth. Gaston Dominici looked the superintendent straight in the eye, the very pattern of the citizen devoted to his duty, respectful of the law and its servants, always ready to lend them assistance. He raised his hand to his head in salute, then turned to take the path to the farm across the orchard, followed by his goats.

'He's a queer one,' Sébeille said to Ranchin when the latter came to join him in the car which was to carry them to Peyruis where they planned to lodge. 'He talked to me as if he had actually witnessed the crime.'

2

. . . Michèle Gamelin, 14, grand-daughter of the general, drowned near Dieppe . . . Clark Gable and Errol Flynn arrive at Deauville . . . Rich oil magnate, Mme M, robbed of fifteen millions in jewels on a beach at St Jean-Cap-Ferrat . . . At Capri ex-King Farouk acts the playboy . . . Three gold medalists back from Helsinki . . . Syngman Rhee re-elected in South Korea . . . An eight-column headline – THE HOLIDAYS REIGN SUPREME . . .

France was resting, and so was the news, that August 5. Items from Indo-China were relegated to obscure corners of the dailies. The fighting was still furious; the negotiations at Panmunjon were dragging on; the Americans were threatening to bomb seventy-one cities in North Korea.

The tragedy at Lurs thus created a stir in the French and British newspapers. Opinion in general was that the murderer would soon be caught; the weapon would betray him.

On Grand'Terre and on the adjoining orchard the moon's rays fell paler than on the previous night, its milky light reflected in the Durance silently flowing in silver wavelets between its banks. No sound, no sign of life came from Grand'Terre itself. They retired early at the farm. By 10.0 p.m. at latest everybody was in bed.

'When I don't sleep,' the old man said one day, 'I go back over my life.'

It was something which could and did give him a sense of immense pride. Handicapped from birth by circumstances which might well have destined him to become a pariah, one of those vagrants in constant trouble with the police as they wander the roads shiftlessly between one odd job and the next, Gaston Dominici was instead at 75 the owner of some well-cultivated acres; not an opulent estate, but a working farm which had enabled him to bring up nine children without privation. If one considers his early beginnings and what he had attained by August 5, 1952, he could be said to have made a success of his life.

He was born on January 23, 1877, at Digne, rue Montée-des-Prisons, at about 5.0 a.m. The law courts were two steps away. In a poor furnished room giving on to the walls of Saint-Charles Prison, Clémence Dominici had awaited through the night the birth of her son. The father was unknown. Clémence was twenty, daughter of a Calabrian couple, who had arrived with a large exodus of their compatriots drawn by the proposed Marseilles–Grenoble railway line. Labourers, masons, lumbermen, not all of whom, their job done, returned home. Many took root and produced a sturdy, hard-working frugal stock.

Clémence at first wanted to entrust her child to a public institution. Neither her father nor her mother took morality lightly. They considered she had sinned. But the midwife's protests decided her to keep the child with her, while working as a domestic servant. She was to bear two more children, a son and a daughter, also by an unknown father. When Gaston was ten his mother reverted to her original idea, and the three children became wards of charity. Not until the girl, Berthe, was twenty did she get to know her brother, thanks to the social service workers. 'He was always very nice to me,' she was to say. 'He worked like a madman.'

Until then Gaston had spent several years in a Catholic school. It did him little good; he could barely read or write. But some people were suspicious of the uncouthness he affected from his youth. It is not impossible that Gaston strove to pass as illiterate in order to hide his undoubted intelligence and cunning.

He was already being accused of a tricky and quarrelsome disposition, but it should be made clear that these accusations only came to light much later. Justice has at times a tendency to base the picture of the accused on the crime with which he is charged, assisted by witnesses who discover in someone they know fairly well faults which seem to stem not from his previous behaviour but from the crime committed.

In 1898 Gaston was drafted into the 7th Regiment of Cuirassiers at Lyons. The tattoo marks on his chest and forearms may date from this period. At one time it was thought that these indelible ornamentations betrayed his transfer to the notorious Bat'd'Af, the disciplinary battalion for irredeemable troublemakers. It seems unlikely. He was discharged in 1901 and settled in Brunet, a small village in the valley of the Assa, 'a score of black houses in black woods on the black flank of the Valensole Plateau', as Jean Giono describes it. There he was a shepherd. He is said to have been a hard drinker and given at times to fighting. It may be so; even now there are Sunday distractions of the kind in remote regions.

On October 3, 1903, he married Marie Germain, a farmer's daughter. She was pregnant, though later he asserted that he was not responsible but had agreed because of her parents' pleas. At first he worked with them, but in 1909 left to settle in Ganagobie, where he was primarily interested in exploiting the land he had rented which had belonged to the abbey before the law separated Church and State. He also hunted game and at times poached, but the gendarmes looked the other way, perhaps in return for services rendered, reporting fugitives hidden in the maquis.[1] He already had four children, two boys and two girls, among them Clovis, born in 1907. Each time he himself assisted at the birth.

When the First World War broke out he was thirty-seven. But he was not called up because of his children – seven of them by then.

He reared sheep, cultivated olives. It was at this time that he made the acquaintance of Father Lorenzi, the last monk living in the monastery. He even offered him a statue of Joan of Arc because, he said, he had a special devotion to the saint, which often led him to curse the English. This historic grudge would later be remembered. It was at Ganagobie that Gustave was born in 1919. Two years later Gaston moved again; forsaking the mountains for the plain, he settled at another farm, La Serre, three kilometres from Peyruis on the road from Digne to Sisteron. This land also belonged to the abbey of Ganagobie, but it seemed to Gaston more fertile. It was here that he achieved his hour of glory: in 1923 he engaged in a victorious struggle with an escaped criminal.

Two bandits, one of them named Gauthier, had committed a crime in the neighbouring village of Claret. They then fled with a horse and carriage. The gendarmes gave chase. They knew that the men were armed. The populace were warned to be on their guard.

At Château-Arnoux the fugitives separated. One was captured almost immediately. The other plunged into the woods alongside Peyruis in the direction of Ganagobie. His course led him to Pont-Bernard where Gaston with his son Clovis was tending his flock. The farmer – forty-six at the time – was as always carrying his shotgun. He challenged the man with a direct, 'Are you the robber?'

[1] The scrubby underbrush which was much later to give its name to the French resistance fighters against the Nazis.

Gauthier's answer was to fire a shot which hit the target in astounding fashion, the bullet entering the barrel of the shotgun. He tried to reload; the weapon jammed. So Gaston, whose life had just been miraculously spared, grappled with him. Clovis dared not fire his own gun for fear of hitting his father. Fortunately the police arrived, guided by the shot. Gaston received a certificate of bravery and an official note of thanks signed by the prefect of the department. He had them framed and hung in his room. 'My pictures,' he was fond of saying.

In 1932 he moved to Grand'Terre, a small house which he had bought several years earlier. He was described as thrifty, even miserly, but however one views this trait, it enabled him to become a landed proprietor. For the first time in his life he was his own master. It was the crown of his striving, the dream fulfilled, the turning of the tables on his beginnings.

He had paid 10,000 old francs, unquestionably a low price. But the buildings had to be restored and the land cleared from top to bottom. Gaston buckled to, helped by his sons, who had reached manhood. He rounded off the property by buying in at intervals adjacent plots as well as more distant ones. He planted fruit trees and vines. He mixed with local notables, and at one time the Calabrian bastard even toyed with the ambition of becoming mayor of Lurs. He had done well, on this everyone agreed, even those who disapproved of his violence and pointed out occasions when he had 'done the dirty' on those he didn't like.

He enjoyed gathering his own around him. Of the nine children he had had by Marie, whom he nicknamed the Sardine, only Gustave remained at his side. He would have preferred Clovis who was a harder worker, with a character much resembling his own. But at the end of his military service, Clovis announced that he was leaving to get married and work on the railway. This so angered Gaston that he refused to have anything further to do with this ingrate. For years the two did not meet. The Sardine's tears had no effect on Gaston. Until one day he agreed to see the renegade. Clovis had just had a son and Gaston was eager for a sight of his new grandson. A duck was killed and the Sardine sobbed in her son's arms. Did the father and son retain any residue of their quarrel? In the family it would be maintained that Clovis had always nursed the desire for revenge on his father.

Of the others, Ida, the eldest, was the first to leave, marrying a Savoyard who took her to the shores of Lake Bourget, where he farmed the land of the Abbey of Hautecombe. The three other daughters, Augusta, Clotilde and Germaine, married locally, the first a level-crossing keeper, the second a labourer, the third a farmer, Roger Perrin. Germaine was the freest, the most detached from the family circle, the most independent. As for the sons, the youngest, Aimé, became a tenant farmer near Marseilles. Gaston was a lock-keeper at Saint-Auban, not far from Lurs. Marcel, a farmer at Notre-Dame-des-Anges, had married a widow fifteen years older than himself.

Gustave remained at Grand'Terre. Two or three times he had missed marrying, first the daughter of a nearby farmer, M. Roche, then a girl from Marseilles whom he met while doing his military service. At the time he had the reputation of being a womanizer and trouble-seeker; for him dances were often the occasion for fist fights – reminiscent of his father at the same age. Then, settling down, he met and married Yvette Barth, ten years his junior; he had just turned thirty. She was the daughter of a well-to-do farmer at Lurs, somewhat richer than Gaston Dominici. The two men had not, it seemed, entertained any great affection for each other, but since the marriage, relations had been friendly. Yvette, dark and rather pretty, quickly showed that despite her bare twenty years she had spirit and would never become submissive and docile like her mother-in-law.

So Gaston's life unfolded. In the surrounding country the family was held up as an example. It was not uncommon on festive occasions for as many as twenty guests, children and grandchildren, to assemble round the table. Gaston was a jovial host, at least when he was not drunk. A sheep would be killed and roasted on the spit. Friends who called were given a slice and welcome. Gaston would sing in Provençal, run a rakish eye over the women and girls, let his hand linger on the rounder parts of his grand-daughters and nieces – but was this not the prerogative of the master of the house, of the 'patriarch' he had become? With his wife, the Sardine – no one ever knew why he had given her this nickname – he was somewhat rough. He had threatened her, so report had it, with a pitchfork, let alone the stick he was accustomed to lean upon when working. One thing was certain: after fifty years of marriage the two had little to say to each other. Usually Gaston ate alone in the kitchen and, having swallowed his final glass of wine, withdrew either to his room or the courtyard. The Sardine for her part was a woman whose voice was rarely heard, a dark shadow shuffling about inside the Grand'Terre enclosure which she hardly ever left.

In about 1950, Gaston handed over to his son Gustave the cultivation of the fields. It was his way of going into semi-retirement. Gustave set aside for him part of the profits. The older man passed his days with his goats, taking them most often to the mountains on the Ganagobie side where he could recapture the fragrances of his younger years.

However, it did not seem that this new, less active life brought him the happiness he expected. Like many men who all their lives have managed a property or a business and are induced to hand it over, Gaston Dominici took badly to being on the outside and no longer in command. His character, already difficult, became more so. According to him, Gustave was an incompetent who instead of improving what he had received, allowed it, little by little, to run down. Gaston's gruff voice was often heard reprimanding his son as a lazy good-for-nothing. Gustave took it, never answering back. He was entirely dominated by his father, having little personality of his own, at once obstinate yet easily influenced, retaining from his youth a memory of the paternal rages and his terror of them.

There is no doubt that Gaston possessed enormous self-control and excelled at making on others whatever impression he wanted. He could be warm, gay, picturesque, could make one smile, at which times he became one of those old men it is a pleasure to like. But if carried away, his rage and resentment attained such vehemence that it was impossible to imagine their serving only as a smoke-screen for trickery. That is why he is difficult to define. He produced an effect on those who came in contact with him such as is occasioned only by certain remarkable human beings: those who would have to pass judgment on his fundamental nature would not only passionately contradict one another, but would often find they were just as suddenly contradicting themselves.

'Ask the Sardine and my children what I'm like,' he would repeat. 'Just a simple peasant . . .'

But the Sardine remained silent as always. Was she terrified? Did she remember the time when to raise a laugh among his friends Gaston handed her a banknote, saying, 'Cry . . .' And the Sardine wept without it being possible to say whether she could cry at will or nursed some perpetual sorrow.

As for the children, now grown up, they recalled a father who had brought them up without special tenderness but had settled them in life reasonably well. He perhaps had his faults, he drank heavily and at such times it was better to keep out of his way. But he had worked and struggled so hard in order that the nine children should never want food or warmth that, looking back, they forgave him everything and liked to return to Grand'Terre to eat and drink in his company. Affection is not quite the word; what united the Dominici clan was above all the feeling of complicity, of a profound alliance in the struggle for existence which had lasted so many years. They felt one with their father because of the position he had enabled them to achieve in turn in the light of his own humble origins. The children and later the grandchildren had the same sentiment for Gaston as soldiers for a victorious chief. They joked with him, though the nieces and grand-daughters stepped back quickly the moment they had grazed his yellowed moustache with a kiss, for his hand was nimble, and his sons less and less tolerated his admonitions and advice. Were they to break up because one evening in August 1952 three English people had chosen to sleep on a stony bit of ground by the side of the Route Nationale which few campers would have selected?

It was the attitude Gaston Dominici was determined to maintain. He permitted no discussion in his hearing of what had occurred the previous night at Grand'Terre, in the orchard, the lucerne[1] field, or on the Department of Roads and Bridges' gravel patch.

That first night Gaston had only one thought: to save Grand'Terre, those few acres wrested from adversity and held by unremitting struggle. They represented not only material goods, a means of livelihood, but the prize and justification of an entire life.

Alone in the steel-blue night, his back to the mulberry tree, which cast its shadow across the scene of the previous night's horror, a man waited. Occasionally he looked at his watch and, when a light at the bend in the road announced the approach of a car, he quickly drew back behind the tree. Most of the motorists slowed down automatically by now, as if hoping to surprise a presence at this already notorious spot. When they had passed, the man resumed his position facing Grand'Terre, his gaze fixed on the windows of the room where Gustave and Yvette slept.

It was past 2.0 when he left his post and walked the few hundred metres along the Route Nationale to where he had left his car. He had the information he had come for: the Dominicis had lied. Of course it involved no more than a point of detail insufficient to build a theory on or offer a lead. Nevertheless it was disturbing. On this

[1] US alfalfa.

night Yvette had not got up to nurse her baby, Alain. There had been no light in the windows. Yet that day the young woman had stated that she had heard the shots at the moment when, as on every night, she was feeding her baby. If there was one human mechanism on which one could depend, which admitted of no oversight or delay, it was a baby's stomach. It was scarcely likely that young Alain, accustomed to his feed at one in the morning, would on this night decide to let his parents enjoy their rest. What truth did this small untruth conceal?

The man who put this question to himself as he started his car was Captain Albert, head of Forcalquier's gendarmerie. His experience had taught him that an investigation is above all the accumulation of small facts which at first seem unimportant.

An oppressive, almost suffocating heat enveloped Lurs, Peyruis and Forcalquier that night. Not one of all those drawn into the affair was able to sleep. It was not only the dog days, it was the sense of something in the air, an offensive, the explosion of a situation which had been maturing all day. The journalists, by now around fifty of them, had not gone to their rooms; they slept for the most part in their cars parked in front of the town hall near the boarding-house where Edmond Sébeille had taken shelter, ready for a quick start the moment information or instinct should guide him to a suspect.

That moment had not yet come. Theories became jumbled and contradicted each other in Sébeille's mind. At times he got up to make a note, record a fact to be verified. But the police officer's thoughts constantly led him back to two elements of the problem. First, the rifle. It was impossible that some day a witness should not recognize it. It had been used, the patching up was proof. Sébeille knew the peasants of the Basses-Alpes, all hunters at heart. They knew it was forbidden to use an army weapon, but how to stop them when boar was among the most coveted game, furnishing the locals with perhaps their favourite competitive sport? Surely if the gun were shown to enough people one of them would one day, covertly or openly, divulge the name of the owner and the case would be all but over?

Sébeille's whole inquiry would centre on the gun. He had had no difficulty in obtaining permission from the magistrate Périès to keep it for a few days. For the moment it was carefully wrapped up, but from tomorrow it would be displayed on the mantelpiece of the local inn where everyone could see it.

But the superintendent also found his mind reverting increasingly to the Dominicis. They had not told the whole truth, that was plain. Was it really possible that, having discovered so atrocious a crime, their concern should have ended once the police were notified? Their indifference was unnatural. Their composed attitude suggested people who knew more than they were telling but would not admit it, presenting themselves as witnesses whose only connection with the case was topographical. But they were like actors who had not entirely adopted their roles and were overacting.

Little by little during the course of the night Sébeille became convinced that he must concentrate his efforts on the Dominici family. It made both logical and intuitive sense. In the quiet of his room, where he caught only brief snatches of sleep, Sébeille mentally reviewed the inhabitants of Grand'Terre and wondered about the placidity they displayed; did it accord with their evasive looks, their awkward or vague replies? Of course one could to some extent explain their embarrassment: it is never agreeable to be the principal witness of an event in the news, especially one of such dimensions. But it was difficult to believe that this was the only explanation.

A few score metres distant from the superintendent, in Peyruis itself, another man was tossing and turning in his bed, but for a reason diametrically opposed to Sébeille's. He was obsessed by a secret. Clovis Dominici knew that his brother had lied to the police on a capital point. It was he himself who had advised concealing the truth. Disclosed, it would get Gustave into serious trouble.

When Clovis arrived with his workmates at Grand'Terre at 5.0 a.m. he had at once gone forward to meet his brother. The linesman Boyer, already on the spot, remained a few steps behind.

'There's been a crime – a little girl,' Gustave told Clovis.

'Is she dead?'

Gustave looked away. 'No, I don't think so. She was breathing noisily and I saw her arm move.'

'Have you called a doctor?'

'I told a motor-cyclist to notify the police.'

Clovis was surprised. Surely the first need was for a doctor to save the child's life! He put it to Gustave but got no response.

'I'll have a look,' said Clovis. 'Where is she?'

'At the bottom of the bank, just below the bridge.'

'Stay here.'

And, followed by Boyer, then Drac, the other workman who had joined them by now, Clovis went towards the Durance. He found the body, only to be less than forthright with his mates and later, as we have already seen, with Roure the foreman. Had he really leaned over the body, as he claimed? Or had he contented himself with examining it from a distance? His reason for keeping Roure, Drac and Boyer away from it was obvious. If there had been any intimation that the child was still alive, they would have indignantly demanded why Gustave had not at once gone off on his motor-cycle to get a doctor. And Clovis's first thought was to protect his brother. He was the elder and had always acted as shield between his father and Gustave. He was the only one to have stood up to the old man. He passed for the strong man of the family, not the most intelligent perhaps but the sturdiest. He had stood for a few moments looking at the body. There was no sound, no movement. It was enough for him. Gustave must have come upon the last convulsions, the death-rattle. A doctor would serve no purpose now. 'She's dead,' he pronounced.

The others agreed with him; the child appeared lifeless, they could see the terrible wounds on her head. They had not overheard Gustave, they could only accept Clovis's diagnosis.

Back at Grand'Terre his first words to his brother after a mumbled 'She's dead now' were a whispered warning not to talk. 'Never say the child was still alive when you found her,' he murmured, 'otherwise you'll be in for trouble.'

Gustave needed no persuading. His brother merely confirmed him in the attitude he had straightway adopted. To the motor-cyclist Olivier sent to alert the police, to Boyer the linesman, he had already spoken of a 'corpse'. Gustave knew very well that if he ever admitted that the child had still shown signs of life he would find himself in a tight corner. But he valued Clovis's opinion, so the advice none the less did him good and incited him to a further confidence.

'After the shots I heard what sounded like screams.'

'And you didn't get up?'

'No.'

'Don't ever tell that to anyone either.'

It needed only those few furtive exchanges between the brothers to keep the secret within the walls of Grand'Terre. For the moment the danger of its spreading farther was practically nil, since it rested with Clovis, who loved his brother dearly and would go to any lengths to save him.

Clovis could not conceive that the key to the mystery lay within

Grand'Terre. Yet should it be found there, he would align himself firmly with his kindred. This at least was his first reaction. He was, he remained, a Dominici, a member of the clan. He might have his differences with his father, entertain a more clear-headed and qualified affection for him than the others, but he would still do nothing to injure him. Clovis no longer belonged to Grand'Terre, yet at this moment he was alone in sharing with its inmates some part of the truth. Without hesitation he brought his stone to the barricades being erected in expectation of attack. Clovis Dominici had no intention of being a traitor. He had too strong a family feeling for that; Grand'Terre and its inmates must be saved at all costs. The fleeting conversation on the morning of the drama would stay buried deep inside him.

'It was very hot today, the night will certainly be delightful. We'll camp out.' With these words Sir Jack Drummond, on the evening of August 4, took leave of M. and Mme Roland who kept the Grand Hotel at Digne. He had lunched there with his wife and daughter. On the 1st the family had stopped there for the night. The Hillman had been disembarked from the Dunkirk ferry on July 27. The Drummonds had then travelled to Rheims, Domrémy, Joan of Arc's birthplace, as a treat for the child Elizabeth, Aix-les-Bains, and finally Digne. It was there that, while her father was paying the bill, the child saw a poster announcing a bullfight. To Elizabeth it meant a *corrida*, although in fact it was only what in the south-west is called a *charlottade*, an entertainment despised by the *aficionados*. She wanted to go, and Sir Jack at once agreed, which was how he came to be back in Digne three days later.

From the morning of the 6th the gendarmes were in possession of these facts. There still remained the task of finding anything out about the victims beyond their name. The English newspapers supplied this information. Sir Jack was a British scientist of considerable distinction. HE SAVED OUR BABIES, screamed the headlines in large type.

Sir Jack Drummond was born in 1891. His early career was an academic one. Until 1939 he taught biochemistry at the University of London. He was a quiet, retiring man, devoted to the study of dietetics and the problems of nutrition. The Second World War, however, brought him a measure of eminence; his activities, though behind the scenes, contributed in no small part to victory. In 1939 he was called in by the Ministry of Food to work out a fitting ration for armies in the field. He had aroused attention by a book he had published some time before: *The Englishman's Food*. He had written it in collaboration with the woman who was to become his second wife, since he was divorced; it was his first wife who was to inherit from him. He had known Ann Wilbraham, fifteen years his junior, at the university, where she had been a student. She was entrusted with the actual writing of the book because she had a clear, humorous style. The book enjoyed a certain success.

The invasion of Europe and the blockade of Britain by Hitler's forces increased his importance. Fifty million British had to be fed from the island's own resources and what could be slipped through the submarine blockade from America. Sir Jack applied himself to the problem and soon made his recommendations: the population should be fed on dark bread, herrings, raw vegetables and dried eggs. 'He starved us but he saved us,' the British were to say. Sir Jack's comment was that a man with a pint of beer in one hand and a plate of herrings with fried potatoes in the other was getting 2,400 calories which were enough to live on. 'Three thousand would be better,' he added, 'but that will come.'

His knowledge of chemistry was used to develop a rationing scheme of whose gastronomic qualities he made no boast but which, in his opinion, would permit survival without ill effects through the lean years. And if he did have a weakness for his National Loaf – soon to become the basic nourishment for children – and mistakenly declare that white bread would never reappear because his would triumph on its own merits come peace, what scientist does not have a favourite among his brain children?

He also launched a campaign to provide fruit juice free in the schools and reorganized school meals, basing them on vitamins. 'If Carnot is called in France the organizer of victory,' one journal wrote at the time, 'Sir Jack Drummond has been the organizer of health.'

He had other assignments, always connected with the nourishment of groups of human beings threatened by famine. He worked out the rationing system for submarines bound for Malta, then besieged by the Germans, and the division and quantity of food parachuted to the European Resistance, notably in France. In the last months of the war he perfected his outstanding invention: a mixture of pre-digested proteins, glucose and vitamins in liquid form for intravenous injection. When the Allied armies invaded Germany and discovered the concentration camps, the 'Drummond mixture' was dispatched to them in large quantities. It saved thousands of displaced persons, the condition of whose stomachs prevented them from absorbing the nourishment they so sorely needed.

It was at this time that Drummond accomplished a mission which was to start sensational, though rapidly discredited, rumours. In May 1945, while a last pocket of Nazis still held out in north-east Holland, Sir Jack decided to go there himself. He had learned that women and children were dying of hunger because of these last desperate struggles by the vanquished. He made contact with the Dutch authorities and suggested that they propose a truce. Then with two other scientists he boarded a military aircraft, landed at Utrecht, and from there directed food trucks towards the German lines. He himself conducted the negotiations with enemy officers, and with some difficulty crossed their lines, forced at every step to parley with soldiers astounded at the arrival of a man in the uniform of the Home Guard, the only military organization to which Sir Jack had ever belonged.

'Coming back,' said one of his companions, 'we were much more frightened than going. We constantly ran into German officers completely drunk – they had just heard of the surrender.'

Peace, of course, brought him his deserved share of honours: the title which he never used, preferring to be called by his second name, Cecil, rather than Sir Jack; Dutch and American decorations, election to various learned institutions, including the Royal Society. He remained what he had always been: a gay, modest man who, having forced the British to diet, became a member of the Wine and Food Society, where they preferred a Château-Lafite to powdered milk, and foie gras to grated carrots. 'At home,' he would say, 'I never set foot in the kitchen. I just eat what my wife gives me and it's always very good.'

When young, Sir Jack somewhat resembled the dancer Fred Astaire. At the time of his death he was still a vigorous man, with reddish blond hair thinning slightly, a full face and a neat moustache.

In 1946 he left public service for private industry, becoming technical adviser to Boots the Chemists on the manufacture of food products, and going to live at Spencer House, a large two-storied house standing in its own grounds at Nuthall, near Nottingham. For six years he enjoyed what appeared to be perfect happiness. An only child, Elizabeth, was born to the Drummonds in 1942. Sir Jack was 51, and fatherhood means much to a man of that age. Notes later turned up which he had made about his daughter. They reflect the tenderness of a father who not only loved but observed her attentively and recorded an almost scientific analysis of her character and temperament:

She is a healthy little person, alert, intelligent and knows what she wants . . . Her handwriting has acquired a personal and definitive character; she now writes much better than I do. She is weak in arithmetic, like her father and mother, but she adores geography and poetry . . . She is very meticulous about the meaning of words . . . She still has very little appetite. She can't eat eggs. She picks about in her food and makes a sharp distinction between fat and the rest. She adores mushrooms and would give her share of paradise for olives . . . She continues to be a glutton for reading. Every morning at six she takes up the nearest book and dives into it. Her reading is not always of a very high level. Dickens gives way quickly to Walt Disney. She retains everything. I infer this from the endless questions that follow her readings. She adores her little pony Frisky and he returns her affection.

Then there are lines which one cannot read without emotion since they were written only a short time before the Drummonds' departure for the Continent:

She has always had a morbid fear of physical pain: she cannot bear the thought of an injection or a vaccination. She imagines fearful pains and sometimes wakes up in tears crying for help . . . She is wild with joy at the idea of the trip we are going to take to France. She already has a mass of projects and itineraries, and a month would not be enough to visit the list of cities she has drawn up.

Thanks to some friends of the Drummonds, the Marrians, it is possible to reconstruct the family's itinerary across France. On August 1, after leaving Digne, Sir Jack made for Villefranche-sur-Mer where the Marrians had rented a property, Le Beau Cyprès. Mr Marrian was a former colleague of Sir Jack's. He had not reached the same eminence but he taught at Edinburgh and they had always remained on good terms. He had therefore invited Sir Jack to spend some days with him on the Côte d'Azur. The Drummonds had arrived at Villefranche in the late afternoon. Sir Jack had at once informed his friend that on the 4th they would be returning to Digne for the *corrida*. They would camp on the way. This mode of travel did not especially appeal to Sir Jack, who enjoyed his creature comforts, but Elizabeth wanted it; her father had therefore brought along two camp-beds to please her. They would take the opportunity to follow the valley of the Durance, which was said to be very beautiful.

Until the 4th the Drummonds and the Marrians were inseparable. Elizabeth found two friends, Valerie and Jacqueline, the hosts' daughters. The former was the same age, and was to identify the dark glasses Elizabeth bought while with her. In addition, Valerie lent her a bathing suit, which was to figure among the objects strewn round the Hillman.

But why did Sir Jack choose so uncomfortable a spot to spend the night, a gravel patch near a highway and not far from a railway? They had been seen driving down the Boulevard Gassendi at about 7.0 p.m., so they left Digne quite late. They could not travel very far looking for a suitable site and they had little time before night fell to make their choice. Moreover, Sir Jack wanted to be back at Villefranche next day for lunch. They would therefore have to leave early in the morning. Farms are infrequent on this road. On arriving at Grand'Terre the traveller finds that the next village, La Brillanne, is six kilometres distant. It was about 7.30 when Sir Jack skirted the Dominici fields and saw the century-old mulberry tree sheltering a space where he could park his car. There was a house near by. The scientist reckoned that the place, though not ideal, had its advantages. For himself and his wife, who would have preferred a room and a good bed, this halt beneath the stars was a sacrifice made for Elizabeth. The Durance was near and the site was no uglier than any other. Sir Jack stopped the Hillman.

At about 8.0 p.m. the Drummonds ate a frugal picnic meal. Half an hour later Elizabeth and her mother undressed for bed. Meanwhile Sir Jack took the two camp-beds out of the car and set them up in the open air. He and his wife were to occupy them, while Elizabeth slept in the back of the car. By about 9.0 p.m. all three had retired.

Driven by Inspector Girolami, the Marseilles squad car climbed the rough road to the village of Lurs. Chewing on his cigarette-holder, Edmond Sébeille thought about the day before him. Though he had scarcely slept a wink, he felt in good form. Turning round, he could see on Inspector Ranchin's lap the precious carbine wrapped in the paper Gustave Dominici had voluntarily supplied after being shown the weapon the evening before. The superintendent was not so naïve as to suppose that the owner of the forbidden Rock-Ola had openly carried it about the countryside, but vanity would have led him to show it to a few close friends. Sooner or later, one of them would covertly betray him.

The car stopped before the town hall of Lurs, an old building on a narrow grey square. The mayor, M. Estoublon, was a large, solid man who headed a municipal council with communist leanings. Inspector Ranchin unwrapped the rifle and M. Estoublon considered it for a moment. Then he shook his head. 'I've never seen it,' he said.

'Do you shoot?'

'Of course.'

The municipal councillors arrived in their turn. MM. Boucher, Armand, Jolifier. Sébeille showed the rifle to each of them. They none of them recognized it. The police officer questioned them: which of the inhabitants of Lurs were the most enthusiastic huntsmen? Names were given him, albeit with a certain reluctance; it was obvious they took part in this inquiry with only qualified readiness. Sébeille was not surprised; he had been warned by the gendarmes the evening before that the triple murder, the police invasion, the investigation and check-ups would beyond doubt sow panic among the possessors of forbidden wartime firearms, certain that there would be searches, that the gendarmes would take advantage of the occasion to make as big a haul as possible. A cordial spirit of co-operation was therefore not to be looked for.

A large part of the morning was next spent going from house to house, from farm to farm, offering the broken carbine for inspection. Faces froze or turned away, lips compressed, the answer was everywhere the same – no one had seen the weapon. Sébeille warned those he questioned that the possession of such a rifle was expressly forbidden. A prosecution might follow if one were discovered. It was a pointless warning.

Two hours later the police went back to Grand'Terre. The operation had been unrewarding but Sébeille had not expected immediate results.

Girolami stopped the car in front of the courtyard, which Sébeille entered followed by Ranchin. It was as hot as the day before and Gaston Dominici was sitting in his favourite place under the tree near the shed. He did not get up when the police arrived, and watched their approach with indifference. The superintendent noticed that, unlike the previous day, his shirt was buttoned to the neck and his sleeves rolled down to his wrists – perhaps to cover his tattoo marks. 'I want a word with you,' said the superintendent.

Gaston got to his feet and leaned on his stick. 'Let's go in,' he said. 'It's too hot out here.'

Sébeille and Ranchin followed him into the kitchen, where Marie, the Sardine, was at work. Gaston sat down near the table, inviting the police officers to do the same. Without giving Sébeille a chance to speak, he told them that he knew very little; he had heard shots, that was all.

So began the first serious conversation between Sébeille and the old farmer. With an air of authority Gaston addressed the policeman with the familiar *tu*, answering either in French or Provençal or in a jargon intermingling the two. The superintendent called him Grandad, which seemed all right with Gaston, who never took his bright eyes off him.

'I should like to know how you spent your time on the evening and the night of the fourth,' said the police officer.

Gaston did not seem offended. He shook his head, reflected a moment, then began, 'I saw the English family for the first time the day before yesterday evening, when I brought my flock back to the farm. It must have been between seven-thirty and eight. I passed a few metres from the car, which was drawn up at the side of the road facing in the direction of Manosque. There were three people, a man, a woman and a little girl. I think they had just arrived since nothing had yet been taken out of the car. They saw me pass, the child kept staring after my goats.'

'Didn't they speak to you?'

'No, nor I to them,' Gaston answered firmly.

Sébeille was surprised: a family occupies a piece of ground within the Dominici property and the owner himself doesn't say a word to them? Hardly the custom of the country.

'I heard them talking,' replied Gaston simply. 'They were foreigners and I didn't understand anything of what they were saying.'

He had then gone on to Grand'Terre, shut up his goats, had a bite to eat alone as usual, then gone to bed at about 8.0, that is to say almost at once. At about 11.0 he had been awakened by noises from the courtyard, which his bedroom overlooked. 'Somebody called,' he said, 'and I got up. I went to the window and saw a man who asked me something I didn't understand. He wasn't speaking French. He went away almost at once, and I called after him, "Go to bed." A few seconds later I heard a car start on the road. I couldn't tell which way it went. I went back to sleep. Then at about ten past one

I was again woken up, this time by the dogs barking. Almost at once I heard the shots.'

'How many?'

'Four, I think. I said to myself, "Hey, that's no shotgun." The reports were too sharp.'

'Where did they come from?'

'I'm not sure. I thought it might be youngsters shooting rabbits. It was bright moonlight.' The old man smiled; in his youth he too had gone poaching at night. He knew the pleasure of tracking game by moonlight. 'I thought it might be happening the other side of the Durance, or on the little islands.'

'You didn't hear any screams?'

'No. Then I went back to sleep. At five I got up and went off with the animals towards La Brillanne.'

'Which means you had your back to the car.'

'That's right.' Gaston fell silent. His face exuded innocence and detachment. It was almost as though he were enjoying the superintendent's questions.

'When did you hear about the crime?'

'When I got back to Grand'Terre at about eight.'

Yvette, then Gustave, had told him of it while his goats munched the hard grass of the hills. 'Gustave told me he had found three dead bodies.' He at once recovered himself. 'Or rather the body of a little girl.'

It was then that he had gone down the bank to the Durance. He had seen the body which he had covered with a blanket. It was while doing this that he found the splinter from the rifle-butt. 'I gave it to the gendarmes,' he said again.

He tapped his pipe on the corner of the table to empty it and then refilled it. His movements were slow and easy. His look was alert under half-closed eyelids. Sébeille considered what he had just heard. Could a whole family have been massacred without the Dominicis hearing one cry? It seemed highly unlikely. But it was still too soon to press the old man. Sébeille exchanged a few more words with him, studying him, trying to classify him. If, as everything seemed to indicate, the motive of the crime was robbery, then Gaston had nothing to do with it. Nor Gustave. So why did these two give the impression of hiding something?

Sébeille next went on to question the son – a very different character from the father; obviously less intelligent, less shrewd, undoubtedly less tough. But difficult to deal with because he was not only fearful of others but of himself and of words, of which he was clearly no master. He uttered as few of them as possible, always putting off as long as he could the moment when he would have to answer. His interrogations would be interminable. Later the superintendent and his colleague Constant were both to use the same analogy: it was like trying to pinch a pane of glass.

Having taken his father's place facing Sébeille, Gustave repeated what he had told the gendarmes the day before, adding some details. The superintendent had sent Gaston back to the courtyard. Yvette and her mother-in-law were there also, together with the baby whose cries at times reached the three men in the kitchen. Gustave placed his arms on the table. His prominent cheekbones were a little strained and Sébeille could tell that the son was more tense than the father.

He had, he said, first seen the English people on the evening of August 4, when he went to have a look at the landslide to which his father had called his attention. He had not spoken to them, any more than had the old man. He had gone to bed a little later than Gaston and like him had been awakened at about 11.30 by the unknown person who had come into the courtyard. No one, he asserted, had gone to the window, yet Gustave could affirm that there had been a motor-cycle, perhaps a three-wheeler, carrying a woman and a child as well. He was more precise than his father: according to him the vehicle had left in the direction of La Brillanne. His room, it is true, was nearer the Route Nationale than Gaston's. Later, at about 1.0 a.m., there were the shots. Two at first, close together, then three or four more spread out.

Had the English entered his mind?

'Yes and no,' he answered. 'I said to myself, "Somebody's being attacked." Then I thought of the campers. But I didn't want to believe it.'

'Weren't there any screams?' asked Sébeille.

'We didn't hear any. Besides, the dog started to bark. He howled like mad.'

'And you didn't do anything?'

Gustave lowered his eyes. 'We were very frightened. The farm is isolated and I am the only man.'

'But your father . . .'

'He's too old.'

'You didn't even go to the window?'

55

'No.'

For a moment the two men stared at each other, then Gustave quickly looked away.

'Tell me again how you discovered the body.'

Gustave studied the table and the silence dragged on. Sébeille waited patiently, knowing that it often did no good to hustle a witness.

'It was in the morning while going to look at the landslide. Faustin Roure had ordered me to as soon as I woke up.'

He had not noticed the English people and assumed they were sleeping. It was only on his way back that he saw the body of the child, her face bathed in blood. He had been terrified and had at once realized that she was dead.

'You were sure of it?'

'Absolutely,' replied Gustave.

He had then run up to the road and there stopped the motor-cyclist, Jean-Marie Olivier.

Sébeille motioned to Ranchin, who took up the carbine at his side and held it out to Gustave in its open wrapping.

'Have you ever seen this before?' asked the superintendent.

'No.'

'Nor one like it?'

'Never.'

Sweat dripped down Gustave's forehead, but it did down Sébeille's also. It was in fact very hot.

'Let's go over the route you took,' the superintendent suggested.

In the courtyard the rest of the family waited. Sébeille put several questions to Yvette and the Sardine. The answers were uncommunicative. Yvette, evasive, confirmed her husband's statements. At 1.0 a.m. she awoke in any event to feed Alain.

'The English people didn't come to the house – to ask for water, for instance?' asked the superintendent.

The answer came almost in chorus. 'We didn't see any of them.'

Sébeille, Ranchin and Girolami accompanied Gustave to the Durance. They followed the Route Nationale, then the cart track, crossed the bridge and turned left. Sébeille was struck by the way in which Gustave took the turn. Instead of keeping close in to the left to get a good look at the railway line, the original objective, he made a wide sweep towards the Durance. This, he asserted, was how he came to see the body which the bank would otherwise have hidden.

Sébeille again went over the ground. The landslide could certainly be seen from the bridge. Why had Gustave gone farther? And why had he made such a wide sweep that he could look right down to the Durance? It is difficult of course to ask a man to explain his most mechanical actions. But police investigation is like that; the minutest details have to be scrutinized to determine if they contain the slightest anomaly. If one appears, an explanation, sometimes even a justification, has to be found.

But it was not on this point that Sébeille sought to catch Gustave out. 'You didn't go near the body?'

'No.'

The superintendent studied Gustave as he asked slowly, 'And what if she had been alive?'

Only the chirping of the crickets answered him; Gustave remained stubbornly silent. Sébeille repeated his question. Then he waited, hands in pockets, like his colleagues who stood by, watching. 'Didn't you think of the parents?'

Silence from Gustave.

'You could have gone back to the car, warned them, seen what had become of them.'

Then Gustave made up his mind. 'I thought it was the parents who had killed her.'

Sébeille was startled. Where had Gustave dug up that notion? But the farmer did not falter. 'You've heard of things like that, haven't you?'

'One's heard of everything,' Sébeille mumbled.

Gustave shut up like a clam. Was he aware of the enormity of what he had said or merely scared by the amazed faces of the inspectors? Sébeille let him go. 'A strange fellow,' he commented.

From this point on Gustave became for Sébeille witness number one, a classification often only a step before that of suspect. But how to corner him? By a knock-out blow – metaphorically, of course, Sébeille being known for his abhorrence of certain more drastic measures – or by a progressive gruelling, a slow, inexorable closing in? Sébeille favoured the second method. He already sensed that with Gustave endurance was needed.

He therefore left Grand'Terre that day conscious that he had uncovered nothing conclusive, merely a road to pursue. There was no lack of improbabilities and inconsistencies in Gaston's and Gustave's stories.

There was the arrival of the motor-cyclist who had entered the courtyard at 11.30. For three years, until the end of the second or counter-investigation, this mysterious visitor would continue to be conjured up. Everyone who studied the files would be surprised at the persistence with which the Dominicis mentioned him. It was as if for them the chief event of the night of August 4, 1952 was not the horrible massacre but the unexpected and inexplicable intrusion of this stranger. Their stress on it at the start had an undeniable logic: to impress on the investigators that there had been some odd characters circulating on the Digne–Marseilles road that night. For honest farmers it was better to pull the sheets over their heads than go poking their noses out of doors.

But how did they know that a motor-cycle or three-wheeler was involved? According to Gustave, no one had gone to the window – contrary to Gaston's assertion. The father claimed that he had seen the man, while the son declared that he had not. It was Gustave, however, who mentioned a three-wheeler, though he would have had to lean out to distinguish the vehicle.

In fact, it was eventually determined that a three-wheeler did pass on the road that evening, although the times do not coincide exactly. It is thus quite possible that the Dominicis had noticed it. But why did they continue to harp on it throughout? It was a question which Sébeille was often to ask himself and to which he never could find an answer. The occurrence seemed to have nothing to do with the crime, it was an irrelevance. Why did the Dominicis attach such great importance to it?

Another question-mark: did the English people come to Grand' Terre on the evening of August 4? It was one of the points most argued at the two inquiries. Sébeille asked and was given a negative answer. Yet on August 9 the newspaper *France-Soir*, under the by-line of its special correspondent Jacques Chapus, wrote: 'Elizabeth might have saved herself by running to the right, towards the Dominici farmhouse, which she knew to be inhabited because she had gone there for water between six and seven.'

Chapus certainly made a mistake in the timing since it was established that the Drummonds arrived after 7.0 p.m. But where did he get his information? Not from Sébeille or a policeman because they had been told otherwise. Chapus cannot after such a lapse of time give his source. But it can only have been an inhabitant of Grand'Terre letting slip an indiscretion.

What comes to the surface during a criminal inquiry, especially a sensational one, is astounding. All the derelicts of society try to get into the act. Tramps, lunatics, visionaries, charlatans, swindlers, invade the stage, recite a line or two, strive for a role.

The Dominici affair was no exception and the gendarmes, under the direction of Captain Albert, found themselves inundated from the beginning with reports of strange happenings, few of which they could afford to disregard out of hand. They had one distinct disappointment: the Italian deserter from the Foreign Legion whose uniform they found on the bank of the Durance had nothing to do with the drama. Young Severino Donati was at Pegli near Genoa with his brother, who had come to France to fetch him, Severino having tired of the military life. On July 17 he had crossed the frontier and surrendered to the carabinieri, who kept him until the 22nd. Since then he had not left Pegli.

On the 6th a tramp was found living it up in the cafés of Digne, paying for drinks with foreign money. He did not get far and was at once interrogated by the police. He was able to justify his exotic wealth: a stranger crossing the frontier had handed him some left-over change, French and other. He was also able to prove that on the night of the 4th–5th he was sleeping peacefully ten kilomètres from Lurs. Another tramp was arrested because of some careless remarks made. Luckily for him he had a railway ticket in his possession issued at Nice the morning of August 5, which he had not surrendered on arrival, doubtless hoping to use it a second time.

A young man in a highly excited state had disappeared on the evening of the 4th, but was found in a wood living idyllically with a girl of fifteen. The lovers were separated.

A Lurs farmer reported that on the 4th a labourer had walked out on him in a rage, leaving no trace. He was a violent type, according to his late employer. Twenty-four hours later the missing man reappeared. To calm his nerves, he had decided to return to his home near Marseilles on foot. He had slept far from Lurs on the night of the crime.

So the files accumulated in Captain Albert's office for the use of Superintendent Sébeille. There were the two barmen who, after attacking a motorist at Sainte-Maxime, had gone off with his car in the direction of Paris. But they were arrested in the capital and produced an unshakable alibi. A search was instituted for two young men in shorts, but they had disappeared into the blue. Finally, a Belfast industrialist related how at Aix-en-Provence a car had swerved in front of him, whereupon two men had leaped out and threatened him with a revolver. Another car coming along had saved him. He had taken the number, which was broadcast across France. Nothing came of it.

From the entire region the telegrams piled up on Captain Albert's desk. On each an inquiry was opened, usually disappointing, leaving slight doubt but not enough to warrant thorough investigation. Every day brought its quota. Soon the reports came from all over France.

Then something turned up that looked as if it might be more than a flash in the pan. The Lyons police circulated the description of an English drop-head[1] sports car, black with green leather upholstery, abandoned in a garage at 11 Quai de Tilsit on the 4th or 5th. It had English licence plates and an inquiry was broadcast by Interpol. From the English police came the information that it had been sold at Peckham on the outskirts of London to two young Canadians giving the names of Peter Martin and George Johnson. The transaction had been concluded on July 7. The young men had asked the seller to send the insurance certificate to the Royal Bank of Canada but the Bank knew neither of them. Their behaviour seemed suspicious and the garage attendant recalled that they had seemed in a hurry to get away. Their names and description were at once circulated throughout France. Soon hope faded. From the Lyons garage it was learned that although the car had only been registered on the evening of the 5th, the reason for this was that the customers had arrived very late on the 4th. On reflection, the attendant was certain of this. The Canadians remained undiscoverable, but were said to be in Spain. Their consciences may not have been absolutely clear, but they were innocent of the Drummond crime.

A second deserter, this time a parachutist, was next investigated. He had one advantage over the first from the police point of view: he was English and had left Germany in a jeep three weeks earlier. He had arrived in the region not long before and signalled his presence by starting a fire in the woods near Vidauban. But he managed to prove that he had not been in Lurs on the evening of the 4th. He was charged with arson.

The gendarmes also had found themselves plagued with clairvoyants, visionaries and seers who came offering their services. When the authorities would have none of them, they addressed themselves to the press, which obligingly published their divinations. One of them affirmed that the Drummonds had been victims of a

[1] Convertible.

60

mysterious organization to which Sir Jack belonged – like a celebrated gangster of the period who as it happened had just been caught in a burst of machine-gun fire. In London a well-known fortune-teller, not wishing to be outdone, declared that he knew 'the way that would lead straight to the murderer.' He boasted of having helped the police when the Coronation Stone had been stolen.

But out of all this one silhouette, a shadow almost, emerged, and during the trial was resurrected by the lawyers. This was a tramp who was to be the Old Man of the Mountains of the affair, someone of whom everyone spoke but whom no one had seen. He was first introduced by Germain Champsaur, a radio-electrician at Peyruis. To increase his income, Champsaur went about the district with a travelling cinema. On the 5th, at 1.0 a.m., he was driving down from Lurs, where he had just given a performance. He saw the Hillman at the side of the road but paid no attention to it. It was very near the time the crime was committed.

'A kilometre farther on,' he said, 'I passed a man with a bundle on his back; I believed I recognized him as a man who had been living for a time with a woman in an abandoned house on the outskirts of Peyruis.'

The gendarmes of Barjols in the Var had just reported that they had in custody a tramp, Lereboullet, who might be worth questioning; he had spent the night of the 3rd/4th in the grass near Grand' Terre. The next day he was at Manosque, where he asked for and received a soup coupon. Did he then go back to Lurs? Was he the man Champsaur thought he saw? The defence later criticized Sébeille for neglecting this lead. As for the couple living in the derelict house, they were traced: snail-catchers from Port Bouc. Champsaur did not recognize the man as the unknown figure in the night.

The nets the investigators cast constantly did enable them to catch a few useful facts. The testimony they dredged up made it possible to build up a clearer picture of the interval immediately preceding and following the murders. Those nearest, the inmates of Grand' Terre, had seen and heard nothing except distant shots, but the Route Nationale had been no emptier than on any other night. It does not seem that there were any witnesses of the crime itself, for one may suppose that they would have reported it, even if they had not dared to intervene. But on the night of the 4th–5th no one presented himself at the nearby gendarmerie.

A tradesman from Château-Arnoux, M. Ode Arnaud, was the first to appear. He had passed the site of the crime at about 11.30 p.m. on the 4th. 'I saw the Hillman,' he said. 'Behind it there was a man sitting on the ground. I was driving towards La Brillanne and passed two young people in shorts without any luggage. They were going towards Peyruis. Opposite the first houses in Manosque I passed a three-wheeler with, if I saw right, a man and a woman in it.'

Later the police received a visit from a student who had been aboard a truck driven by a public works contractor at Peyruis, M. Conil. It was about 2.0 a.m. Like M. Arnaud, he had seen the English car and it seemed to him that 'something was moving round it.' When questioned, M. Conil confirmed his passenger's story. But he could not be precise about what he had seen. At Grand'Terre the road zigzags and drivers are too concentrated on their driving to take an interest in the scenery. 'I really believe I saw a shadow behind the car,' he said.

The inspectors listened, made notes, passed them on to Sébeille. But what deductions were to be drawn from them? Who had been near the car, the murderer or a scavenger picking over the loot? The crime had taken place around 1.0 a.m., later rather than earlier. On this point the Dominicis had been found correct. On the other side of the Durance, near Dabisse, a village from which one can see across the river the roof of Grand'Terre, a farmer, M. Roger Roche, had distinctly heard the shots – at first two sharp reports with an interval between, then three or four closer together. He had had the same thought as Gaston Dominici: 'Hey, that's no shotgun.'

That was why, on reflection, he thought the shots had been aimed not at a rabbit but at some prowler. A little later he lit a lamp and looked at his watch – it said 1.30. Had he heard screams? He could not swear to it. Possibly, between the two bursts of firing. On nights of full moon, dry and clear, sounds easily traversed the 1800-metre width of the bed of the Durance.

It is worth noting an item of testimony which Sébeille did not collect until August 8. He at once realized it could be important, but he got little out of it. Later during the trial the lawyers cited it several times as an illustration of how the investigators had not, in their view, exhausted the possibilities their inquiries had opened up.

On August 8, Lucien Duc, a young fruit merchant from La Roche-de-Rame in the Hautes-Alpes, sat opposite Superintendent Sébeille in the town hall of Peyruis. He had passed Grand'Terre in his truck on the fatal night. It was about 12.20. His brother Georges was with him and both were making for the Cavaillon market. 'After a bend,' recounted Lucien Duc, 'my headlights picked out a car drawn up at the side of the road. A little farther on I saw a man who at sight of our truck didn't move. He was like a man standing at attention. He was quite stout and about six feet tall. I'd put him at around forty. He was bareheaded, so I could see his thick hair. He was wearing a shirt and trousers of some dark colour.

'When I passed in front of him I looked at him hard. With my left-hand drive I was about one and a half metres from him. He didn't look at us, didn't bat an eyelid. Just stood there frozen stiff. I wondered what he was up to.' M. Duc was so struck by the apparition that he at once said to his brother, 'If he'd signalled for a lift I wouldn't have stopped.'

When he learned of the crime, Lucien Duc telephoned the local gendarmes. Sébeille thought that the description might apply to Gustave, though he was only thirty-two. But it does not seem that M. Duc was confronted with Gustave; the record makes no mention of it. Doubtless a regrettable omission. In fairness to the superintendent, it should be added that when the first reconstruction of the crime took place on August 17, Lucien Duc was summoned. It was at night, the same time to within a few minutes as on August 5. The fruit merchant arrived at the wheel of his truck and in his headlights, at the same spot, he saw a man. He pulled up, leaped to the ground and ran to Sébeille.

'It's him, I'm sure,' he said.

But he was designating Inspector Girolami, whose height and weight corresponded to the description given. Would it have been prudent to replace Girolami by Gustave and begin again? Nothing is more deceptive than an identification by witnesses required to recognize a man glimpsed in the space of a lightning flash.

Moreover, while listening to M. Duc, Sébeille had thought of another suspect. The witness had spoken of 'ugly teeth and a horse face'. The description fitted a road-mender from Peyruis who had hung about on the first day, wanting to be of help to everybody, constantly hovering near the police to eavesdrop. Sébeille called him in, only for him to deny – to the superintendent's astonishment – having been at Grand'Terre on the afternoon of August 5. For two hours he stuck to this position. Finally he admitted that he had been there 'but after my day's work'. Fearful that he had been at fault in this, he had lied even to the point of incurring suspicion for the crime, although he had a perfectly good alibi for the night which it had not occurred to him to mention.

Working in the furnace-like heat, particularly scorching that summer, foreheads and necks dripping with sweat, shirts permanently wet, having trouble sleeping as dawn approached, the superintendent and his colleagues slogged away at probing that night's events. Much more had happened between 11.0 p.m. on the 4th and 5.30 a.m. on the 5th than the Dominicis had said.

It was by no means enough to collect depositions. They had to be worked over, compared and contrasted, pieced together like a film on the cutting-room floor.

On August 6 or 7 two men appeared, one before the Forcalquier gendarmes, the other before the criminal investigation officers at Nice. Their depositions were taken down and forwarded to Sébeille who classified them in his rapidly swelling files.

Jean Ricard was a Marseilles tradesman with a passion for walking and the open country. On the morning of the crime he had passed Grand'Terre to take the bus from Forcalquier for his home, his holiday being over. He had seen the disorder round the Hillman and noticed Lady Drummond's body. He had taken it to be a camper sleeping out of doors. The bus arrived and M. Ricard quickly climbed aboard. It was only then that he was struck by a 'peculiarity': the woman was on the ground beside a camp-bed; a perverse whim, thought M. Ricard, smiling to himself. Then from the papers he learned of the crime and thought it his duty to tell the police. His deposition squared with the established facts, so they did not pursue the matter. Certainly, no one thought of showing him the photograph taken by the Marseilles police photographers. Champsaur had mentioned a man with a bundle on his back walking swiftly in the direction of Lurs station. The gendarmes were now satisfied they knew the identity of the unknown: it was M. Ricard.

At Nice it was a doctor who went to the police. At 50, Dr Morin remained an inveterate camper. In 1951, in company with his wife, he had pitched his tent near Grand'Terre. In this way he became acquainted with the family and especially Gustave, with whom he had embarked on discussions about shooting. They had found each other sympathetic and Gustave had even invited him one evening to take part in a shoot. His brother Clovis and his nephew Roger Perrin went with them. Dr Morin had at first been surprised at the way the beating was organized. He had been placed near a hedge and told that the rabbits would come. He waited, but nothing appeared. But he had heard shots in the distance, and the suspicion came to him that he might have been kept deliberately far from the tent because Gustave and Roger had designs on his wife – a notion he soon dismissed as unworthy. Admittedly he had seen no sign of game, but shooting has its uncertainties. No one had come near the tent, his wife had confirmed on his return. Gustave apologized for his bad luck. If Dr Morin returned next year, he would do better.

Since it was said in the press that Dr Morin had made a statement unfavourable to the Dominicis – they had threatened him with a firearm, so it was reported – the doctor issued a communiqué: he could only express gratitude for the welcome he had received at Grand'Terre. He had met Gaston only once or twice. He had visited the farm and been offered a glass of white wine.

The arrival in the Basses-Alpes of the Marrian family, the Drummonds' friends, enabled an exact inventory of their belongings to be made. According to the Marrians nothing had been stolen, Sir Jack having left most of his money and his wife's jewellery as well as their passports at Villefranche. But this did not exclude the possibility of robbery as motive. The guilty person or persons might have been disturbed while ransacking the car and going through the clothing. It could also be that they had been disappointed; they would not be the first to have killed for nothing.

Records accumulated, pages which seemed to consist of nothing but words, often repetitious, for the storage of banal facts and descriptions with little apparent relevance to the event whose secret was being sought. Sébeille would reach for each fresh document as it came in and wonder whether this one might not at last provide some valid hint, a clue.

3

When the superintendent or his colleagues left Peyruis town hall to take a witness's statement, conduct a check or carry out an interrogation, they mobilized a party of ministerial dimensions. Whatever their direction or mission, there were cars right behind them crammed with journalists, all with columns to fill daily for their papers for which the whole of Europe waited.

Sébeille was as co-operative as his duties allowed. But they were like a ball and chain he dragged after him. Sometimes he had to use force to keep them at a distance – often in vain. One of them once went so far as to conceal himself in a cupboard to eavesdrop on an interrogation.

In order to resume his questioning of Gustave on August 7, Sébeille had to spread a screen of gendarmes between himself and his pursuers. When he entered the courtyard of the farm, it was neither Gaston nor Gustave who received him but Yvette with a sharp 'My husband is in bed ill.'

Sébeille was surprised. What kind of illness could have struck him so suddenly? 'I'll go up and see him,' he said.

Gustave was in fact lying, fully dressed, on his bed. 'Not feeling well?' Sébeille asked.

The farmer's only answer was to hand him a medical certificate signed by Dr Nalin: '. . . certifies that the condition of M. Gustave Dominici, of Grand'Terre, Lurs (Basses-Alpes), necessitates his remaining in bed and complete mental rest.'

The policeman finished reading with a sarcastic laugh which didn't seem to trouble Gustave. 'All those journalists, all those gendarmes,' he explained. He did not add, 'and the police officials,' but his obstinate and uneasy expression spoke for him.

'You can show the journalists the door, can't you?' And when there was no answer, 'I'll come for you tomorrow, I warn you, and sick or not I'll take you with me, one way or another.'

Gustave seemed on the point of tears, wrote Sébeille later. He was convinced it was not the gendarmes or the reporters Gustave wanted to flee, but the questions. It was additional proof that Gustave knew more and was afraid he wasn't strong enough to hide it.

In order to impress him, Sébeille drafted a regular form of summons requiring his presence at Peyruis town hall at 8.0 the next morning, 'And you'll be there,' he ordered.

'Yes,' Gustave said feebly.

Sébeille went downstairs, out through the kitchen, followed by Yvette's hostile glare, and into the courtyard. Gaston was peaceably smoking his pipe under the tree. Sébeille strolled over to him. 'Look here, Grandad, couldn't the people who came into the courtyard that night have been the Drummonds, frightened by people prowling round them?'

'Certainly not.'

'Why?'

Gaston smiled widely. 'Because they were talking in Italian and not in English.'

Sébeille pretended to be surprised. 'Didn't you tell me yesterday that they were using an unfamiliar language?'

For the first time the superintendent then witnessed one of the old man's furies, sudden and astounding in its violence. As if on springs, Gaston rose and rushed at Sébeille, holding his stick by its tip, brandishing it over the superintendent as if he would knock him down. 'Let me alone!' he roared. 'You want to catch me out but you won't. Get out!'

'A splendid outburst,' wrote Sébeille. And at once a thought crossed his mind: the old man's action had been the same as the murderer's when crushing Elizabeth's skull, except that instead of a stick the killer had swung a carbine by the barrel. It was not the only pointer Gaston had just given the police officer: he had exposed himself in a new light. Peaceable patriarch, elegiac shepherd perhaps, but capable also of excesses of rage, of unexpected violence.

'Why are you so angry, Grandad?' asked Sébeille with a smile.

As quickly as he had been carried away Gaston calmed down. 'You're right, my boy. Come on, let's have a drink . . .'

He at once went off to fetch glasses. Sébeille beckoned to Ranchin. Even without Gustave, the visit might not be fruitless. Why not take advantage of it to search the place to see if they could find cartridges or some other clues which might put them on the track of the carbine?

For an hour they ransacked the farmhouse and its outbuildings, followed closely by Gaston and Yvette who both signed the report. They went to the unused upper floor and noted that from there they had an unimpeded view of the scene of the crime. It was the only result of the operation. 'We found no object, no document, no fire-arm or ammunition relevant to the current investigation,' wrote Sébeille in his report.

The lawyers would later severely criticize the manner in which the search was conducted. Had the police officers thought of other objects – besides cartridges and things related to the carbine – which might be useful? Shoes which corresponded to the footprints the gendarmes had measured, clothes with stains which might be dried blood – not a word on these in the reports; a very serious omission, the lawyers declared, negligence which had perhaps decisively influenced the course of the inquiry.

Sébeille and the inspectors left Grand'Terre at 4.30 p.m. The inspector decided to see Dr Nalin, who had issued a certificate to Gustave apparently from a mere willingness to oblige. The doctor was at first surprised by the visit but, faced with the police officer's insistence and his threat to have an expert second opinion, he talked. 'This morning,' he admitted, 'I received a telephone call asking me to call in at Grand'Terre and see Gustave. I found him very low-spirited, harried by the journalists, wanting to run away. So I signed the certificate for him.'

A ridiculous performance by any standard. How could the doctor not have realized that Gustave's major fear was not the journalists, who would have had small respect for a medical certificate, but the police who could have been disarmed by it? Sébeille did not press the matter. Tomorrow he could be tougher with the young farmer, whose health demanded no special consideration. Something could be got out of him, Sébeille reckoned, the big drawback being his comparative weak-mindedness. He was rough and uncouth in body as in mind, it was exhausting work to manage him, but in the end it should be possible.

The afternoon was over but for the police the setting sun brought no rest. Getting back into the car and seeing the carbine lying on the seat, Sébeille had an idea. Why not show the weapon to Clovis, the eldest son who he had already learned had had a quarrel with his father? At this hour he would be at work near the Lurs station, and Sébeille thought up a little scene for his benefit. The Rock-Ola was placed on top of a stone wall near the road and covered with a newspaper. Inspector Ranchin then went to fetch Clovis. On his arrival Sébeille uncovered the rifle. The result was unexpected.

'At the sight,' Sébeille wrote in his report, 'Clovis Dominici had such a shock that he fell on his knees, biting his lips and opening his eyes wide. He remained for a long moment without uttering a word. I then questioned him, telling him that if he recognized the weapon, he must at once tell me the owner's name. Clovis Dominici recovered himself and assured us that he had never seen the rifle.'

The staged scene came to nothing. Sébeille's questions were stone-walled. 'You know this gun,' he kept repeating. 'Tell me who it belongs to.' But Clovis, kneeling on the line, petrified, open-mouthed, eyes distended, remained silent.

'Come along, Clovis . . .'

The linesman, staring at the gun, continually swallowing his saliva, still said nothing. Then he shut his eyes, struggling to recover his calm, searching for words, and finally gasped out, 'No, no, I don't know whose it is.'

It is worth pausing briefly because many official commentators on the case – lawyers, magistrates, or police – considered that the fate of the investigation turned on this moment. For two days Sébeille had been repeating to all and sundry that 'the weapon will speak.' And here was a man overcome at the sight of it; someone, moreover, closely connected with Grand'Terre. The situation was striking: on the one hand the carbine, on which Sébeille placed all his hopes; on the other the farm bordering the road and its inmates, to which all lines of inquiry seemed to lead. It might be assumed that Sébeille would press his advantage, demand that Clovis explain why his emotion had been so intense, and not let him go until he had disgorged the truth.

He did nothing of the sort. Why? It is hard to know what really happened afterwards. In his memoirs Sébeille asserts that he then asked Clovis to accompany him to the Peyruis town hall where for two hours he questioned him without result. Clovis shook his head and kept repeating, 'No, no, I don't know whose it is.'

When Sébeille asked why in that case he had fallen on his knees, Clovis fell back on his habit of working on his knees on the railway line. But in his report, a more official document than a volume of memoirs, Sébeille's story is slightly different. There is no mention of a prolonged interrogation on that day: 'We were struck by the man's attitude, but we did not insist further because we were only at the beginning of the inquiry and, not knowing him, we were not in a position to interpret his demeanour with certainty.' Moreover, no formal record was made that day and it was only on the 12th, five days later, that Clovis signed the following statement:

You have just shown me the carbine you found in the Durance. I can positively assure you that I do not know it and that I have never seen it in the hands of anyone. I can equally assure you that it does not belong to me and if I had had such a weapon in my hands which was subsequently stolen, I should not have failed to tell you.

So Clovis returned to work, taking with him any knowledge he might have. Sébeille returned to Peyruis, where the journalists sitting round the café tables were waiting for any news he might give them. He did not tell them of Clovis's agitation at the sight of the carbine; he only revealed it later.

The charge has often been made against Sébeille that on August 7 he missed a chance that would not come again. On Sébeille's behalf it should be pointed out that he had no aces up his sleeve on August 7. What could he prove against Clovis? His sudden shock. He could only go on repeating to him hour after hour: 'Your attitude is such that you cannot deny knowing the carbine.' Was that enough? Perhaps Clovis would have broken down. We shall never know.

All we do know is that Superintendent Sébeille did not try the experiment and that Clovis gave a great sigh of relief when he rejoined his comrades. The disparity between the memoirs and the official report indicates that the police officers would one day be aware of his mistake: his book is a defence of his investigation, the report part of the record. In the one it is difficult to play with facts, in the other the pen can run on. It is not a matter of reproaching or excusing a man, but of understanding him. If Sébeille let a chance slip, it was doubtless because of a trait in his character which would later be more clearly demonstrated. Sébeille did not play things by ear. He preferred to reflect, prepare his attacks, take every precaution, multiply safeguards. He laid ambushes, set traps, avoided counter-attacks. The recent scene he stored away inside himself. It served to fortify his conviction. He would use it later to break Clovis's silence.

In the afternoon of August 7, a pathetic ceremony took place at the Forcalquier cemetery. This Provençal necropolis is undoubtedly one of the prettiest and strangest in France. It could be somewhere near

Florence in a Botticelli setting: plantations of carefully trimmed yews arranged like cloisters of greenery among which the graves are dispersed. One of them was open to receive the three murdered victims. A godson of Sir Jack's, Mr Austin Smith, came over from London, and he and the Marrian family were the chief mourners, the two little daughters in front weeping for their friend Elizabeth. Representing the Queen was the British Consul-General at Marseilles, Mr Pateman.

An anonymous crowd followed the procession and gathered at the graveside. Was the murderer in the crowd? Many wondered if the murderer was in the crowd. Whoever he was, he must be punished, and as soon as possible.

There were the inevitable eulogies. One of them ended rhetorically: 'They rest in this corner of our land, sacred symbols of the eternal friendship which unites France and England.' But the marble slab to be placed there bore the moving epitaph, 'They were lovely and pleasant in their lives, and in their death they were not divided.'

Simultaneously Gaston was driving his goats to the hills; Gustave, terrified, not daring to put his nose out of doors, stayed in his room. He allowed the journalists, however, to take some photographs of him. He was a good deal less afraid of them than he professed to be.

Clovis carefully shut the door of the shed facing the entrance to the kitchen. Then, thoughtful, he leaned against the wall. He could no longer doubt; he knew where he had seen the broken rifle Sébeille had shown him.

Gustave appeared on the path that ran alongside Grand'Terre, saw his brother and came up to him. The two looked at each other. 'You've seen the carbine is no longer where it was,' said Clovis.

He waited for a reply from Gustave that would comfort him. They had not had it for a long time, had lent it, given or thrown it away so as to have no more trouble since once already the gendarmes had seized prohibited arms at Grand'Terre. The carbine had escaped their vigilance but it had nevertheless been deemed more prudent not to keep it. This was what Clovis hoped to hear.

'What carbine?' asked Gustave with a sidelong glance.

'You know perfectly well.' Then as Gustave said nothing, 'Was it you who used it?'

Gustave heaved a deep sigh. 'No,' he murmured, 'it was Father.'

To Clovis the revelation was like a body-blow. He would not accept it. The old man killing three people! Running in the night

71

after a frantic small girl, catching her, brutally striking her down –
no! 'It's impossible,' he said.

Gustave shook his head. 'He told me so.'

'When?'

'In the morning, when he left with the goats.'

'I don't believe it.'

'It's the truth, all the same.'

Clovis tried to imagine the scene. It was years since his father had
gone shooting. He was not even sure that he knew how the Rock-Ola
worked, being used only to shotguns like the ancient Gras in his room.
Whereas Gustave, who at times tracked boar, might have used it.

'How did you know that the Rock-Ola was in the shed?' asked
Gustave.

Clovis explained. One day in May or June 1951 he had been working at the farm. He had needed some binding cord, and not finding
the ball of twine in the shed, had climbed on a log to see if it wasn't
on the top shelf. It was then that he saw the carbine. It was lying flat
on the shelf, the butt towards the back of the shed, hidden under
some empty sacks except for the breech and barrel. He had assumed
it came from the Maquis, of which his brothers Gustave and Aimé
had been members.

'Why did he do it?' asked Clovis.

Gustave shrugged his ignorance. Their father had said nothing
else and refused to answer questions, going off at once with his goats
and declining to be questioned since.

'You know what he's like.'

Clovis acquiesced silently, only to be seized by a suspicion:
perhaps the murderer was Gustave and not his father? The idea
shocked him as much as the other; he could no more imagine his
brother in the guise of a monster than his father. Gustave was not a
man to kill, strangers especially. Might he have been drunk? But
Gustave denied it; that evening they had gone to bed as usual.

'You'd nothing to do with it?' Clovis asked for the last time.

'I swear it.'

'Why did you get up so early? Father leaves about four.'

'I had work to do,' Gustave replied shortly.

'Where were you?'

Gustave gestured at the courtyard where they were talking.
'Here.'

'When he did it you were with him,' Clovis suggested, hoping for
a denial.

'No,' said Gustave.

A long silence between the two brothers was finally broken by Clovis. 'Nothing must ever be said about it,' he said at last.

'No.'

'Does Yvette know?'

'Yes.'

'And Mother?'

'I don't think so.'

Heavy-hearted, Clovis turned back to the road without entering the kitchen. He had left his bicycle against the wall of the farm. He mounted it and pedalled off towards Peyruis where his wife was waiting for him. His thoughts were in a turmoil. The carbine was indeed the one he had previously seen in the shed. But who had used it? He evaded the answer. He was inclined to believe that it had been Gustave, but why? What devil had possessed him? Alcohol, the brandy his father made? A delayed panic laid hold of him. With a word he could brand Grand'Terre, deliver his family – Gustave especially – to the pack of police and press hounds, drag them to ruin and dishonour. He had held his tongue before but had that deceived the superintendent? His lack of reaction – had that not been a cunning pretence, a trap? And wouldn't the inspectors return tomorrow or the next day to take him away and subject him to a hammering which would beat down his resistance? Anguish lodged in Clovis's heart, never to leave it.

Sitting in the room where weddings took place in the Peyruis town hall, Sébeille waited. The day had begun early for the police. At 7.0 a.m. the Citroën had brought Sébeille to Grand'Terre, but he did not go to the house. He wanted to see the road again, the railway bridge, the bank where Elizabeth was found. Then he had returned to Peyruis where his first visitor was Faustin Roure, the railway foreman, who brought him two details.

'I never ordered Gustave to go to the site of the landslide the morning of the 5th,' he said. 'I intended to go there myself to see if the express could pass.'

He also described a scene at which he had been present at about 8.0 that morning. After having made his inspection and seen the body of the little girl, he had gone to warn the Inspector of Posts and Telegraphs about the telephone lines threatened by the broken branches. Then in order to return to the station at Lurs he had again passed by Grand'Térre. At that exact moment Gaston Dominici had just got back from the mountains with his goats. Faustin went into the courtyard. The old farmer was with his wife and Yvette who appeared at the same time.

Yvette said to him, 'Oh, Papa, there was a murder last night.'

Gaston asked, 'Where?'

'On the gravel patch,' she told him.

The old man went off to have a look.

Sébeille took it in. If Roure had reported the dialogue faithfully, it had to be assumed that Gaston, absent since 4.0 a.m., had known nothing. But at the moment it was Gustave who interested him most.

A car braked suddenly. Sébeille did not have to leave his seat to know what was happening in the little square of Peyruis. The inspectors were back and the commotion among the journalists could only mean that they were bringing in Gustave. A few seconds later the farmer appeared.

'Well, Gustave, are you any better?' Sébeille greeted him ironically. He made him sit opposite him, telling him that he first wanted to confront him with Roure. 'He never asked you to have a look at the landslide, at least so he assures me.'

The two men came face to face. Roure repeated that Gustave came to see him on the evening of the 4th to warn him of the landslide and reassure him he had cleared the way for the evening train. The conversation had been short and had taken place in the café run by Mme Roure in Peyruis. But the foreman was categorical: he had given Gustave no precise instruction.

It was therefore on his own initiative that the farmer had gone to the railway as soon as he got up, so discovering the child's body.

Gustave said nothing. When Sébeille pressed him, he said, 'You must have misunderstood me.'

'Probably,' admitted the superintendent with a smile.

Gustave's interrogation thus began with a strategic withdrawal. He claimed he had no other thought in mind except the landslide and had forgotten the shots in the night. It was why he had not stopped near the car, noticing only the cushion under the mulberry tree. When he found the child's body he fell into such a panic that he thought only of alerting the gendarmes.

Sébeille returned to the events of the night. Had Yvette and he heard no cry, no sound of a motor or footsteps?

'None,' Gustave replied without hesitation.

'You saw nobody?'

'No.'

Patiently Sébeille began going into details, but the dialogue became a virtual monologue. Sébeille noted that during three hours of questioning Gustave spoke only a quarter of an hour. 'With Gustave,' he wrote in his report, 'questions remained unanswered.'

And he sketched a portrait of the farmer. 'Of agreeable appearance, his open expression suggests a superior peasant type, but despite his expression, he is by nature uncommunicative. Unlike his father, he is not the least talkative. His reasoning is simple, and he goes on the principle that the less one says, the less one risks making a mistake. His behaviour, too, is the opposite of his father's; in fact, Gustave, rather apathetic, shows no apparent reaction. He told us several times that he would always repeat the same things, having nothing more to add. Like all the rest of his folk, he unfailingly displays a disarming peace of mind.'

Sébeille was first of all surprised that Gustave had not gone to the window at the sound of the shots. Certainly Grand'Terre was isolated and the officer well understood that Gustave had not thought of going out; he might fear an attack the moment he stepped out of doors. But the window was open; he could have approached it cautiously to see what was going on, while remaining hidden.

Gustave listened attentively to the superintendent's arguments; they provoked no response from him. Sébeille resumed his discourse in another form – in vain. At the third attempt Gustave decided to speak. 'And what if there'd been a fellow near the farm, watching? He'd have shot me like a rabbit.'

'You can look without being seen.'

But Gustave felt that his answer ought to be sufficient. His gaze remained fixed on the superintendent, expressionless, dejected. He sweated heavily. From time to time he passed his hand through his dishevelled hair.

Sébeille did not let up. He made fun of Gustave: a strapping fellow like him, a hunter and a good shot, to tremble like a silly woman ready to hide under the bedclothes because of shots fired off somewhere. 'You never know who the people are who knock at our door at night,' Gustave said finally. 'And it's not uncommon. Look at those motor-cyclists the night of the crime.'

He repeated that the shots had been fired at 1.0 a.m., adding in confirmation that his father's clock in the kitchen on the ground floor had struck immediately after the last report. He was absolutely certain it was caused by a military weapon.

For three hours Sébeille laboured to make Gustave change his story. He exhausted himself, noting only with some satisfaction towards the end that Gustave was not invulnerable. His features became drawn, his cheeks lost their colour, his eyes grew dull, sometimes his chin or throat quivered. The man was afraid of betraying himself. Sébeille became more and more convinced that if he agreed to talk, Gustave might part with some of the keys to the riddle. No question seemed to trouble him. Yet he was not really the solid rock he appeared to be. He suffered and he grieved. His nerves were raw. The self-control was only on the surface. 'I will never change my story,' he ended one of his brief replies, 'it will always be the same as I gave the gendarmes.'

It was noon when the door of the town hall opened for Gustave and exposed him to the full impact of the impatient journalists. They had been waiting eagerly for three hours. From an interview between the superintendent and witness number one anything might emerge – even an arrest, for many of them had already fixed their suspicions on Gustave. But he was emerging free, nervous and sweating. He returned monosyllabic answers to their questions and then allowed himself to be pushed into a police car which would take him back to Grand'Terre.

Behind him Superintendent Sébeille made a brief statement: the witness had confirmed his first story. 'We have learned nothing more. He is not involved in the crime.'

He seemed disappointed and refused any further details. The journalists piled into their cars to follow the one containing Gustave. The procession moved on to Lurs.

In the courtyard of the farm friends and relations awaited Gustave's return. There was no doubt that they feared he would be detained. Their faces cleared when he turned up, followed at a distance by the police.

'All the same, it's a terrible existence,' sobbed Yvette, shaken by a sudden bout of nerves. 'We are innocent.'

She was speaking to the journalists who were assailing Gustave with questions and getting answers much more easily than the superintendent had.

'I'm very tired,' he said. 'It's natural that I should be questioned since I'm the first witness. But it's nothing to do with me.'

Gaston took no part in the excitement. He remained aloof and when the journalists questioned him he grumbled, 'In my son's place I wouldn't have gone with them. But he's so stupid,' and he added, 'He's innocent. He's got nothing to do with the crime.' Then he turned on his heels and walked off to his orchard. The intruders annoyed him.

In the evening, at the apéritif hour, while the journalists questioned him, Sébeille sought to escape them by saying, 'For goodness' sake, don't press me too much. The murderer isn't far away, let's not tell him anything. Don't give him a chance to prepare his story. At the moment he's watching and listening to us.'

At one point Sébeille was close to giving up the case. He reconsidered his decision only at the urging of his superiors. Sébeille had learned that a distinguished lawyer, Maître de Moro-Giafferi, President of the Committee of Justice in the National Assembly, had addressed to the Lord Chancellor,[1] M. Martinaud-Déplat, a forceful protest against the 'brutality' with which the interrogation of Gustave Dominici was conducted by Superintendent Sébeille. He emphasized the fact that the witness was in poor health as attested to by a medical certificate. In short, Sébeille was denounced as a torturer, an accusation which certainly could not be made against him. The superintendent was understandably cut to the quick but his superiors reassured him. They had never doubted his correctness.

But Moro-Giafferi was not alone. He was joined by one of the most eminent French lawyers, Maurice Garçon, member of the Académie Française, who attacked the police investigations even more fiercely. He accused the police officers of trying to rival Maigret in popularity and of giving press conferences and organizing reconstructions of the crime without regard to the pain they caused those unjustly suspected as a result of these blundering procedures conducted in the full glare of publicity. The British press joined in along the same lines, declaring that the police had neglected the most elementary routine, such as taking prints – a charge which Sébeille was forced to deny.

These were not the only external difficulties Sébeille encountered. He quickly recognized that a very special atmosphere surrounded the case. The region had long been notorious for its history of criminal violence. In the last hundred years or so there had been at least three brutal murders – and (by a curious coincidence) in two of the cases there were three victims.

In 1841 a Lurs farmer had been found gravely wounded with the mutilated corpses of three of his employees, a man and two girls,

[1] In French *Garde des Sceaux*, the highest legal authority, equivalent to the Lord Chancellor in England and the Attorney-General in the US.

one half-naked, at various distances from him. The murderer was soon caught – an escaped convict, arrested three days later for killing a gendarme. He was condemned to the guillotine on that charge since it proved too difficult to pin the other on him and he always denied his guilt. In 1871 a gang of Italian criminals who had been terrorizing the countryside, robbing and murdering, were finally caught after the massacre of a Lurs farmer – coincidentally living on the same farm as the previous victims – together with his wife and daughter. Two of the gang were publicly executed at Digne. And in 1928 came the killing at Valensoles for which the murderers were brought to justice by Edmond Sébeille's father. These crimes became local folk legends and the perpetrator of the first, Larderay, the subject of song and story throughout France. The site of the farm, only five hundred metres from Grand'Terre, remained desolate as if accursed.

But it was not formally defined crimes such as these that now concerned the superintendent and his colleagues. From the beginning they were conscious of a very special climate of opinion enveloping the affair and the Grand'Terre inmates. Furtive warnings reached them. Let them beware: they were raising a stone under which reptiles swarmed. Many recent events which were better forgotten, out of fear or love of peace at any price, would come to light. The period of the Liberation was not yet distant. Strange things had happened round 1945 in the Basses-Alpes and more particularly near Lurs and the neighbouring hills.

Also, from the moment suspicion first fell on Gustave's sincerity and the truth of his story, a Marseilles paper and then another, in Paris, came vigorously to his defence. *La Marseillaise*, the Communist Party organ of that city, and *L'Humanité*, the Party's national organ, bitterly criticized Sébeille's conduct of the inquiry and the direction it was taking. From August 9, *L'Humanité* took up the cudgels for Gustave. He was 'cleared of any suspicion', while his family 'enjoyed an excellent reputation'. No doubt it was true. But Sébeille could not ignore the way the Party press insistently emphasized the fact, as if wishing to make it clear to the police that there could be no question of meddling with the Dominicis. The nearer Sébeille came to Grand'Terre, the clearer the warnings became: the whole family must be kept out of the affair.

One theory widely disseminated in the Communist press and repeated by other newspapers was that the murder was only an episode in a secret war. That in reality Sir Jack Drummond was a highly placed spy whom enemy agents had finally struck down on August 5, taking advantage of his impromptu camping-out after having followed him all across France. The assassins were, according to one's political predilections, Americans, Russians, or Germans.

Imaginations exploded. A whole fable was created. The agents were looking for a document. Under the masterly direction of 'technicians', place and circumstances had been coldly chosen to incite the investigators to believe in a foul crime committed by local inhabitants. How could one avoid thinking of members of the Intelligence Corps or CIA seeking to infiltrate the Mediterranean where the British already had a start of several decades? For others, it was the executioners of the NKVD via members of the underground.

The theory had very little to support it, but the police could not fail to notice the presence of unexpected visitors at Grand'Terre, including the local heads of the Communist Party and the municipal councillors of Lurs. At such times everybody remained shut up in the kitchen and no word filtered out of what had been said. The wildest rumours circulated. One was that Marcel Servin and Charles Tillon, then the stalwarts of the Party and members of its National Political Bureau, had taken the trouble to come in person for a secret meeting with the Dominicis – rumours no more confirmed than Drummond's membership in a secret service. Then another theory sprouted: it was Lady Drummond who had been involved in espionage – a story no more able to withstand scrutiny than the others. But public opinion abandons its myths with reluctance. The investigators had to take note of all the theories.

What had occurred at Lurs during the war, and especially after the German withdrawal? The investigators' requests for files met with little response, but it emerged that in this corner of the Basses-Alpes the purge had not been gentle and that the settlement of numerous personal grudges had played a large part in it. Of course Sir Jack had not been involved in the brutal liquidations of an epoch when passions ran wild. The police very quickly determined that this was the first time that he had been in Haute-Provence. He had no tie, friendly, professional, or military, with the region. But again the climate of opinion had to be considered. The silence, the circumspection, the evasiveness of witnesses, the faces shut tight when asked a question – to what fear could these be attributed? Those who agreed to talk invariably stopped short in their admissions. They recalled summary executions like those of the mayor of Peyruis or the two brothers of a neighbouring miller which were later proved to have been so unjustified that the head of the Maquis had to offer belated apologies to the survivor. When the miller demanded the names of the murderers, he encountered first silence, then threats.

Sébeille did not leave this avenue unexplored. He had secret meetings with members of the Resistance, the true, the honest and patriotic, who after helping in the allied landing returned to their jobs as if nothing had happened. They belonged to all manner of political groups – Communist, FTP,[1] FFI,[2] a clandestine army – and in their company Sébeille could take stock of the Resistance and the bands who had lived in the surrounding mountains. It emerged that under cover of the Resistance gangs had formed for plunder, extortion, even the murder of victims guilty of only one wrong, the possession of jewels or hidden gold.

Moreover, treasure was apparently hidden more or less everywhere: relics of parachute drops which had been diverted, pounds sterling or counterfeit French banknotes printed in London but which the Bank of France would redeem, all lures for the criminal. Prowlers and nocturnal hunters were not necessarily seeking furred or feathered game; shots which at times wakened farmers or villagers were not always meant for badgers or boars. No one reported them to the authorities. No one was interested in doing so. One plausible theory was that Sir Jack Drummond had found himself on the night of August 4–5 face to face with one of these hunters after easy treasure. It was not impossible.

No one was anxious for the superintendent to burrow too deep. He was in fact dissuaded from all sides. The uneasiness was general and genuine. World War II collaborators were only too ready to discredit the whole Resistance movement and would start a smear campaign at the first opportunity. Sébeille had to advance on tiptoe. He was advised never to probe into what the individuals he questioned might or might not have done during the Liberation. But a lawyer appointed by the British Consulate at Marseilles, Maître Claude Delorme, declared openly that the mystery of Lurs would not be solved so long as the secret of the massacre which took place during the summer of 1944 at the château of Peyrolles remained hidden. Maître Delorme himself had no axe to grind since he had been a courageous member of the Resistance.

[1] Franc-Tireurs et Partisans, a clandestine movement during the Occupation under communist obedience.
[2] Forces Françaises de l'Intérieur: the Maquis.

He was referring to the murder of M. and Mme Cartier at their château on the left bank of the Durance, nearly opposite Grand'Terre. M. Cartier, retired, lived with his wife, his aged mother and his grandson. During the occupation he had supplied the neighbouring Maquis. He had even contributed a hundred thousand francs on one occasion but refused to give more.

One morning the servant found the bodies of M. and Mme Cartier in the hall, with several bullets in their heads. On the first floor the grandmother and child had been locked into their rooms. The evening before they had heard cries and shots. It seems certain that M. Cartier had known his assailants, since after nightfall he opened the door only to callers whom he knew. Everything had been ransacked, the safe was open and empty, and the jewellery had disappeared.

A superintendent from Nice, M. Stigny, sent to investigate, was discovered dead in a nearby irrigation ditch with a bullet through his head the day after he reported that the case was solved and 'I've got the killers.' His colleagues, bent on avenging him, arrived in force in the Basses-Alpes and their inquiries eventually resulted in two arrests: that of a departmental head of the FTP known as 'Serge', and a colleague of the police whom they knew well, Inspector Lapontre, seconded from Nice to Peyruis. It was he who had asked Serge for the 'execution' of M. Stigny on the pretext that he was a 'collaborator'. In 1951 he was sentenced to ten years' solitary confinement. But he continued to deny his guilt and the Cartier killers remained unknown. 'Find them,' those who had lived in the region at the time whispered to Sébeille, 'and you will have the murderers of the Drummonds.'

To each of these well-meaning but perhaps not entirely disinterested counsellors Sébeille put the question, 'How are the two cases linked?' He could even go along with the invariable argument: 'He who has killed will kill again.' But no one furnished anything concrete, he collected only vague assertions, accusations unsupported by facts, simple gossip relayed at second or third hand. Whatever its source, the superintendent classified the data in his files.

Sébeille's freedom of movement was at times restricted. Requests came for caution: do nothing that might start political controversy; proceed against the Dominicis only with the greatest circumspection.

This resulted in criticism by the newspapers of the way the case was being handled. The tone was set by the British press which presented Sébeille as a man thirsting for publicity, playing the inspired and mysterious detective. British reporters accused the investigators of not having made a serious check of fingerprints and of having allowed the crowd to trample the site of the crime, obliterating all traces. And in London a campaign was started to send out competent people as soon as possible, meaning, of course, men from Scotland Yard.

Sébeille shrugged his shoulders; it had never occurred to him to call in a clairvoyant, as the British press accused him of doing. If the professional seers flocked to gather some unwholesome publicity there was nothing he could do about it. One of these seers actually rendered him a service by discovering the bullet which had ricocheted off the parapet of the little bridge, leaving a mark noticed earlier by an employee of the Department of Roads and Bridges. Divination? Hardly. The magus had simply trodden on it. It was one hundred metres from the bridge; the murderer must therefore have fired at the child to stop her flight and missed.

The French press debated the affair as if it were an item in the cold war then raging. *Le Figaro* asserted that the 'murderer could be an FTP who had taken part in summary executions during the Liberation.' The Communist papers exploded with remarkable unanimity. The National Association of Former Combatants of the French Resistance issued an indignant communiqué: '*Le Figaro* is attempting to besmirch the honour of the whole Resistance . . . By presenting those who executed traitors as murderers capable of any crime, *Le Figaro* once more identifies itself with the traitors.' It was a long way from the tragic death of an English family. But the Lurs affair in the first month of the inquiry was also a breeding-ground for old passions. 'One fears,' wrote *France-Soir*, 'that in this atmosphere the police have not always been as free to act as is desirable in such an affair.'

Paul Maillet was something of a character. Shrewder and more intelligent than Gustave Dominici, during the war he had been chief of the parachute section at Mirabeau for the FTP in the area. He had been courageous and honest. No ugly rumour touched him, although suspicion was quick to fall on men like him who had handled money, supplies and arms dropped from the sky. Paul Maillet had displayed an absolute integrity and had become the secretary of the local branch of the Communist Party. Here also he was untouched by criticism. He led his militants with wisdom and camaraderie. The Communist Party is regarded as uncompromising with those in responsible positions, expecting them to be above suspicion. Paul Maillet enjoyed the confidence of his superiors.

There was one small black mark against him, however, though it was a mere peccadillo. Like most of his friends, Maillet enjoyed poaching. One of his passions was to set out at night, gun in hand, for the hills and valleys. Ginette, his wife, complained of it; during the day, if Paul saw game on the wing or caught the scent of boar, there was no keeping him in bed that night. He would go off alone, sniffing the wind, tracking the spoor. The gendarmes were not unaware of it, but shut their eyes; if they were to round up all the poachers, half the area would be up before the magistrates.

But Paul's brother Auguste interested the police. At 30 he had no regular employment. It was not altogether his fault; he had been detailed to Germany for forced labour and returned ill, his lungs affected, his stomach tormented by an ulcer. He lived either with his parents or with another brother, Pierre, a locksmith at Manosque. On the evening of the crime he had been with his father and mother at Lurs.

It was reported, however, that he had spent the night of August 4–5 in the disused railway station at Lurs. What was he doing there? The police came to question him at home. He was said to be irascible and embittered, always ready for a brawl. Like his brother, he worried little about the regulations when he felt like going shooting. The police had been assured that he bore on his chest the marks of a violent struggle.

The inspectors asked him to undress. With obvious reluctance, Auguste complied. His skin was intact. The allegation was only a malicious revenge or a stupid joke. But did he have an alibi?

'I went to bed at nine,' he said, 'and didn't get up.'

His parents upheld him and the police were convinced that they were not lying. The gendarmes then suggested that the same test be applied to Paul. Sébeille and his colleagues went to Paul's farm, La Maréchale, and he accompanied them to Peyruis town hall.

The account of his time squared with that of his brother. He had gone to bed early and not risen until 5.0 a.m. Auguste had then joined him and until 7.0 they cut hay. It was the postman, Francis Perrin, who told them of the crime during the morning. Paul Maillet made a good impression on Sébeille. He answered without anxiety or hesitation. He appeared to have nothing to hide. 'If I knew anything,' he declared, 'I would tell you.'

His wife Ginette and his parents were again questioned. Sébeille's impression was confirmed; there was neither contradiction nor withholding. Very different from the Dominicis. Nevertheless, he didn't close the Maillet chapter. It was not only his intuition. Maillet was considered the closest intimate of the Dominicis both socially and politically. He was often at the house. The police had seen him disappear when they arrived. Did he know anything further? In his capacity as head of a cell had he been in on a conspiracy? Sébeille, who was now proceeding with caution, might legitimately ask himself the question. But he was less and less disposed to a brusque move before holding more trumps.

One piece of encouragement had come his way this first week, only to fizzle out. In the café where he was taking his apéritif, one of his inspectors had heard that a local inhabitant had seen Gaston Dominici buying a rifle from an American soldier. It was almost too good to be true and Sébeille did not dare believe it. However, he hurried off to see the man in question, a mason named Abel Bastide who devoted his spare time to searching for truffles.

Abel Bastide was a strange character. Doubtless not very bright, he was colourful, fond of the bottle, and expressed himself with his hands as well as his lips, an incessant talker who had seen and heard everything, worked when he felt like it, which was as little as possible, lived alone in a hovel, and was always cheerful and delighted to have an audience. It took Sébeille little time to assess this witness. Even if he was telling the truth, it would be necessary to snatch it from a torrent of boasts, lies and gossip all offered with equal conviction. The more he talked, the more Sébeille regretted that he failed to come up to expectations, for his tale was intriguing.

In August 1944 Abel was working at Grand'Terre, repairing the roof of an outbuilding. Military trucks passed along the road; he could hear their roar. Now and then one of them stopped and the soldiers got down to ask for water, wine or fruit. 'One day,' Bastide related, 'Gaston himself received them. I was on my roof and didn't hear very well what they were saying. But I saw Gaston point to a rifle a soldier was carrying on his shoulder. The old man's quite a hunter. And he's a good shot. The American showed him the gun, explained how it worked and even fired a few shots in the air. It seemed to get Gaston all excited.'

'Did he buy one?'

'I can't say.'

'Was he alone or with Gustave?'

'Alone, I think, but I'm not sure.'

When Sébeille repeated this conversation to Gaston he openly derided it. 'You're listening to nitwits now, are you?'

'Did he do work for you?'

'Yes.'

'In August 1944?'

'It's quite possible.'

'And the American?'

Dominici shrugged his shoulders. 'No American ever stopped here.'

Whom to believe, the exuberant Abel or the placid Gaston? Sébeille had several more conversations with the mason. But Bastide became noticeably more and more cautious. If put against the wall, he would deny everything. Had pressure been put on him, or had it dawned on him that if he co-operated with the police he would expose himself to general contempt and hostility? The Dominicis always posed as good people persecuted by the investigators because of an unlucky circumstance: they had been the nearest neighbours to the triple crime. Their complaints seemed well founded to many, and whoever helped the police was immediately suspect. Bastide lost his warm and welcoming disposition. As soon as Sébeille appeared he clammed up and his memories dissolved. Perhaps the scene had not taken place at all, or it happened elsewhere and he had confused one employer with another. Sébeille abandoned the idea of a confrontation between the mason and Gaston, which might have given the latter too easy a victory.

Yvette Dominici had just turned twenty. She was quite an attractive girl, full-faced, with a matt complexion, black hair, more coquettish without doubt than farmers' wives commonly were at that time. That was perhaps why her father-in-law at times expressed himself forcefully about her. According to Gaston's firm convictions, the model wife should diverge only slightly from the example set by the Sardine – silent, docile, dressed in black or sober colours, a scarf on her head, wasting as little time as possible on her appearance, spending little or nothing on adornment. The old man freely evoked the virtues of another age and the disastrous influence of fashion on the ways of the traditional family. It could also be that he found it hard to tolerate the sight of radiant youth which would never again be his.

He had met his match in Yvette. The young woman never brooked interference. In her family, the Barths, the father certainly commanded and the wives obeyed. But her father was the head who did the producing and continued to reign. At Grand'Terre, Gustave worked and Gaston, who no longer did anything, still wanted to give the orders. This did not accord with Yvette's notions: he who made the land yield was the master. After having studied the people around her she had staked out her position. The father-in-law had no illusions about it; he would not govern his son's household, Yvette would not allow it.

It was under her influence that Gustave announced to his father that henceforth Grand'Terre was to be divided in two even to the point of cooking independently. To achieve this had required a certain obstinacy on Yvette's part. Gustave did not dare impose it on his father. Gaston resisted but in the end he had to yield; either that or the couple would leave. He needed Gustave, the last pair of hands which could preserve the value of his soil. As for Yvette, resolute, sharp-tongued, not easy to live with, she had one compensating factor which Gaston was well able to appreciate: she was a worker, clean, orderly, with solid good sense, who had served her apprenticeship on her father's farm. Gaston always settled when he had to. He even had a certain respect for her.

That Yvette was not easy to handle was clear to Sergeant Louis Romanet even before she sat down in front of him. The gendarmes had arrived at the farm that morning led by Romanet. Sébeille had asked them to clear up a number of points with the Dominicis. Romanet had selected Yvette, whom he knew well. She had obstinacy in her blood. It was no use trying to outstare her. She had already ordered out of the house journalists whom she didn't like. She would not have minded doing the same with Sébeille, and the same went for the gendarmes, although they were local men and their faces familiar. Inwardly Sébeille had already wondered about this couple who seemed to him ill-matched. Yvette deserved better. Not in the least stupid, cold or harsh in her judgments, how could she have let herself fall for the so much cruder Gustave? Of course he was well built, virile to look at, broad-shouldered – a physique which might well have titillated the girl. Perhaps she had already realized that above the neck the endowment was more moderate.

Romanet opened his attack with the night of the crime: what

had she seen and heard? He knew the answer beforehand: Yvette's story would correspond with her father-in-law's and her husband's. But Sébeille's instructions were strict: to go into the most minute details. Contradictions would inevitably emerge. Does a witness stumble more easily in proffering undeniable facts or in repeating a prepared and concerted version? Does one remember better what one has seen or the lie learned by heart? If Yvette's and Gustave's answers coincided literally, contained the same set phrases, at least two conclusions could be drawn – proof of sincerity or of total docility. Sébeille intended to compare carefully the actual words used by the young wife. When a witness repeats a pre-arranged story he has a tendency to use the same terms without ever resorting to synonyms for fear of dangerous deviations.

Romanet first asked Yvette to tell him very simply what had happened that night. 'About half past eleven,' she said, 'I woke up to arrange my child's covers. Almost at once I heard a large motor-cycle or three-wheeler which stopped near the house.' (Gustave: 'At half past eleven we were wakened by the noise of a large motor-cycle or three-wheeler.') Thus there was a slight discrepancy between the couple as to the reason for the awakening. But the same words recurred: large motor-cycle or three-wheeler.

'Did you see it?' asked Romanet.

'No, a man came into the courtyard and spoke to my father-in-law. He also had a woman and child with him. The woman burst out laughing, I don't know why.'

'Did you go to the window?'

'Yes, with my husband.'

(Gustave: 'No one went to the window.') To the investigators the difference had its interest: if Gustave denied approaching the window during the incident of the 'large motor-cycle or three-wheeler' he perhaps intended this to justify his failure to stir when the shots were fired. But how could the two in bed know so well what was going on outside?

'You didn't go down?'

Yvette shook her head. 'At night we never leave our room for any reason. We're too isolated.'

At 1.0 a.m. there had been shots while the baby was feeding. 'I didn't hear any cry or call for help,' said Yvette, 'but I was afraid because the dog began to bark.' She even added a detail. 'He didn't do it with any strength, as if he were afraid of something.'

'This time you didn't even get up?'

'No, my husband reassured me. He said it didn't mean there was anything dangerous about. Then he added that the shots might have come from farther off.'

She had then finished feeding the baby and they went back to sleep. They rose at 5.30. Gustave went off to check the condition of the landslide. He made no allusion to the shots the night before. Then he returned running. He told her of the little girl on the bank of the Durance. Yvette here added something which intrigued the gendarme. 'He went back to the mulberry tree to note the details of the car.'

'Why?' asked Romanet, surprised.

'In case it should drive off,' answered Yvette.

The girl's sentence echoed the curious remark of Gustave: the child might have been killed by her parents. But on what evidence could they have based such a notion? Had they seen the Drummonds the previous evening? Had the parents seemed to them capable of something so inhuman? Had they, for instance, witnessed a scene of violence, heard threats directed at Elizabeth? Yvette would not be drawn. She had no idea about the crime, so could report only what she had seen and heard. At 7.0 Gustave had merely spoken of 'a child'. Not until after the arrival of the gendarmes did she know that there were three victims.

'Nevertheless you connected them with the shots?' the sergeant suggested.

From Yvette came the disconcerting reply, 'We didn't go into it.'

They showed her the rifle, which she did not recognize. Had she ever seen any like it? 'No,' she said, 'but in 1944 I was only twelve; American weapons didn't interest me.'

In another corner of the courtyard the gendarmes were listening to Gustave. He now modified his first statements. During the appearance of the motor-cyclists he had gone to the window, but he had not done so during the shots. He thus tallied with his wife on this point. Had he realized that he ought not to admit to anyone his profound indifference to strangers intruding on his home at night – he, the family's protector? Or was it Yvette who had sensed the weakness of this position? A scrutiny of these contradictions and variations did not lead to much – except to wonder that the inmates of Grand'Terre should work so hard to offer a coherent and unanimous account of the night's incidents.

Sébeille, meanwhile, had spent the whole day running round the countryside on unrewarding pursuits. In the evening he received the minutes of the interrogations. From Captain Albert he learned that nothing by way of a clue had been discovered. But Gustave's oscillations disturbed and irritated him. They confirmed that the young farmer was uneasy. He was afraid of betraying himself and advanced like a man venturing on thin ice, fearful at every step that it would give under him. During the day Sébeille had also been to see Clovis. It had been another routine performance: Gustave's brother repeated what he had said on the morning of the 5th. It was he who had notified Gustave that there was another body. 'He told me,' Clovis definitely asserted, 'that he had not gone near the car.'

Sébeille could not fail to notice the insistence of the members of the Dominici family that Gustave, contrary to all logic, had not in returning from the bank of the Durance approached the car. Why stubbornly emphasize abnormal behaviour? The instinctive reaction would have been to run and warn the parents that their child lay dead not far off. But by now Sébeille knew that he could not trap Gustave with simple questions. Somehow or other he had to be faced with the reality of his lie. Even then Sébeille might not succeed; Gustave's powers of inertia seemed limitless. Still, Sébeille planned to try the experiment one day. It would yield results only if he found an unshakable witness whom Gustave could not challenge. Night after night Sébeille read and re-read the thick file already accumulated in an effort to discover the fault or flaw which would give him a hold over Gustave. At this point, Gustave was undoubtedly the superintendent's prime suspect.

Her eyes wide, the little girl listened, attentive and willing, as the journalist Jacques Chapus gave his instructions. She was blonde and of the same age as Elizabeth Drummond. The daughter of an engineer with the Department of Roads and Bridges at Marseilles, she was spending her holiday with her grandparents at Peyruis. Jacqueline Dubois knitted her brows. She was proud of having been chosen for the experiment Chapus had in mind.

'First you'll take off your sandals,' he told her.

They were on the gravel at the exact spot where the Hillman had been found. Before them was the stony path leading to the bridge, the railway cutting and the slope to the Durance. 'You will run as fast as you can to the slope,' said the journalist, 'even if it hurts your feet a little, OK?' Jacqueline nodded her agreement. 'And don't fall.'

In his hands he held a stopwatch, souvenir of his days as a sports reporter. He raised his arm and then brought it down abruptly. 'Go!' he ordered.

The child shot forward, elbows pressed to her sides. It could have been Elizabeth fleeing from her attacker towards the refuge of the bushes. Jacqueline followed the journalist's directions; running without attention to the rough contact her feet made with the ground, the stones and the harsh vegetation.

Chapus rejoined her where she stood breathless at the spot on which Elizabeth's body had lain. 'Twenty-five seconds,' he said. Then he told Jacqueline to show him her feet. They bore no scratches, only the red marks Sébeille had noticed on the little corpse. The object of the journalist's experiment was twofold: to measure the exact time Elizabeth had taken to flee from the car in which she slept to the slope, and to verify if in her desperate flight she might have wounded her feet.

Of course the test did not permit hard and fast conclusions. It had taken place by day for one thing, and Elizabeth had fled before her murderer at night. Moreover, Jacqueline had nothing to fear, while Elizabeth was running in terror.

That same evening Sébeille returned to the spot at midnight, accompanied by Chapus who had informed him of his experiment. As on the night of the crime, the weather was exceptionally fine. The moon, very high, lit up the orchard and the Durance. The dark pile of Grand'Terre was like an inert, dead mass on the landscape. The police officer and the journalist posted themselves on the gravel. Jacques Chapus explained the results of his test.

They were to wait nearly three hours, noting that the traffic on the road was less than they had expected: fifteen cars in all. It was therefore possible that the murderer had remained at the site of the crime quite a while, hiding each time headlights swept the nearby trees. This strengthened the testimony of the Duc brothers that they had seen a man: it might well have been the murderer. Moreover, at no time had the lights in Yvette's room been on. It seemed that the night of the crime was the only one on which little Alain had been given his feed at 1.0 a.m.

Captain Albert had already, on August 6, watched during the night from near Grand'Terre. No one had wakened. If the couple had not slept on the 5th it was for another reason.

Sébeille tried to imagine the minute-by-minute unfolding of the crime. The murderer had probably tried to open the door of the car where Elizabeth slept. She had cried out and wakened her parents. The murderer had first attacked Sir Jack, who fled to the other side of the road and died there. Lady Drummond was killed almost immediately thereafter, since she had had no time to move. It was in this brief interval that Elizabeth had leaped from the back of the Hillman and run towards the Durance in an effort to escape. The superintendent himself went through the actions required for the murder of the parents, it took him forty-five seconds. If Jacqueline had taken twenty-five seconds to follow by day a path she knew in advance, it was probable that the English girl's flight had taken a little longer, thirty-five or forty. She therefore had a slight start on the murderer, who fired at her and missed. He then dashed in pursuit of the child, who probably fell or tried to hide in the deep grass.

When the superintendent and the journalist left for Peyruis, there was no sign of life at Grand'Terre, not a window lighted up. Only the dogs barked when the two passers-by deliberately brushed against the walls of the farmhouse and took several steps along the path that led to the courtyard.

4

Every year on August 15 France to a man retires to rest. The only exceptions are those whose work is indispensable to life. It is the summer counterpart of the Christmas festivities, an opportunity to draw breath, a collective pause. In many villages and towns these two or three days mark the annual holiday. People dance in the squares, dodgem cars and shooting galleries invade the shady open spaces, beer, cider and white wine flow in rivers, and showers of confetti float through the air before sinking down into muddy piles.

Peyruis was one of these towns. But Gaston Dominici had not altered his morning routine. He rose at 3.30 a.m., drew on his thick shoes, tied his canvas belt round his waist, put on his battered hat, and drank his rosemary tea well laced with white wine. It was his breakfast, together with the solid chunk of bread into which he sandwiched a sausage or slice of pâté which he would eat when he reached the mountain. Rosemary was for health, a secret he had discovered in a book by an old healer. (He also treated his rheumatism with a tisane of rye.)

Then he whistled for his dog Dick, who accompanied him to the pen where the goats were waiting. They grouped themselves intelligently. In the distance beyond the Durance the first light of day defined the horizon. From the orchard drifted scents that delighted Gaston every day. A blow from his stick on the backside of the nearest goat and he was on his way. He did not turn his back on the gravel patch but directed his flock straight towards Peyruis. It was in this direction that the best grass was to be found in the summer. And thanks to the morning dew, it was fresher. He lighted his pipe and with his supple gait followed the animals. He was happy.

Gustave got up a little later. He had little to do that day but the horse was waiting for his hay. Then he returned for his breakfast. Yvette was lazing in bed and his mother served him; it was the usual coffee, bread and cold meat. Then he went up again to the bedroom where Yvette had fed Alain and was taking her time with her morning routine.

At about 8.0 Gaston returned. But he did not, as on other days, seat himself under the tree in the courtyard. He went up to his room, replaced his cotton shirt with a white one and a cravat, took a dark suit from his closet and put it on. In this Sunday dress he took his accustomed place and waited for visitors. The white wine – five or six bottles – was cooling in the kitchen. The old man would drink half of them. Possibly, if there were reason for it, he would go to Lurs or even Peyruis. But Gaston Dominici did not often pay visits. People came to him, he did not go to others, the Maillets or even his children. If anyone put themselves out, it would be the others. Gaston laid down his own laws.

This year, August 15 was to be marred by a disagreeable incident. A car stopped before Grand'Terre which Gaston recognized as belonging to the police. Sébeille got out. So they never stopped working, these people. His face surly, puffing his pipe, Gaston watched the superintendent's approach.

Sébeille came straight to the point. 'Grandad,' he said, 'sorry to disturb you on the 15th but I've got a letter to show you.'

He drew a paper from his pocket, but Gaston made no move to take it. 'You read it,' he said.

Sébeille obeyed. 'Dear Superintendent,' it began, 'I have some useful information for you . . .'

As he read, the scowl on Gaston's face deepened. Gustave and Yvette appeared, only to disappear when they saw the visitor. 'Who's your letter from?' the old man broke in.

'It's not signed. It comes from Paris. It seems that you are a great enemy of campers.'

It was not the only accusation in the letter. According to its anonymous author, Gaston Dominici had a few years previously bought a rifle from an American soldier named John Monte for 8000 francs. 'He goes on to say,' the superintendent continued, 'that if you deny the fact, he will reveal his identity.'

Abruptly the old man stood up. His face turned purple and he raised his stick over the police officer. 'He's a swine,' he shouted.

'Is it true or not?' Sébeille asked evenly.

But Gaston did not answer except with a string of oaths. Thrusting the superintendent aside with his stick, he made for the kitchen. Before closing the door he snapped at Sébeille, 'It's lies – let him

93

show himself.' Then he slammed the door. The police heard him muttering behind it.

For Gaston the day was spoiled. It would not be completely for the young couple. That afternoon the fête at Peyruis broke all the annual attendance records. People came from all round; Sébeille and his men were an additional attraction which the rival villages could not offer. They flocked to Peyruis to sniff the atmosphere of the crime which was intriguing the whole world, to scrutinize those connected with it, to pick up a shred of gossip or rumour which they could thrive on for a week or more. The journalists had remained, hoping to see the Dominicis at the rural country fête.

At about 4.0 p.m. a car stopped near the war memorial in the square where an orchestra was playing for whirling couples. Yvette and Gustave got out, and all eyes were upon them. Cameras clicked. They found the role of 'stars' not displeasing and posed obligingly. Gustave was wearing a dark suit, with a cravat round his neck, his collar open. His large bony face wore a satisfied smile, while his sunken eyes looked round as if to ask, 'Are you shocked because I'm here?' There was a challenge in Yvette's expression too; she looked very pretty in a close-fitting flowered dress, her hair tightly permed.

The welcome they received did not lack warmth. People shook their hands, asked how they were, and they responded cordially, even to journalists whom normally they couldn't bear the sight of. They called out to friends and acquaintances who were holding back. Their attitude was that of a couple on display. Someone asked if they were going to dance – and there they were dancing. They had nothing to hide, nothing to regret, nothing to fret about. They wanted to enjoy themselves and dance, like all those at Peyruis who had forgotten the Drummonds and little Elizabeth. Gustave put his arm around Yvette and led her into the square. Way was made for them. He had formerly been an excellent dancer.

Sébeille had not missed the festivity either. Together with his inspectors, he mingled with the crowd, circulating among the couples, watching the dancers, Gustave and Yvette especially. He noted that the man seemed less serene than his wife, who wore a permanent smile. The superintendent was convinced that their presence at the fête was a deliberate reaction to his visit that morning. The young people had been sent to demonstrate the lack of fear at Grand'Terre. Or else Yvette, the cool one of the family, had inveigled her husband into it.

When night fell the dancing continued under arc lights. Gustave and Yvette lingered a while longer, then left in the friends' car which had brought them. Sébeille, thoughtful, watched them leave. For him too the festivity was over. He slowly returned to his room and, with the music still echoing in his ears, once more opened his files.

The problem which preoccupied Sébeille at the moment was motive. The most probable explanation was certainly robbery. But police good sense dictated that no theory be ruled out, even if it seemed fantastic at first. Espionage? Apart from the fact that Sir Jack Drummond had never been involved in it, Sébeille discarded this hypothesis because of the patched-up rifle. It was hardly the weapon of a professional executioner. Mistaken identity? The suggestion had been put forward because of the presence in the area of a second Hillman of the same colour. But the Drummonds had arrived at Lurs by day. It would be difficult for pursuers, who knew the car's registration number, to make a mistake on this point. A family quarrel? Scotland Yard's investigation proved the Drummonds to be a particularly devoted couple. Sadism? No sign of any perverse violence had been found either on the mother or the child. So perhaps it was a haphazard crime committed by a prowler, some poacher or sinister type who had got ideas at the sight of the Hillman. A poacher would have already been armed; a prowler would have had to return home for his rifle.

At this stage of his analysis Sébeille found himself in difficulty. He could not bring himself to attach the name of a Dominici to the person who had perpetrated such a massacre for a few banknotes. Gaston would not have sold for so little the fruit of his life's work, the social position of which he was so proud. Moreover, he was not poor or in financial difficulties. He always had plenty of money. He was not the man to kill for theft, especially not 150 metres from his house. To swindle a neighbour, to buy a piece of land while profiting from the seller's need, to give short weight, might be allowable. It was common practice; almost every rural property rests on a modicum of deceit, a rule of the game which enters into all transactions, even legal ones. But Gaston would not sacrifice a human life to his greed for money, if only out of prudence. Gustave being more timorous would be even less disposed to. So Sébeille, convinced of the logic of his analysis, dismissed the Dominicis from the immediate range of his suspicions. But out of the corner of his eye he continued to observe them, just as he had during the festivities of August 15.

*

Shaking his head energetically, Jean-Marie Olivier, a tall 27-year-old with the look of an athlete, emphasized every sentence with a gesture of his fingers. No, he didn't agree and he was sure he was right. 'When I saw Gustave,' he repeated, 'he was coming out from behind the car. I told the gendarmes so.'

The superintendent nodded. It was true that at his first interview with Sergeant Romanet, Jean-Marie Olivier had declared that Gustave 'was coming out from behind a car with a British registration number.' It was the gendarmes who had drawn the superintendent's attention to the fact that their first witness directly contradicted the young farmer.

Jean-Marie was a driver for a factory at Saint-Auban. On the morning of August 5 he was returning from his night's work on his motor-cycle. It would have been about 5.30. 'Immediately after the bend,' he said, 'I saw the car on the gravel. I didn't pay any attention. But when I drew level with it a man suddenly appeared. He must have been hiding behind the car.'

'Were you going fast?'

'About sixty kilometres an hour.'

'Possibly you didn't estimate the distance correctly,' said Sébeille. 'On a motor-cycle you don't pay much attention.'

Jean-Marie Olivier made another gesture of denial. 'No,' he said, 'I remember well. I first noticed an arm, which surprised me. Only after did I see the man. I knew him as the farmer of the place.'

'Did he stop you?'

'Yes, I braked at once. But I only stopped thirty metres on. He came up to me and said, "Telephone the gendarmerie at Forcalquier or go to the one at Oraison. I've found someone killed over there." That's what I did. I even thought the body was near the car.'

But at that moment Gustave had found only the little girl lying on the bank of the Durance. At least that was what he said. In which case it was understandable that he specified that at the moment he signalled Jean-Marie Olivier he was fifteen metres in front of the car. If at any time he had passed behind the car, he must have seen the other body, that of the woman. If he was to be believed, he had run up the slope to the Route Nationale and alerted the first passer-by, not taking time to check what had become of the parents. But if he was lying, why? Wasn't it because he wanted to hide the fact that he had been wandering around the site?

'If he had been where he says,' concluded Jean-Marie, 'I would have seen him from the bend and not been surprised when he appeared.'

Sébeille was impressed. For the first time he could contradict Gustave Dominici. Jean-Marie Olivier could not be suspected of partiality and he did not grasp the import of his statement. The superintendent took the young man to Lurs in his car. Olivier pointed out the position of the Hillman, then the place where he had stopped. He passed the test successfully; it exactly confirmed his statement.

But the superintendent did not make for the farm, get hold of Gustave and confront him on the spot with Jean-Marie Olivier. 'I waited,' he wrote in his report, 'because I counted on collecting other evidence which would enable me to interrogate Gustave Dominici in a way that would prove decisive.'

So Sébeille held back. A few days earlier, taking the gendarmes on duty with him, he had questioned Yvette. She had told the story of the night of August 5, contradicting Gustave on one point: they had not gone to sleep again after the shots. Therefore they had been uneasy. Yet she had not asked her husband any question about the campers. And in the morning it hadn't even entered their heads that they might have been attacked.

'Isn't all that utterly inconsistent?' Sébeille asked her.

Yvette remained untroubled. 'I know what you're thinking,' she answered, 'but I can't tell you anything else. It wouldn't be true.'

What was to be done in the face of such self-possession? Every form of attack fell into an unfathomable abyss, shattered against a wall of total indifference. It would require a bulldozer to disturb the Dominici rock.

This was why Sébeille was planning a reconstruction of the crime by night and not including Jean-Marie Olivier in the operation. He was keeping him in reserve, like the Maillets. Nor did he speak of it to the journalists dogging his every step. It was among the surprises he was keeping up his sleeve for the Dominicis while ostensibly following other trails – seasonal workers, North Africans in neighbouring construction gangs, and suchlike.

The press was running out of wind. It was now admitted that the killer had vanished for ever, an anonymous assassin whom only chance would produce. The British papers redoubled their derision of the French police. Sébeille hunched his shoulders and kept his thoughts to himself.

Nevertheless, on August 20 Gustave caused a certain sensation by putting in an appearance of his own accord at Peyruis town hall. He arrived with an air of triumph on a superb red motor-cycle. In his hand he held a letter which he passed to Sébeille. 'It's from one of my brothers,' he said.

The superintendent learned from reading it that one René-Marcel Castang, a resident of Lurs dead since 1946, had owned some fire-arms which were stolen from his house the very day of his burial. And Gustave, like his brother Clovis, connected the initials RMC engraved on the butt of the rifle with those of the deceased. Sébeille shrugged his shoulders; he knew it was the manufacturer's trade-mark.

'I know,' said Gustave boldly, 'but that might have given Castang the idea of buying it.'

Truly a remarkable clue: a dead man, arms stolen by heaven knows whom! Gustave retreated and a little later left the town hall. But not before Sébeille ironically thanked him. 'Are you after the reward?' he asked. For two newspapers, one English, the *Sunday Dispatch*, and one French, *Samedi-Soir*, were each offering 500,000 francs to whoever supplied the decisive lead. The notices posted at Lurs, Peyruis and throughout the region were mutilated by unknown persons as soon as they were up.

The man seemed to hesitate between the various offices opening before him at the Marseilles headquarters of the Brigade Mobile. He was small and round, with a slight limp, a plump face, a sketchy moustache of a nondescript colour, black hair, soberly dressed. Superintendent Icard, passing by, asked whom he was looking for. He answered that he wanted to see Superintendent Harzic, the chief, and him alone. If he wasn't there he would return. Icard was used to these visitors. Usually they were gossip merchants or dealers in unsavoury denunciations. The police could not afford too sensitive a nose; a good tip never smelled bad. 'It's about the Lurs business,' the man said.

Icard pricked up his ears. Harzic wasn't there, but Superintendent Constant was acting for him. The visitor refused – it was Harzic he wanted. The voice was mysterious, the tone that of a man who knew his own importance. Icard grew irritated; if the stranger knew any-thing, let him speak up. The officer then noticed the ribbon of the Legion of Honour on the lapel, proof that the man was not just a nobody.

With difficulty he managed to coax the visitor into Superintendent

Constant's office. 'I'll tell you what I know,' he began, 'but you won't believe me.'

He revealed his identity: Aristide Panayotou, aged 36, born in Piraeus, Greece, tradesman, divorced, father of three children, decorated for his activities in the Resistance. He talked fluently and listed his decorations with evident satisfaction.

Constant studied him. The superintendent was a man of 40, tall and thin, but athletic, with a boxer's nose, short curly grey hair, clear blue eyes, a nonchalant and imperturbable bearing. But this was only in outward appearance. Constant was an enthusiast. He had chosen to be a policeman although he had wanted to be a teacher, and had taken his arts degree. He was a sensitive man who loved both action and more reflective pursuits. Since the Liberation he had taken part in all the notable activities of the Marseilles police. Along the wharves of the Old Port the gangs had taken advantage of the period to bring off some remarkable exploits. He was a redoubtable father confessor whose gentle manner misled his penitents. He discovered their lies instinctively, let them entangle themselves, then went for them bluntly. Constant's cold rages were famous in Marseilles. 'Go on,' he said to Panayotou.

But the merchant wanted a guarantee of absolute secrecy, otherwise disaster would follow. Constant didn't quite understand why. Panayotou was afraid of his wife, who was in fact his mistress. On the night of the 4th–5th he had been out on an 'escapade'. Constant promised, and began to pump this odd witness. If he had anything to say, let him speak up. 'I saw the crime,' Panayotou finally said.

Constant showed no reaction, but became all ears. The Lurs affair excited him, and not only for professional reasons. He had been born at Forcalquier and had passed his whole childhood in the region. If he had not been on vacation on August 5 the matter would almost certainly have been entrusted to him. He knew the country and its inhabitants as well as anybody.

'I was coming from Grenoble to Marseilles by road,' Panayotou went on. 'After I had passed Digne and a village beyond, the lights on my Lincoln failed. I looked at my watch – it was ten past one. I stopped and looked at the panel. I needed only a few seconds to see what had happened: the switch had come loose. I felt a call of nature and got out. At that moment I heard frightful screams, then shots. I hid behind the car. I saw a tall man cross the road, reeling, and collapse on the slope. I quickly got into my car to escape. A second man appeared who seemed to be holding some object in his left hand, the arm raised. The right fist was closed on something, he bent over the body he had shot down. Then he crossed the road again and disappeared.'

M. Panayotou gave this description of the murderer: tall, bare-headed, hair a little dishevelled, dressed in dark clothes but without a coat, trousers gaping at the waist. The witness had also noticed prominent cheekbones.

'It still gives me gooseflesh,' he ended.

Constant quickly came to the conclusion that M. Panayotou's statement was not to be taken at its face value, which raised the question of the million-franc reward, a possible stimulus to the imagination of a businessman whose affairs were not – as was in fact learned later – as prosperous as he had suggested. 'What were you doing on the road in the middle of the night?' asked the superintendent. 'Was your journey all that urgent?'

Panayotou explained that he had gone to explore the Digne and Grenoble areas to promote his trade in cheeses. But Constant did not let it rest there. When had he decided on this journey? What had been his itinerary and his schedule? What was the last village he had passed through? After his stop at the scene of the crime, how had he got back to Marseilles? Had he been frightened at this point, he, a decorated hero of the Resistance? And even if he had been afraid for his life, why had he not stopped at the first populated area to notify the police?

The tradesman faltered, stammered, spluttered. He had been reluctant to come, even after thirteen days. 'A family matter,' he repeated, 'a disaster, if it were known.' Constant began to doubt and suspect Panayotou. He could be the murderer. Sometimes a guilty man is so afraid of the police turning up that he flings himself into their arms.

When Superintendent Harzic arrived, Constant at once let him know. Panayotou was taken in to him: as it happened, he knew the man. M. Harzic listened to his story, then asked abruptly, 'How was the victim dressed?'

'In something dark.'

'Odd,' said Harzic. 'Sir Jack Drummond was wearing light-coloured pyjamas, and it was he who crossed the road in order to get away.'

M. Panayotou was dismissed but told to hold himself at the disposal of the police. As soon as possible he would be taken to Lurs and asked to repeat his story on the site itself. Constant telephoned

Sébeille to say that a witness claimed to have actually seen the murder. But his knowledge seemed to come straight out of the newspapers.

The following week Panayotou was asked to accompany the officers to Lurs. Meanwhile inquiries had been made about him. The results were not unfavourable. His Legion of Honour had not been bogus, though somewhat excessive for someone who had done no more than any average member of the Resistance. But this was not something to quibble about; he had wangled it through the good offices of a friend in one of the ministries. His affairs seemed prosperous (an impression subsequently proved to be erroneous). As he had said, he had been involved in a wholesale deal in cheeses. The police were thus inclined to credit him; why should a man like him spin such a tale?

Constant was nevertheless surprised to learn that Panayotou now declared that on the night of August 4–5 he was going from Marseilles to Grenoble: a glaring contradiction.

At Peyruis the journalists were summoned by Harzic for a talk. He proposed an agreement: if they would stop following the police around, he would supply the special correspondents with full details at the end of the operation. The matter related to 'a witness of prime importance'. The journalists agreed and rushed to the telephone to notify their editors.

The officers then went to Grand'Terre where this time the barrier of gendarmes rendered it inaccessible to the curious. Panayotou pointed out the place where he had stopped and which corresponded closely to that where the Duc brothers had seen the unknown man, but the press had already given this testimony wide publicity. On the other hand, Panayotou hesitated before designating the mulberry tree which marked the limit of the gravel tip. The officers were especially surprised that he had been able in the darkest part of the night to distinguish the features of a face. For unlike M. Duc's, his headlights had been off, due to the temporary breakdown. Thanks to this, the murderer had paid no attention to the Lincoln and its occupant. But how had M. Panayotou himself been able to catch so clear a glimpse of the scene?

Sébeille then brought him to the sub-prefecture at Forcalquier where he questioned him for two hours – an interview which left the superintendent perplexed. He suggested, for instance, bringing M. Panayotou face to face with Gustave Dominici. But the merchant energetically refused. What was he afraid of? He reiterated that he was frightened of a 'domestic drama'. The superintendent let him leave in the car that had brought him from Marseilles. Sébeille was torn between two feelings. He distrusted Panayotou and tended to regard him as the very prototype of the false witness, but what could have been his motive, when it seemed that Panayotou had nothing to gain? Sébeille would have liked to be able to believe the story he had just heard, the first real picture of a crime until now peopled with shadows.

M. Harzic kept his promise. At noon he called the journalists together to hear the story. He limited his account to Panayotou's words without divulging his name, and made no comment. The Marseilles merchant became for the press Mr X, or 'the phantom witness'. His disclosures were flashed all over the world and given prominent coverage in all the newspapers. The journalists were understandably struck by the screams which he had heard, and hurried to Grand'Terre.

'We only heard shots,' Gustave claimed, 'neither screams nor a car starting: it's a pity, because then they wouldn't be looking for the killer among us.'

The anonymity preserved by M. Panayotou led the journalists to speculate that he might be a witness radio-controlled by the police in order to induce the murderer to give himself away.

From the beginning of the investigation Sergeant Louis Romanet had been hard at it. It was he who had found the bodies on the morning of August 5. Next he had been sent to verify and check from one district to another. With the gendarme Bouchier he had dissected the whole region, stopping in the most obscure hamlets. He had asked questions, listened, let people run on, received innumerable confidences, most of which were worthless. But today an indiscretion seemed to him of a kind to interest Sébeille. So he at once hastened to Peyruis town hall where the superintendent was preparing to leave. 'I'd like to have the carbine for a little while,' he said.

He explained that he had been interrogating a farmer's wife who was a neighbour of Paul Maillet's. Under the seal of the closest secrecy she had confided her suspicions: it could well be that the weapon belonged to the railwayman-farmer, who was quite a hunter.

'Has she seen it?' asked Sébeille, at once interested.

'It's possible.'

The sergeant informed the superintendent in a few words that two years ago the woman had forgotten some tools – a spade, a pick, a pitchfork – in a field south of Lurs. Two days later she went back for them, but they had disappeared. Suspecting Paul Maillet, she had gone to his house on a vague pretext. She had found his father, who was alone. While talking to him, she had noticed hanging on the wall a shotgun and a weapon that looked to her like an automatic rifle. On reading the papers and seeing a photograph of the weapon with which the crime had been committed, she connected it with the Maillets' gun. She thought she would be able to recognize it if it were shown her.

'It's not a case of revenge?' Sébeille asked doubtfully.

'No,' said Romanet. 'Because the next day she found the tools in the hollow of an olive tree. They had been hidden for safety.'

Inspector Ranchin went to get the Rock-Ola and gave it to the gendarme who took it to his informant. He returned almost at once, beaming. 'She recognized it,' he announced.

She had even specified that the weapon she had seen at Maillet's had no clip. Romanet had thereupon removed that of the carbine. Then the farmer's wife had been definite: Maillet's gun was the same model. The gendarme had even offered to hang the weapon in the witness's kitchen but she had refused, she was certain without that. The spotlight was thus diverted from Grand'Terre to a man who now became the new favourite for the role of monster.

'Get to work,' Sébeille ordered Romanet. 'Gather all possible information. Ask everyone you can, and go on asking, if that was seen in his kitchen.' He took Maillet's file, which he had never definitely closed. Suspicions already existed. The new accusation increased them, because unfavourable reports had reached him about Paul's brother, Auguste, former prisoner-of-war, idle and not, it was said, in full possession of his faculties.

For two days the gendarmes discreetly questioned all who knew the Maillet farm, pledging never to divulge their names. No one had seen the carbine except the first informant. Even she was now less positive. At the same time information about Maillet flowed in. Agreement was general that, apart from his exaggerated love for every form of hunting, legal or otherwise, there was nothing against him. He lived peaceably with his wife and four children. He devoted long hours to the activities of the local Communist cell. He was sensible and moderate, neither hot-headed nor fanatical. Sébeille, in agreement with the prosecutor and the magistrate, nevertheless decided to search his farm. Professional instinct told him that it would not be a waste of time to put a little pressure on Paul Maillet. The pretext would be to find out if he had any cartridges which could be used with the Rock-Ola. But the gendarmes were not forbidden to discover anything else that might put Maillet on the spot.

At 7.30 a.m. on August 20 the police surrounded the Maillet farm. The display of force was to impress the occupants. Not wanting to be followed by a horde of journalists, Sébeille and his inspectors slipped away on foot, leaving their cars in the square at Peyruis and joining up with the gendarmes' cars on the outskirts of the village. When they realized they had been tricked, the reporters organized an extensive search. But they only found the police when the operation was over.

Paul Maillet had already left for work when Sébeille and his colleagues searched the farm. Ginette, a 29-year-old brunette already growing plump, received the superintendent. She was surrounded by her four children ranging in age from two to ten. Gendarmes and inspectors spread through the house to search the store-room, the barn, the cellar, dig holes in the garden. In the inner oven of the kitchen range they found two Sten-guns in separate pieces – an offence whose importance Sébeille at once made clear to Mme Maillet. 'My husband brought them back from the Maquis,' she explained.

Sébeille had brought the carbine. To the elder children he put the question, 'Have you ever seen this?' They answered in the negative, unflustered.

'Have you had any money worries lately?' he asked Ginette Maillet.

The woman answered straightforwardly. 'Yes, little Nicole had an accident which cost us a good deal. The Welfare hasn't yet compensated us.'

But among the cartridges taken none matched the rather special calibre of the Rock-Ola.

At noon, while at the Café des Alpes, Paul Maillet learned from the journalists what had happened at his home that morning. 'They're hammering at us because I'm a Communist,' he declared. Yet he did not protest when an inspector came a little later to conduct him to Forcalquier, where Sébeille was waiting for him in a room at the town hall. His wife and parents joined him there. They were all questioned until nightfall. The journalists, parked in the square under the supervision of the gendarmes, waited. A rumour circulated that an arrest was imminent.

Paul Maillet was by now thoroughly upset. The Stens were from the Maquis, but if he were to be prosecuted, that would not stop him from being condemned. The Party wouldn't forgive him for this unfavourable publicity. The bourgeois papers charged often enough that at its headquarters in the rue de Châteaudun they dreamed of installing a Popular Democracy by means of a coup like that in Czechoslovakia in 1948. It was mortifying to provide them with 'evidence', even so slight as a linesman's private arsenal. 'Will they send me for trial?' he fretted.

'That depends on the prosecutor,' said Sébeille.

Maillet repeated that he had had nothing to do with the business; he was in bed at 9.30 on August 4 and rose at about 6.0.

'You've never had an American carbine?'

'Never.'

'One was seen at your house.'

'By whom?'

The neighbour had refused to testify if her name were mentioned. So Sébeille remained evasive. 'People.'

'They're dreaming. Or else they've got something against me on political grounds.'

Sébeille heard the father, the mother, the wife. He never caught them out once. He came back to Paul Maillet. The linesman was undoubtedly innocent but Sébeille remained convinced that he could help. 'It's in your interest not to hide anything,' he repeated.

Each time, Paul Maillet turned his head away in embarrassment. Finally he made up his mind. Did the superintendent know that on the afternoon of August 4 a shot from a military weapon was fired in the bushes along the Durance? 'I was working down on the line and I've an ear; it wasn't a shotgun.'

'Why haven't you mentioned it?' Maillet remained silent. 'Is that all you know?'

'Yes.'

At 7.0 p.m. the Maillet family was released. The avid journalists learned only of the Sten-guns and of a system of electric wiring which suggested that Maillet was stealing current. Would he be prosecuted? The superintendent replied that it was for the prosecutor to decide. But before allowing Maillet to leave, Sébeille took him aside.

'All these,' he told him, 'are minor crimes. But they could cost you dear. I know you're OK. I think the Dominicis are in the clear too. But there are things you're hiding. They say that there's nothing you don't know about what went on at Grand'Terre the night of the crime.' Sébeille was alluding to the meetings which had been held at the Dominici house on the days following the tragedy. Maillet and Communist municipal councillors had been present. 'I'm sure you weren't only talking politics.' Maillet said nothing. 'We've been easy with you,' Sébeille ended. 'Remember that.'

Maillet hesitated a moment, then shook his head. 'I'll help you,' he said, 'because I've got nothing on my conscience and I don't want people to suspect either me or my brother.'

Police officers and magistrates held a conference that evening to consider whether to start proceedings against Paul Maillet. Sébeille advanced two objections. First, if he were charged, other possessors of arms would take fright. Instead of coming to the gendarmes on the quiet to get rid of the compromising relics on the strength of promised immunity, they would hide them and wait for better days. The harvest so far had not been too bad. In the second place, it would be a good thing for Paul Maillet to feel the sword suspended over his head. Under such conditions thoughts move fast. The prosecutor declared that for the time being Paul Maillet would be treated with leniency. Sébeille considered the day to have been auspicious.

A gun on his shoulder, wearing an old shooting jacket which puffed out his back like a hump, Gustave Dominici walked slowly along the lane leading to the courtyard of Grand'Terre. It was 7.0 a.m. on September 3. He had taken no more than a few leisurely steps when he came to a halt. He had caught sight of the rear of a Citroën car. So the police were there. When they came that early it was to take him away, or Yvette or his father, for questioning. He was tempted to turn round and hole up until evening in the mountain from which he had just come and where it was so pleasant. But what was the point? They would come back tomorrow if it was his turn.

Three inspectors were waiting for him and one of them addressed him sharply as he rounded the corner of the house. 'Gustave, you're coming with us.'

'Without breakfast?'

'It won't be for long.'

Gustave indicated his shooting jacket. 'Can I at least get out of this?' he asked sullenly.

The officers escorted him to the kitchen. Without haste he drew from the back pockets of his jacket a rabbit and a fox, still covered with blood, which he deposited on the table.

'A good shot!' exclaimed an admiring policeman.

Yvette and his mother had followed them from the courtyard. 'Let him at least have his breakfast,' said the younger woman.

But the police said they were in a hurry. Gustave shed his jacket. The inspector who had first spoken to him thrust him towards the door. The car left at once in a cloud of dust.

The police car did not turn in the direction of Peyruis and Gustave became uneasy, wondering where they were taking him. To Forcal-quier, they replied. Gustave placed his large red hands on his thighs and fell silent.

They stopped outside the gendarmerie. In Captain Albert's office three men were already waiting – Superintendent Constant, M. Mével, deputy chief of the squad, and Sébeille. Gustave at once realized that this interrogation was not going to be like the others.

He was shown to a seat. The four packed the very small room, their faces almost touching. The blinds were closed to discourage the photographers. An inspector had placed his typewriter on a little table. Sébeille, looking haggard, was exhausted. Since August 5 he had not had one good night. He slept in catnaps, obsessed by the investigation and the meagre results. This was why he had asked Constant to be present; they could take turns.

'Now, Gustave,' he began, 'tell us what you did when you found the child Elizabeth.'

Gustave bristled. 'I've already told you three times.'

'Maybe our memories are bad,' smiled Sébeille.

The farmer scowled, and repeated his story. He had seen the body while going to inspect the landslide, returned quickly and stopped the motor-cyclist.

'At once, without delay?'

'Almost.'

'Which means?'

'Another motor-cycle passed before Olivier,' Gustave replied, 'but it had a Swiss licence. So I didn't stop it.'

'What did it matter whether it was Swiss or French since it was only to notify the police?'

Gustave hesitated and fell into one of those profound silences which Sébeille already knew and which could outlast questions, pleas, threats. 'I saw Olivier coming round the bend,' he said finally. 'I knew him.'

'Where were you when you stopped him?'

The three officers scanned Gustave's face, alert for the answer which might provide the springboard for their interrogation.

'I've already told you,' Gustave sighed. 'At the end of the path.'

'And not in front of the Hillman?'

'No.'

Sébeille switched to something else – the screams. He had heard none, answered Gustave. But a witness had, Sébeille tested him. Gustave shrugged his shoulders and said nothing. The superintendent read out M. Panayotou's deposition. He paused at every word, questioning the farmer with his glance, repeating the details furnished by the Marseilles tradesman, including the description of the murderer. Gustave became confused and irritated. Suddenly he burst out, so loudly that the reporters massed in the square heard and noted down his words: 'Why don't you confront me with him?'

Constant took over from Sébeille. He concentrated on Gustave's itinerary the morning of August 5. It was false to claim that the body could have been seen without making a detour, he said. Constant's manner was different from Sébeille's. He was a cold logician. He could go on repeating the same question until he had an answer that satisfied him, tirelessly warning the sufferer that he would not give up until the facts interlocked perfectly. But in Gustave he had a worthy adversary. Very quickly Constant capitulated; he didn't have Sébeille's mastery of the affair at the moment. Both tackled Gustave on the subject of the weapon. Things went no better; Gustave repeated that he had never seen it.

'Why are you contradicting your wife?' Gustave raised his head, surprised. 'And on many other points,' Sébeille went on relentlessly. 'For instance, on the fact that you did not go back to sleep after the shots. Who is right, you or she?'

Gustave's expression hardened. For a long time there was total silence in the room. Then abruptly he exploded, 'You can question me till Doomsday, you won't get any more out of me.'

Occasionally one or another of the superintendents went out on to the balcony giving on to the room. Not until 1.10 p.m. was the interrogation adjourned. The police officers refused to answer any questions. They lunched at the nearby Provençal inn and the journalists did likewise; the restaurant did its best business of the year. But neither Sébeille nor Constant consented to be interviewed. Gustave remained at the gendarmerie where a snack and a bottle of beer were brought to him.

While they were at lunch the police officers saw a car arrive in the square and Yvette and her father, M. Barth, get out. They made straight for the gendarmerie. The young woman seemed very angry. To the gendarme who received her she exclaimed indignantly that Gustave had supposedly been taken away for only a short while but he hadn't returned; where was he? M. Barth supported her. 'No doubt you imagine you've got the guilty man,' he said furiously.

Sébeille left the restaurant only to be intercepted by an outraged Yvette. 'Where is he? What are you doing to him?'

The superintendent smiled. 'Calm down, we're not torturing him. We only want him to tell us the truth.'

'He has told you!'

The journalists were crowding round the officer and the girl. Under the sun burning down on the square, Sébeille felt the sweat pouring down his face. 'It's as well you came,' he told Yvette. 'I want you to answer some questions.'

Captain Albert, arriving at this moment, led her into an office. The interrogation of Yvette, prolonged until 6.0 p.m., yielded nothing.

When the police officers returned to the small room Gustave was sitting in the same chair, his body bent forward, his shoulders bowed, his expression sullen. He made no movement, no gesture, he ignored his examiners and, it seemed, the whole world. Sébeille sat down beside him. 'We've sent for Olivier. You shall have a confrontation with him.'

Constant opened the door for the young workman. Gustave, his eyes expressionless, watched Olivier enter. A single bulb cast a feeble yellow light.

'Let's have your testimony again,' Sébeille said to Olivier.

The witness obeyed, not varying a word. He had seen Gustave dash out from the corner of the car, not from several metres in front of it.

'Did you notice another motor-cycle ahead of you with a Swiss registration?'

'Not at that moment. It left Saint-Auban ten minutes before me, which is why I noticed it. I thought I'd catch it up a little farther on.'

'If it had preceded you by only a few seconds, you would have seen it in line with Grand'Terre?'

'Definitely.'

Sébeille, then Constant, turned to Gustave and asked if he understood the inference of this contradiction. Gustave shook his head. The two superintendents then patiently explained. The Swiss motor-cycle was not an invention; Olivier had seen it. But between the moment when it passed and that at which Olivier arrived there had been an interval of time. Gustave had therefore lied; he had been at the camp site for some while.

'No,' he protested.

'The proof,' persisted Sébeille, 'is that Olivier saw you very near the Hillman. What were you doing?'

But Gustave denied this; he had not been near the car.

Still alternating with Constant, Sébeille resumed. Did Gustave feel that the questions being put to him were offensive? Basically, what did it matter if he had been near or far from the Hillman? Or if he had found one, two or three corpses? It was the distortions of the truth that interested the police. For if Gustave were lying about details of no apparent consequence in themselves, it must be because they embarrassed him. Why? How long had he been at the scene of the crime? What was he doing there? Was he looking for something, missing cartridges for instance?

The rain of questions that beat down upon Gustave Dominici was drowned in the depth of his silence as he sat staring at the floor. 'Olivier is mistaken,' was all he said.

With the same impassivity he withstood another assault. To the police officers' twenty or thirty questions he responded with a single word or none. The catechism was carried on by Sébeille, Constant and Mével like participants in a litany. Was he listening? At times the officers wondered if he was not thinking of something entirely different. Or nothing at all. Olivier was allowed to go. Dejected, Gustave watched his departure in silence.

The inquisition went on, Sébeille and Constant incessantly baiting him with the same questions. They no longer had any faith in him, they said, and had decided to keep him until he furnished a coherent explanation. As the hours passed, Gustave showed signs of impatience. His nerves were on edge; he was no longer immobile as he had been in the morning. He moved constantly, waved his hands, shuffled his feet. The police officers continued to press him.

At about 6.0 p.m. Gustave cracked. He felt Sébeille's breath on his cheek as the latter repeated for the hundredth time that he was lying. In a tired voice he admitted it; the police did not believe their ears. 'It's true,' he said. 'I didn't follow the path to the road, I cut across and came to the bonnet of the car. There was a camp-bed to the left with rugs on it. Across the road I saw another camp-bed upside down.' But he would not admit that Olivier was right; when he signalled him, Gustave insisted, he was several metres from the Hillman. The police did not press the point.

'Why did you hide all this?' asked Sébeille.

'You can't think of everything,' Gustave answered in all simplicity.

Had his tormentors finished with him? He seemed to hope so and got up as if to leave the room. But Sébeille detained him with a hand on his shoulder. 'Not so fast. If you saw the camp-beds, how is it you didn't think of warning the Drummonds?'

Gustave opened his arms wide in a gesture of helplessness. 'I called out, "Is anybody there?" Nobody answered.'

The three superintendents exchanged looks. Should they rest content with this admission or follow up their advantage, go on until they finally broke Gustave's resistance which now seemed weakened once and for all? The tacit agreement was immediate – it was the moment to test Gustave's endurance. 'Read this letter,' Sébeille said to him.

He held out a paper, unsigned and badly spelled, posted at Sisteron on August 25:

Mr Superintendent, you will have a hard time proving who the Lurs murderer is. In the end if it isn't him, you can always try Lauzier and Estève at Peyruis – each has an automatic rifle. I only decided to write you since I am a friend of the Dominicis and hope he will speak . . . This is why I don't want to betray him, but as he hasn't spoken I can tell you that between 11.30 and midnight on the day of the crime, Dominici was still up, because I passed him on my bicycle in front of the farm. Who was the man who was with him near the farm? He alone can tell you. I clearly saw the Hillman at the side of the road but there was nothing unusual so I don't know any more.

Gustave glanced through the letter, then handed it back to Sébeille. 'It's a lie since I was asleep.'

Sébeille drew from the file another unsigned letter whose bad writing seemed to him to resemble the other. It was addressed to the gendarmes and its author described the murderer: tall, thin, curly-haired, bare-headed. 'Like you,' the officer remarked. 'I will read you the last sentence: "Pity that M. Dominici doesn't talk. Good luck, and don't leave Peyruis." '

Confronted with Gustave's silence, Constant tried another line of attack. How had Gustave known that the child was dead? It was a point that had worried the superintendent ever since he began to take part in the inquiry and he wouldn't let go of it, convinced that it would throw a useful light on Gustave's conduct.

'I saw blood on her face,' said Gustave.

'You can bleed from the head and still be alive.'

'Yes, but she was dead.'

'I repeat, how did you know?'

He got no answer. Sébeille then went into his finances. On these the farmer was even more reticent. It was none of the police's business, he began by saying. Then he grew angry. Did they accuse him of killing three people, including a child, for a few thousand-franc banknotes? He decided to supply figures: he had just sold his harvest of apricots for 72,000 francs in money of that time, and received 65,000 francs in advance for his wheat. It was not a fortune, but average for a comfortably-off farmer.

At about 9.0 p.m. the police decided to suspend the interrogation. They were exhausted, but Gustave seemed to them even more so. And for the first time he was uneasy. His assurance had disappeared. He was afraid of what was to come, of betraying himself. So he had not told everything. He could still be of use. Dinner was ordered for him from the wife of a gendarme. And his visible disappointment when he learned that he would not be allowed to go home seemed to Sébeille, Constant and Mével a good sign; he would not hold out long. An inhuman excess? Some were to say so. But how was one to deal with witnesses so hard to budge?

Gustave's interrogation was resumed briefly at about 10.0 p.m. At 11.0, Superintendent Mével gave a statement to the journalists waiting all this time for a sensation – Gustave Dominici's arrest. Instead, the superintendent read out a communiqué which astonished them: 'On the advice of M. Orsatelli, Attorney-General of the Republic of Aix-en-Provence, the examination of M. Gustave Dominici was suspended at 10.45 and will be resumed tomorrow morning at 9.0. M. Dominici will be detained at the Forcalquier gendarmerie.'

It was obvious to the journalists that the police officers were deeply chagrined at the respite granted to Gustave. 'Justice has let slip her opportunity,' as one of the reporters put it. If there was a moment when the truth might have been dislodged and brought to light, it was that which found Gustave at a loss, without the support of the father he feared or the wife to whom he was devoted, reeling

112

under Sébeille's and Constant's questions. For many the interrupted interrogation of September 3 would remain the capital mistake of the whole affair.

The attorney-general, M. Orsatelli, small, dry, thin, had a very high sense of duty. At the time he was making a difficult recovery from a serious car accident. Nevertheless he had hastened to resume his post, the Chancellery following the Lurs inquiry closely. Every evening it was M. Orsatelli's task to forward a report of the day's proceedings to Paris.

On September 3 he was taking a few days' holiday at Castellane, though still remaining in touch with events in the Basses-Alpes. And that evening the Digne prosecutor, who had come to Forcalquier with the magistrate Périès, telephoned M. Orsatelli to report that since morning Gustave Dominici had been questioned without intermission. 'Better to let him have some rest,' said M. Orsatelli.

He was obeying both a personal feeling and a desire to spare the judicial system the criticisms which for some time now had been mounting in vehemence. A number of cases had brought to light the excesses of certain police officers. A Nantes docker, Deshays, for example, had been found innocent of a crime for which he had been sentenced and confessed his guilt. He had apparently been beaten. The Bordeaux police had been accused of knocking out a suspect. Protests multiplied against confessions obtained by exhaustion. Their value was put in doubt. But were the attorney-general's words an order or advice? The prosecutor interpreted them as, 'It is preferable to let Gustave Dominici alone for the present.' Sébeille submitted without protest. The journalists took note of his discomfiture. But a criminal investigation officer is closely dependent on the Public Prosecutor's office. He has little choice but to submit. 'Moreover,' Sébeille wrote in his memoirs, 'contrary to what might be thought, I had no truly valid new argument to pit against it.'

Gendarmes went to Forcalquier hospital to fetch sheets, a blanket and a pillow. A bed was made up for Gustave, who at once dropped off to sleep. The following morning Sébeille privately envied him; he himself had not slept a wink the whole night.

Without much conviction the superintendent tried to draw the net tight once more. It was no good. Gustave had recovered his capacity for inertia unimpaired. He had cut his losses, and let it go at that. Admittedly he had lied. But the error was really almost involuntary. It in no way involved him in guilt. He had rallied very quickly, much more so than the superintendent. At 11.30, Gustave appeared on the balcony before the eyes of the journalists, triumphant. Ten minutes later a car brought him back to Grand'Terre, where a weeping Yvette flung herself into his arms.

'At last they've realized we're innocent,' Gaston kept repeating.

Yvette hadn't spent the night at Grand'Terre. As soon as she was released from the interrogation she had undergone she had had herself driven to her father's farm, taking little Alain with her with scarcely any explanation to her father and mother-in-law. They had not tried to detain her. She obviously did not want to be alone with her parents-in-law, Gaston especially. So it was at her father's house that the journalists found her. And she made a curious statement to them: 'I should regard myself as a criminal if I knew the murderer and did not denounce him. Even if he were one of the family, my husband, my brother, a nephew, an uncle, I would not let the crime go unpunished.' And, in the voice of a judge, the young woman added, 'I would kill him with my own hand.'

At Forcalquier, M. Mével read a final communiqué to the journalists. 'No proof of guilt has been found against Gustave Dominici. He is therefore free. He has modified his first statements on points that contradicted M. Olivier.'

The newsmen promptly asked Gustave why he had committed these 'errors'. 'I'd like to know what you'd have done,' he answered. 'The horrible sight was enough to make me lose my head.'

Sébeille was worn out. His official leave had begun three days earlier; he wondered if he should take it and was urged to do so; he would collapse if he didn't. Constant promised to take over for a month. It was time to begin, if not from scratch, at least with a fresh eye. The ammunition was exhausted, it had to be replenished. An interrogation like the one just ended was an ordeal comparable to a gruelling race, especially if the result was disappointing. As it had been. Of course it had been proved that Gustave had lied, and his powers of endurance had been probed. But only at the price of laying bare the fruits of a month's investigation. Sébeille was still sure that the solution of the enigma lay at Grand'Terre. But who was the guilty person, Gustave or Gaston? The superintendent inclined towards the old man. He knew him better now, having begun to study him. He saw him as being both brutal and profoundly egotistical. But why should Gaston have indulged in such a massacre? The handing over of the fragment from the gun-butt also troubled the officer. If guilty, would the old man have had such a sense of impunity that he could afford the luxury of delivering to the gendarmes an essential exhibit to prove that the child had been felled with a rifle?

'I'm quite sure that while I'm on leave I won't be able to think of anything else,' Sébeille told Constant before they separated.

Clovis on the railway line falling on his knees at sight of the carbine; Gustave with drawn features at the Forcalquier gendarmerie – the two pictures floated incessantly before Sébeille's eyes. Had he twice missed out? 'On September 6, physically and mentally exhausted, I resigned myself to leaving Lurs,' he wrote in his report.

5

The end of summer is perhaps the best time of year in the Durance valley. The days are bright and clear, for the heat mists have disappeared and the fogs of the first cold haven't yet arrived. After the dog days have dried up the river-bed, one can breathe; a light, fresh air comes from the mountains in the late afternoon.

To this feeling of deliverance another was added for the Dominicis: the enemy had decamped. Sébeille had left the region and his inspectors, Ranchin and Tardieu, who had stayed on with Constant, were no longer in evidence. The superintendent appeared to have lost interest in Grand'Terre. He was getting through a lot of work, it was said, roaming tirelessly round the district. Let him, so long as he forgot the Dominicis. The heavy work of the season was over, and for Gustave the holidays had begun. He devoted his spare time to shooting. The valley resounded every day with shots, for the peasants' relaxation was to lie in wait for rabbit, pheasant or boar. The Drummonds and their tragedy were to a large extent forgotten. But, every day unknown hands brought flowers to their grave in the pretty Forcalquier cemetery.

So long as the police were assailing Grand'Terre there had been talk of forming a committee for the defence of the Dominicis. The sub-prefect of Forcalquier had had to threaten that if these makeshift lawyers meddled in the inquiry they would be prosecuted. No one had a right to hamper the course of justice, even – and especially – if it were desperately slow.

Leisure gave Gustave a taste for writing letters. He wrote a long one which was published by a Communist evening paper, *Ce Soir*, founded after the Liberation by the writer Louis Aragon. In it the farmer announced his intention of proceeding against all those who had 'given it out that he was a murderer or a coward' – the whole of the French press, in effect, except for the Communist papers. The text

116

was obviously not from Gustave's hand. He had gone to Marseilles where he had met a lawyer who was already a name in the south, Maître Emile Pollak, who probably helped him to compose his protest:

> I am neither a murderer nor a coward, indifferent to the fate of respectable people struck down in a mad fury while I could have gone to their help. Nor am I so lacking in moral sense that I would protect a monster from the wrath of all decent people. I have therefore decided to seek redress without regard to the rank of those who have done me this unpardonable wrong, whatever their functions or motives . . . my attitude had been above criticism since the tragic events of which all know . . . My one misfortune is to have lived near the scene of the drama and my sole part in it is to have notified the local police . . . My conscience and my courage have upheld me throughout. I ask no more than attainment of my aim, that justice shall restore my honour and my peace before the eyes of all.

Most of the journalists had left Peyruis and Forcalquier, except for a small group the papers had left there just in case. Constant was much less co-operative with them. Besides, he was engaged in a dull task, eliminating false trails.

Constant shared Sébeille's conviction that the solution lay at Grand'Terre. But what it was and how to get at it eluded him as much as it had his colleague. One of the first steps was to eliminate Aristide Panayotou. He hadn't the slightest doubt about him – he was inventing. Constant summoned the Marseilles merchant and put him through an intensive grilling. It emerged that on the evening of August 4 Panayotou was in a bar in the Cours Belzunce at Marseilles when at 11.0 p.m. he suddenly decided, for no real motive, to leave for Grenoble. He told no one, neither his wife nor his partner. He had, he said, received a letter from a former girl-friend who lived in the Isère. When? In June. And it was only on August 4 in the middle of the night that he set out? It didn't make sense. Panayotou stammered and stuttered – all the more when the woman whom he introduced to Constant as his wife stated that on August 6 while reading the paper he had said something like, 'Another massacre,' without showing any particular emotion. As for her jealousy, when Constant alluded to it, she burst out laughing, remarking that Aristide might dredge up all the girls he liked, she couldn't care less. In the end, with the aid of a psychiatrist and the

Military Intelligence in the area whom Panayotou had often plagued with his spy fantasies, he was dismissed as mentally unbalanced.

Constant next suffered a disappointment. He was hoping for results from an investigation started by Sébeille of the aluminium identity disc on the barrel of the Rock-Ola carbine. It was, as already mentioned, the sort used to identify bicycles and motor-cycles. The supplier came forward on his own initiative: Joseph Chauve, a resident of Marseilles. He visited all the fairs of the region to sell his discs, which he engraved himself. He recognized the one on the rifle as one he had sold – but to whom? It was impossible to say as he did not keep the names of his customers. He simply engraved them on the discs. But this one was blank – why? He explained that people sometimes took them away as they were. In his opinion it had been bought recently as there was no corrosion on it. It was possible that the buyer had carried it around in his wallet before using it to repair the gun. The screw that went with it indicated that it had been meant for a motorized bicycle.

Patiently Constant sifted the first suspects. He looked into the alibi of Paul Maillet, questioning his relatives and friends, trying to find a contradiction; the result was favourable to the linesman. The only doubtful point, and that purely theoretical, was that he owned a motorized bicycle. Constant's examination of Paul's brother, Auguste, who might have patched up the rifle with the aluminium disc, produced the same result. The superintendent accused, bullied, threatened, and argued with him for two solid hours. He stood by his story that he had slept through the night. Constant came away convinced.

A little later he received confirmation that Paul Maillet was a truthful witness. He had not invented the shot in the afternoon of August 4. The man who fired it was discovered – Aimé Perrin, the brother of Gaston Dominici's son-in-law who farmed near the Durance, some distance from Grand'Terre. The gendarmes had learned through a denunciation that Perrin possessed a military weapon. He handed it over regretfully, an American rifle he had found abandoned on the road in September 1944. He had used it to shoot magpies. Constant was not convinced that Perrin was telling the whole truth, but found nothing to warrant suspicion.

He examined individually each of thirteen Algerians employed in re-laying the road to Ganagobie. All belonged to the same *douar*.[1]

[1] North African village.

118

They were good, orderly workers, never a fight or an incident. Everybody spoke well of them. In any event, how could they have hidden a carbine in their encampment?

The seasonal threshers, a migratory population, were counted, traced, questioned, their way of life scrutinized. The results were the same as for the North Africans – no record of any misconduct, little possibility of concealing a military weapon. Constant thus closed both these files.

He then moved on to consider the carbine. What had made those nicks and scratches? He put the question to two friends at Manosque, M. Vernucci, a cabinet-maker, and M. Granier, a cooper. They replied that the nicks came from rubbing, possibly against a bicycle frame. An inspector who was helping Constant suggested that a groove cut into the barrel was to accommodate the gear-lever if the weapon was mounted on the frame of a motorized bicycle; but it would then have to be assumed, in view of the measurements, that the gear-lever of the bicycle in question had buckled. So Constant's team and the gendarmes started looking for a bicycle with a buckled gear-lever. Hundreds of machines were inspected but none fitted the description.

Constant next reviewed the poachers. The night of August 4–5 had been favourable for them; there had been a full moon. Stalking is then rewarding, especially of boar. And for bigger game a military weapon is most suitable. The gendarmes checked on known lovers of this sport, but their alibis were satisfactory. One of them, intimated a retired gendarme, was Gaston Dominici. But on being questioned by Constant the gendarme could not add to this. He did not even know if the Dominicis had a military weapon.

The superintendent was the first to question a strange lad, Gustave's nephew, and grandson of the patriarch of Grand'Terre. Roger Perrin, at 16, was small, round-faced, always laughing, empty-headed, a ball of muscle in constant movement, head and legs unco-ordinated, babbling anything and everything for fun, for a joke. Despite his youth, he had a passion for guns and shooting. The Nice doctor, Dr Morin, had already testified to that.

Constant questioned him only about his alibi. The boy answered that he had spent the night of the 4th–5th in his parents' old farmhouse, La Serre, in the Ganagobie district three kilometres from Grand'Terre. He had been alone, since his parents were taking over a new property, La Cassine, near Saint-Auban. He had gone to bed at 10.30 and had not gone out until morning. He had learned of the crime directly from Faustin Roure, the railway foreman. For the moment this statement satisfied Constant.

All these activities did not keep the superintendent from speculating on the way the crime could have been committed. On this point he differed sharply from Sébeille. Undoubtedly Sir Jack Drummond and his wife had been killed as his colleague thought, the former shot in the back but crossing the road before dying, the latter struck down on the spot. But to Constant it seemed probable that Elizabeth had not run along the path. She had been carried by the murderer, who wanted to finish her off out of sight near the riverbank. In short, Constant did not believe the child could have run along the path without injuring her feet. The journalist Jacques Chapus's experiment seemed valueless to him. As a native of the region, he knew well that Provençal paths were not mossy carpets. The stones and rough grass would have hurt the soles of Elizabeth's feet; she fled from a murderer in the dead of night and not by day under the harmless observation of a journalist. To him the difference was vital. Moreover, he was convinced that the child had been struck while lying on the ground. He had consulted the pathologists; in their opinion, had she been upright, the blows from the rifle-butt would not have caused such fearful injuries to the skull. The murderer had thrown her to the ground and attacked her before she could get up.

The superintendent concluded that the Drummond murders were unpremeditated. A man came to the camp site armed with a carbine. An incident occurred and he fired in a rage, suppressing the witnesses who might identify him. Beyond all doubt he was local; one doesn't take a stroll at night carrying an illegal carbine. Constant's conclusion was reinforced by the camp-beds which had covered the bodies. The killer had sought to delay discovery of the crime as long as possible. That would give him time either to get away or to take immediate precautions, such as harmonizing certain testimonies, which the police would not fail to elicit. Between the lines of Constant's report it is impossible to miss the hint, 'Follow the direction of my eyes.' No one did miss it.

Sébeille had finished his holiday. It was high time; he was restless. In the Aveyron where he had been staying he never stopped thinking of the affair and scribbling on bits of paper countless notes of his ideas, sifting his recollections, reading the papers, listening to the radio, watching for the slightest news, maintaining a regular correspondence with Ranchin, grumbling when a letter failed to arrive. To his wife Andrée, his unfailing confidante, he reiterated 'Another hour and I'd have had it,' meaning he would have made Gustave disgorge what he knew. So on reflection the interrupted session of September 3 now seemed to him a mistake.

On October 6 he was back in Marseilles. He sought out Constant, who gave him a detailed account of his own inquiries. Sébeille thought he detected a certain reticence in his chief, M. Harzic, who perhaps would have preferred Superintendent Constant to remain in charge; his knowledge of the country was invaluable. But Sébeille did not want to drop the case; he even announced that if necessary he would continue to pursue it at his own expense and in his own time. He even thought of resigning in order to have a freer hand. He was obsessed by the mystery, as if he had made a vow to bring the murderer to justice, as if failure would dishonour him in his own eyes. M. Harzic yielded and so did Constant. Sébeille was in charge again.

He did not at once go to the Basses-Alpes. During his vacation, he realized that he must do something: re-read the documents in the case and make notes. He had never had time for this during his month's investigation. Perhaps in those hundreds of grimy pages he would find a clue that had been overlooked. With Inspector Ranchin he began re-examining the mountain of words, statements, replies. Constant returned to Lurs.

A few days later news was brought to Sébeille by the branch of the Intelligence Corps at Digne. This was the organization charged with the gathering of all possible information about offenders, whether potential or already sentenced, political or otherwise. Members of this organization, in fact, kept the police records. They were the listening-post, their ears to the ground, in touch with 'correspondents' in circles which might interest the police, their job to anticipate crime or political agitation. In this capacity the Intelligence Corps in the early 1950s kept a close watch throughout France on the activities of the Communist Party launched on behalf of the cold war in the struggle against 'American Imperialism' and its allies – meaning in this context the government of the Fourth Republic. As far as they could, the police kept in touch with the Party militants. Often they were friends or neighbours, playing a cat-and-mouse game in a spirit of cordial rivalry.

It was an inspector of the corps who learned from the lips of a Party member that Paul Maillet knew all about the murder of the

Drummonds and especially the responsibility of Gustave Dominici. 'The child was still breathing when he found her,' the informer stated.

'Impossible,' said the officer.

'Ask Maillet; he had it from Gustave himself.'

Constant was notified. He applauded and congratulated his colleagues at Digne. But how was the information to be exploited, and was the informer ready to confirm it officially? When the question was put to him he said that it must be referred to the 'chiefs'. In an organization as hierarchical as the Communist Party was then, it was impossible to act otherwise. Forty-eight hours later Constant received the answer: not only had the militant been invited to speak but he had been given a formal directive which applied to Paul Maillet as well: if he knew anything, it was his duty to reveal it. The Dominicis had been protected as long as it seemed they were being wrongly harassed in an attempt, through them, to sully the glorious memories of the common struggle against the Occupation. But if they had done wrong they must pay for it. The departmental secretary, Hauteville, was clear on this point. He knew Constant and his integrity; he would in no way meddle in the investigation.

At 8.30 a.m. on October 15 Constant arrived at Grand'Terre and sharply ordered Gustave to come with him. The family was astounded. They suspected nothing; for a month they had been free of these invasions. Constant intimidated the Dominicis much more than Sébeille did. His blue eyes were rarely friendly, he seldom smiled. The old man protested as a matter of form. Gustave silently put on a grey suit over a blue jersey and light brown shoes. He did not say a word when Yvette embraced him. Meanwhile another police car went to collect Paul Maillet, who was working on the lines.

For this phase, which might be all-important, Constant chose the office of Superintendent Canal, head of the Intelligence Corps at Digne. He had asked the young magistrate Roger Périès to be present. Maillet was kept in a room out of Gustave's sight; he must not suspect why he had been brought to the Criminal Investigation Department.

Paul Maillet was questioned first. 'You hid something very important from us,' Constant began.

The linesman nodded his acquiescence.

'Why?'

'We were friends.'

'*Were?*'

Maillet smiled feebly. 'We shan't be much longer, shall we?'

'Tell me.'

Without any fuss he sat down at the table. It was true, he had known from the beginning that Gustave was lying. When Gustave found Elizabeth she was still breathing. It was in fact the child's death rattle that drew the young farmer's attention. This was the first logical explanation of the way in which he had come on the body. He hadn't made a detour as he said, or rather, if he had, it was because he had heard an unusual sound. Constant was satisfied; logic had returned.

'Clovis also knew,' added Maillet.

'How do you know that?'

'He was there when Gustave was talking to me.'

'Where was this?'

'In the courtyard of the farm, I think.'

'Did he volunteer this information?'

'No, it was after I questioned him.'

Gustave was brought in. He seemed perplexed and uneasy. Constant didn't keep him waiting; he told him in a few words what he had just learned. Gustave's reaction did not surprise him. 'Maillet's a liar,' he said angrily.

Constant pointed at the door. 'He's there. We'll soon see.'

Paul Maillet was recalled. He slowly entered the room where Gustave sat facing Constant and Périès. The two stared at each other. A violent outburst seemed likely, and Constant swiftly tried to evaluate the balance of forces. On the one hand Gustave and his stolidity, on the other Paul Maillet, equally tough and reinforced by Hauteville's directive to co-operate with the police. Obviously Maillet had decided to do so. The thin bony face was tense. He did not lower his eyes despite Gustave's look of hatred.

'Repeat what you told me,' Constant began.

Maillet obeyed. Every word pierced Gustave's flesh. Suddenly he straightened up, his face hard. 'Swine!' he shouted.

'Is he lying?' asked Constant.

'Of course he is.'

Insults gushed from Gustave's mouth. Paul Maillet, livid, did not react.

'Remember, Gustave,' Constant said, 'you denied what Olivier said, then you had to accept it. He was telling the truth and you were lying. It will be the same with Maillet, I'm quite sure.'

Gustave sat down again, scowling, his hands on his thighs, his shoulders bowed. Constant pretended to ignore him, addressing himself to Maillet to get as many details from him as possible – the time, the words used by Gustave, the questions Maillet had put to him. Finally Gustave raised his head. Red with anger he said, 'So you're helping the cops now, Maillet.'

'Because it's the truth.'

'Lies, you mean.'

The two men were facing each other, and Constant and the magistrate Pèriès were merely spectators of the quarrel boiling up, ready to step in only if a fight started. But they limited themselves to uninhibited insults. Soon Maillet was trembling with rage. He had four children and Gustave one, with another shortly to be born. They were fathers of families and Maillet couldn't understand how Gustave had allowed a child to die without doing anything about it. He had called him a bastard when he had heard his admission and asked why he hadn't called a doctor. And Gustave had admitted it, hadn't he? Gustave protested less and less. He had been beaten; his assurance deserted him. Uneasy, he cast furtive looks in Constant's direction.

'You'd better come clean,' the superintendent suggested.

Gustave slumped in his chair. 'Yes, it's true,' he admitted. 'I heard the death rattle.'

Constant motioned Maillet to go; he had performed his task and well, leading the investigators to a decisive turning-point, though at the expense of Gustave's friendship.

The police officer and the magistrate were now alone with the young farmer. 'We're listening,' said Constant.

'Beyond the bridge I saw a white blob on the grass. I went towards it. I heard the sound.'

'Did you see or hear first?'

'I heard and saw her at the same time.'

Constant did not quibble; for the moment he let it pass. 'Was she groaning?'

'It was a kind of snoring.'

'A rattle?'

'If you like,' said Gustave reluctantly.

'Was she moving?'

Gustave remained silent and Constant repeated the question with no more success. But Constant knew by now that when Gustave would not speak it was because he was uneasy. The superintendent faced him squarely, his elbows on the desk, his expression merciless. 'Was she moving?'

'Yes,' Gustave finally admitted. 'I saw her left arm stir slightly. Then it sank back on the ground. That's when I said to myself I must call the gendarmes.'

'And not the doctor?'

There was no response; a despondent look merely, the lips parted but no sound issuing from them.

'Why did you tell Olivier there was a corpse when she was still moving?'

The only answer Constant could elicit was, 'I wasn't paying attention.'

'Did you tell your mother and your wife that she was still alive?'

'That she was at her last gasp.'

'And neither offered to go and see if they could do anything for her?'

'No.'

'Heartless, aren't they?'

Gustave looked angry. In a hard voice Constant repeated the sentence.

'Yvette is pregnant,' Gustave mumbled in defence of his wife.

'And your mother?'

'She's very sensitive.'

'Sensitive as a stone.'

This time it was Constant who fell silent. He did not believe that Gustave was yet telling the whole truth. He had been forced to retreat and abandon the position previously held. But the one he now occupied was not definitive. Without knowing where he was vulnerable, Constant vaguely felt that he should continue the offensive. The advantage the superintendent had just gained was not the objective he sought but a means of throwing his adversary off balance and making him fall before he could recover himself. Constant therefore wanted to press on.

He suspended the interrogation around midday. But it was only a tactical pause. He used it to telephone the pathologists, the doctors Girard and Nalin, to ask a single question: how long could Elizabeth have survived her injuries?

'Not more than an hour,' they answered.

So Gustave was lying and Constant had caught him out on one point: the time at which he had found the body. The shots had

125

occurred at 1.0 a.m., therefore it was 2.0 a.m. at the latest when he was at the scene of the crime.

To make Gustave acknowledge this, Constant devised a plan of attack with Sébeille, who had returned from an inquiry in the Isère. He would take charge of Gustave while Sébeille went to Grand'Terre to question Gaston, Yvette and the Sardine.

The first step was to question Clovis. Sébeille and Constant went to look for him on the railway line. He came clean immediately. Quite right; Gustave had admitted to him at once, that is at 7.0 a.m. on August 5, that the child had been moving.

'And you advised him to say nothing.'

Clovis looked away. 'To spare him trouble.'

'You've very carefully not mentioned it to the police. You the honest man . . .'

The linesman flushed. 'No one asked me,' he said.

'Of course not – the police couldn't guess.'

At a little after 3.0 p.m. Constant had Gustave brought before him. 'I've been thinking it over,' the superintendent said. 'Your story won't stand up. Not for a moment.'

'Why?'

'Take one example. You say, "I saw a Swiss motor-cycle but I didn't stop it." All right if the child was dead. But she was alive – you ought to have stopped the first comer.'

Gustave opened his eyes wide, not comprehending. After a long moment he said, 'That's true.'

'It's also true that you didn't go near the body when you might have seen if it was possible to save the child.'

'I didn't want to.'

'Why?' asked the astonished superintendent.

'I didn't want to leave my footprints.'

Constant leaned towards Gustave with a look of scorn. 'Are you serious?'

'I didn't want it said I'd been wandering around.'

'And you preferred to let her die?'

'They might have blamed me.'

'I don't believe it,' said Constant softly.

He studied Gustave, trying to understand what sort of man he was. Into Constant's mind drifted an idea which the farmer's answers strengthened: he had the murderer right there in front of him.

'What time was it?'

Gustave was surprised; he had answered that question more than once. 'Five-thirty.'

'That's impossible. The doctors are categorical.'

'They could be mistaken, couldn't they?'

'Not on this point.' The superintendent's voice hardened. 'You're still only a witness, Gustave. You have taken an oath to tell the truth. Until now we've ignored your lies. Now that's over. We no longer believe you. When you left your home it was two in the morning at the outside.'

'No.' It was a weak protest. Gustave was helpless. Face to face, Constant didn't give him a moment's rest, overwhelming him with crisp, short questions, castigating his attitude, pointing out the clumsy contradictions underlying his every word. But time was now working against the police officer. The witness's anxiety remained, but a kind of tactic was taking shape: let the storm pass, don't struggle, take shelter under a tree and wait for the skies to spend their fury. All that Constant heard were sentences like, 'I don't know.' 'I can't tell you anything different.' 'That's how it was . . .'

'You say you were afraid of being pestered. You have been. You still are being. On September 3 you could have told me everything. Why didn't you?'

'I had lied, I was afraid to change.'

'Today you've been forced to speak. Spill it all and we'll stop bothering you. Otherwise you'll make us think you know a good deal more. In fact, that you're the murderer.'

The accusation did not outrage Gustave. His worst misfortune was to find himself in the hands of the police. Given that disagreeable situation, it didn't much matter what was said to him. Words seemed to slide off him. Constant tried another argument. 'You didn't go up to the body because you didn't want to leave footprints. Therefore you already knew it was not an accident but a crime.'

'I didn't know.'

'Then if you thought it was an accident, why didn't you try to help the child?'

The reasoning was flawless and would have nonplussed any man subject to the laws of logic. But Gustave kept a discreet silence.

'In ten seconds you thought it all out, and cut short the natural reaction which would have been to hurry to the victim, especially a child. You said to yourself, "Careful, I'll get into trouble."'

Gustave agreed. 'That's right,' he said calmly, 'I told myself I'd better not go wandering around.'

'And to Olivier you spoke of "a corpse"?'

'Yes.'

'Again, why?'

Gustave gave the superintendent a sullen stare but said nothing.

'And you didn't get in touch with the parents?'

'I didn't think of it.'

Constant shook his head. 'Gustave, you are unspeakable. After having stopped Olivier, you didn't even go back to see if the child needed you.'

'I was afraid.'

'Of whom? The poor little kid?'

But the police officer's contempt in no way embarrassed Gustave. It slid off his thick hide, arousing no remorse in him, no regrets. He had about him the air of thinking of something else, of not hearing, as if his eardrums were incapable of registering displeasing remarks.

Night had long since fallen as the interview continued without let-up. As in September, it was a contest of patience and endurance. But Gustave had steeled himself. He showed no sign of weakness. The moment arrived when Constant became convinced that he would get no more out of him. 'Your story is totally improbable,' he said, 'and for a simple reason: you have had to invent in proportion to your lies – one thing that proves you are no stranger to the affair.'

Gustave shrugged his shoulders.

'You know the murderer.'

'I do not.'

Constant still held on, although by now he cherished few illusions. Gustave did not budge from his disconcerting immovability. This formidable impassivity, this apparently infinite indifference to others, was his way of escape. 'Can I go home?' he asked.

It was about midnight. Constant shook his head; Gustave was to be kept under observation. The farmer sighed. 'Isn't there any way of proving to you that I'm telling the truth?'

'Give us some likely answers.'

'Isn't there a truth drug?'

'Yes.'

'Then try it on me.'

Constant nearly burst out laughing at the very thought. On a man like Gustave Pentothal would have about as much effect as water. 'We'll see,' he said.

Gustave was already lying full length on the camp-bed made up for him; sleep always came easily to him.

Sébeille and his inspectors invaded Grand'Terre on the morning of October 16. Gaston was not pleased to see his persecutors reappear. His first words were to ask what they had done with Gustave. He scowled when Sébeille answered that the police had detained him. 'He is innocent,' the old man said.

Yvette was questioned in the kitchen. Sébeille told her of Gustave's admission. The young wife at first refused to believe it, but gave way when given the details. She also knew. 'He told me her arm moved.'

'And that he heard the death rattle?'

'No!'

Sébeille was surprised. Why deny it when Gustave himself had admitted it? But Yvette did not elaborate, perhaps to ward off the inevitable reproach that she, a mother herself, had lacked elementary charity and made no move to aid a child suffering near at hand. Not that she seemed any more embarrassed than her husband, even though she had recently told reporters that the crime so horrified her that she would kill the murderer with her own hands, even if he were someone close to her. Grand'Terre was obviously not the place to have an accident. 'We were only thinking of the gendarmes who would soon turn up,' she said.

'Why, if you didn't know that a crime had been committed?'

Sébeille was no more successful with Yvette than Constant had been with Gustave. Sébeille next tackled Gaston, whom he questioned in his room. Every now and then the old man made a point of looking at his 'picture', the certificate awarded him long ago for bringing about the arrest of a malefactor. He was a good citizen and had never ceased to be one. He respected the police and would always help them. But in order to do that he had to know something, and he didn't. Half in dialect, half in French, the words coming in a sort of chant through his thick moustache, either angry with or weeping for his family, Gaston declared that he was the only one at Grand'Terre to know nothing. 'Everybody hid everything from me.'

'That's not possible,' Sébeille said.

'It is.'

'You didn't know that the child was still moving?'

'No.'

'Your daughter-in-law and your wife did.' An inspector had questioned the Sardine; she had made the same admission as Yvette.

'You see,' observed Gaston philosophically, 'nobody ever tells the old anything any more.' Now the very symbol of imperturbable wisdom and honesty, he added, 'If he had told me, I should have advised him to speak.'

He himself had done everything the situation required. On his own initiative he had covered the body, the ants having begun to crawl over the face. It was also he who had handed over the fragment of wood. If anyone was above reproach, he was. But he contradicted himself and Sébeille pointed it out to him. Once he had stated that Yvette had mentioned a dead child, at another time it had been the gendarmes. Calmly the old man amended his statement. Yvette had said, 'There's been a crime committed.' He had gone to the spot and it had been the gendarmes who had told him that the body of a child was lying at the end of the path. As for Clovis's advice to Gustave to say nothing, he had been told about it only this morning, and he was still very indignant; a Dominici owed it to himself to be straightforward, especially to the police. Sébeille congratulated him on his admirable principles. But he held to his opinion. If the Sardine knew, so did Gaston. He noted also a slight discrepancy – now it was in the morning that Gaston had discovered the fragment of wood, while in his first statement it had been the afternoon.

Meantime Constant had resumed the interrogation of Gustave, who had breakfasted heartily on coffee and croissants. But for the police officer it was only a matter of duty. It was just a long monologue, scarcely interrupted by Gustave except for an occasional trite response. Expressionless in word and look, he barely followed the superintendent's arguments.

Towards noon Constant left Digne for Grand'Terre. Gaston fiercely demanded news of Gustave. If he told the truth he would have him back, answered the superintendent. Afterwards Constant conferred with Sébeille and Périès. The prosecutor, M. Sabatier, was consulted. The decision was made to charge Gustave with failure to assist a person in danger.

At 5.30 p.m. this was conveyed to him by M. Périès. Gustave had lost some of his assurance. Ill-shaven, features drawn, eyes vacant, he was led away. For the first time he wore handcuffs. The prison was not far from the law courts, a few yards from the place where his father had been born seventy-five years before, at the end of a steep lane almost at the town's highest point.

'Why have they got it in for us?' Gaston complained to the journalists. 'I don't even know what a justice of the peace is.'

*

The first cold. The rain-soaked earth grew mushy underfoot. The vines, stripped of their fruit, retained only the black wood of stock in the soil from which they would draw nourishment during the winter. The apricot and peach trees shed their leaves which had become unnecessary trappings. The old silver of the olive leaves grew tarnished. Each morning a sharp wind whipped the countryside. The swollen Durance overflowed. A chilly sun lit a sky still often blue.

At Grand'Terre, Gaston wandered aimlessly through the day, listening to the Sardine in the kitchen tirelessly moving her pots and pans. He was bored and lonely. Gustave was at Saint-Pierre, and had been refused release on bail. His lawyers, Emile Pollak and Pierre Charrier, had applied for it and M. Périès had agreed, but the prosecutor, M. Sabatier, appealed. The court at Aix-en-Provence which had issued the indictment upheld it. Gustave would not be freed to go home; he had lied too much.

Yvette had left with little Alain. It was a shock and there were rumours that she was no longer on good terms with her parents-in-law, with Gaston especially, reproaching him for having done nothing to spare Gustave his present predicament. When asked, she denied these rumours. She was, after all, five or six months pregnant. In the event of an accident – and after the emotions she had gone through anything was possible – who would take her to the hospital? Gaston had no car, and he was old. It was Mme Barth, her mother, who had decided that she should come and live with her parents until Gustave's return. There was no need to look further.

Gaston had asked Clovis to replace Gustave. There was not much work at this time of year, apart from looking after the animals. Clovis came after his day's work at the Lurs station and stayed the night. 'Your mother's frightened,' Gaston said.

The evenings were longer than they had been at Grand'Terre. Gaston complained of not being able to sleep since Gustave was in prison. He and Clovis installed themselves in the kitchen. The old man was drinking more than usual; after dinner – a thick soup and cheese – he drank a litre or two of his white wine. He went to bed at about 11.0 and Clovis realized he was leaning on his stick to keep himself from falling. His heavy shoes shook the wooden stairs. Gaston groused about everything. Everyone was against him. They had never accepted that he, an Italian bastard, had become a well-to-do farmer. The police had taken it into their heads that someone at Grand'Terre was a murderer. 'You know it isn't so, don't you?' he would ask.

131

'I know,' Clovis would reply.

Silent, self-effacing, almost invisible, the Sardine would move round the kitchen without listening to the two men, at times followed by the sarcasms of her husband who mocked her and abused her when he had had one too many. But no matter how coarse he became she took no notice, never answered back. Clovis would see her wince and often came to her defence, but his father would turn on him. If he didn't like it he could clear out! He had already left once without warning and they got on without him. Clovis let him talk. He was patient. He knew his father, and stayed because of his mother. When she said she was afraid, he wondered if it wasn't simply of her husband.

Gaston could not speak to his wife without recalling the past, the grievances he nursed against her. They were as old as the hills – and probably imaginary – but for Gaston these old tales were an obsession. The Sardine had been pregnant when he married her – and not by him. She had gone on having her fun whenever she felt like it. She had cuckolded him and he had revenged himself by mistreating her. Natural justice. An old whore who had no right to complain. Seated at the table, glass in hand, Gaston spewed out his insults between swallows.

'That's enough, Father,' Clovis said one evening. 'If you go on like that at Mother, I won't set foot in this house again.'

Clovis's tone surprised Gaston. Contemplating his son, he knew he was capable of keeping his word. Gaston muttered something and then fell silent, saying nothing more during the meal. But his anger had not left him. To sustain it, he drank more than usual, and when the Sardine left the room for a moment he started to mumble, watching Clovis with anything but affection. Clovis pretended not to notice. At last Gaston banged on the table and said in dialect, 'I'm the one who killed the three of them. If I have to kill one more, I will.' He stared hard at Clovis.

'What do you mean?' his son asked.

'I did in those three.'

Clovis looked his astonishment. His father continued to watch him, glassy-eyed. The old man seemed delighted with the effect he had produced.

'Why did you do it?'

'I went to look at the landslide. I came back past the car and had an argument with Drummond.'

132

'Impossible!'

'Why is it impossible?'

Clovis was familiar with that arrogant tone. It was the one his father used when he was finished with answers and expected his word to be taken as gospel. At such a moment curiosity was useless; it only served to provoke insults and oaths. Besides, his mother had returned and Gaston had taken up the bottle to refill his glass. A little later he got up and went to the staircase, his moustache bristling, his eyes glazed. Before retiring, he hurled at everyone and no one, 'I'm not afraid of anybody.'

Clovis remained seated in the kitchen, even after his mother had also gone up to bed. His father was hopelessly drunk, that was sure. With age he could no longer carry his liquor. He too must have gone over and over the affair in his mind; alcohol was responsible for the notion that he was the killer. And who was the fourth he proposed to do away with? Himself, Clovis, because he had told him off when he abused his mother? Or Maillet, whom Gaston often accused of being at the bottom of all the family's troubles?

Slowly Clovis bolted the wooden door which converted Grand' Terre into an enclosed universe. His thoughts went to Gustave in prison. For the time being he was charged only with a minor offence. But it was possible that one day the indictment could be transformed into one involving a monstrous, inexplicable crime. Clovis miserably recalled Gustave's telling him that their father was the murderer. Strangely, that accusation had rebounded in Clovis's mind against the one who made it. A few minutes before that, he had recognized the carbine in Sébeille's hands and nearly given himself away, falling on his knees as if in supplication. Then he had hurried to Grand' Terre. At the door of the shed he had collided with Gustave, who seemed terribly upset and stammered incoherently. Later Clovis gained the impression that his brother was improvising his answers, accusing his father to distract attention from himself. But Gustave was lying most. Clovis had to get answers from him syllable by syllable. For Gustave knew. He had not lied to the police alone. This could only mean that his mind was uneasy. Without realizing it, Clovis was wrestling with the same arguments as Sébeille and asking himself the same questions.

A heart-to-heart talk with both Gaston and Gustave would be necessary to learn the secret of that dreadful night, to escape the fear that a lie lurked behind every word. But Clovis did not know how to go about it. The Dominicis were not in the habit of exchanging intimate confidences; they had neither the taste nor the technique for it. Clovis recalled that Gustave as a small boy had been given to odd pastimes: killing lizards, prowling through ruins to ferret out rats and crush them with stones. But he wasn't the only child to do that. You couldn't judge a man a murderer because of cruel amusements he had indulged in as a child.

As for his father, Clovis had witnessed his struggle with the bandit from a few steps away. He had admired Gaston's courage and guts, as well as his savage strength. True, he had been under fifty then. Could he now at seventy-five pursue a child, seize her, strike her down? But why destroy in a few seconds a prudently conducted life of which he was so proud? Clovis had seen him work like a slave, carry on an unending struggle with the soil, reclaim the land, slowly put aside a small fortune, depriving himself so as not to have to beg for a state pension, and proudly enjoy a semi-retirement which owed nothing to anyone. It was difficult to believe that so much effort would be risked in a single act. The old man would have to drink less, Clovis concluded; otherwise he would begin blurting out this nonsense to anyone within earshot.

Two or three days later he tried to raise the subject again. His father seemed fairly sober, neither more nor less than usual. Drawing on his pipe, he responded with an air of mystery between two puffs, 'What's happened is too bad, but we mustn't talk about it any more.'

Clovis was left with his doubts, and from this moment they were to give him no peace. What had happened that night at Grand'Terre? And what was going to happen?

Gaston Dominici had dressed in his dark brown corduroy suit, wound a long woollen scarf round his neck, and put on his broad-brimmed Sunday hat. In his right hand he carried a stick, under his arm a net shopping-bag. At the side of the road he waited for the bus to Digne, where he was going to answer the summons of the examining magistrate, M. Périès. He had received it two days earlier and had taken no exception to it. For a magistrate you put yourself out – more than for a police officer, who in his peasant eyes always smelt of the constabulary, the universal enemy.

Roger Périès who, as examining magistrate, would from now on be in charge of the case, was only 33. A tall, thin man with a friendly face, he was easily approachable. If anything, he was regarded as too easy-going, especially regarding bail. He had already been overruled by the court at Aix-en-Provence in the matter of Gustave, and an official rap on the knuckles was never a good thing for a young magistrate. But it hadn't affected his good humour and kindliness, which were known to every lawyer in the south of France. Roger Périès was esteemed by all for his integrity and his respect for the rights of the individual. Originally from Béarn, he had got himself appointed to Digne because he was in love with a Provençal girl who had since become his wife. Until now he had had to deal only with petty theft and bar-room brawls. Apart from a recent air disaster, the murder at Lurs was his first big case.

M. Périès's office was lighted by two wide bay windows. Gaston entered it half an hour late and deposited his hat, umbrella and bag on a chair. M. Périès hung a sign on the door: Please do not disturb.

'I've asked you to come to clear up a few details,' he said quietly.

'I've already told everything.'

'Well, tell it again,' returned M. Périès with a smile.

He did not expect much from this interview, aware that if the police had got so little out of the old man, he had no better chance, unless Gaston allowed himself to be impressed by the prestige of the judicial office. Périès quickly realized that he was not. The interview lasted less than two hours. Gaston had seen the English people only on August 4 from a distance as he was returning with his goats. They had not come to Grand'Terre. He had never owned a carbine like the one used for the crime. He had never seen one in the hands of his neighbours or his shooting companions.

'Would you like to visit your son?' asked M. Périès.

Gaston shook his head. 'No, I wouldn't have the courage.'

'I can give you a permit.'

'I've never crossed the threshold of a prison and I don't want to. Besides, if I were face to face with Gustave, we'd both cry. It would be unmanly.'

M. Périès nevertheless handed him a visitor's permit in case he changed his mind. But Gaston, after lunching in a small restaurant, went to see some friends and at about 5.0 p.m. took the bus back without going near the prison.

Gustave, however, was not forgotten. He received several visits, especially from Constant and Sébeille. The former questioned him about an incident which turned out to be of no great consequence. The police learned that Yvette had spoken of a certain 'Jo', who may have slept at the farm and to whom the Dominicis had given money. Blackmail, services rendered? The investigation led to a half-wit, Marcel Cheyland, who sometimes slept in the Dominici sheepfold.

Was he there the night of the crime? Had he seen anything? Could he be the murderer? After questioning Yvette and her parents-in-law, Constant went to the prison. Gustave said he knew nothing about it. The superintendent used the occasion to return to a point that puzzled him: a landslide had to be kept under observation from hour to hour. Was it possible that on the night of August 4–5 Gustave had not gone out between 10.0 p.m. and 5.30 a.m.? Had he slept peacefully with this menace hanging over his head?

'I had let Faustin Roure know,' Gustave maintained. 'He told me, "Go to sleep and don't worry, I'll come by tomorrow morning, just have a look when you get up." That's what I did.'

The police officers meanwhile had been surprised by a curious small fact reported to them. A fellow inmate of Gustave's came one day to tell him that he knew the Grand'Terre murderer, someone living at Volx in the Basses-Alpes. It was undoubtedly the sort of false tip that often circulates among prisoners. Imprisonment stimulates the imagination. It takes a cool head for a prisoner not to be caught in the trap of hope.

Gustave, who had never ceased to proclaim his innocence, listened to the informer and said only, 'Better tell it to the police.'

It showed surprising self-control. Gustave may have thought that with his arrest the police were no longer interested in him. Or that it was pointless to start a dormant inquiry going again. If he thought either, he was mistaken. The police were never more convinced that the solution was to be found at Grand'Terre.

When Maître Emile Pollak came to inform Gustave that the application for his release had been refused, the young farmer simply remarked, 'I always pay for the others.' He said no more.

One of the preoccupations of French justice seems to be to take up as little space as possible. It is hard to imagine the cramped cupboard into which all the components of a tribunal are packed: the presiding judge and his two assessors, the clerk, the usher, the counsel for the prosecution, the lawyers for the defence, the defendants and the witnesses, not to mention the public as required by law, the journalists and the curious. A positive crowd is somehow squeezed into a few square metres. In official eyes comfort has no right to exist. French justice has always had a zero rating for the welcome extended to her visitors.

The trial of Gustave Dominici on the morning of November 13 was no exception. By 8.0 a.m. a dense crowd was gathered before the railing of the Palais de Justice at Digne. It was very cold; the thermometer had dropped below freezing for the first time. Fog hid the neighbouring mountains and was still drifting through the streets, pursued by an icy wind. When the doors opened there was a scramble up the steps. Reporters and photographers elbowed one another for the best places. The photographers climbed on to the tables. It was a first-rate crush.

The Dominicis turned up in strength, Gaston and Yvette first. Gaston was in excellent humour. He was convinced that Gustave would be back at the farm and that their worries would be over. The son had been in prison for a month, which would be deducted from any penalty inflicted, and according to the forecasts this would be the maximum awarded for the offence of non-assistance. The defence counsel, Maîtres Emile Pollak and Pierre Charrier, had been assured by an expert, Dr Jouve, that the child's condition had been such as to preclude any hope of survival – she had been beyond help.

To the great disappointment of the newsmen, no witnesses were called. 'The confessions are sufficient,' declared M. Jean Builly, who was presiding.

The trial was therefore kept within strict limits – Gustave's interrogation, the charge, and the pleadings. All that did not directly concern the offence, such as Gustave's indifference to a child in her death throes, was ruled out. While waiting for the court's entry, Gaston made a rude gesture at the photographers raking him with their cameras. The room broke into loud laughter.

Gustave, between two gendarmes, entered at a little after 9.0, wearing a sheepskin jacket with a fur collar. He nodded to his father and his wife, then took his place in the dock, blinded by the flashbulbs of the cameras. His face was calm, his hair carefully brushed, his deep-sunk eyes reflected nothing but boredom. His thin lips barely opened.

The court entered amid deep silence. M. Builly came to the point at once, stating the charge against Gustave Dominici: 'You failed to give help to Elizabeth Drummond whom you found dying on the morning of August 5th. The previous evening the Drummonds had camped in a small enclave requisitioned on your land by the Department of Roads and Bridges. At one in the morning you heard the sound of shots and recognized them as coming from a military weapon. You said to your wife, "Something's happened to the English campers." Next morning you took care to check the condition of a landslide but did nothing to learn what had occurred.'

Gustave said nothing, his power of silence arousing public wonder for the first time. When the president urged him to answer, he repeated in a few sentences what he had already said five or six times: he had seen a white blob, the child in light-coloured pyjamas; she was 'snoring'; her left arm, lying across her abdomen, had moved slightly. He had alerted a motor-cyclist 'as quickly as he could'.

'It did not occur to you to call a doctor or help the little girl? Nor to your mother or your wife?'

'No,' said Dominici.

A rustle passed through the room, but Gustave was unaffected. 'The sight upset me too much,' he said. 'I was afraid and didn't want any trouble.' It was true that he had not gone close, but at six metres he could tell that with the skull as bloody as that he could do nothing for the child.

'That's not true,' rejoined the president drily. 'You couldn't tell. At the place where you were standing you should have thought there might still be a chance to save her. In any event it was your duty to find out.'

'I didn't think of it.' He added that he had hoped the gendarmes would arrive quicker than they did. But they came on bicycles, he explained, which was untrue; Romanet and Bouchier had taken the police motor-cycle.

'According to your evidence,' the president went on, 'the movement of the arm you saw was not the last, since Dr Dragon found the body lying on its back, the arms extended like a cross.'

Gustave reiterated that he hadn't wanted any trouble. The president observed that the defendant had not waited for Clovis's advice to say nothing, because he had already told Olivier that there was a 'corpse' on the bank. If he lied, it was on his own initiative.

The interrogation ended there. Gustave sat down in the dock, knees together, hands clasped, an outsider at his own trial. Next came M. Sabatier's speech for the prosecution. The facts were established and he spoke without heat. One should forget the sensational character of the case, take into account only the offence charged, allow for the defendant's 'honourable' past, remember that Elizabeth was dying anyway, and impose only a moderate sentence.

'Our client should be acquitted,' responded Maître Pierre Charrier. 'Didn't he at once notify the gendarmes? Was it his fault if they were late?'

'Gustave Dominici is harassed because he is weak and unable to defend himself,' said Maître Pollak. 'This trial is an alibi for the police who want to disguise their total failure. The murderer is still at large. But they had to have a scapegoat, at least that was their hope, and they picked on Gustave Dominici.'

The verdict was deferred for a week, bail was refused. The Dominicis were stunned. Before leaving the dock, Gustave collapsed in tears in his father's arms. A week later, at the same hour, sentence was pronounced – two months' imprisonment. His hands gripping the lapels of his sheepskin, Gustave heard the president's judgment read out. His father was not present, having been kept at Grand'Terre by a slight attack of flu. 'It'll finish him,' Yvette predicted.

The reasons given for the decision were particularly severe. Gustave, declared the magistrates, had the duty of calling immediately for medical assistance. He deliberately refrained from doing so, and his inaction was not due to any moral constraint or irresistible force, for this farmer, by no means primitive, and in the prime of life, could not have remained upset for so long that he did not realize where his duty lay . . . The offence must be judged harshly, taking into account the strange and still inexplicable attitude of this man who violated both French traditions of brotherly love and the accepted notions of human solidarity . . . However, he should be granted the benefit of extenuating circumstances because of his family position, favourable testimony as to his character and the absence of any previous convictions.

In a low voice Gustave acknowledged this last sentence with a muted 'thank you'. Yvette followed him into the corridor where she held him in a long embrace. An appeal was lodged on the spot. The sentence was severer than had generally been expected. It was clear that the magistrates intended to punish the reticence displayed by the inhabitants of Grand'Terre towards the police; the sentence struck not only at Gustave but at all who lived there. At noon the doors of the house shut behind the old couple, and a nephew from the Haute-Savoie, Ida's son, Gaston Balmonet, took over for Clovis.

Less than a month elapsed before the case came before the Court of Appeal at Aix-en-Provence. The proceedings were even shorter than at Digne. The deputy public prosecutor asked for the sentence to be confirmed and opposed the release again demanded by Maîtres Pollak and Charrier. But the court had already freed Gustave before confirming now, on Christmas Eve, the penalty imposed in November. The previous judgment was upheld; Gustave had abandoned without help a child who still showed signs of life.

139

Gustave was not present at the hearing, at which he was represented by Maître Charrier. He had already been back at Grand'Terre for a week, joined there again by his wife and son Alain. His reception had been almost a triumph. Gustave, however, was suffering from eczema, the result of an allergy. His hands became covered with blotches whenever he was very upset. This had happened at the time of the Liberation when he found a dead German hanging by his feet in a tree. He does not seem to have displayed any such symptoms on August 5 and the days immediately following.

'They've been hard on me,' he said to the reporters awaiting him at Lurs. 'I didn't deserve it.'

Then he lunched with his family, which included brothers and sisters who had come flocking from the entire region. From the courtyard the journalists occasionally heard the sounds of a lively discussion and also of singing. One of the sisters, Augusta Caillat, came out to tell them to go away. Then she made the following statement which they recorded: 'My brother is a fool, an imbecile, he didn't know how to defend himself. If the police had knocked on the right door instead of swarming round us, the truth would have been known long ago.'

Christmas came. There was a truce, even for the police. Lurs regained its solitude. The cold December sky lighted the village's old houses and the abbey of Ganagobie. Father Lorenzi, the recluse, commemorated the birth of Christ before a crowd of the faithful. A child carried in a lamb to be blessed by the monk. At Grand'Terre they were content with revelry. As on every December 25, Gaston welcomed his children. But the atmosphere was less festive than usual. Only the old man did not seem affected. He joked and caressed the women with his moustache. No use fussing, it was all over; the policemen were at Marseilles, let them stay there. It was noticed that Clovis was in low spirits. He had no appetite and barely picked at the food, which was unusual. They teased him, but he only responded with a joyless expression. They decided that he had troubles he didn't want to talk about.

Constant and Sébeille were back at their desks in the Bishop's Palace at Marseilles, but still preoccupied with the case. It had been decided that Sébeille should go on with the investigation. The first stage had ended with Gustave's conviction – a tangible result, certainly, but less than satisfactory, as the two superintendents were only too well aware. The murderer had won the first round.

The Confessions

6

As if to hide it from view of its enemies, a light fog enveloped Grand'Terre. Winter on the banks of the Durance is harsh, for in this region the seasons are extreme. Ice covers the road surfaces which in summer melt in the heat. On the hills, the north wind bends the short, gnarled trees.

Under the mulberry tree which provided the Drummonds' last shelter, two men were standing. They seemed to be contemplating the earth cracked by frost. One of them pointed out to the other where the car had stopped, where Lady Drummond had been killed, where Sir Jack had been struck down. Then his finger traced the route along which Elizabeth had fled. Edmond Sébeille had returned to the scene and his companion was none other than his father, the retired inspector. The superintendent had waited until Lurs was abandoned to its winter isolation, the journalists absorbed in other dramas. Edmond Sébeille now needed solitude.

For weeks he and Inspector Ranchin had worked on his files: invisible, tedious work whose importance outsiders fail to appreciate but which no investigator neglects when a problem defies solution. Days were spent in collecting documents previously scattered among the various services taking part in the inquiry. Minutes and reports are not necessarily composed on the same day as the operations with which they are concerned. Constantly on the move or keeping watch, police officers have to wait for a slack period. Then these documents, amounting to several volumes, must be minutely studied. Until December Sébeille hadn't had the time to get down to this work.

By the beginning of 1953 he had a card index in which he had entered all the Dominici family's evasions and contradictions. The fullest entry was of course Gustave's, liberally interspersed with cross-references in red. When Sébeille re-read it, he realized that there was not one point on which the young farmer had not lied at some time or other, whether about the visit of the mysterious motor-cyclists to the courtyard, his itinerary on the morning of the crime, or the instructions given him the evening before by the railway foreman Faustin Roure. With him, truth slid into a shadowy abyss and emerged as a tissue of mist. Like that now enfolding Grand' Terre.

This was the first time Robert Sébeille, the father, had been at Grand'Terre since the start of the investigation. He knew the region by heart; it brought back old memories. He had often made inquiries there and Edmond Sébeille followed his methods: to ferret everywhere, listen, chat, open the doors of the farmhouses, sit in the courtyard with the owners, judge men and their reactions, provoke them if necessary, keep on coming back with a kind of irritating naïveté to disturbing questions, drawing out with care the discrepancies and contradictions. Robert Sébeille had won many a case by this procedure.

He had frequently discussed the Lurs affair with his son and probably knew it as well as he. Despite his age, Robert Sébeille's memory was excellent. He wanted to know all about the people, urged the superintendent to repeat word by word what they said, how they looked and behaved, their way of lying or evading. Edmond submitted to this grilling partly out of filial tenderness – he greatly admired his father – partly because the old man could give him useful advice.

Even before setting foot in Lurs, Robert Sébeille was convinced that the answer would be found at Grand'Terre. He even had a favourite – Gaston. His prediction rose from the depths of unwritten experience: the majority of crimes against children were either the work of the very young, or the very old satisfying an obscure need for revenge on those who are hurrying them to the grave. Gustave was certainly not to be ruled out, but Robert Sébeille judged him to be too spineless for so horrible a crime. The former inspector also distrusted a character who had made only brief appearances on the scene – Roger Perrin, the now 17-year-old grandson who had already shown a sturdy talent for distorting the truth.

'In any event,' Robert Sébeille emphasized to his son, 'it will be a long business. The Dominicis are tough. Your only chance is in their number. Wait . . .'

This was indeed the superintendent's intention. The end-of-the-year festivities had given him a chance for reflection. He must now start a patient siege of Grand'Terre. The second phase of the attack

144

was beginning. The first had been noisy and tumultuous, the next would be secret and invisible. Instead of working in the glare of floodlights, he would advance in the dark. No more reporters, no more communiqués, no more news. Perhaps it would be said that the police had given up and that one or several murderers had got off. It didn't matter; until the final attack it was better that the case should not appear on the front page of the newspapers. There on the other side of the wall, inside the enemy camp, confidence would revive, a misleading confidence which could be shaken occasionally so that nerves might little by little be strained. The days would pass by, apparently tranquil, the weeks mount up without bringing new dangers, the months slide past without a sign of battle. But Sébeille would always make his presence felt. That was how uprisings began inside a besieged city; when people are fearful for their lives and liberty, there are always individuals ready to break away from the group. Sébeille believed Gustave was destined for this role.

'I had so often read and re-read his statements,' he later admitted to a journalist, 'that I caught myself repeating them by heart when I woke up at night.'

Towards the end of January, Sébeille made his first reappearance at the farm. Snow had invaded the valleys and covered the hilltops. The Dominicis were hibernating. Gaston seemed surprised to see the superintendent again. 'I thought you'd let the matter drop,' he said.

Sébeille smiled. He had been passing by and dropped in to greet him. The old man's scowl was eloquent; he didn't mind being forgotten. 'Since it's you, all right,' he said, 'but the other one, Constant, I'd have chucked him out.'

He was angry with Constant for having led Gustave into contradicting himself, then admitting the offence which sent him to prison. Sébeille sat down in front of the large fireplace where Gaston was warming his legs. 'Well, Grandad, what sort of winter have you had?'

Gustave's diversion during the bad weather was the local form of bowls. He got up a little later, at dawn, about 7.0 a.m. The work was quickly accomplished – looking after the animals, attending to the trees and vines, inspecting the soil. In the afternoon he rode his motor-cycle or bicycle to Peyruis where he engaged in countless bowls matches. Often he went with the local club to take part in regional tournaments. The local game had the advantage of requiring no meticulously laid-out piece of ground. After nightfall the players retired to cafés for endless games of lotto.

Gustave had lost one of his team-mates, Paul Maillet. The two were on bad terms, not even greeting each other when they met. No one was surprised but no one took sides. At Peyruis they preferred to forget the whole business. The journalists had left and that was all to the good; they had published too many unpleasant things.

Paul Maillet had troubles of his own. The Communist Party had asked him to explain the sub-machine-guns found in his kitchen. When he confirmed the fact, he had been dismissed from his post of secretary of the cell and proceedings were under way for his expulsion. Maillet was furious. He announced that he 'would speak up', indicating that he had a weight on his mind that he could well be rid of.

Clovis was morose. He continued to come to Grand'Terre but much less often than before. He seldom spoke with Gustave and still less with his father. When he came, as often as not his mother would start weeping, causing Gaston to flare up, stamp out and disappear. Yvette was anything but friendly disposed towards her brother-in-law, but at least part of this could have been caused by the latter stages of her pregnancy. The child, a daughter, was born on January 23, 1953. When Yvette returned to Grand'Terre the whole family filed past her bed, rejoicing. Gaston took his nineteenth grandchild in his arms. The art of being a grandfather held no mysteries for him.

A violent argument had divided the family a short time before. M. Barth, Yvette's father, had begun it by saying at dinner one day, 'Gustave shouldn't have to bear the whole expense of the trial.' And without pause he went on to propose that the brothers and sisters should share it equally. Those present accepted this with varying degrees of enthusiasm. Germaine Perrin, who was not at the dinner, said no, frankly and unhesitatingly. She had been the outsider for a long time and had never forgiven her father for having once said that she kept a hospitable bed. To Gaston it was of no importance; if a girl was pretty, no reason for her to be unsociable. But Germaine hadn't liked it. The matter in hand, however, had nothing to do with her father. Why should she help her brother Gustave? Her brothers and sisters-in-law were sharply critical; if there was a defect in the family, let her take a look at her son Roger, who had no more sense in his head than a ten-year-old.

When the crime was spoken of in the family, it was only to incriminate Paul Maillet. Gaston and Gustave were categorical; he had denounced Gustave in order to divert suspicion from himself. How else could his behaviour be explained? The worst of it was that he had succeeded. Beyond any doubt the carbine belonged to him. When Clovis was asked his opinion, he agreed awkwardly; Maillet did seem to him suspect. And the police were wrong not to go for him first. Unless it was a tactical move.

The word about Maillet passed from mouth to mouth, gaining strength with each repetition. Paul Maillet was no more pleased than Gaston Dominici had been to see Superintendent Sébeille and Inspector Ranchin turn up on the morning of January 27. His welcome too was a scowl. Sébeille was amused. 'Anyone would think you weren't overjoyed to see me, Paul.'

'Not after all that people are saying.'

'Quite so.' Sébeille sat down at the kitchen table. 'You fooled me nicely. Last September I was kind to you. I arranged for the little matter of the sub-machine-guns to be dropped. And you waited until I left to confide in Superintendent Constant.'

It was partly to embarrass Paul Maillet, partly perhaps a touch of professional jealousy. Constant had first obtained the result Sébeille had sought for five weeks.

'You weren't at Lurs.'

'For a month you were leading me up the garden path.'

Maillet half-heartedly defended himself. Gustave was his friend, he did not want to betray him. And now they had fallen out, and Gustave was saying mean things about him, let alone the old man. It used to be that no two days would go by without Maillet dropping in at Grand'Terre. It was one of his chief pleasures. Now that was over, thanks to this damned business which had brought other troubles on him as well. Sébeille commiserated. 'The Communist Party doesn't take things lightly,' he remarked.

'Oh, them!' exclaimed Maillet spitefully.

'In short,' Sébeille concluded, 'you're in bad now with everybody, including me.'

'I didn't want to be the first to talk,' Maillet said. 'I waited for Gustave to do something about it. He didn't.'

Sébeille didn't refresh his memory. If he had broken his silence it was because one of his comrades had confided in the Intelligence Corps. Constant had had the luck which had escaped Sébeille. But it was still true that almost from the first Maillet could have expedited the investigation. Sébeille hadn't forgotten those sticky hours when he felt as if he were moving through bird lime. 'You haven't played very fair with me,' he said.

Maillet looked almost apologetic. Sébeille had come to see him more or less by chance, impelled by a feeling which was based only on intuition: Maillet had divulged only a part of what he knew. Like all the actors in this drama, he was capable of a momentary gleam of sincerity which had to be exploited instantly. Otherwise they relapsed into their chosen darkness, only too glad to ignore, forget even, the disagreeable problems involved. Maillet, however, knew that this was only an illusion, since it had already lost him a friend and his position in the neighbourhood.

'All right,' he said, 'I've more for you.'

Hands on the table, his eyes at first lowered, he began his story. 'Since Gustave doesn't want to tell you what he knows I'll do it for him. It's too bad, but at the point we've reached it doesn't much matter any more. I've given him time to think it over, haven't I?'

Sébeille merely listened, impatient to hear what was coming.

'It was last September, between the 1st and 5th, I believe. One evening at about six I went to Grand'Terre to buy some potatoes. I found Gustave and Yvette under the big tree in the courtyard. We talked about the case, naturally. I must have said that it was surprising they hadn't heard screams, because the English family must have made some sort of noise when they were fired on. Both assured me that they had heard only shots. I didn't insist and asked Yvette how many kilos of potatoes she could spare me. She said she would have a look and went to the shed, leaving me alone with Gustave.'

He fell silent for a moment. 'Then,' he resumed, 'he grasped his head between his hands as if he were in pain. "God," he said, "if you'd seen, if you'd heard those screams! I didn't know what to do with myself."'

'Did he say it in French or dialect?'

'In dialect.'

'Was he answering a question or talking on his own?'

'I had the impression he'd been waiting to be alone with me.'

'So he just came out with it point-blank. Why, do you think?'

Maillet shrugged his shoulders. 'Maybe it was torturing him.'

'He waited until Yvette had gone?'

'Yes.'

'You didn't ask him any questions?'

'Yvette came back with the potatoes.'

'You might have spoken earlier,' the superintendent said brusquely.

148

Maillet repeated that he wanted to give Gustave, his long-time friend, the opportunity. He himself had been surprised when in his confession to Superintendent Constant he had failed to mention the screams. 'Such silence wasn't normal,' he said.

'What about yours?' returned Sébeille. He gave Maillet no time to answer, going straight on to the suspicions he had entertained. The linesman would have made, if not an ideal, at least a reasonable suspect. But by a word, by concealing nothing, he could have cleared himself. Maillet acknowledged that this was true. The police had not been alone in suspecting him. His colleagues, his neighbours, his Party comrades had all cold-shouldered him. He had suffered a good deal.

'By your own fault,' remarked Sébeille.

'All the same,' Maillet said, 'I'd like you to catch the murderer.'

Sébeille was surprised; with witnesses like Maillet, murderers didn't have to worry.

'Did you never try to find out any more about the screams?'

'Two or three days later I went back to Grand'Terre to buy more potatoes. I tried to ask Gustave some questions then, but he told me to clear out.'

Maillet did not hide from Sébeille that he was uneasy. He had been threatened, and shortly before Gustave's arrest he had been the victim of a curious accident while riding his motor-cycle. 'Look –' he pointed to the door – 'on the lane you came up which leads to the road, I fell over: a wire had been stretched across it. Not meant to kill me, maybe, but a warning for sure.'

Another day he had encountered old Gaston. Without a word the old man had levelled his stick at him as if it were a gun and pretended to pull the trigger. 'Quite apart from the anonymous letters I've had,' he added.

He claimed he had no hatred of the Dominicis. If he was aiding justice, it was because he thought it his duty to reveal the truth. No place could go on in the atmosphere of distrust and fear that weighed on Lurs. Maillet said he would bless the day when Sébeille laid hands on the murderer.

'Meanwhile,' Sébeille ordered, 'you are to say nothing to anyone of our conversation – especially to the Dominicis.'

Maillet promised and Sébeille left. Sébeille was torn between bitterness and hope; bitterness because four months earlier this evidence would have confirmed what everyone thought – that the couple had heard screams – and would have forced an admission on this point from the Grand'Terre farmer. Without the means of pinning him to the wall, his confession had remained unfinished. Constant had had to give up. With Maillet's help, he could have hustled Gustave into a confession.

Yet there was hope now because the overheard screams removed all trace of doubt about Gustave and Yvette's behaviour on the morning of August 5. How could Gustave now maintain that his natural reaction on getting up was not to run to the camp site to learn what had happened? Or that he was only worried about the landslide? How could he continue to declare that, having seen the body of the child, he had not hurried to tell the parents? It was impossible that he hadn't connected the shots, the screams, and a tragedy that occurred 150 metres from where he lived.

Yvette's position also became untenable. And her story took on its full meaning. They had not 'looked thoroughly into the matter', she had said, suggesting that they had not interpreted the shots as having anything to do with an incident near by. But if they had heard the screams, there could be no doubt that since 1.0 a.m. on August 5 they had known that a tragic event had taken place. If they wanted to know nothing about it, it was because of the fearful implications of the truth. If they took great care not to let it touch them, it was because they were afraid of being implicated.

However, Sébeille didn't run to Grand'Terre to exploit his new advantage. His method was to mine Grand'Terre's defences so that when the right day came he could blow them up. Maillet's revelation had only brought about a few inches of progress. Now it was necessary to press forward in the tunnel noiselessly, without alerting the enemy, and if necessary to multiply the diversionary manœuvres.

A fragment of wood nine centimetres long is not much. When Sébeille re-read the file it was like a splinter under his skin. Impossible to forget, it was also impossible to disregard, because it had provided a starting-point; on August 5 it had given Sébeille an understanding of how Elizabeth had been killed. Like the carbine that had not revealed the name of its owner, the fragment had ceased to be one exhibit among many. For the superintendent it was packed with some unknown meaning.

Sébeille re-read the gendarmes' report. The wooden fragment appeared on page five: 'At 3.30 p.m.,' Captain Albert had written, 'the victims were removed to the hospital at Forcalquier. Under the body of the little girl was found a piece of wood from the weapon used in the crime. The piece was 9 centimetres long and seemed to be a fragment of the butt of something like a carbine or a shotgun.'

Then, early on, Gaston Dominici had said to the superintendent in passing, as if it were a matter of no importance, that it was he who had noticed the fragment when the child's body was taken up and had handed it over to the gendarmes. He had immediately thought it was a fragment of the weapon. At the time Sébeille hadn't paid much attention. It hadn't occurred to him to suspect the old man or any of the residents of Grand'Terre. But he had questioned the gendarmes, who had replied that it was quite possible.

Days had passed. Sébeille had dealt with Gustave's lies and gained an insight into Gaston. Were they guilty? But each time the superintendent considered the old man's guilt, whether alone at night or in the company of his father or Inspector Ranchin, he had to overcome the objection that if Gaston were guilty he would have pocketed the fragment of wood and got rid of it at the first opportunity. What would be the advantage in handing over to the investigators an exhibit whose origin no one knew better than he?

Twice Sébeille had put the question to the old shepherd: how had he found the fragment? Gaston had seemed delighted that the superintendent should ask him about this. He had answered willingly, sure of his ground, easy of conscience. Unfortunately he had contradicted himself. Once it was in the morning that he had made the discovery, the next time in the afternoon when the body was removed. Sébeille had noticed the discrepancy, and kept it in mind.

'We decided,' he wrote in his report, 'to reconstruct the smallest facts down to their minutest details as they unfolded in the course of the inquiries. Under these conditions we wanted, despite old Dominici's explanation, to have the fullest light thrown on the discovery of the fragment from the butt.'

It was the mayor of Forcalquier, M. Esparlat, who had taken charge of the removal of the bodies. Sébeille asked him for the names of the men he had recruited for this task: a road-mender, M. Robert Eyroux, a retired night-watchman, Simon Orsatti, as well as a resident of Lurs, M. Figuière. Sébeille questioned each of them.

Robert Eyroux burst out laughing when Sébeille told him that Gaston Dominici claimed to have found the fragment. 'He's got a nerve!' exclaimed the road-mender. 'I'm the one who found it, not him.'

'Exactly where was it?' asked Sébeille.

'In the grass, about ten centimetres from the child's head.'

'Could you see it clearly?'

'You had to bend over, as I did, in order to lift the body.'

'What did you do with it?'

'I showed it to the others who were there. I must have said, "Look, a bit of a gun."'

'Was Gaston Dominici present?'

'Very near, about two or three metres away, near the child's feet.'

'Who handed it over to the gendarmes?'

'I did, of course.'

Sébeille went to find Simon Orsatti, who confirmed Eyroux's story.

'I'm sure,' he said, 'that it wasn't old Gaston who found the bit of wood. The road-mender showed it to us and even had us pass it round.'

So Gaston Dominici had lied and Sébeille could follow his train of thought. He had been present at the discovery of the fragment and at once realized the danger it represented. He had to avert it. So he had said that he handed over the fragment to the gendarmes and promptly claimed credit for the act from Sébeille. A clever defence, demonstrating remarkable reflexes and presence of mind. But Sébeille now knew where he stood. Gaston's lie had turned against him and it benefited Sébeille in two ways. First it proved that the fragment was of prime importance and that Gaston knew it; therefore he, like Clovis, recognized the carbine. Second, it opened to Sébeille an unexpected field of psychological exploration. Thanks to this incident, he understood in a flash Gaston Dominici's behaviour. He also knew that the old man was not invulnerable. Like his son Gustave, and even Clovis, he was so entangled in his lies that one day he would crack. When he said that it was perhaps in the morning he had found the fragment, it was because the superintendent had caught him off his guard. So the matter could be dropped for now, as with Gustave. What was required was patience.

'The testimony regarding the fragment from the butt marked a decisive turning-point in the inquiry,' Sébeille wrote in his report. 'In fact it convinced us that the Dominicis were more than eye-witnesses, that they had taken an active part in the business.' He informed the magistrate Périès of the results of his investigation, concluding: 'The old man stood out as big as a house.' The magistrate told him to carry on, that he believed he was right.

Jacques Chapus, the journalist, repeated to Sébeille a conversation he had had with Gaston Dominici which he'd been thinking about.

He had found the farmer near the Roads and Bridges gravel tip. They began talking, and continued under the mulberry tree. 'This is where the kid screamed,' Gaston said suddenly. Chapus was startled and it didn't escape the old man's notice. 'At least,' he resumed, 'this is where she must have screamed.'

In a siege the besiegers wait for any sign of weakening morale. Sébeille now noted with satisfaction the small details which showed that the Dominici citadel was not impregnable.

It is better for a young gendarme to have no memory at all than a delayed-action memory. His superiors will have greater cause for anger if he misses his moment for disclosure and then turns up with it when it is of no further use. Henri Marque, aged 25, belonged to the Valensoles squad 20 kilometres from Lurs. Until now he had performed the tasks appropriate to his modest rank – keeping the peace, verifying details, checking suspects, the routine duties of the gendarmerie. Then one day he talked too much, and it was his ill luck that a journalist was within earshot. 'There were two Hillmans,' he declared, 'one following the other, and in the second I remember a woman in black.'

He was, he stated, on duty in front of a large hotel in Digne on the evening of August 4. He had first seen the Drummonds, whom he of course did not know but had subsequently identified thanks to the newspapers – a couple and girl of about ten. The car had stopped and Sir Jack got out to ask him the way to Château-Arnoux; then he set out in that direction. A few minutes later another car of the same make arrived, also with British licence plates. The driver stopped in front of Marque, asked him where to find the nearest telephone, went into the café indicated by the gendarme, and came out shortly afterwards. He took off immediately at high speed along the Château-Arnoux road. During the halt a woman in black got out and nervously smoked a cigarette.

'Why didn't you mention it earlier?' Marque's superiors asked him.

'I didn't think of it,' he answered.

The testimony itself was of no great importance, especially after seven or eight months. But it echoed rumours which had circulated during the very first days. Sir Jack's Hillman had been followed through the Basses-Alpes by a car of the same make and colour in which rode a 'woman in black'. From this it was only a step to imagining that the murder had its origin in professional or even

sentimental jealousy and not in France but in England. At Grand'
Terre the chance was not missed. A number of times in front of
reporters Yvette and Gustave alluded to this mysterious couple who
had been seen on the road and met all the killer's requirements.

In every respect Marque was wrong. He gave support to this
theory at a time when verification was no longer possible. How could
anyone trace the ghostly 'woman in black' and learn if she were a
flesh and blood reality or a phantom born out of the needs of the
case? When Henri Marque made his revelation the journalists were
wandering round Lurs like lost souls. Sébeille no longer spoke to
them, and Périès, the magistrate, had never been talkative. They
didn't know what was going on; Marque saved them. He was interviewed everywhere, all the newspapers printing his revelations. At
Grand'Terre he became a hero overnight. 'We've always said,' Yvette
kept repeating, 'find this woman in black and there will be no more
mystery.'

To visitors, passing friends and journalists, the Dominicis offered
with a glass of wine their version of the Marque story, revised and
improved of course. The Drummonds had been spied on until they
fell asleep. The little girl had been killed because of course she knew
the murderers. It was the perfect crime and the Dominicis themselves
were victims; the pair of killers had got back to England and must
be laughing at the misfortunes they had caused the poor French
farmers.

'A sum total of zero,' Sébeille declared when the newsmen
questioned him about Marque's evidence.

'Hillmans,' he added, 'must be circulating by the dozen on the
Côte d'Azur in August. Also women in black.' He referred back to
the argument already used at the outset: a pair of murderers could
hardly be imagined traipsing across Europe with a patched-up Rock-
Ola when it was so easy for anyone interested to procure a 6·35 mm
or 7·65 mm of the best quality. But the Dominicis' eagerness to leap
at the wildest theories to distract attention from themselves made
sense to Sébeille: they were on the defensive.

Sometimes Sébeille would visit Grand'Terre himself. His visits
were necessarily brief; inside the house a tête-à-tête with anyone was
difficult. With the return of the good weather, he intended to show
himself more often. In the courtyard or orchard, or at the edge of
the field that separated them, he would dawdle with the old man
and, if possible, with Gustave.

One day on the Canebière he met a gendarme from Forcalquier

who was passing through Marseilles. 'Wouldn't you like some news of Gaston?' he asked Sébeille.

'Very much.'

'They say he's dying.'

Sébeille was startled. 'Dominici?' The gendarme was astonished; the superintendent hadn't been told? 'He's been very ill since yesterday. Pneumonia.'

The superintendent rushed to telephone Digne, where the news was confirmed. Dr Caccia, the doctor at Oraison, had prescribed penicillin. Sébeille was deeply troubled. At 76 pneumonia could well finish the old man. And if Gaston died, the Lurs affair would, at least in part, preserve its secret. Sébeille recalled cases he had dealt with where if suspects had the luck to number among their closer acquaintances someone recently dead, he would be saddled with the crime. If Gaston Dominici died suddenly, he would surely be denounced as the guilty one without any possibility of irrefutable proof. Never had Sébeille prayed so heartily for the recovery of one of his suspects. But after three days of fever the patriarch recovered. He resumed his place in the kitchen, and if he was a little thinner, his cheeks hollow and his colour pale, his white wine quickly revived him. Sébeille was thankful.

From the first day a bicycle left leaning against the mulberry tree worried Captain Albert. The head of the Forcalquier squad was a tall, thin man with a long face, a prominent, slightly aquiline nose, thick eyebrows over eyes always on the alert, a képi perched high above a wide forehead. He knew his area like the back of his hand and he travelled through it ceaselessly. Generally liked, he was able to shut his eyes on suitable occasions, which was not held against him. The role of a responsible official of the gendarmerie involves not only gaining the confidence of the notables and the sub-prefect, but also of the general public. Captain Albert had; he could say almost immediately who inhabited the most remote farmhouse and supply information on the moral condition of the place.

Albert had actively seconded Superintendent Sébeille, often taking the initiative, his task being to check possible clues, petty thieves and suspects of every kind. He was of course intensely interested in the case and in his theory of it. Like the superintendent, he believed that the solution would be found at Grand'Terre. But he did not exclude the possibility that the Dominicis were shielding a murderer who, though closely related to them, did not necessarily live at the farm.

The bicycle he had seen on August 5 belonged to Gustave. It seemed odd to Captain Albert that the farmer should have used it to go only 150 metres. At the same time he remembered a statement made to him. Gustave's nephew, young Roger Perrin, told him that on the morning of August 5 he had come by bicycle from his parents' farm, La Serre, four or five kilometres distant. But Captain Albert had seen only one bicycle on the farm. In the turmoil of the first few minutes it was a detail which might have escaped him, and he might have given it no particular thought if his attention hadn't been caught by the discrepancy between Roger Perrin's version and that of his other uncle, Clovis. The boy declared that he had used a bicycle belonging to Gilbert, Clovis's son, who worked in a bakery near Paris. But according to Clovis, Roger Perrin had not borrowed it until August 18. It was a point of reference – the date of the Peyruis fête.

Why had Perrin been unwilling to admit that he used Gustave's bicycle? The question troubled Captain Albert, who decided to examine Roger Perrin; the boy was invited to describe in detail how he had passed his time between the evening of the 4th and the morning of the 5th.

Perrin was 16 at the time. He was born at Grand'Terre where his mother, Germaine, Gaston's daughter, was still living. He had spent a large part of his childhood at his grandparents'. A deep affection linked him to his Uncle Gustave, from whom he had acquired his taste for shooting. In the course of the inquiry and the trial Roger earned the title of 'King of Liars' in a competition where formidable rivals laid claim to that crown.

The starting-point for the investigators was Roger Perrin's statement to Superintendent Constant on September 23. The boy then affirmed that he had passed the afternoon alone in a field worked by his parents near Ganagobie; he had been instructed to water the beans, which he had done until 7.0 p.m. His father and mother were at another farm, La Cassine, which they had recently taken over. But for Captain Albert he altered this timetable. On March 17, 1953, he declared that on August 4, 1952, he had worked at Pont-Bernard for a farmer called Daniel Garcin. Then he had gone to his garden in the Saint-Pons quarter. He had even had a discussion with a neighbour, M. Delclitte, on the subject of watering. Then he had returned to his parents' old farm, La Serre, for the night.

'I don't remember having young Roger with me that day,' declared M. Daniel Garcin.

'I didn't see Roger the afternoon of August 4th,' asserted M. Delclitte.

Had he moved from La Serre the night of the 4th–5th? 'No,' he answered. 'I watered the horses, ate the meal my mother had prepared, and went to bed.'

Captain Albert informed the magistrate Périès of Roger Perrin's inconsistencies. Wouldn't they interest Superintendent Sébeille? The magistrate telephoned Marseilles and Sébeille, followed by the faithful Ranchin, drove up to the Basses-Alpes. There he encountered Roger Perrin and his ways with truth.

The first question put to the boy by Captain Albert had been how he learned of the crime. 'From Faustin Roure,' he answered. 'At about six-thirty I was at Daniel Garcin's at Pont-Bernard. Faustin Roure came in to buy a bottle of wine and I was drinking my milk. He told us there had been a murder at Grand'Terre.'

But on the afternoon of the same day his story to Sébeille was different. 'Faustin Roure,' he said, 'came to the farm to buy his litre of wine same as every morning. "Last night," he told me, "people were camping at the bridge, beyond the apricot trees. During the night they fought with revolvers and a little girl was killed. She's under the bridge between the railway and the Durance." After Faustin Roure left I took my bike and went to Grand'Terre. I got there at about eight.'

In Roger Perrin's story to Superintendent Sébeille the 'woman in black' figured. Gustave had seen her the evening before when returning from the landslide. But she was not one of the victims, therefore she could be the murderer. So he told his nephew when they first spoke on August 5.

Sébeille pressed on with his questioning, using the technique of exhausting the smallest detail. The milk Roger had had for his breakfast, for instance, who brought it to him if he hadn't gone to Daniel Garcin's to fetch it? 'My mother,' he replied.

But an hour later the picture changed. 'I must tell you,' he admitted, 'that on that morning I got up at five. I looked after the livestock and at about six I went to Peyruis on my bike. I bought my bread, then I wanted to get some milk so I went to the Puissant dairy. But the dairymaid's father, M. Puissant, told me that the Garcin servant, Jean Galizzi, had taken the litre. So I went to Pont-Bernard where I found the milk in Galizzi's room. I went back to La Serre and Faustin Roure had arrived. With his wine I even gave him a piece of ham.'

Sébeille wondered at the precision and minute detail with which Roger Perrin reconstructed this somewhat confused timetable. 'All these people will, of course, confirm what you say?' he asked quizzically.

'Sure,' answered Roger. 'Except M. Puissant.'

'I suppose he's dead,' suggested the police officer with gentle irony.

'Correct.'

'A pity . . .'

A pity indeed. M. Puissant had died in November 1951, eight months before the tragedy at Lurs. He could not have told Roger that morning what had become of his milk. It seemed a bad slip but it took more than that to trouble a temperament like Roger's. Nor was he noticeably upset when Jean Galizzi denied any memory of taking his friend's milk that morning. Why should he? Roger was asked.

'I don't know,' he answered. 'I said it like I might have said anything.'

For the police officer, a liar's brain has its intriguing aspect. A scrutiny of his motives for departing from the truth in the first place is often more revealing than the occasional relapse into honesty. Tell me why you lie and I'll tell you who you are.

Sébeille could at a pinch understand why Roger Perrin let his imagination run away with him when accounting for the morning of August 5. But August 4? What difference did it make whether Roger had watered the beans at Ganagobie or his garden at Saint-Pons? What importance did he attach to an argument about watering with a neighbour who denied it? It could be a malicious pleasure in finding himself at odds with the whole world and not merely 'saying the same as the others'. But if he lied to hide his presence on the morning of August 5 at some place other than La Serre, how could he call to witness a man he knew perfectly well was dead? The only answer seemed to be that sometimes he lied for the fun of it and sometimes out of self-interest – except that it was practically impossible to sort out which he was doing when.

In May, Sébeille decided to launch a major offensive against the young tale-spinner, to corner him with his own lies. At 7.0 p.m. on the 7th he sent for him at the butcher's at Digne where he had been employed for some time and had him brought to the police station. Roger showed not the slightest uneasiness. He was delighted, it seemed, with a role that gave him importance in the eyes of his friends. An interview with the police was a heady adventure.

Sébeille concentrated on the morning of August 5. Roger Perrin confirmed that he had learned the news from Faustin Roure. He had set off at once for Grand'Terre after leaving a note for his mother; there had been an accident at Grandfather's, he wrote. At the farm he had found his grandmother and Yvette. Her parents, the Barths, had turned up shortly afterwards and come into the kitchen. Yvette had related that English campers had spent the night under the mulberry tree and during the night had been attacked. They had arrived the evening before at about 7.0. 'A little later,' the boy added, 'they went to the house.'

Sébeille cut in abruptly, 'What's that you're saying?'

'The English people came to Grand'Terre to ask for some water.'

'How do you know?'

'From Yvette – she told us so.'

The superintendent stared at the young man. Was he telling the truth or was this one of his yarns? Did he realize the value that the investigators would put on this revelation? He was providing what might be a decisive weapon since, thanks to him, they had found that the Dominicis' lies embraced not only the crime itself but the hours preceding it.

'It was the lady and the little girl who came,' Roger Perrin added. 'Yvette, my grandmother and grandfather were in the courtyard and received them. It was the girl who spoke; my relatives thought that the lady did not speak French, because every time any one spoke to the girl, she translated into English for her mother. Yvette led them over to the pump. They had brought along a little canvas bucket.'

'Are you imagining that they had a little canvas bucket or do you know it?'

'Yvette mentioned it.'

'What happened next?'

'Yvette chatted with them for a moment, or rather with the girl. She asked where they had come from and the girl said Digne. Yvette then suggested that they had not chosen a very good place to stop; she advised them to go beyond the bridge. At the bottom of the field there was a hut where they would be better off for the night. But the girl answered that they were all right on the gravel patch. Before leaving, they went over to the stable where my grandfather opened the door to show them the goats.'

Sébeille had difficulty hiding his satisfaction. It was his happiest moment since the August afternoon when he had first come to the

Basses-Alpes. For Roger Perrin had mentioned a detail which the superintendent recognized gave his story authenticity. The 'King of Liars' had for a moment told the truth.

It was quite true that Elizabeth spoke French while her mother was ignorant of the language. Sébeille knew this from the Drummonds' friends, the Marrians, but Roger could not know it. He therefore could not have invented the conversation Lady Drummond had held with the Dominicis through the intermediary of her daughter.

So the Dominicis had lied with splendid assurance about their contacts with the victims. Not only had they seen them, they had spoken with them. With the good nature of which he was capable, Gaston had shown Elizabeth his goats. The family's defensive system was crumbling and had now received another blow: how could Gustave and Yvette now maintain that after hearing the shots they hadn't the next morning thought the victims might be the woman and child they had seen the night before? Moreover, they were well aware that they were still under the mulberry tree, since Elizabeth had declined the offer of the hut. Yvette and her parents-in-law, then, had good reason not to mention the English visitors: their lofty detachment about the campers would otherwise become utterly implausible.

'Is that all you heard?' asked Sébeille.

'No,' replied Roger. 'Yvette said that Gustave had got up a little earlier than usual, about a quarter to four, to have a look at the landslide and also at what had happened. He came back a little later and said he had discovered a body.'

Another revelation, and a serious blow to Gustave's position. He had insisted against every probability that it was 5.30 when he heard the child's death-rattle. The timetable supplied by Roger Perrin conformed better to medical reason and common sense. How had Gustave occupied his time between getting up and stopping Olivier on the road – three hours during which he had known what had happened without trying to summon help or notify the gendarmes?

Roger was the first to betray his family, but why had he now become an ally of the police? Certainly their success of that May 7 had been cunningly prepared by Captain Albert's gendarmes, who during the preceding weeks had devoted themselves to baiting him every time they ran into him. They reminded him that they were keeping an eye on him, that they didn't like his attitude, they asked disagreeable questions about him. A liar would not be left in peace until he had made some effort at telling the truth. One day or another he would have to make an admission.

'And what time did your grandfather get up?'

'At about three-thirty.'

'Earlier than usual, that is?'

'Yes, and he left the other way. Ordinarily he turns to the right, but that morning he turned left.' (Away, that is, from the mulberry tree and the gravel patch.) Even Roger had been surprised and had asked Gaston if he had been able to see the way. The old man had replied that there had been bright moonlight.

The boy had not remained at Grand'Terre the whole morning. He returned to La Serre for lunch, where his mother, Germaine Perrin, had found his note and from various people learned what had happened at her father's. Roger, while eating, told her the whole story of the morning, repeating what he had heard. In the afternoon they went to Grand'Terre. Roger remained for some time near the gravel patch with Gustave, who told him about the night and repeated that he had risen at about 3.45 a.m.

Sébeille sent for Germaine Perrin. She was a sturdy woman of 38 who confirmed her son's statement. She had learned what had happened at about 9.0 a.m. on August 5, passers-by having told her almost as soon as she found the note Roger had left. Two or three days later her sister-in-law Yvette told her about the English coming to the farm. She even added, 'Next time we won't do anything for anybody.'

Germaine did not realize the implications of what she had said. What link could there be between the crime and so commonplace a thing as the English people coming to ask for a little water?

Sébeille was not entirely satisfied with his interviews with mother and son. From several sources he heard that Roger's indiscretions stemmed from a fear of being suspected. Perhaps he had spent the night of the 4th–5th at Grand'Terre. Captain Albert had the impression that he had and it was with the intention of establishing this fact that he had begun to take an interest in Roger. Sébeille had the boy in to see him again. It was only the matter of his alibi, he was told. But the boy was a good deal shiftier this time – as was his mother.

On the essential point he did not vary; he had slept alone at La Serre. But – and this was something new – at about 8.30 p.m. Gustave had passed by the farm sounding his horn. Roger Perrin had even mentioned it to his mother, they were having dinner. Half an hour later, while Mme Perrin was on her way to join her husband at the other farm, Gustave had shown up. He had just warned Faustin Roure about the landslide and was returning to Grand'Terre. He had only stopped to exchange a few words with his nephew, especially about having watered his field too much, which was worrying him. Roure had ordered him to watch it. Then he left because he had not yet eaten.

'And didn't he suggest taking you along to Grand'Terre instead of letting you sleep alone?' asked Sébeille.

'No.'

'Yet you're so nervous.'

'Not really.'

Sébeille smiled. 'So nervous that you're afraid to go to the bathroom alone at night.'

Roger Perrin blushed furiously. 'It's not true.' The proof, he added, was that he went to bed at once, sleeping soundly by 9.30.

'Why did you ask Galizzi to lie?'

Again Roger seemed annoyed. The farmworker, servant on the same farm where Roger had worked, had admitted that his friend had asked him to tell the gendarmes that he had received Roger's bottle of milk the morning of August 5.

'For no special reason.'

'Like other things,' remarked Sébeille ironically.

'I did it without thinking.'

'I can see another explanation. Since you were not at La Serre but at Grand'Terre, you thought up this lie to make us believe that you slept at home as on other nights.'

Roger protested vehemently. Gustave had not been worried about his being alone and had not proposed taking him with him on his motor-cycle.

His mother Germaine succeeded him in Sébeille's office at the Digne police station. She differed from her son. She had certainly had dinner with him before leaving him alone. But she had not seen her brother Gustave and had not known that he had passed by La Serre that evening. She did not know why her son said he had; he must have his days mixed up. 'I am sure,' she added, 'that if Gustave had seen Roger alone at La Serre he would have taken him along to Grand'Terre. My son passed his childhood there, Gustave often looked after him.'

Sébeille did not confront mother and son. They contradicted each other on an important point and it would be interesting to know why. But more important was the part of Roger's statement concerning the appearance of Lady Drummond and Elizabeth at the farmhouse and the time Gustave got up. He now understood why the child had fled towards the river instead of making for the farmhouse: the murderer came from Grand'Terre and she had recognized him. In the manœuvre he was planning, Roger Perrin would play an important part. If he had been present at the crime, had participated in it, he would be involved in the general offensive, and Sébeille meant to spare no one. It would be a game of massacre in which the players would fell one another; only those with clear consciences would remain standing. Between two tactics, that of immediately overwhelming Roger Perrin with his lies, or temporizing after carefully recording them, Sébeille chose the second. He had just achieved a major step forward. He would swear Roger and his mother to secrecy, threatening them with the worst if they warned Gustave or Yvette. They would keep their word. Sébeille had gained what he wanted: the division of the clan.

When they were together in the courtyard near the fig tree, in the orchard among the apricot trees, or the olives which springtime was reviving, they looked like two friends, the younger listening with respect to the advice and wise recollections of the elder. Sébeille had returned to Grand'Terre. He let no week pass without visiting Lurs. Often cars were lacking at Marseilles, mobilized for an investigation. The superintendent then went by train or bus. At Digne he always found a friend or colleague who would drop him near Grand'Terre. The remaining distance he covered on foot, appearing at the entrance to the courtyard. If Gaston was not in his usual place, Sébeille pushed open the kitchen door and the old man would welcome him with a qualified smile.

Sometimes Gaston sulked as if to remind the superintendent that he would prefer him elsewhere. The superintendent's arrival disturbed him, it spoiled his day. But he rallied quickly. The kindly grandfather's mask of good humour slowly took over. Then Sébeille sat down and on good days Gaston offered him a cup of coffee or a glass of wine. Yvette or the Sardine served them. Yvette was rarely friendly. Sébeille knew by now that her brusque voice and gestures were only the reflections of her anxiety.

Most often Sébeille came with Inspector Ranchin if the inspector wasn't occupied with another case. Ranchin's mission was to keep alert to every word that fell from the lips of the inmates of Grand'

163

Terre and engrave them on his memory. At the same time he observed their looks and behaviour. In the evening during their return journey the officers took stock of what they had seen and heard, then recorded it on their file cards. In this way Sébeille obtained a faithful portrait of the Dominicis – of Gaston and Yvette chiefly, Gustave having a tendency to take flight when he saw the superintendent coming and hide out for the duration of his visit.

The superintendent had quickly ascertained that there were two very different persons in Gaston Dominici: the impish old fellow and the irascible one. With an evil glare from under half-shut lids, he could suddenly be malicious and hateful. A number of times Sébeille had witnessed one of these metamorphoses. What triggered it off was always something to do with the case. Gaston became crotchety whenever he realized that Sébeille's visit was not disinterested. Or rather he pretended to be. If the superintendent persisted, his face would close up and he would start in with reproaches, followed by undisguised anger if the officer indicated that he was not being taken in. Sébeille remembered the day Gaston had raised his stick to him, in a gesture which irresistibly recalled that of the murderer smashing the little girl's skull.

Gaston Dominici could pass in a flash from tranquillity to fury without any sound reason at all. Sébeille had seen this happen several times. One day in the spring of 1953, he, Ranchin and Gaston were together near the mulberry tree. The conversation was friendly, Sébeille avoiding dangerous topics. They discussed the coming season. Gaston made predictions about the harvest. A few metres away the goats and the dog were idling. Suddenly the goats scattered and Dick pursued them, driving them towards the bank where Elizabeth had died. Gaston jumped up, cursing in dialect, bawling at his dog. Then he seized a large stone and threw it at Dick with all his might. It caught the dog square in the ribs. Only then did he calm down, as if the animal's pain had satisfied him.

A banal incident doubtless, but it impressed Sébeille because it contradicted the image of philosophic benevolence which Gaston usually assumed towards people and things. The superintendent was also struck by the terror of the animal, who seemed accustomed to these outbreaks of sudden violent anger. Gaston Dominici always professed to love his dog best of all beings because it was the most faithful to him. But if he could display such blind brutality towards him, what about strangers and intruders?

Certain types of news could trigger off one of his outbursts, as when a rumour got around that a monument to the Drummonds was to be put up on the spot where they had met their death. Gaston's reaction was so coarse that it surprised even Sébeille. 'It seems they're going to erect a monument to the carcases,' he said. And when the superintendent remained silent he continued, 'Well, they'd better fence it off or the goats will shit on it.'

Seeing him so angry, Sébeille decided to goad him a little. He confirmed the news, embroidering it with invented details. 'I've heard it talked about,' he said. 'I even believe they're going to put up a life-size statue of Elizabeth in marble.'

Gaston knitted his brows malignantly.

'She'll be wearing a pretty white dress,' Sébeille went on remorselessly, 'and pointing her finger.'

'Pointing it where?' asked the old man uneasily.

'At Grand'Terre, I think,' the police officer replied smoothly. He slyly watched Gaston, goggle-eyed, the veins in his neck swollen. The old man swore in dialect and turned his back on Sébeille.

One of Gaston Dominici's great preoccupations was sex, the pleasures he had had from it and his regrets at not being able ever to repeat them. He was in fact obsessed; the old man never stopped talking about it, thus confirming the rumours about him – his insistent attentions to the female members of his family, young and not so young.

'How are things?' Sébeille would ask on arrival.

'OK,' Gaston would reply, 'except for one thing.'

'And what's that, Grandad?'

'You know, young fellow, ass!'

He loved to brag of his former conquests. He had made plenty of trouble in the neighbourhood. In the cemetery lay a good number of his contemporaries who had worn horns because of him. He worked fast and women didn't do too badly; they asked for more and he was ready. Seated in his courtyard or on the parapet of the bridge, he would pour out all his memories, which Sébeille listened to with polite wonder. 'And now no more, you realize,' the old man would conclude sadly. Nevertheless he could still look. Whenever a girl passed along the road on foot or on a bicycle, Gaston's eyes followed her until she was out of sight.

'You know,' he would say occasionally, 'once upon a time I would have gone for her.'

One day a glider passed over them coming from the gliding centre near Saint-Auban. Gaston at first showed some irritation. 'There he goes again!'

What did he have against the glider, which didn't even make any noise? Couldn't he bear any intruder, even at a thousand metres overhead? But his spasm of anger did not last. He calmed down and, turning to Sébeille, said, 'They're in luck.'

'Why, Dad?'

'Just think, from up there they can see all that's going on in the bushes.'

Thanks to the many dossiers he had compiled in the course of his career, Sébeille knew that the voyeur is often an elderly man who through this mania tries to compensate for lost delights.

For years Gaston and his wife had occupied separate bedrooms. As he grew older, his manner towards her daily became coarser. Even in front of Sébeille he addressed her as 'old slut'. The superintendent was embarrassed, especially because Marie Dominici did not answer but made herself even smaller as she bent over the kitchen range.

Sébeille noted another fact: it was impossible for him to talk with Gustave or Yvette alone if Gaston was prowling in the vicinity. Several times he succeeded in cornering Gustave, but each time Gaston surprised them, came over to them, asked jokingly what they were hatching, and stayed on, his ears wide open. Gustave did not conceal from Sébeille that his father's authority was becoming increasingly irksome. But he was bound to Grand'Terre like a prisoner. And although the father kept repeating that his son was idle and incompetent, he was obviously glad enough to have him there. Who else would keep Grand'Terre going?

One of Sébeille's aims was to catch Gaston in a flagrant lie. Not necessarily to do with the crime but something more casual, bearing on commonplace incidents, his habits, his tastes, his everyday affairs. Gaston, never quite sure of the superintendent, usually watched his words. Until he made a slip without realizing it. Sébeille was careful to keep him from noticing.

'I never read the papers,' the old man said repeatedly.

It was his regular formula for cutting short questions whenever Sébeille asked him what he thought of such and such an article about the Lurs murder; the suspicions expressed by this or that paper about the Dominicis; the threat of a libel suit most of them had made public. Gaston maintained that it was his son who was annoyed. He himself never opened a newspaper.

But one day an aeroplane passed low over Grand'Terre, barely skimming the roofs. Gaston grunted, 'I hope that thing isn't going to fall on my house,' and added, 'Like at Marseilles.'

A few days earlier a Mystère had in fact crashed in Marseilles. The local press had published long reports and photographs. Gaston could only have known of the accident by reading the dailies.

Put together, his words little by little lost their simple anecdotal value. They cracked the image of a man whom Sébeille never stopped studying. In his report he included an observation from which he had derived one of his insights into Gaston Dominici. He had long turned over in his mind two incidents. On the evening of August 5 the old man had made a slip of the tongue. 'The woman fell there,' he said to Sébeille. Then he corrected himself. 'Or so I suppose.' To the journalist Jacques Chapus he remarked, 'The kid screamed just beyond the mulberry tree.' He caught himself – 'She must have.' Odd slips; if each time the first sentence was true, it was conclusive proof that the old man knew all about the affair. But another inference could be drawn: that his self-control was less than it had at first appeared. And Sébeille tried to reconstruct the mechanism which determined his mental functioning.

'These incidents,' he wrote, 'enabled us to define a propensity we found in him and which should emerge clearly in other circumstances. When Gaston Dominici wants to lie and in his explanations he happens to speak of a material fact common alike to a lie and the truth, he inclines towards the latter . . . This trait of character seems to us in the circumstances a weakness if one considers that Gaston Dominici is a born actor, playing his part with ease.'

An effective lie is always based in part on truth and, like all crafty people, Gaston was not ignorant of this fact. His defect was not sufficiently guarding the division between them, thereby giving himself away. Something handy to know for the future.

There were enough indications for Sébeille to sense that the situation was slowly maturing. An incident was reported to him concerning Yvette. Two journalists from Digne came to see her. She knew them, they being from the region, so she welcomed them more readily than the Paris reporters whom she thoroughly disliked. The journalists quickly recognized that the young woman was nervous and tense. Suddenly she burst into tears. 'I've had enough,' she said, 'I'm going to tell you the truth.'

The two men were stunned. One of them, noticing Yvette's father in the courtyard, went to fetch him, not wanting later to be accused

167

of having played the policeman. M. Barth, seeing his daughter in tears, reacted violently. 'What's the matter with you? You don't know anything, keep quiet.'

The spell was broken. Yvette recovered her self-control. The journalists paid for their scruples, they had robbed themselves of a heady scoop. Sébeille, when informed, was confirmed in his belief that the seed was germinating at Grand'Terre.

Holding the photograph in both hands, Jean Ricard studied it carefully.

'Take your time,' Sébeille recommended. A man in his forties was sitting before the superintendent in his office at the Bishop's Palace in Marseilles. Re-reading the files, Sébeille had noticed that no one had followed up the testimony of a very early witness – understandable since Ricard had contributed nothing of particular interest. But it was Sébeille's policy to neglect nothing in his files. Ricard had evidently passed the scene of the crime at the moment Gustave was there; Gustave himself had mentioned a man with a bundle. It seemed to Sébeille worthwhile to have a chat with M. Ricard now that he knew that Gustave had been near the car quite a while before the motor-cyclist Olivier had passed by.

'There's something not right about this,' said Jean Ricard.

The photograph was one of those taken by the gendarmes of Forcalquier shortly after their arrival. It showed the body of Lady Drummond near the Hillman.

'Why?' asked Sébeille.

'The body wasn't in this position.' On the print it was at right-angles to the car. 'When I saw it,' declared Ricard, 'it was parallel.'

'Are you sure?'

'Absolutely. And it was on its back, the toes upward.'

Sébeille examined the picture. Lady Drummond was lying face down.

'The head towards Peyruis, the feet towards Grand'Terre,' added Ricard.

The superintendent was reluctant to believe him despite his certainty. The deduction to be drawn from this new statement was incredible. Inspector Ranchin, behind Ricard, was also sceptical, and suggested his doubt to Sébeille with a gesture.

'Let's go over it again,' said Sébeille patiently. 'You were at Lurs the morning of August 5th . . .'

Ricard repeated what he had already told the Forcalquier police in the first place. He had been camping at Ganagobie and on August 5, his holiday over, left by way of the road to catch the bus for Marseilles. He passed near Grand'Terre at about 7.0. He noticed such disorder round the Hillman that he thought there had been an accident. He came close and walked round the car. He saw a camp-bed and beside it a woman who seemed to be asleep. He had only thought how odd the sight was. Why wasn't the woman on the camp-bed? It was this that decided him to go to the nearest gendarmerie. Until now no one had thought of showing him a photograph, other-wise he would have immediately supplied the detail he had provided today.

'It's of prime importance,' said Sébeille. 'Did you see any one about?'

'Nobody.'

'And near the farmhouse?'

'I hardly noticed it, I must admit.'

Gustave Dominici could not have been far off, although he might have hidden on seeing Ricard appear, warned by a signal from Yvette who had spoken of a pedestrian with a rucksack. 'How long did you stop near the car?'

'A minute or two, not more.'

Sébeille dismissed Ricard with the request that he keep himself available for them; there would soon be need of his testimony. Alone with Ranchin, Sébeille expressed his astonishment. 'You see what it means – between seven and seven-thirty that morning the body was moved.'

It was a stupid thing to do, since the police would be along at any moment; anybody found carrying or manipulating a body would have a lot of explaining to do. But at that hour Gaston was on the mountain with his goats. It could only have been the usually faint-hearted Gustave. But what had been so urgent as to give him the courage? One answer came immediately to mind: Gustave was looking for cartridge cases or unexploded cartridges.

Of course, Ricard could have been mistaken; after all, it had all happened nearly a year ago. How could they check on the reliability of his deposition then and his memory now? 'Faustin Roure,' sug-gested Sébeille, suddenly recalling the railway foreman.

The next morning Sébeille and Ranchin made for the Basses-Alpes, and the Lurs station where Faustin Roure worked. Roure agreed to come with them. Sébeille drew the car up exactly where the Hillman had been, pointing towards Grand'Terre.

169

'Do you remember precisely what you saw when you arrived here the first time at six thirty-five on August 5th?' Sébeille asked.

'Yes.'

'The body especially, just where was it?'

'I'll show you . . .'

Faustin Roure lay down on the ground. His back was parallel to the car, confirming Ricard's statement: at 6.35, as at 7.0, the body was parallel and not at right-angles to the Hillman. The foreman got up and went on to describe the scene. 'I didn't see the body, because it was covered from head to foot.'

Another revelation for Sébeille – the gendarmes had found the rug so arranged that the legs could be seen. It was both a confirmation and a piece of supplementary evidence. Between the arrival of Faustin Roure at 6.35 and Jean Ricard at 7.0, Lady Drummond's body had been found, since the man from Marseilles had at that time noticed the sleeper's legs. Then between 7.0 and 7.30 the body had been moved. It was obvious that some unknown person had hidden each time he heard steps or the sound of an engine. When the passer-by had moved off, he had resumed his work.

To Sébeille, Gustave seemed the most obvious suspect, although he didn't at the start altogether rule out Clovis. But even if Clovis had been able to move the rug, it was impossible for him to have moved the body, since at 7.0 or 7.5 at the latest he was at work at the Lurs station. That left Gustave alone on the site. Increasingly, all Sébeille's thinking brought him back to the same starting-point. Gustave seemed the most deeply involved. Guilty or not, it was against him that the assault must be launched.

If there hadn't been such a delay in uncovering all the small facts, if they had been known when Gustave was cornered for not having helped Elizabeth, the investigation might have been shortened by months.

The police certainly hadn't been aided by the witnesses, who had restricted themselves to answering questions without volunteering anything essential on their own. The Dominicis' conspiracy of silence had spread to the whole neighbourhood. There was distrust and, since no one knew what stand to take, they all preferred to say nothing. It was true of Paul Maillet and Roger Perrin, true of Faustin Roure. A photograph had to be shown to Jean Ricard, a stranger to the district, for the thread to unwind.

It was a broiling August. A year had passed since a happy family chose a flat strip of earth sheltered by a mulberry tree as a camping site. Death had struck three times and the guilty person remained unpunished. From the end of July 1953 the newspapers again filled their columns with accounts of the affair and of the first inquiry. Their tone was sharp, seldom flattering to the investigators. One big daily carried the lead: 'The police have nothing to hide: they have found nothing.'

However, one of them, Alain Ancelot, apparently had premonitions when he wrote in *Le Parisien Libéré* that Sébeille knew the murderer, had talked with him throughout the winter, noting his reactions, measuring his patience, estimating his endurance. According to Ancelot, Sébeille intended to wait another month or two before launching his grand offensive.

At the Forcalquier cemetery a slab was placed over the Drummonds' grave. A committee had been formed for this purpose – which had aroused Gaston's spite. On August 5 three sprays of flowers had arrived from England addressed to the cemetery keeper and sent by the Marrians. Each bore a card testifying to their friendship and affection. At the scene of the crime an anonymous hand had laid out a cross in white pebbles. Bunches of lavender or modest bouquets had been deposited on the ground.

That night only a few French and British journalists wandered along the bank of the Durance. M. Périès had recently left for his vacation. Sébeille stayed in Marseilles. Not even Albert's tall figure appeared; he had not stirred from Digne. No one expected the investigation to start up again on the first anniversary of the crime. The Dominicis did not show themselves, but remained holed up on their farm – like the year before, if they were to be believed.

In the afternoon a short ceremony took place in the cemetery. The British vice-consul at Marseilles, Mr Pateman, officiated. He was accompanied by the sub-prefect of Forcalquier, the mayor of the town and his colleagues from the neighbouring communes. Official wreaths were placed on the grave. Then came a long procession of little girls in white who bowed over the slab beneath which lay a child of ten whom they had heard about from their parents. In London it was announced that £25,000 had been given to establish a research scholarship in nutrition, the science in which Sir Jack Drummond had been a noted specialist.

Gaston Dominici kept away from the journalists and photographers, as did those round him. A few days before, the family had reassembled for a special occasion: on August 1 a grandson, Gaston

Balmonet, from Savoy, married the sister of a son-in-law, Yvette Perrin, consequently the young aunt of the flighty Roger. The couple had met at Christmas when the family was celebrating Gustave's return from prison. The marriage had followed the best tradition, singing and drinking both unrestrained. Gaston had not fallen behind; he had even had one too many. The old man didn't seem to notice that Clovis wasn't there. He had sent word that he was ill and couldn't make it.

Clovis's trouble was not physical. For some months he had avoided Grand'Terre and had barely spoken to his father. Clovis also kept his distance from Gustave.

The family wasn't altogether surprised by this estrangement. Clovis had been on bad terms with his father for years, for obscure motives disputed by both sides. Along with Germaine Perrin, he was the outsider. She had never forgotten her father's remarks on her conduct.

Gaston showed no affection towards either of them. Because of their bad dispositions, he would suggest; their greed to lay hold of the lion's share of the inheritance. The Dominicis were inclined to believe Gaston. Among heirs it was easy to imagine that one or the other wanted more than his share. And Clovis's firm refusal to merge with the clan aggravated the suspicions.

'You're not well,' said his wife Marie-Rose when she saw that her husband was worried.

'Drop it,' he grumbled.

Sébeille learned about it. He held his mental picture of the family up to the light: slippery Gustave; melancholy Clovis; Yvette, always nervous; Roger the liar; his mother who would defend him against everybody. From the superintendent's point of view, the mercury was rising – and fever makes even the taciturn talk.

One after another the gendarmes began coming forward. Fernand Gilbert, aged 42, had been the one on duty between 6.15 and 6.30 a.m. on August 5 when Jean-Marie Olivier, the motor-cyclist whom Gustave had stopped on the road near Grand'Terre, arrived at Oraison. It was he, then, who had set the affair going, alerting his superiors who sent Sergeant Romanet to the scene. Like his colleague Marque of Valensoles, a memory recurred to him that summer of 1953, a detail which merely by chance he passed on to his chief, Captain Albert, who at once grasped its importance and sent his subordinate to Sébeille.

172

On first hearing, Gilbert's revelation may not have seemed very significant. It had to do only with Olivier's way of putting things when he turned up at the Oraison gendarmerie. Yet it is still surprising in the circumstances that no one had noticed the slight discrepancy.

Gustave had declared that after stopping Olivier to ask him to notify the gendarmes, he had said without further particulars, 'I've just found a corpse.'

But according to the gendarme, Jean-Marie Olivier had been a good deal more talkative. 'He arrived at the station,' Gilbert affirmed, 'and said to me, "Come quickly, there's been a crime. I've just been stopped by a peasant whom I know only by sight, near the Lurs station. He told me he'd found a body, apparently dead, lying on the bank. There must be other bodies."'

Sébeille was no longer surprised at discovering things like this a year after the fact. Thanks to Ricard, Sébeille knew that a man, probably Gustave, had been wandering round the place long enough beforehand to have known that there were several victims. Olivier brought him additional support. That is why he now summoned him.

'The gendarme's right,' Olivier acknowledged. 'It's just what I said.'

'You spoke of a crime?'

'I repeated what Gustave Dominici told me.'

'And several bodies?'

'I didn't invent them.'

Before writing up his notes, Sébeille asked the motor-cyclist if he knew anything else he had omitted to state. After some hesitation Olivier nodded. 'While Gustave was talking to me I stayed on my motor-cycle with the engine running. As I left and passed in front of Grand'Terre, I saw Mother Dominici and Gustave's wife at the edge of the road where it borders the house. They watched me go by without saying anything.'

The superintendent asked the eternal question: why such a long delay in making a complete statement? Jean-Marie Olivier's answer was similar to Maillet's. 'It's up to Gustave to speak, not me.'

'No doubt, but why did you change your mind today?'

'Because I saw you were groping in the dark.'

Jean-Marie Olivier, unlike Paul Maillet, was not Gustave's friend. He owed him no special consideration and Gustave could do nothing to him. Yet he had kept silent, even though he had some idea of the strength of evidence he could offer Sébeille.

Sébeille added this new evidence to the rest. It was important because it showed that the Sardine, like Yvette, had known of the discovery of the bodies. They had been anxiously awaiting Gustave's return. Why else would they have taken up a position at the edge of the road at an hour of the morning when normally they would have been going about the first tasks of the day? The new evidence also discredited the farmer's statement that he had informed his wife and his mother while they were in the courtyard, totally ignorant of what happened. Indirectly Roger Perrin's testimony was thus corroborated. Gustave had not risen at 5.30, but earlier. Otherwise he would not have had time to go to the mulberry tree or the bank of the Durance, discover the tragedy, tell the two women, then set off again to stop Jean-Marie Olivier. To him, as to Ricard, Maillet and Perrin, stern orders were given to say nothing. The conspiracy of silence had worked against Sébeille; now it was operating in his favour.

Towards the end of August 1953, Sébeille was ready to act, having extracted from the files everything he was counting on. For a last time he shut himself up alone in his office in Marseilles, keeping out everybody except Ranchin. Smoking cigarette after cigarette, covering dozens of pages with notes and sketches, breaking off only to munch a sandwich or snatch a few hours of sleep, he dug everywhere in search of any further contradictions and peculiarities he could exploit. He found nothing new. At times he despaired, remarking to Ranchin, 'We're starting with a small pair.'

Ranchin shrugged his shoulders; if they waited for a royal flush, retirement would come first or old Dominici would die. Better take advantage of what they had. They had to forge ahead.

This was very much in line with the opinion of ex-Chief Inspector Robert Sébeille, whom his son had kept in touch. In his view they would never have a better grip on the Dominicis, there was no use waiting any longer. From now on time would work against the police.

Edmond Sébeille's luck was to have involved Yvette, thanks to Roger Perrin's evidence.

'A woman,' Sébeille's father asserted, 'is easier to convince than a man. She recognizes danger more quickly. You have gained an important point by implicating her, don't lose it.'

Sébeille spent his nights, as he was to write, 'in going over my records like a student on the eve of exams.' He had only small facts up his sleeve and could imagine the sport his adversaries would have with them. Olivier and the presence of the women on the road? They were in the courtyard – why shouldn't they not have taken a few steps outside? The moving of the body? Sébeille could imagine Gustave's absent expression and hear his vague answers. Maillet and the screams heard in the lucerne field? The hostility between the two men was such that Gustave would put it down to malice. For him the linesman was motivated by the desire to do him harm. All year the Dominicis had believed him to be a police auxiliary, interested above all in diverting suspicion. Confronted with Maillet, Gustave was quite capable of holding his ground against defeat by a man the family so heartily detested.

The strong point was obviously Roger Perrin's statement. With any other witness Sébeille would have felt victory to be within reach. But what could the boy say? Would he stand firm? Or would he with his irritating smile retract, saying calmly that he had spoken of the visit of the English mother and daughter because it amused him to? Sébeille was convinced that on this point the boy was not lying; the details he gave rang too true.

Deep down, whatever he may have said, Sébeille was anything but sure of what he would find behind the breached walls. He always maintained subsequently that from the autumn of 1953 he was advancing step by step towards Gaston Dominici and that the old man was his sole target. But it was against Gustave that he concentrated his attack. It was Gustave whom he intended to confront with the witnesses.

The superintendent was working all this time in full agreement with the examining magistrate, Périès, and the prosecutor, Sabatier. He received more sympathy and encouragement from them than from certain of his superiors who feared the reactions. He had long talks – with Périès especially – during which the two planned their attack down to the last detail. Like Sébeille, the magistrate was determined to succeed. He shared the superintendent's hopes and disappointments, and was aware that if they missed this time, they might never have another chance. With Sébeille he had read and re-read the depositions they would use. Would they be sufficient? 'We must try playing poker,' Sébeille said more than once.

Roger Périès was persuaded. But his point of view was not altogether that of a police officer. As examining magistrate, he was responsible for the inquiry. Sébeille was acting only on a formal commission issued at his request. The Supreme Court of Appeal could be quite suspicious in examining the limits within which a magistrate and his police collaborators operated. The ultimate legal counsellors, guardians of the law, guarantors of individual liberty, were already irritated enough by recent criticisms of the judicial corps, the increasing protests against excesses or maltreatment, real or exaggerated. Any such incident would discredit M. Périès.

'You know very well,' said Sébeille, 'that Gustave will be treated properly. He'll eat and he'll sleep. He'll be allowed to rest when he feels the need. But we mustn't give up any of the time that has been granted us. He will remain in our custody and we'll question him as long as the law allows.'

Périès agreed. But first he wanted assurances. He didn't want to make any promises to the superintendent he couldn't keep. So he consulted the prosecutor's office and that of the Director of Public Prosecutions. A few days later the Director gave his answer: within the limits of the law Sébeille would have full freedom of action. Among other things, the superintendent obtained approval to prohibit any contact between Gustave and his relatives until he had divulged all he knew.

Normally the interrogations would be held at a police station, that at Digne for instance. But Sébeille urged that the hearings and confrontations should take place where they could be supervised and at the same time not be overheard by indiscreet ears. 'That's why I ask to be allowed to work in the Palais de Justice (the Law Courts' building),' he said.

In principle the police are not authorized to conduct proceedings in such premises; a physical application of the separation of powers. But there was no specific prohibition. M. Sabatier, the prosecutor, gave his consent.

It remained to fix the date. Summer being over, the tourists no longer streamed along the roads, stopping as they passed Grand'Terre, at times forming small groups.

But then came the harvest and the grape-picking. The witnesses would submit better to the inconveniences they would have to undergo if they were not preoccupied by urgent domestic tasks. They had to be entirely available, not balk at being detained for a morning or a whole day. Calendar in hand, Sébeille and Périès considered the most favourable dates. Their choice fell on the first fortnight in November. But they had to avoid two holidays, All Saints and Armistice Day, which meant waiting until after the 11th. Sébeille suggested the 12th. Périès agreed. Sébeille informed his superiors, who merely wished him good luck.

On the morning of November 11, the superintendent again set out for Digne. The evening before in his office in Marseilles he had assembled the 198 files comprising the dossier, as well as his personal notes and the carbine. On his arrival he went to the Palais de Justice, where Sabatier and Périès were waiting for him. A few days earlier the three had conferred at length on how to keep the operation secret as long as possible. The object was to avoid alerting the Dominicis. The French Code allows for delays in issuing summonses and subpœnas, so Edmond Sébeille had arranged that witnesses would not be informed until the last minute. He had also asked that the inspectors and drivers needed should only be told during the night on which they were to be mobilized. He demanded the same discretion from the gendarmes who would cordon off the site during the reconstruction of the crime.

While the dead of two world wars were being commemorated before their monuments, Sébeille, Périès and Sabatier went over the superintendent's plans. The start would be a series of checks on the site. Then, whatever the results, they would go for Gustave. During the day Sébeille made appointments with Olivier, Ricard, Faustin Roure and Clovis. At midnight he telephoned his superior, Harzic. 'Everything's ready. I'll expect your reinforcements at dawn.'

At 3.0 a.m. the drivers were awakened at Marseilles and summoned at once to the Bishop's Palace. None of them knew the reason. A half-hour later the mobile laboratory left the port for the Basses-Alpes. Jean Ricard was picked up in a car already crammed with inspectors. The invasion of the Dominici citadel had begun.

7

The sky was grey and cold. Thick fog covered the hills and swirled down over the ground. Winter was on its way. The early morning passers-by huddled in their clothes. Grand'Terre was silent and showed no sign of life. But round it, even before dawn, strange things were happening.

Before 5.0 a.m. the gendarmes' barriers had been placed on the Route Nationale, a kilometre each side of Grand'Terre; other gendarmes had slipped into the countryside and were checking the roads and lanes. An hour later, the plan now being in effect, the first radio signal had been issued, forbidding all traffic on Route 96. Cars and trucks were diverted to the other side of the Durance. No explanation was given for the measure, which also affected pedestrians; neither by road nor field could anyone reach Grand'Terre, temporarily cut off from the world.

At 5.30 a.m. the barricade opened to admit a car. For the first time since August 5, 1952, the Drummonds' Hillman was in motion. Since then it had been kept in a garage at Digne. The inspector now at the wheel drew it up near the mulberry tree exactly where the gendarmes had found it on the morning of the crime. A quarter of an hour later two Citroëns, a mobile laboratory and a van from the gendarmerie followed the English car and parked on the dirt road leading to the railway bridge.

A little before 7.0 a Citroën and a grey Peugeot 203 drove up to Grand'Terre and entered the courtyard. Some inspectors got out, followed by Périès. In the courtyard were Gaston Dominici and his son. They had known since they got up that morning that something was going on. But they remained faithful to their rule: not to show themselves when they sensed commotion, to affect the same indifference as they had towards the crime itself. This is why Sébeille had ordered that anyone trying to reach Grand'Terre should be turned back; the Dominicis always had informers eager to pass on news.

The magistrate went up to Gaston, who greeted him sourly. What did he want now?

Roger Périès said brusquely, 'I must ask you to mind your manners or I shall charge you with contempt. We've been very patient with you. We'll be less so if you go on this way.'

The old man seemed surprised by the magistrate's tone of voice and retreated at once, contenting himself with a grumbled 'This is no life.' He looked puzzled over this unexpected invasion. Apparently nothing had leaked out about Sébeille's intentions, and for the Dominicis this was a bolt from the blue.

'I request you,' the magistrate went on, 'not to leave Grand'Terre until you are permitted to.' He gestured towards Inspectors Erny and Culioli. 'These gentlemen will stay here to keep an eye on everything. It won't be long, you may be sure. Only the time necessary to make certain checks.'

Périès's real purpose was to prevent the Dominicis from seeing even at a distance anything that was taking place on the far side of their orchard; the presence of Faustin Roure, Jean-Marie Olivier and Jean Ricard might well give them a clue and allow them to agree on their answers to questions. A small risk, perhaps, but no use taking chances.

Meanwhile Sébeille had arrived. He gave the order to scatter round the car all the articles that had been there the morning of August 5. The camp-beds were placed as the gendarmes had seen them. An inspector, wrapped in a rug, assumed the role of Lady Drummond. Everything was ready. Except that it was cold and cloudy, it might have been that tragic daybreak in August 1952.

Faustin Roure was brought in first. He retraced the path he had followed from the landslide. Roure looked down at the body of the inspector; it was exactly as he had seen the corpse of Lady Drummond – entirely covered and parallel to the Hillman.

He was asked to withdraw and Ricard to take his place on the road some distance from the gravel patch, and to go through his movements as before. It was the first time he had been back to the scene. As on August 5, when he was going to catch his bus, he approached at a good pace, and stopped on seeing the car and especially the disorder around it. He came closer, studied the prone form for a moment. He was positive that the corpse had been

179

parallel. 'But,' he added, 'this confirms my impression that I saw the legs up to the knees.'

Next were Sergeant Louis Romanet and the gendarme Bouchier. They were just as sure that they had found the body at right-angles to the car. Their notes taken at the time were evidence of that. Sébeille had also summoned Dr Dragon who had conducted the first examination; only a simple confirmation, but Sébeille wanted no loose ends. Through all of this the inspectors from the Identification Section were photographing their colleague stretched out in the alternate positions indicated by the witnesses. The film they would assemble would serve to prove that the body had changed position between Jean Ricard's passing it at 7.0 and the gendarmes' arrival at 7.30.

While all these preliminaries were being gone through, two inspectors went to fetch Clovis Dominici from the Lurs station. He faced Sébeille with ill-concealed anxiety. Faustin Roure and Jean Ricard had been dismissed; on the stretch of gravel there remained only Sébeille, Périès and the inspectors. 'You saw the body of Lady Drummond at seven o'clock,' said the superintendent. 'In what position was it?'

Clovis hesitated. 'Has the inspector taken the position in which you saw the victim?' Sébeille asked.

The linesman indicated with his hand the position the police officer should take: at right-angles to the Hillman.

'Are you sure?' queried Sébeille.

'Yes.'

The two men appraised each other in silence for a moment. Clovis seemed uncomfortable. Then Sébeille motioned a colleague to produce Faustin Roure and Jean Ricard. Clovis's eyes shifted suspiciously from one to the other as he watched them approach. 'Clovis Dominici declares that the body was at right-angles to the car,' Sébeille told them without preamble.

Faustin Roure was adamant in protest; he had been at Clovis's side and remembered the scene as if it were yesterday. He could not be mistaken. Jean Ricard repeated once more that he was in no doubt whatsoever.

'Well, Clovis?' Sébeille turned to him.

The linesman hunched his broad shoulders helplessly; he no longer remembered. Sébeille expressed surprise; until now, Clovis's memory had been excellent.

'It may well have been parallel,' he said finally.

Clovis was asked to follow an inspector who had him get into a Citroën parked some distance away. Two other police officers went to Grand'Terre. Father and son were in the kitchen. Gaston was huddled before the hearth, where a black cauldron hung over the glowing embers. He did not even raise his head when the police led Gustave away. Gustave himself went without a word.

To break him down Sébeille intended to go over everything from scratch. The young farmer had begun to stumble when he was confronted with the motor-cyclist Jean-Marie Olivier in September 1952. He had declared that he had been unable to see Lady Drummond's body because he had not gone near the car. But when Olivier asserted that Gustave had emerged from in front of the car, the farmer had yielded; he had vaguely noticed the camp-beds and rugs but had thought nothing of it.

Gustave had never, however, been confronted with Olivier on the spot, something Sébeille now considered essential both as a matter of procedure and psychologically. Gustave must learn that the police were tenacious, he must have no more illusions; he would only have peace the day he proved that he had nothing more to hide.

Jean-Marie Olivier had stationed himself on his motor-cycle a little beyond the bend in the road, awaiting the signal to go. 'Gustave, you will show M. Périès where you were when you stopped Olivier.'

Gustave walked to within about 35 metres of the car, thereby contradicting himself, since in the presence of Constant on September 3, 1952, while refusing to admit that he had been near the car, he had said he had taken only two or three steps. Sébeille made no comment. He gave Olivier the starting signal.

When the motor-cyclist arrived abreast of Gustave, the former waved his arm to stop him. But Olivier, at the risk of skidding, gestured an emphatic refusal. Pulling up some 20 metres farther on, he swerved back and called out, 'It wasn't there.'

Sébeille and Périès went to meet him. 'Where was he?' asked the superintendent.

Olivier dismounted and, pushing his machine, led the police officer and the magistrate towards the Hillman. 'Here,' he said, stopping behind the Hillman's bonnet.

'Go over there,' Sébeille ordered.

But the farmer shook his head; why should he go where Olivier said, since he hadn't been there? 'To take a picture,' said Sébeille.

Reluctantly Gustave yielded with bad grace. Olivier went by again. The experiment confirmed his testimony that Gustave had emerged on the road in front of the car, but the farmer refused to admit it.

'Did you none the less notice a rug?' Sébeille asked.

'Yes,' said Gustave feebly.

'And camp-beds?'

'Yes.'

He therefore reaffirmed part of his statement to Constant. But why did he continue to claim that he was far from the Hillman as Olivier passed, yet on the other hand admit to having gone near it?

'Put the rug back as you saw it,' said Sébeille, offering him Lady Drummond's plaid.

Suddenly Gustave was close to rage. 'I will not!' he exploded.

Sébeille held it out. 'Take it,' he commanded.

But Gustave still refused. He backed away, as if the sight all at once disturbed him. What was he scared of? Not even for a second did Sébeille think it was memories. It must be that he scented a trap.

With some force Sébeille threw the rug at Gustave, who put up his hands to protect himself and disappeared under it. He clumsily disengaged himself. 'Will you show us or not?' Sébeille roared.

Gustave surrendered. He bent over and spread the rug at the edge of the irrigation ditch where Lady Drummond had lain at right-angles to the car, as the gendarmes had found her at 7.30.

Sébeille said nothing. His last doubt was settled; it was indeed Gustave who had disturbed the body between 7.0 and 7.30, since he was now contradicted not only by Roure and Ricard but by Clovis. For Sébeille the rift between the two brothers was the most important. 'You will go to the house to get a jacket and come with us to Digne,' he ordered. There was no mistaking the panic in Gustave's eyes.

At Grand'Terre itself there was an outbreak of hysteria when Gustave returned with the announcement that he must go with the inspectors to Digne. Yvette had one of her nerve storms. Gaston hurled curses all over the courtyard, the Sardine wept quietly. Surprise had achieved the maximum effect. Sébeille and Périès were kept discreetly informed of everyone's reaction. They congratulated themselves. Each of their moves had been directed not only at the minds but at the emotions.

In the course of the morning the reporters were told of the offensive just launched. They learned it from a communiqué issued by the prosecutor, Sabatier, whose firm and unequivocal tone evoked some surprise. 'There was an abscess to lance at Grand'Terre,' it ran. 'We have therefore made a surprise attack. We still lack proof but we

182

remain convinced that the Dominicis can provide the key to the riddle. We shall question everybody as long as necessary. Justice must be done in the Drummonds' memory.'

At 10.30 two cars drew up before the Palais de Justice at Digne. Gustave and Clovis were led in by a private entrance to screen them from observation. Faustin Roure, Olivier and Ricard followed, and a little later Paul Maillet and Roger Perrin. Then the doors were shut and gendarmes posted outside. A veil of secrecy had temporarily descended on the Lurs affair. From it would emerge either light or unending darkness.

For his interrogations Sébeille chose the library. It was a rectangular room, its walls lined with books – works on law, case histories, most of them shabby with use – and old-fashioned decor of another era, where a jurist of the last century would not have felt out of place. It was in this library that the tribunal at times deliberated, as the previous December when the magistrates had tried Gustave for failure to help a person in danger.

The farmer sat down on a red velvet-covered armchair ordinarily used by lawyers and magistrates checking on some point of law. Gustave sagged with dejection, and hardly moved. Sébeille was not the only one with him. Ranchin was present, as well as other inspectors who would take over from time to time.

From opening commonplaces about wine and shooting, the superintendent passed rapidly to the attack. 'You and your wife really didn't hear any screams when the shots were fired?'

Gustave looked him straight in the face. 'No.'

'Are you quite sure?'

'I've told you so all along.'

'Maybe because you've always lied.'

Without another word Sébeille asked an inspector to bring in Paul Maillet. This was a major confrontation from which he expected a lot; if it failed, the entire operation might be jeopardized.

Paul Maillet was calm. He had nothing to lose. The case had already cost him dearly; he had no interest in lying, whitewashing or accusing. He was no longer under suspicion, as he had been, but he was kept under constant supervision and no longer able to poach, since the gendarmes now had their eyes on him. Before Gustave he repeated what the farmer had told him one day at Grand'Terre – the screams heard in the night.

Gustave flared with anger. 'I never said that.'

'So I'm a liar?'

'Always have been.'

'Remember, Gustave,' Maillet went on, 'I'd come to you to buy some potatoes. Your wife made a mistake, she gave me eleven kilos instead of six.'

'It's not true.'

Obstinately Gustave stuck to his story. Maillet was lying, inventing in order to make trouble. Sébeille intervened.

'I can't see why you deny such a self-evident fact,' he said. 'It's impossible in the first place that the victims didn't cry out, and in the second that you didn't hear anything. Maillet is only confirming what we all believe.'

His body bent forward, head lowered, Gustave seemed sunk in deep thought.

'Well, how about the screams?' asked Sébeille.

'Maybe so.'

'Maybe so what?'

The long silence that followed seemed an eternity to Sébeille. Gustave continued to study the floor, then slowly raised his head. 'I did hear them,' he said at last.

He acknowledged that Maillet had not lied; the conversation reported by him had in fact taken place. As for the screams, he had heard them at the same time as the shots. They had lasted only a few seconds. Yvette and he had been terrified. 'We realized that people were being attacked,' he said.

'The campers.'

'Yes.'

'And you decided to say nothing about it?'

'Yes.'

'Why?'

'So we wouldn't have any trouble.'

'You wouldn't have had any,' Sébeille said irritably. 'The law doesn't require a person to be heroic, to go risking his life. You would have had a good deal less trouble if you had mentioned the screams you denied right from the start. Do you understand me?'

'Yes.'

'So you kept quiet for another reason.'

'We were frightened.'

'Not the next day you weren't!'

But Gustave's effort at candour was spent. Deep within him the instinct for self-preservation reasserted itself. Sébeille tried another

184

tack. 'You've a genius for getting yourself into trouble. Take Olivier's evidence. Why should he lie? What does it matter if you came from behind the car or from a little in front?'

Gustave once more assumed his gloomy, closed expression. Then he muttered that he had, in fact, been in the place designated by Olivier. 'I came out from between the car and mulberry tree.'

Why had he still lied that morning? Why had he gone back on earlier statements made before Superintendent Constant? Again came the standard answer: he was afraid of trouble. What trouble? Any trouble, never mind what.

Progressively Gustave regained confidence. He had just made a great effort at sincerity. Generally speaking, Sébeille was satisfied, and gave him permission to leave and go home. Until: 'Do you know what Roger Perrin says?' the superintendent asked abruptly.

The blow hit home. Gustave shuddered. The danger was proving more extensive than he had bargained for. The police's underground work had penetrated far indeed if it had reached down to his unpredictable young nephew Roger. 'Him,' grunted Gustave.

'He says that the mother and daughter came to the house the evening of the 4th.'

'It's a lie.'

'You told him so yourself,' Sébeille went on ruthlessly.

'He can always say so.'

Sébeille smiled. 'He had also a number of other most interesting statements.'

He drew from his dossier the notes of the previous May 7 containing Roger Perrin's interrogation. Sentence by sentence he read the principal passages to Gustave, who relapsed into a sullen silence.

' "My Uncle Gustave got up a little earlier than usual on August 5th, around four. He wanted to know where the shots had come from. He saw the little girl and went back to the farm to tell his wife." '

Roger was shown into the library. Gustave began by being highhanded with him – what did the kid think he was doing? But Roger stood his ground. 'You told me all that in the kitchen,' he said.

'It's a lie.'

'And Aunt Yvette also told me about the English people's visit.'

To Gustave it seemed that part of his universe had collapsed. How had the police pickaxe dug so near him without his suspecting? Isolated, cut off from his base, he could not even know how far they had penetrated.

'Did they come or not?' demanded Sébeille with deliberate brutality.

Gustave raised a hand to his forehead as if his memory had miraculously returned. 'The boy's right. It comes back to me – they came in the evening. Yvette told me when I returned. But I didn't pay any attention; I was thinking only of the landslide.'

'And what time did you get up?'

'At four.'

Sébeille motioned to Roger Perrin to leave. The method to which Gustave had clung for fifteen months was falling apart. To the superintendent what was immediately important was not so much any revelations he might hear now, as the moment when Gustave, harassed and ignorant of what else might have been unearthed, would begin committing himself, unlocking the core of the truth.

'It's true,' Gustave began, 'when I got up I wanted to know what had happened. I went to the landslide not by the main road but by following the ditch that separates the road from the field. So I skirted the path to reach the stone bridge. As soon as I had passed it, I saw a white form and recognized the little girl I had seen with her parents the evening before. I then made for the car to find out what had happened to the parents. First I saw the father on the other side of the road, then the mother near the car. In fact at that moment I didn't know which was the man and which the woman. I didn't touch anything and ran back to the house.'

'Was the body near the car parallel or at right-angles to it?'

'At right-angles.' Without realizing it, Gustave had just supplied Sébeille with a weapon.

'Go on,' said the superintendent.

'I told Yvette and my mother. I only went back to the camp site at five forty-five.'

'What did you do in the meantime?'

'I tended the animals.'

Sébeille heaved a deep sigh. 'Now you're starting to lie again. You'll never make me believe that you quietly fed your pigs after just finding three bodies on your land, or practically on it.'

'I swear . . .'

Night had by now fallen. Sébeille was as tired as Gustave. Since 10.30 a.m. there had been no let-up. Sébeille decided to call a short halt before the second round. In any case, Gustave was no longer reacting; it took more time than ever to get a word out of him. The interrogation was suspended until 8.30 p.m.

Like Sébeille, Gustave had recovered some of his strength by then. But the superintendent had held fresh reinforcements in reserve – the testimonies of Faustin Roure and Jean Ricard. He started off by recapitulating Gustave's last statements. 'You got up at four. You found the bodies. For more than an hour after that you fed your animals. A little before six you informed Jean-Marie Olivier. Between six forty-five and seven three people saw the bodies: Faustin Roure; a camper walking along the road, Jean Ricard; and your brother Clovis.' With hardly a pause after those last four carefully spaced words, Sébeille went on deliberately, 'All three assure me that the body was lying parallel to the car. But when the gendarmes arrived they found it at right-angles. How do you explain that?'

Gustave was stunned by this new blow. 'I've nothing to explain,' he mumbled.

'On the contrary, only you can enable me to understand what happened. The body was moved between seven and seven-thirty. By whom?'

'It wasn't me.'

'I can't see how it could have been anybody else.'

But Gustave persisted in his denial – until Sébeille erupted with rage, part genuine, part tactical. How long would Gustave go on mocking everybody? Did he realize that he could no longer be believed? Did he imagine that Sébeille would let him go today without getting to the bottom of his lies and evasions? They were in this library surrounded by old books and they would stay here until the end of time if need be. But Gustave would talk. No one would find fault with him, Sébeille. The whole world appreciated that the police had been very patient with the Dominicis. They had reached the limit. No defender would come forward this time.

Gustave was dumbfounded by this outburst. He continued his resistance a little longer while Sébeille went on rubbing his nose in his lies. Then abruptly he gave in.

'You're right,' he said. 'I did move the woman's body. When I found it, it was parallel and completely covered.'

'When did you do it?'

'After Clovis and Faustin Roure left.'

He had gone to the camp site and first completely uncovered the body. Lady Drummond was wearing a red dress dotted with pale flowers. Her legs were bare and one arm was folded on her breast, the other on her stomach. She was wearing neither shoes nor stockings.

'Just then I heard steps. They seemed to be coming from Peyruis. I dropped the rug and hid in the ditch among the oaks. I didn't see anybody but I followed whoever it was by the noise made. He stopped for some minutes, five maybe. Then I heard him go away and went back to the gravel patch.'

Gustave thus corroborated Jean Ricard's evidence except for one variation: Ricard estimated the time he paused at a minute or two, Gustave at five. But for Gustave, fearful of being discovered, the seconds went slowly.

'It was then,' Gustave went on, 'that I took the body by the feet. I turned it face down and placed the feet towards the ditch, the head by the car. Then I put back the rug and spread it, leaving the legs exposed.'

'Why did you do that?'

Sébeille awaited the answer with a certain curiosity. It was too much to hope that it would correspond with his own thinking, but Gustave's fictions always threw light on the working of his mind. 'I wanted to find out if she was dead or only wounded.'

The superintendent feigned admiration. 'A proper sentiment,' he said sarcastically. 'But you found her at four. You waited over three hours to ascertain whether she was dead. I know your mind works slowly, but you certainly took your time.'

'I didn't think about it.'

'Granted. But to know if she was dead you didn't have to turn her over. On the contrary, it would have been enough to touch her, to see if the heart was still beating.'

'I acted automatically.'

'Was the body cold or still warm?'

'Cold.'

'Then you had no need to turn it over.' Sébeille waited. 'Unless you had another motive.'

Gustave remained silent. He was completely hemmed in, cornered. In less than a day the superintendent had got out of him what he had denied for fifteen months: that he had lied from beginning to end about that fatal dawn. Sébeille could no longer catch his eye. Collapsed in the armchair, Gustave stubbornly kept his head down.

'Were you looking for something?'

Gustave almost yelled, 'No!'

'Did you do the same with Sir Jack Drummond's body?'

'No.'

'Why not?'

'I had seen that he was dead.'

'How?'

'He was cold.'

'So was she, yet you turned her over. Why didn't you do the same with him? One body you say was cold and that was enough for you, the other you moved. Explain. You surely had some reason.'

For a moment Sébeille thought he had the solution in his grasp. Gustave seemed to have reached the limit of endurance.

'What were you looking for?' prompted Sébeille.

'Nothing,' Gustave returned dully.

He repeated as if to convince himself that he only wanted to make sure that 'the English woman was really dead.' Whatever arguments Sébeille now dinned into Gustave's ears had no effect. It was nearly midnight. Sébeille decided to rest. 'You will sleep here,' he directed, 'and we'll resume our talk tomorrow. I'm sure you haven't told me everything.'

Two inspectors joined Gustave, who had slumped in his chair, ready to cry. Sébeille didn't go to bed at once. He knew that in any event he wouldn't get much sleep. He briefly questioned Clovis and Roger Perrin's father, who had been waiting all day at the Palais de Justice. Clovis acknowledged that Gustave had told him of the screams he had heard. The elder Roger Perrin affirmed that his son had slept at La Serre.

In the neighbouring streets the reporters, frozen and impatient, waited for news. They had tried everything to get some, but in vain. Towards 1.0 a.m., thanks to indiscretions, they did gather a few shreds of the interrogation. On the morning of November 13 they announced a sensational development: Gustave Dominici had admitted lying on three important points. They considered this only a beginning.

When Superintendent Sébeille and his colleagues returned to the library at 7.30 next morning, Gustave was already awake. He had had coffee and eaten with a good appetite, but complained that he had not slept well.

'I didn't either,' said Sébeille, 'if that's any consolation to you. I did nothing but think of your lies.'

Gustave bristled. 'I've told you the truth.'

'Not all of it. I've given it a lot of thought, Gustave. Your version won't stand up. It wasn't to see if she was dead that you moved Lady Drummond's body. You won't get anybody to believe that.'

'But it's true.'

Tirelessly Sébeille listed the improbabilities. Why had he waited three hours before finding out if the victims were dead? Why had he moved Lady Drummond's body and not Sir Jack's?

'What a risk you were taking. Suppose someone had arrived while you had hold of her by the feet? You'd have looked fine!'

'But I had to find out if she was alive.'

'Try something else . . .'

Gustave nervously shook his head as if warding off something. Sébeille had no intention of letting go. The dialogue, broken by long silences, went on. Sometimes the superintendent got up, took a book, leafed through the pages. Gustave dared look at him only when his back was turned.

'It wouldn't have been cartridges you were looking for?' suggested the superintendent. Standing, he looked down at Gustave, slumped in the armchair. 'Come on, Gustave, admit it, you expected to find cartridges under Lady Drummond's body.'

The farmer still kept his face down, but Sébeille heard his answer. 'Yes, that's what I was looking for.'

'Why?'

'To see if they came from the house.'

'And did you find any?'

'No.'

Sébeille made a quick calculation. The murderer had fired six shots. Four cartridges had been found, and two of them had not been fired. Therefore eight had been ejected. What had become of the four missing?

'I don't know,' Gustave declared.

Sébeille detected a change of attitude. Generally Gustave regained a little courage after he made a concession, undoubtedly hoping that the superintendent would call it quits as a reward for his candour. But now he stammered, his face red and crumpled with entreaty. He was paralysed by fear, incapable of a coherent defence.

'If you were afraid of finding cartridges that came from your house,' Sébeille went on implacably, 'it's because you know the murderer, know he lives at Grand'Terre.'

'NO!' It was a cry of anguish.

'You're shielding someone, Gustave. Who?'

'Nobody.'

It was nearly 1.0 p.m. Gustave's silences had filled most of the time.

190

'Have a bite to eat,' suggested Sébeille. 'Meantime think it over.

The examining magistrate Périès had not been idle that morning. He sent some officers to Grand'Terre with instructions to fetch Yvette. She went through the routine motions of protest: she was pregnant again, and the evening before, when they had taken away her husband, had had a bout of nerves which had gone on all day. The officers weren't impressed, and she drove off with them to the magistrate's office.

'It seems that the English visitors came to the house the evening of the 4th,' the magistrate began.

'Not at all,' Yvette objected.

'Your nephew, Roger Perrin, says so.'

'He's a little liar.'

'Your husband has admitted it.'

For a moment Yvette was bewildered. But she quickly recovered herself. 'I can't imagine why he said that.' She demanded to see him. But the time had not come to bring the couple face to face. The magistrate had been kept informed step by step of Sébeille's gradual progress. The momentum must not be broken.

'You yourself told Germaine Perrin so.'

'It's not true,' Yvette replied, extremely annoyed. 'I didn't leave Grand'Terre the whole day. If the mother and daughter had come I would have seen them.'

There remained no doubt in the magistrate's mind that the Dominicis had come to an understanding to keep Lady Drummond and Elizabeth's visit a secret. It was an essential part of the conspiracy of silence to act as if they didn't know that the campers had definitely stopped for the night near the mulberry tree.

When he re-entered the library, Sébeille took a seat facing Gustave. One glance convinced him that the waiting had done the trick. Gustave looked at the superintendent as if seeking help from him.

'Get it off your conscience,' Sébeille told him. 'There's no other way.'

Gustave wept and the superintendent remained silent. Suddenly leaning his forehead on Sébeille's shoulder, the farmer burst into sobs. Sébeille's throat tightened, as much for the distress of the man near him as for joy in perhaps having reached his goal. 'For the first time in sixteen months,' he wrote in his report, 'Gustave shed the attitude he had until then never abandoned.'

He allowed a few seconds to pass. Then he put his hand on the nape of Gustave's neck. 'Come on,' he said.

Gustave raised his head, his eyes full of tears. 'He told me,' Sébeille went on in his report, 'that at four o'clock on the morning of August 5th, 1952, his father had confided to him that he had committed the murders.'

When giving his official permission for Gustave's examination, Périès had asked Sébeille to inform him as soon as there was any positive result.

'You can tell it to the magistrate,' Sébeille said.

Contenting himself with drawing up a fifteen-line statement which he had Gustave sign, the superintendent hurried along to the magistrate's office. Périès let out a great sigh – he hadn't slept the night before either. 'Bring him along at once.'

Sébeille went to fetch Gustave, who now seemed infinitely weary. Roger Périès set him down in front of him. At the typewriter his clerk, Pierre Barras, prepared to record the statement. An examining magistrate's interrogation is more formal than that of police officers, which gives it a certain solemnity. Périès himself was very moved. It was, after all, quite something for a man of 30 to receive a confession concluding such an important affair.

'Gustave Dominici, I am listening to you.'

Gustave's story still came out spasmodically, but he spoke more freely to the magistrate. Perhaps he was frightened of this man who, after all, had sent him to prison in October 1952.

'In the morning,' began Gustave, 'when my father was leaving the house with his goats, I came downstairs. I asked him if he had heard the shots. He said yes. I pressed him. Then he said, "I fired them." '

'You don't usually get up so early.'

'No, but after the shots I couldn't get to sleep again. So I came down as soon as I heard my father's footsteps. I wanted to ask him what had happened at one in the morning.'

'Did you suspect?'

'No.' At times a sob choked Gustave's voice. Périès gave him time to calm down. 'He made this confession quite calmly,' Gustave began again. 'I asked him if he was crazy. He said no. I was stunned. Why had he done it? He told me that he had gone for a walk and on the way met the English people who had come to the house the evening before. Then he left with his goats.'

The magistrate expressed astonishment. How could Gustave be satisfied with such a feeble explanation when his father had just admitted a triple murder including that of a child? The time was past for the vague and inexact truths Gustave had used up to now.

'He did say something more,' Gustave acknowledged.

'I'm listening.'

'At about one he had gone out for some shooting. He followed the Route Nationale in the direction of Peyruis. Near the camp site he ran into a man coming towards him. They had an argument but he didn't say who started it. Nor at whom he fired first. But he killed the whole family. "What gun did you use?" I asked him. "A carbine I'd kept hidden away," he answered.'

Gustave denied knowing of the weapon's existence. He thought his father owned only the old Gras shotgun converted for shooting big game and a very antique twelve-bore. He must have hidden the carbine in his room or in the goats' pen. 'I asked him, "What did you do it with?" and he answered that he had thrown it away without telling me where.'

'You didn't ask your father how and why he killed the child?' Périès queried in wonder.

'No.'

However, he revised one of his statements; the old man had acknowledged shooting the man first. 'But Elizabeth?' the magistrate persisted.

Gustave shook his head; the question hadn't arisen.

'Did you confide your secret to anybody?' asked Périés.

'To Clovis. Father also told him.'

'You spoke of it at Grand'Terre, I suppose?'

Gustave hung his head. 'Never.'

'Why?'

'When he left me, Father said, "Above all, never say a word about it." Later I tried to learn more, but he told me to get out.'

'And you accepted two months in prison without saying anything? Without protest?'

Gustave did not answer.

'When you returned to Grand'Terre, didn't your father say anything? Didn't he thank you?'

Gustave's face contracted. 'No, nothing.' Then with bitter irony, 'He didn't give a damn if I spent two or three months inside.'

The magistrate went back over how Gustave had spent his time that morning. The farmer reiterated that he had only gone to the spot after his father had left. It was then that he saw the child's arm move. He had hurried back to tell his mother and his wife. Then before 6.0

he paid another visit to the camp site. He had seen the cartridges – something he had previously denied – but hadn't collected them. Therefore there was no need to move Lady Drummond's body. He didn't know why he had done it. He wanted to make sure that there was nothing belonging to his father near the car. But the cartridges? Gustave turned a perplexed look on the magistrate. It was true he might have put them in his pocket, but the fact was that he hadn't.

He had no more to tell. The clerk handed the transcript to the magistrate. Périès read through it rapidly and passed it to Gustave. 'Read and sign it.'

There was a long silence while Gustave obeyed. The magistrate handed him a pen and Gustave signed. But as he returned the authenticated document to the magistrate he pleaded, 'I don't want you to tell my father that I denounced him.'

'That will be difficult,' Périès observed.

Tears welled again in Gustave's eyes. 'Have it come from farther off,' he begged.

The magistrate made no promise.

Clovis was not surprised to find himself before the superintendent once more. He had foreseen that some day he would have to confess, though that didn't make the ordeal any less painful. Clovis had never fooled himself that the patience of the police would be less than the clan's. He had lived in expectation and his nerves had suffered from it. Nevertheless he still refused to give in.

After his questioning at the site on the 12th, he had waited the rest of the day at the Palais de Justice. In the evening the superintendent had heard him briefly, after which he was sent home. Just an interlude, he thought. He was not wrong. At 5.0 p.m. on the 13th police officers came to bring him back to the Palais de Justice at Digne.

'Clovis, you know the guilty person.'

His expression mulish, his small eyes blank, Clovis shook his head. 'No.'

'It's your father and you know it.'

Clovis almost lost his temper. 'Who told you so?'

'You in the first place, when I showed you the carbine and you fell on your knees on the tracks.'

'I don't know the carbine.'

'Gustave has told us everything.'

'He may know. I don't.'

194

'He assures us that you do.'

'Never!'

Sébeille's tactic was an old one, but he had no further need of it. 'You don't believe me?' he asked.

'No.'

'Would you like to see Gustave?'

Clovis nodded and Sébeille had Gustave brought in. He was in a pitiable state, his eyes red, lips trembling, utterly deflated. When he saw Clovis he went over to him and fell on his shoulder, as he had on Sébeille's. 'I've told everything, Clovis,' he confessed. 'I couldn't, not any more.'

For the first time Clovis broke. His jaw tightened, tears ran down his cheeks.

'Well, Clovis,' Sébeille asked gently.

'Since Gustave has talked.' He added, 'It will be better for everybody.'

Gustave was taken into another room and Clovis related how he had learned the truth; first from Gustave after the scene with the carbine, then when he was at Grand'Terre during his brother's imprisonment. Even so, he'd been in doubt until the day he talked to Gustave about it after his release.

'We were cutting wood in the mountains,' Clovis said. 'Near Saint-Pons. It was haunting me – I couldn't bring myself to believe it. I wanted to convince myself that Father was drunk when he spoke. I told the story to Gustave and he said he knew all about it.'

'Did you speak to anyone else about it?'

'To nobody, not even my wife. Not even to our other brothers.'

'Why did you keep such a secret between the two of you?'

Clovis's answer was the same as Gustave's; their father had forbidden any reference to it. If a secret is to be well kept, it is best never to speak of it, even among those who know.

Clovis denied knowing, however, that his father owned a carbine.

'You recognized it,' Sébeille objected.

But Clovis would not be shaken on this. He had never seen it, he insisted.

The superintendent did not press the point. Périès was waiting for Clovis to hear him in greater detail. Besides, he had another task ahead; to tackle Gaston Dominici on the subject of his sons' accusations. Clovis and Gustave had confirmed what he had always obscurely believed. Their twofold testimony seemed to him unshakable. Clovis would probably be as resolute as his silence had been.

195

Gustave might falter, but Clovis would stand firm. Sébeille could go for the old man, knowing that he had found the guilty one.

For the first time in years Gaston Dominici had neglected to take his goats up to the mountain that morning, Friday, November 13. He had walked along the road, stopped in the olive grove, and sat on a mound of earth. The air was dry but cold. A large woollen scarf round his neck, his battered old hat on his head, he kept mulling things over. Gustave had not returned the evening before. From the papers Gaston had learned that his son had admitted he had lied.

In the afternoon a reporter found him still sitting in the olive grove.

'Heard the latest?' he asked.

Gaston was expressionless.

'Gustave has told the magistrate that he went out three times during the night.'

'Then he's done for.' Angrily Gaston threw a stone at a goat that had strayed off. 'They've framed him,' he went on.

'I don't think so, Grandad. Not the magistrate, anyway.'

The reporter left. Gaston slowly returned to Grand'Terre. At the house a family group had gathered – as always when there was trouble. Augusta Caillat, her husband Clément and their 17-year-old daughter Marie-Claude were the first to arrive. They remained the whole afternoon. They were still in the kitchen when a black car rolled up and Captain Bernier appeared.

Sébeille had a good reason for assigning an officer to fetch Gaston Dominici. The superintendent didn't want to start this offensive with an incident. He feared that if he went himself or sent one of his colleagues, the old man would be stung to more or less genuine anger. The sight of a uniform, on the other hand, especially if decorated with gold braid, had always reassured him. 'Superintendent Sébeille would like to see you,' Captain Bernier told him.

'I'll come tomorrow,' ventured Gaston.

'It's urgent,' the officer said shortly. 'You must come at once.'

Gaston gestured to the Sardine. 'There's time for a drink at least,' he said.

The captain accepted. He had orders to proceed gently. He sat down opposite the old man, clinked glasses with him, and sipped the rough wine. Gaston Dominici then stood up, wiped his moustache, wound the woollen scarf round his neck, put on his old hat and said, 'Let's go.'

In the car he seemed perfectly at ease, chatting easily with the captain about the harvests. When the car stopped in front of the Palais de Justice at Digne, night was falling. The journalists crowded close, and the captain had to force a passage for Gaston, to the accompaniment of flashlights, a barrage of questions. Gaston waved them away. With a firm step he crossed the courtyard and followed Bernier to the library, where Sébeille was waiting for them with Inspector Ranchin. It was Ranchin who first addressed the old man. 'Lend me your knife,' he said.

Surprised, Gaston drew his knife from the pocket of his baggy velvet trousers.

'Don't you have another?'

'A penknife.'

'Let's have it.'

Anything might be expected from a man as violent and passionate as Gaston Dominici, even an attempt to take his own life. But all he did now was turn to Sébeille with a direct, 'What have you done with Gustave?'

'He's never been better.'

'So you say,' growled Gaston.

'Sit down, Grandad.'

Gaston took the armchair Gustave had sat in for an entire day. He took off his hat, put his stick within reach, and crossed his hands on his chest.

'I've a good many questions to ask you,' Sébeille began. Ranchin and his colleagues were there in support.

His first concern was with the fragment of wood near Elizabeth's head. Did Gaston still maintain that he gave it to the gendarmes?

'Was it to ask me that that you brought me here?' the old man asked, surprised.

'That and other things. Answer.'

'Of course it was me.'

'You're lying.'

'What's wrong with you?' the old farmer asked almost sadly.

But this time Sébeille was in no mood for banter. 'What's wrong is that we've had enough of your tricks.' From the file on the table he extracted three statements by the men who had removed the bodies on August 5. Slowly he read them to Gaston, who listened attentively.

'I'm the one who gave the bit of wood to the gendarmes,' he maintained.

197

'So they're liars.'

'Why me and not them?'

'Because they are not the only ones to contradict you.'

'Who else does?'

'The gendarme Bouchier for one.'

Gaston frowned. Sébeille pointed out that the gendarme formally denied the old man's version of having gone to cover the child's face to shield it from the crawling ants. Gaston seemed upset. He got up, pipe in mouth, saying nothing, and went over to the bookcase, where he stroked the backs of the bindings. 'They're fine books,' he remarked. 'They must have cost a lot.'

'Sit down,' Sébeille ordered.

The old man obeyed, but showed his displeasure. He showed it by discharging a volley of insults at Sébeille in dialect. When the storm passed, the superintendent resumed in an even tone, 'There's also Roger Perrin.'

Gaston opened his eyes wide. 'The halfwit.'

'Why is he a halfwit?'

'If you've questioned him you'll know.'

Sébeille took up the file containing the boy's statements. After listening for a moment, Gaston pretended indifference, sank back into his chair whistling, and gazed at the ceiling where he seemed to make some exciting discoveries.

'Did they or didn't they come to the house?' No answer. 'Did you hear me?'

'I'm not deaf.'

'Well then?'

'No one saw them, at any rate.'

'But it was you who told Roger Perrin.'

Gaston lolled back in his chair, his elbows on its arms, his legs spread out. 'These chairs are comfortable, make you feel like a minister.'

Sébeille barely kept his temper. What the old man needed was a good jolt.

'Dominici, you are, I know, a first-class actor. But we're not at the Comédie Française here. Answer simply and drop the nonsense.'

Gaston's face registered genuine grief. Had Sébeille stopped being a friend? Where were the pleasant chats, the good jokes, the exchange of broad stories, the police officer's deference? The old man suddenly got up and started for the door, grabbing his hat and stick on the way. 'You're beginning to bore me,' he said. 'I'm going.'

Sébeille exploded. 'That's enough,' he cried, banging his fist on the table. 'Sit down and don't move again.'

But Gaston kept going. Sébeille went after him, followed by Ranchin. The two took hold of the old man and tried to bring him back to the armchair. Gaston swore and threatened in dialect. The colourful, sonorous words poured out with such violence that Sébeille didn't understand half of them. After a short struggle Gaston consented to resume his seat.

'I forbid you to *tutoyer* me,' Sébeille warned. 'This affair has gone on all too long simply because you've never stopped making a fool of me. You've insulted me, your coarseness has gone beyond all bounds. I let you go on and said nothing because of your age, but today you're in a house of justice and we want the truth. So you're to mind your manners and tell me what you know, everything you know.'

Gaston seemed temporarily subdued. Sébeille, Ranchin, then Culioli or Amédée, an inspector who had joined them, put their questions one by one: the fragment of wood, the English people's visit, what he did during the night. But Gaston did not yield an inch. There were no quips, no show of indignation, no vulgarities, no insults in French or dialect. His face closed tight, not a feature moved. Only his look unwaveringly fixed on the police officers showed that his rage was still present.

At 9.0 p.m. Sébeille had a plate of soup brought to him. Dominici carefully cut a slice of bread into squares which he dipped in the broth. He ate with a good appetite, then lit his pipe. Meanwhile Sébeille had gone with Ranchin to have dinner in a nearby restaurant. Half an hour later the interrogation was resumed.

Did Superintendent Sébeille and his colleagues continue their interrogation of Gaston Dominici through the night? Did they press him with questions until dawn, threatening, harassing? Did they employ the technique of exhaustion, the grilling practised by all the world's police? Later, Gaston Dominici several times claimed that they did, while Sébeille defended himself against the charge. 'At 10.30 p.m. on November 13, 1953,' he wrote in his report, 'the interrogation of the old farmer was suspended and not resumed until the next morning, November 14, at 7.0.'

Reporters milling about outside, however, were convinced that inside the building there had been no nocturnal break; the lights had stayed on all night. At 10.0 p.m. Superintendent Harzic, head of the Criminal Investigation Department in the region, told the reporters that Gaston was being questioned. There was a rush to telephones and typewriters with this announcement. There was no more news that night but the windows remained lighted.

Meanwhile the struggle between Gaston and the police assumed a new violence. Sébeille attacked him from every angle before letting go with his big punch. 'A little girl had her head bashed in by a swine. And I know who he is.' Gaston looked at him, petrified by the outburst. 'That swine is you.'

The old man sat up in his chair. 'What are you talking about?'

'It's what your sons have said.'

'The bastards said that! It's a lie, you're having me on.'

'Would you like me to read their statements?'

Sébeille didn't bring father and sons together at this point. He may have thought that the interrogation had gone on long enough, that the old man must have some rest. After all, Sébeille held the whip hand and knew that success couldn't escape him. One fact is sure: Gaston Dominici had triumphantly resisted Sébeille's and his colleagues' most furious attacks. He had stood up to them without giving ground, and survived Friday the 13th. Sébeille acknowledged it. But he didn't feel uneasy about it, because he knew that meanwhile Périès was gaining points in his interrogation of Clovis.

Sitting heavily in his seat facing the magistrate, Clovis was desolate. His square face was contorted, his sharp-angled jaw trembling slightly. He had just parted with a secret which had increasingly weighed him down. He had told what he had heard, he knew no more. It was up to justice now to examine and evaluate what he had contributed.

Roger Périès was only partially satisfied. There was a certain opacity in Clovis's story which the magistrate wanted to clear up.

'Without pressing you for details,' he said, 'would you go over the scene in which your father confessed to the killing.'

In his rough voice with its slight accent, Clovis retold his story: the quarrel in the kitchen; the anger of the old man who had drunk more than usual; the sentence in dialect – 'I'm the one who killed the three of them'; the details he had given; the row with Sir Jack. 'He used the word carbine, but I thought he meant the converted Gras shotgun.'

'You surprise me,' Périès interrupted. 'You recognized the Rock-Ola when Superintendent Sébeille showed it to you.'

Clovis shook his head. 'No, I was merely upset. The crime was so horrible.'

'Why did you think of the Gras shotgun when your father confessed to you?'

'Because it was the only firearm I knew he owned.'

'I don't believe you.'

The sentence came sharply and brought no response. Clovis merely lowered his eyes. Patiently the magistrate went over the ground again. Clovis had been shown a weapon which had been used for the crime and retrieved from the water. He had fallen on his knees, prey to a powerful emotion, and he wanted it believed that it was because he had suddenly been overcome by the horror of the crime! Moreover, how could he have thought of the Gras shotgun, since by the time his father made his revelation the affair was three months old? By then it was universally known that the crime had been committed with an American carbine. Clovis's explanation simply did not hold water.

Caught like that, Clovis gave in. Yes, it was true that he had recognized the carbine in the superintendent's hands. It was usually kept on one of the shelves on the right-hand wall of the shed attached to the Grand'Terre forge, a shed in which the Dominicis stored their farm implements and, if necessary, repaired them. As soon as he could, Clovis went to the farm, and finding the weapon gone, realized that it had been used in the crime. Coming out of the shed, he met Gustave and asked if it had been he. Gustave said no.

Périès sent for the carbine. He showed it to Clovis, who looked at it for a moment in silence. 'That's it. I'm sure of it; it didn't have a handshield, and the barrel was attached to the stock by an aluminium ring.'

It was midnight and the magistrate offered to book a room in a hotel for Clovis so that he could have a few hours' rest. The next day would be hard. But Clovis refused. He preferred to stay with his brother who would not be leaving the building. Périès allowed Clovis to join Gustave in a small office to which he had been taken. The two brothers fell into each other's arms under the eyes of the magistrate and Sébeille.

In Digne there was a rush for newspapers that Saturday morning, November 14. Almost all the headlines ran: 'Father Dominici the murderer of the Drummonds: Clovis and Gustave accuse.' Short of time, the journalists had not been able to spread themselves. Only Gabriel Domenech of Le Méridional had suggested a possible motive.

Since Superintendent Harzic's 10.0 p.m. statement on the Friday there had been much puzzled speculation about what could have possessed the old man. 'While waiting round the palace,' Domenech had written, 'there was endless speculation about the motive for the crime. Father Dominici, one who knows him well told us, is depraved. Doubtless he went prowling round the Hillman in order to observe a scene of intimacy. Sir Jack got up and an argument ensued. The old man, furious, went to get his gun, returned and perhaps unintentionally pulled the trigger, killing the English tourist. After that he had to eliminate any witnesses.'

How had Domenech come up with this theory? In May or June of 1953 an informer had told him that there was no need to look further for the cause. He no longer remembered who had told him, but the piece of gossip stayed in his mind and emerged in time to catch the last editions.

By early morning, what had now become a family drama was once more under way. Like the Dominicis, Sébeille had been satisfied with an armchair in which he slept no more than an hour. Périès had gone home but at 7.0 a.m. was again at the palace. He had given himself one specific task: to make Gustave acknowledge that he, like Clovis, knew of the carbine's existence. The magistrate was convinced, but it was important to know if Gustave would admit it.

As it turned out, he offered little resistance. His eyes red, his face mottled, cheeks hollow and voice almost inaudible, he admitted that the carbine came from Grand'Terre. 'It belonged to my father,' he went on. 'Probably from the time the American troops came through.'

He himself had never used it. His father took it for shooting boar. There were two clips for it, which seemed to be loaded. Like Clovis, Gustave knew it was kept on the shelf in the shed. Not seeing it on the morning of the crime, he had at once guessed that it had been used to kill the Drummonds. But his father hadn't told him that himself. He was only repeating his father's admission to Yvette which she had passed on to him the same day.

Roger Périès was satisfied; there was no longer any divergence between Clovis and Gustave. The next step was none the less to check the statements on the spot; have the two brothers point out exactly where the carbine had lain.

Sébeille had meanwhile visited Gaston. They had both slept badly. The superintendent was not in top form and he had the distinct impression that the old man was in better shape than he. When he entered the library Gaston watched his approach with a mocking eye, already nibbling at his morning pipe. The officer was carrying the morning papers. 'Have a look,' he said, handing them to Gaston.

They were the two Marseilles dailies, *Le Provençal* and *Le Méridional*. In enormous letters his name was coupled with the word murderer. Below were those of the accusers, his sons. Gaston bounded from his chair in a rage. 'The swines! The bastards!'

His anger was real. French and Provençal alternated as Gaston cursed his sons and his whole family. 'They're the murderers,' he shouted. 'Show them to me. Bring them along.'

But Sébeille wasn't going to confront the father with the sons now. That would have to wait until the old man was more tractable.

It was an unproductive session. The old farmer only answered questions with insults, refusing to co-operate. At 10.0 a.m. Sébeille broke off temporarily. Périès had told him that it was time to go to Grand'Terre with Clovis and Gustave.

Dishevelled, beside themselves, sticks in their hands, the five women faced the police like avenging furies and prevented their entry into Grand'Terre. Yvette was there, but overshadowed this time by Augusta Caillat with her daughter, Marie-Claude, and trailed by two sisters-in-law. Assembled at the farm deserted by its menfolk, waiting terrified for what was to come, having learned from the papers of the two brothers' accusations and realizing therefore that the clan was breaking up and that the end might be near, the Dominici women never thought to surrender. The whole force of resistance now seemed concentrated in them.

Surveying the spectacle, Sébeille and Périès could even be moved. The women's distress was understandable; they were living out an unexpected tragedy, some of them at least. Superintendent and magistrate were convinced that Augusta, for instance, had never suspected the truth. Learning it from the papers, she rejected it outright.

The women had surged forward on the arrival of the police cars near Grand'Terre. Shaking their fists and shrieking, they rushed at the first officers to get out. The insults came flying – traitors, swine, assassins. 'You chloroformed our brothers,' Augusta screamed.

When Gustave and Clovis appeared, the police had to protect them. 'You're all mad,' cried Clovis, while Gustave, his head down, not daring to look at Yvette, remained silent.

Augusta Caillat was beside herself. To Sébeille she shouted, 'Where's my father?'

The superintendent tried in vain to calm her. 'You're going to kill him,' she raged on. 'I know it, you've been wanting to for a long time. But then I'll kill you, at least I won't go to prison for nothing.'

Armed with an iron bar, she raised it, threatening. 'If my father is in prison, I want to take his place,' she cried.

For the present, entry into the farm had to be given up. It could only be effected by a battle which neither Sébeille nor Périès wanted. Certainly the women could be overcome, but once freed, the violence would begin again. Taking hold of Augusta, a gendarme tried to draw her into the house. Roger Périès begged the woman to keep quiet. He even gave the order to arrest Augusta. She turned on him a face distorted by hatred. 'You're the magistrate,' she said, 'you're satisfied, today you've won. But don't gloat. We're ten, we're a hundred, and we'll save our father.'

Officers and gendarmes succeeded in carrying her off. A few seconds later she reappeared, carrying little Alain in her arms, mouthing insults. Périès therefore decided to break off the combat, call for reinforcements, and apply the classic formula of showing strength in order not to have to use it. The police beat a tactical retreat and lined up their cars 500 metres off, removing Clovis and Gustave out of sight of the women. For the journalists staying behind the curses continued.

Half an hour later a dozen gendarmes arrived from Forcalquier. The sight provoked a final outburst but the women knew they had no chance. They retreated, taking shelter inside the house. Sébeille could at last get going. Gustave and Clovis were directed to the shed, which stood at the bottom of the courtyard.

One after the other, accompanied by Périès and Sébeille, they entered the shed littered with implements such as every farm in the world possesses. At the far end of the shed were two shelves one above the other, carelessly attached to the wall and loaded with junk.

The magistrate asked the two brothers where the weapon had always lain. Both indicated the same corner between the wall and the lower shelf. Photographs were taken as they did so, hand raised, forefinger pointing to a piece of wood, the remains of a farm tool, lying on the shelf.

Half an hour was enough for the operation. Sébeille and Périès went back to the courtyard. Yvette, on the lookout, was quickly with them, anxious for permission to go with her husband to the Palais de Justice. When the magistrate granted it, she all but leaped into Gustave's arms, clinging to him with tears running down her face. Then she ran to the house, to return a few seconds later with Alain in her arms and followed by her relatives, calmer now, but not letting the police leave without a final gesture of solidarity. They gathered in a circle round Alain, and each with an arm extended over the boy's head, intoned an oath: 'On our children's heads we swear that Gaston Dominici is innocent.'

Handing the child over to the women, Yvette got into the car between Clovis and Gustave. At Peyruis the convoy stopped for a moment before Clovis's house to pick up his wife Marie-Rose. Since it was now 1.0 p.m. a further stop was made for a quick lunch at a nearby restaurant, Sébeille and his colleagues eating at one table, the two Dominici couples at another. Gaston, still in the library, was just then refusing lunch; a sandwich and a dish of noodles brought to him by the concierge. He was not hungry, he said.

The attack resumed at 2.0 p.m. when Sébeille, with Ranchin, Tardieu and Culioli, got back to the library. Gaston was dozing quietly, pipe in mouth. He merely opened one eye and greeted the police officers with a vague phrase they didn't catch. Was the spring broken? Sébeille was soon disillusioned. When he informed the old man of the morning's expedition, his reward was a frown and an obscene oath. 'If they saw a carbine in the shed,' he growled, 'it's because it's theirs.'

'Gustave's or Clovis's?'

'Gustave's, of course.'

The old man seemed satisfied with his answer. Return to sender, he seemed to be saying. Sébeille started afresh; how had Gaston spent his time that night? Gaston complained irritably, 'You keep making me repeat the same thing.'

He could alter nothing of what he had already said, he declared. He had not got up at 1.0 a.m. as his sons claimed, but at 4.0, and driven his goats in the direction of the Lurs station. Of course he had heard the shots but had attributed them to poachers.

'Who were shooting with a military weapon,' Sébeille challenged.

'It happens.' Dominici shrugged it off.

'Like you with the carbine.'

The old man shook his head. 'I never had one.'

The atmosphere once more grew heated as Gaston, recovering his energy, raised his voice and resumed his insults. Sébeille and the inspectors bludgeoned him with questions. There were four of them around him and they heckled him without pause. It was the standard technique to throw the suspect off balance, to give him no time to reflect and to wear him out. But the process has its own built-in hazards; to escape his tormentors the suspect may come up with anything. How much pressure did Sébeille and his colleagues exert? 'They drove me nuts,' the old man said later.

The pitiless duel ended with the confrontation between father and sons. It was extremely painful and yielded nothing. Sébeille does not refer to it either in his report or his memoirs. But Clovis and Gustave later brought it up without being contradicted. It remained one of the grimmest experiences of their lives.

Clovis was the first to be led in to the old man, still seated in his armchair. He remained standing, and the two gazed at each other intently.

'Speak,' ordered the superintendent.

In a distraught voice, his jaw tight, Clovis declared, 'One evening you told me you had killed three people.'

Gaston angrily shrugged his shoulders. 'Liar!'

'You did say so.'

An oath was the answer and Sébeille led the witness out.

Gustave's behaviour was altogether different. He stammered, without looking at his father, who eyed him with contempt. Gustave repeated his accusation and left the library, glad to escape his father's malice.

'Well, Dominici?' asked Sébeille.

'You don't imagine you've changed anything?'

'Are they lying?'

'Of course.'

'Why?'

'Ask them.'

The last sentence of the day's transcript read: 'I am not guilty, I do not understand why my sons accuse me.' It was 6.0 p.m.

Sébeille summed it up for Périès: no progress, Gaston is a rock. The magistrate said he himself would examine Gaston in the morning. After all, a man could be prosecuted without having confessed. The joint accusations of Clovis and Gustave were sufficient legal basis to proceed. 'Keep him under observation,' the magistrate ordered.

Sébeille arranged for Gaston to spend the night in the same room as before. A young policeman, Victor Guérino, had the first watch.

Just 30, he was not particularly happy with the honour. The responsibility was heavy, especially because of Sébeille's instructions. 'You can talk to him, but never utter the word "murderer". Don't bring up the case on your own initiative. If he does, listen but ask no questions, remember what he says and inform me.'

Sébeille and his colleagues had dinner in the restaurant of the Hotel Mistre some 200 metres from the palace. He was neither hungry nor sleepy. Only tired, a deep fatigue. He advised the reporters to do what he was going to do; go to bed. They were grateful. Some of them had been up for 60 hours.

8

Gaston Dominici looked over his new companion and keeper Guérino. Sitting in his armchair, smoking his pipe, he seemed at ease, without a care. 'So you're going to keep me company.'

Guérino nodded.

'You seem a good sort.'

The policeman noticed the dish of cold noodles on the table. 'You haven't eaten?'

'I'm not hungry.'

The two spoke in dialect and Gaston seemed pleased to be talking with someone who could understand him. French was the language of officialdom; it was in Provençal that he thought and liked to converse. 'I've had enough of being questioned like this,' he said. 'Dominici this, Dominici that – I'd be better off in my bed.'

'Me too, Grandad.'

'You'll be there soon. You've spent the day outdoors. I've been kept shut up here.' Then suddenly, 'Do you shoot, lad?'

'Yes.'

'Me too, I've done a good bit in my time.'

'That's what I'm planning on tomorrow; Sunday.'

'Lucky you.'

Dominici sighed. The game was disappearing, dying off. It was not like the old days when in the oak forests or on the heaths every thicket harboured its rabbit or hare. 'Imagine, one day I caught seven hares in a snare.'

'You don't say, Grandad.'

Gaston laughed heartily. 'I didn't set them. But the fellow who did got screwed.' He drew on his pipe, smiling at the memory. 'Do you know my farm, Grand'Terre?'

'I've passed it.'

'Fine place.'

Guérino politely agreed.

'Do you know what I paid for it?'

'No.'

'Ten thousand francs. It's all I had. The house was in ruins and I had to rebuild it. Then I added land, ended up by buying three farms. That made it a property.' Out of the corner of his eye he watched for a sign of admiration which Guérino willingly granted him. 'I've got goats, a vineyard, olives,' the old man went on, consoled by the tally. He had always worked hard, he added. He had to; nine children to feed and bring up. 'But it wasn't there I found my happiness,' he sighed.

'Why not, Grandad?'

Gaston Dominici shrugged, nibbling his pipe which had gone out. 'The Sardine, I never did get anywhere with her.'

'Hm.' He considered for a moment and then went on almost as if to himself. He had made love to the Sardine but she hadn't liked it. So he had run after other women. He had had his good times. He hadn't given up his life in that respect and at his age he still had it in him. And he was a grandfather, not a new one either. 'Sixteen grandchildren, think of that; without counting my brother's four. That makes twenty.'

His musing trailed off into a silence which Guérino did not interrupt. He had been told not to ask questions, not to initiate conversation. Beginning to wonder none the less as the old man's silence continued, Guérino suddenly realized its cause. Gaston Dominici was crying.

Gaston was struggling with his sobs. 'And to think of all the grandchildren I have.'

What was he getting at? That he was ashamed as a grandfather to be accused of killing a child? That it was a fearful calamity to have become a murderer at his age? Guérino interpreted the remark as the beginning of a confession, an expression of remorse. He said casually, 'If you've something to say it's better that you say it right now. At your age one must realize . . .'

In his reply he had mingled French with Provençal. Gaston raised his head, his face wet with tears but with a melancholy smile. He mumbled something Guérino didn't understand. 'Perhaps it was an accident,' the gendarme suggested.

The policeman expected anything except what he actually heard. 'Well, yes,' said Dominici, 'it was an accident. They attacked me and I killed all three of them.'

Guérino was startled almost to the point of embarrassment. He could well have done without this confession the world was waiting for and that had just been handed to him on a platter. At that moment the concierge, M. Giraud, came in to make up the camp-bed for the night. He was a former gendarme and at once sensed that something unusual was going on. Old Dominici was weeping, Guérino looked uncomfortable. Giraud exchanged a look with the young policeman and understood that he should leave. 'I'll come back when the restaurant brings your supper,' he said to Dominici, who did not seem to hear.

Guérino looked at his watch; it was a little after 7.0, still an hour before going off duty. If he rushed off now to notify his superiors, the old man might pull himself together and say that his attendant must have been dreaming – an unpleasant situation that wouldn't help his career. On the other hand, Superintendent Sébeille had been very precise: to ask no direct questions. Guérino felt that he was walking on a razor's edge. At 8.0 p.m. his relief would arrive. What should he do? For twenty-four hours the experts had grilled the old man without getting anything out of him; he had put two questions and the other had crumbled.

What Guérino did was hold his tongue and Gaston talked, disconnected sentences, in dialect, which the policeman sometimes failed to catch, while trying to inscribe every word in his memory. He didn't dare ask Gaston to repeat anything for fear of breaking the spell. What he heard, Sébeille had for months hoped for in vain. 'I went to the landslide,' the old man said, 'taking the gun by chance, out of habit. I was afraid of an accident to the train. If the line had been blocked, there'd have been more than three dead.'

He gave Guérino a questioning glance, as if he had already furnished a justification. 'I passed near the camp site. I was attacked. I realized they took me for a prowler. I fired.' And in a still feebler voice. 'And then the trouble blew up.'

That was the end. He was no longer crying and his eyes had a faraway look.

Eventually, just before being relieved, Guérino said, 'All this must be told to Superintendent Sébeille.'

'Never!' At the sound of his enemy's name Gaston flared up again. 'They can all go to hell. They've done me harm enough. They'd enjoy hearing me too much. For two days they've badgered the shit out of me with their questions. They wanted me to say I did it. Well, I'll say it to somebody else.'

'To whom?'

Gaston seemed to be racking his brains. 'I've got it,' he said suddenly. 'To the president of the court. Go and get him, I'll tell him everything.'

Guérino hesitated – who was the old man talking about? 'I don't know him,' he said.

'Yes you do,' Dominici said impatiently, 'the little fellow with the curly hair. He can draft it for me; I can't write.'

It dawned on the policeman that Gaston had confused things. When Sébeille had given orders at 6.0 p.m. that Gaston should be kept under surveillance, Superintendent Prudhomme, head of the Digne police, had come into the room for a few moments. He had exchanged a few words with Gaston. Seeing that the officer seemed to be at home there, the old man had taken him to be the master of the place, the president of the court, no less. Guérino didn't contradict him. 'As you wish,' he said.

The door opened and Guérino inwardly heaved a sigh of relief; his substitute, Bocca, was on the threshold, followed by the concierge, Giraud. It gave Guérino an idea. To prevent Gaston from retracting, he would make the two arrivals witnesses.

'Do you still acknowledge that it was you?' he asked. 'Do you still want me to go and find M. Prudhomme?'

Dominici seemed disgruntled. 'I've already said yes.'

Guérino gave the old man a last look. Followed by Giraud he left the room, leaving Dominici in the care of Bocca.

The newcomer, a man of 40 with a round face, receding hair and a prominent hooked nose, sat down silently in front of Gaston. They seemed to measure each other for a moment. Then the old man drew a box of lozenges from his pocket and offered it to Bocca. 'For the throat,' he said.

'Is yours sore?'

'Yes.' Putting a lozenge into his mouth, Gaston sucked it for a while before sighing, 'That's not the worst.'

'What's wrong, Grandad?' asked the policeman kindly.

Gaston said in dialect, 'At home they're all against me.'

Like Guérino, Bocca obeyed instructions to ask no direct questions about the case. Only to listen. And there was enough to listen to. 'I went up the mountain with my goats,' Gaston was saying, 'and when I got back Yvette told me that three people had been killed. It was Gustave who bought the American carbine, I don't know where he hid it.'

His talk was curiously confused and Bocca had a good deal of trouble following it. The old man seemed to be suggesting that Gustave had got up several times during the night. Yvette had told him so. He then accused his son of the crime. In any event he had not done it. 'I accuse myself,' he said, 'but it's for the sake of my grandchildren. To safeguard their honour.'

He seemed sad. To go to prison mattered little to him, he declared, so long as he could take his dog. He alone loved him. The family wanted to be rid of him. He no longer had confidence in any of his sons. What concerned him was not to have to sell the farm. He wanted a paper drawn up stating that he would not be obliged to sell.

Bocca extricated himself with vague answers. His anxieties were the same as Guérino's: what would Superintendent Prudhomme say if Gaston Dominici told him with a malicious smile that he had been pulling everybody's leg, or worse, that Bocca, like Guérino, had simply invented his confession?

Superintendent Prudhomme lived not far from the Palais de Justice. So it took only a few minutes for Victor Guérino and Simon Giraud, the concièrge, to get there. The chief of the Digne police was just sitting down to dinner when the two arrived. He was more than surprised by the news Guérino brought him. From the very short interchange he had had with Gaston Dominici he hadn't gained the impression that the old man was given to incriminating confidences. The superintendent had suggested that it would be best to tell the truth and Gaston had merely shaken his head.

Pierre Prudhomme was in something of a quandary. He knew no more about the case than the average newspaper reader. He was therefore hardly in a position to gauge Gaston's sincerity. So he telephoned the restaurant where he knew Sébeille was having dinner and quickly told him Guérino's story. Sébeille wasted no time in coming over and Guérino once more repeated Gaston's confession.

'Since he wants to talk to you,' Sébeille advised Prudhomme, 'go to the palace and listen to him. Try to find out if it's genuine and keep me informed.'

Prudhomme arrived at the palace at about 8.30, accompanied by Guérino and Giraud. Gaston was still being guarded by Joseph Bocca, although they had both settled into silence. Prudhomme asked Gaston if he would repeat what he had told Guérino. 'Make a draft of it and I'll sign it,' said Gaston.

'No,' returned the superintendent. 'I've come so that you may tell me what happened. So far as I'm concerned I know nothing. It's up to you to tell me.'

Gaston Dominici looked the superintendent in the eye and said firmly, 'All I can tell you is that I am innocent.'

'In that case, all I can do is go away,' the superintendent offered.

'Make a draft,' Gaston prompted him again.

'What will you do with it?'

'Tomorrow I'll send it to Sébeille and it will all be over.'

Prudhomme's answer to that was that Gaston's attitude altogether baffled him; either Gaston was innocent and the matter was closed, or he was guilty and it was for him to decide whether he would acknowledge it. In either case no confession could be drafted.

'If I confess,' asked Gaston, 'shall I be able to keep my farm?'

Pierre Prudhomme almost lost his patience. They were not at a fair, he pointed out, to chaffer like this. Beside him Guérino and Giraud were dismayed by this hedging and bargaining.

The superintendent turned to them with the request that they go over the conversation with Dominici in dialect. Giraud chided the old man. Why had he gone back on what he had said? No one had forced him to speak as he had done to Guérino. He had accused himself and been listened to. He had asked to confess to Superintendent Prudhomme because he had seemed to him a decent man, as he was. Surely he was not going to make fools of them. He would not be badly off in prison, added the former gendarme. They would even, he promised, let him have a cask of his own wine.

Gaston listened in silence. 'You will stay alone with M. Prudhomme,' Giraud concluded, 'and tell him your secret.'

No protest. Giraud translated for the superintendent the advice he had just given and signalled Guérino that they should withdraw and leave the chief of police alone with the old man.

Prudhomme drew up a chair and sat down facing Gaston. 'Tell me what happened,' he said.

Gaston remained silent, deep in thought.

'Is there something troubling you about confessing?' asked Prudhomme.

No answer.

'Are you ashamed because it has something to do with sex?' Prudhomme hazarded.

That morning he had read Gabriel Domenech's theory about the crime. The idea seemed to please Gaston, who smiled. 'Yes, that's it,' he said.

Returning from the landslide, he had in fact passed by the camp site. He had stopped behind the mulberry tree and stayed there some twenty minutes. He watched the woman undress. She wore a very short transparent slip and a patterned dress. 'For her age,' he said, 'she was all right; she had what it takes.'

'And that put ideas in your head?'

'Yes.'

He had gone closer to touch the woman. But at that moment the man had intervened and of course had objected. They came to grips but Gaston had had time to pick up the carbine, which he had laid on the ground. 'I fired and wounded him in the hand,' Gaston said. 'I didn't know it, but once when we were talking Sébeille told me that he had a wound.'

Sir Jack had then gone for him again and Gaston had fired at him twice. One shot had done for the woman. As for the child, she had left the car and tried to flee towards the Durance. Gaston had fired at her but missed. 'I ran after her and caught her on the bank. I knocked her down with a blow from the butt.' This particular memory seemed to distress him. His moustache quivered and his eyes closed. 'I didn't know what I was doing any more.'

Afterwards he had washed his hands in the Durance. Then, following the riverbank, he returned to Grand'Terre after crossing the railway line. He sat down for a while in the garden before going up to bed.

Was it the truth? Superintendent Prudhomme had the impression that it was. However, he wanted to verify two or three details. He left Gaston for a short time in the care of Bocca. From the palace he telephoned Sébeille at the restaurant to ask him if there was a mulberry tree at the camp site, and if Sir Jack had been wounded in the hand. Sébeille answered in the affirmative. Prudhomme said that in his opinion 'it was genuine', and that he should come over. Then he returned to the library, again cloistering himself with Gaston. Where had he got the carbine?

'In a shed,' the old man replied. 'Along the wall on the right coming in, at the far end, hidden between a couple of planks which acted as shelves.'

The superintendent considered his mission ended. He went to the door and brought in Guérino, Simon Giraud and a Sergeant Marius Sabatier, come to check his roster. In front of Gaston Dominici he went over the admissions he had just heard, wanting to give them a certain publicity which would make any retraction impossible.

Gaston did not protest. He was now hungry and Giraud went to fetch the meal he had kept hot. Before the policemen, Gaston ate a large bowl of soup into which he broke a large hunk of bread, and drank half a litre of red wine. He had recovered, it seemed, complete self-mastery. Just as he was finishing his short meal, Sébeille came in. Gaston greeted him with a smile. 'All right, lad, you've won.'

When Sergeant Sabatier told him that he had done well to confess to Superintendent Prudhomme because he was a good man, Dominici answered, 'I knew it, that's why I did it.' He was almost grinning, well content with himself. 'It was a crime of passion,' he said as if summing up for himself the drama and his confession.

Edmond Sébeille had the room emptied, keeping with him only Superintendent Prudhomme. He did not even feel the joy which victory brings. It had arrived too unexpectedly. He did not yet understand very clearly, and with Gaston anything was possible; so long as he had not heard the old man himself and made him sign the declaration which incriminated him, Sébeille did not consider the matter ended.

'I'm going to make you happy,' Gaston told him. 'I'm the one who killed the English people.' In his eyes there lurked, oddly, the same mischievous slyness that always greeted the superintendent. Sébeille quickly decided on his tactics – to listen while saying the least possible, not to insist on points of detail. With his pig-headedness Gaston was quite capable, if one wrangled with him, of upsetting everything and playing dumb. There was the same danger if Sébeille allowed himself to cast doubts on his sincerity, even if only on one particular aspect. The superintendent therefore decided to record even the most improbable statements. He suggested that Ranchin should be present, but Gaston refused; the inspector was his *bête noire*. If he were there, he would not open his mouth and Sébeille would have to put up with it. Why? Gaston did not want, he said, to be made a fool of. Sébeille yielded without understanding. The essential thing was that Gaston should speak.

The statement Sébeille received was certainly more detailed than the one Prudhomme had obtained. But on numerous points Gaston varied. Thus he had not inspected the condition of the landslide before going near the camp site – that had been his intention but once outside he had changed his mind and turned towards where the English people were. He had seen them earlier that evening when they were settling down beyond the irrigation ditch, near an olive grove at Saint-Pons. It is in fact quite possible that the Drummonds had changed their place of encampment. Gaston's statement did not seem in this matter to reflect the truth anyway, since he claimed to have spoken to Lady Drummond, and she knew no French. However, Sébeille did not take him up on this.

Gaston asserted that he had taken the carbine 'in the hope of shooting a badger or other animal.' He repeated that he kept it between a couple of planks which acted as shelves, a detail to remember. The magazine was partly loaded, and he had taken two or three additional cartridges. Then he had gone to the mulberry tree. It must have been 11.30 p.m.

'The woman had undressed,' he went on. 'I went up to her. We exchanged a few words in a low voice. Then I reached forward to touch her. She didn't draw back.'

For the remainder it is best to keep to the testimony Sébeille dictated to his colleague Pierre Prudhomme. It rings true and became an essential passage in the dossier:

At a certain moment the man, who was sleeping on a camp-bed towards the back of the car, heard us and got up. He began shouting in his own language. I did not understand and he flung himself on me. We came to grips when I picked up the carbine I had left on the ground near the woman's camp-bed. The man, who was tall, tried to disarm me by seizing the barrel of the gun. I lost my head and pulled the trigger, obviously not knowing what I was doing.

The bullet pierced his hand, which forced him to let go. He ran to the edge of the road and I fired at him twice more. He must have been hit in the back or the side. The woman was screaming, and I then fired at her, only once, I think, and she fell down on the spot. It was then I noticed the little girl, who had got out of the car by the rear doors and run towards the Durance. I fired one cartridge at her but didn't hit her, since she went on running. I saw her run down the bank at the end of the bridge and ran after her to catch her. As I came up with her I found her on her knees. I struck her on the head once with the butt of the gun. Being more and more panicky, I no longer knew what I was doing.

I went straight down to the Durance to a place in line with the child's body where there is a gap through which it is easy to reach the river. I had blood only on my hands. When striking the child on the head the butt broke. After washing my hands in the river I took up my gun and threw it away a few metres from there, at a point where I knew the water was deep and open. I followed the little path and got back to the farm after crossing the railway. I sat down for a moment on my garden wall, then went back to bed. I got up at about four and went to pasture my goats up near Giropey.

When I left I did not see my son Gustave nor did I later tell him anything of what I had done that night, nor did I ever tell any of my family. I did not go back to the scene that night nor try to recover cartridges. I have no idea whether Gustave later came to the spot to find out anything whatever.

I again repeat that I committed this crime without anyone's help. I sincerely regret what I did, and if I shot the man and the woman and struck the child on the head with the gun-butt, I did so in a moment of absolute frenzy. I completely lost control of myself when I saw the man rushing at me; it was fear that made me pull the trigger. I killed the little girl so she wouldn't talk.

So deposed Gaston Dominici, who was still the only witness. His story of the night certainly had elements of fantasy. Sébeille affirms in his report that he was careful not to interrupt the old man or divert him with queries. He respected his silences, only asking him to repeat sentences imperfectly understood in order to dictate them as faithfully as possible to Superintendent Prudhomme, who was acting as stenographer.

A confession is a document subject to the same pitiless criticism to which a historian subjects the memoirs left by a political figure for the edification of future generations and his own posthumous fame. It would be naïve to believe that a murderer's confession represents the exact truth. Every police officer in the world knows that even if a guilty person admits the essential – the crime itself, that is – his statement made under the influence of emotion will include some errors, wilful or no. Also, more than at any other time a guilty person seeks in confession extenuating circumstances or the seeds of justification. He is also influenced by another factor: if his statements do not correspond with material evidence, doubt can later be introduced. The result of all this is that the record of a confession does not exist which does not at some point diverge from the reality as constructed by the investigators. Their work then consists in determining whether, despite these 'holes', the confession is valid.

Edmond Sébeille could easily pick out the most immediate improbabilities in the story. The most glaring was the encounter with a consenting Lady Drummond, welcoming with open arms an old tramp turning up in the night within two steps of her husband. Gaston Dominici had thus improved on his first statement, taking up the motive suggested by Superintendent Prudhomme and transforming it into his own formula of a 'crime of passion'. Neither Sébeille nor his colleague believed for a moment in the authenticity of this scene, but in line with their policy of acting for the time being as transcribers only, they noted it without comment.

It was also hardly probable that Gaston had armed himself with a carbine to kill an animal, still less a badger. One does not fire bullets in the dead of night at small game. It was more plausible that the old man, if his admissions were genuine, had gone out without the weapon and, having quarrelled with Sir Jack, had gone back for the Rock-Ola. Sébeille at once hit upon an explanation: if Gaston asserted that he had casually collected his gun to shoot a badger, it was to intercept any effort to saddle him with a charge of premeditation. It was an accident; he would stick to that. Finally, Sébeille did not believe that Dominici had seen the English family at Saint-Pons. But he was puzzled why he said he had. Was it so that he could deny the visit of Lady Drummond and Elizabeth to Grand'Terre?

None the less, the superintendent found much in Gaston's statement that had the ring of truth. The wound in Sir Jack's hand explained that noted by the pathologists. Until now Sébeille had inclined to the belief that the scientist had cut his hand in grasping the bumper, since a shred of flesh had been found there. In fact, he had had reservations; it seemed to him unlikely that the shred had been torn off in this manner. If a wound already existed, the incident became clearer, and Sir Jack's struggle to turn aside the weapon pointed at him was the logical and instinctive reaction of a man threatened. It was the first time that the beginning of the crime had been described in this fashion. Moreover, Gaston Dominici had confirmed what he said to Sébeille on the evening of August 5, which had surprised him then: the woman had fallen on the spot, she had not suffered. Another essential point: the shot fired at Elizabeth fleeing explained the wound in the ear observed by the experts. Finally Gaston had indicated the place where the rifle was kept – between two planks in the shed. He thus confirmed the statements of his sons. The subject had not been mentioned during the confrontation. The old man therefore did not know the location pointed out by Clovis and Gustave.

It was nearly midnight. Gaston seemed relieved, almost relaxed, Sébeille noted.

'When I'm in prison, will Grand'Terre still belong to me?' he asked.

'Yes, Grandad.'

'Then I'll sell it. The old girl will get half and Gustave can bugger off wherever he likes.' The idea appealed to him – it was his revenge.

'Now, lad,' he went on, 'do me a favour. In prison I'll need money. At the farm you'll find eighty thousand francs in cash and two hundred thousand in securities. They're in two tin boxes on the kitchen dresser. Bring them to me.'

Sébeille promised.

'And my wine? I'd like to have that too, I'll drink it with my guard.'

Smoking his pipe, his face smooth, Gaston Dominici arranged his life. For him, prison was a hospital where one had the good fortune not to be ill.

He sighed. 'At least like that I won't have to get a divorce,' he said.

'Did you want to leave the Sardine?' asked Sébeille, surprised.

In dialect Gaston proceeded to curse wife, children, family. Sébeille and Prudhomme merely listened.

'You'll take me to prison when there's nobody in the streets,' he instructed. He got up, took a few steps, yawned, sat down on the camp-bed. 'I think I'm going to sleep well,' he announced.

Sunday morning in a provincial city. The streets practically deserted. The faithful going to or returning from Mass, shops with their shutters closed. Silence broken only by the distant sound of a church bell. A car stopped in front of the Palais de Justice and Roger Périès got out. He knew nothing of what had occurred during the night; Superintendent Sébeille had not wanted to disturb him. He had acted under the formal commission issued to him, deciding that it was pointless to get the magistrate up at midnight. He had therefore done no more than place the report of the confession on the magistrate's desk.

But the concierge, Simon Giraud, was on the look-out for him. 'Sir, it's done, we've got him to confess.'

It was an obvious surprise for Périès, who had come to the palace to confer with Sébeille, and make up his mind whether to charge the old man.

'The confession is on your desk,' added Giraud.

Périès hurried upstairs. He read the two typed pages at once without pausing to take off his overcoat. The improbabilities stood out, but also the patently true. He had first to know how the unexpected confession had been obtained. Giraud, immediately summoned, told him.

At about 9.30 Sébeille arrived at the palace. First he went to see Gaston Dominici. The old man looked tired. Tears came to his eyes when the superintendent asked him what sort of night he had had. Sébeille then went straight to the magistrate. Périès was blunt; the story in front of him was less than entirely convincing, which Sébeille readily conceded.

Only then did Périès go along to Gaston who was again in the library. He found him in an armchair which he had drawn up to the radiator. His legs were stretched out on a chair. He did not get up when the magistrate entered, unwilling in any circumstances to renounce the privileges of old age. With a motion of his hand he beckoned the magistrate to sit down beside him.

'I am not the murderer of the Drummonds,' he said without waiting to be questioned, 'but don't worry, I'll confirm what I told the superintendent; I want to save my grandchildren's honour.'

'I don't understand how by accusing yourself you save your grandchildren's honour,' Périès calmly replied. 'If their grandfather is the murderer, it's still a stain on the family.'

'I'm the oldest,' said Gaston. 'It's my duty to sacrifice myself.'

The magistrate persisted; he wasn't there to receive a confession intended to mislead justice. If Gaston knew the murderer, let him denounce him. If he was the murderer, let him say so as he had the evening before to Superintendents Sébeille and Prudhomme.

'I am not guilty,' Gaston repeated.

'Who is, then?'

'Try Gustave,' was the sly suggestion, only for the old man to go on immediately, 'Put it down that I'm the murderer.'

Périès refused. 'I'll leave you,' he said. 'Think it over. I'll be back soon.'

'If you won't draw up the document,' said Gaston, 'misfortune will come to Grand'Terre.'

Left alone, he did not move. An hour later, when Périès returned, the old man was still shiveringly huddled close to the radiator. The reek of strong tobacco had thickened. Gaston kept his eyes fixed on the magistrate as he came up to him. 'It's a terrible misfortune that's fallen on me,' he said.

'Tell me calmly how things happened,' the magistrate prompted. 'It's as I told the police,' said Gaston.

The story he told corresponded almost exactly with the one Sébeille had heard. However, certain details were different again, and as the statement drawn up by Périès is one of the very fundamentals of the case, it is essential to give it in full without omitting the crude details supplied by the old man. These indicate that the magistrate had arranged for Gaston's testimony to be taken down verbatim. He did, however, modify certain statements made to the superintendent; the one, for instance, bearing on the time Gaston declared that he had gone out. To Sébeille he had mentioned approximately 11.30 p.m. But one thing was certain: the crime had been committed at 1.0 a.m. This is why Gaston's deposition begins, 'I don't remember exactly at what time I left the house in the middle of the night.'

Then he reiterated that he had seen 'the English' earlier in the evening at Saint-Pons.

I chatted with the lady and the little girl a little before dusk in the part of Saint-Pons where I pasture my goats. The lady spoke French very badly, but the girl spoke it well; we talked about the beauty of the landscape. At the time the husband was reading a short distance away. A little later when I returned to the farm I noticed that the three had pitched their camp on the strip of flat ground at the edge of my property.

On leaving the house a little after the three-wheeler stopped at Grand'Terre, I took my carbine which was in the shed between two planks one above the other forming shelves, at the far end to the right. The clip was lying on it. I knew that it was fully loaded but I took two or three extra cartridges which were near by on the shelf.

I took the weapon because I hoped to find some badgers or rabbits. When I went out I intended to go and look at the state of the landslide, then try to do some shooting.

I took a course along my lucerne field towards the mulberry tree, near which the English people had camped. I noticed that the man was lying on a camp-bed alongside the car and seemed to be sleeping, while the woman was taking off her dress. As for the child, she wasn't in sight. I later learned that she was sleeping inside the car. From behind the mulberry tree I watched the woman undress. All at once I wanted to have her. I had put down the carbine a little before reaching the front of the car. The woman didn't seem frightened at seeing me. I at once stretched my hand out towards her ass. She didn't flinch. I didn't hesitate. I took out my cock. The woman lay down on the ground and I began having her.

We must have made some noise because the husband soon awoke. He got up angrily. I also got up and got my carbine. The man came at me. He tried to take away the gun. We struggled for a moment. We were then at the back of the car. The man got hold of the barrel. I don't know how a shot was fired without my intentionally pulling the trigger. I insist on this point, that the first shot was accidental. The bullet caught my opponent's hand but he still tried to seize me by the throat. As I realized that he was getting the better of me (I felt in fact that he was stronger), I fired a second time point blank. He ran away behind the car. I followed and as he was crossing the road I fired again, and he fell once and for all.

The woman began screaming. Turning towards her I fired in her direction. I don't remember whether it was once or twice. At that moment the child came out of the car by the rear door. She hardly cried out at all. She started running towards the railway bridge, taking a short-cut between the mulberry tree and the hedge. I followed her. I fired once, but missed; the second time as well. Then I noticed I had nothing left in the clip. I can't explain this, as I thought the clip was full. I must certainly have lost some cartridges on the way. I must also have lost the two or three I had put in my pocket.

I saw the child cross the bridge and run down the bank. I don't know how I caught her. When I did she was on her knees. She looked at me but didn't say anything. She didn't cry out. I took the carbine by the barrel and brought it down on her head. I was drunk. I no longer knew what I was doing. I was off my head.

I affirm that the carbine broke at the first blow. The child sank down without even a groan. I took a few steps to the Durance and threw my carbine into the stream. Afterwards I washed my hands which were covered with blood. To be exact, I got rid of the carbine at a place some twenty metres above where I had struck the child, in the direction of the farm. Then I retraced my steps. I could tell that the child was dead because she wasn't moving; it was after that I went to wash my hands.

Later I went back to the camp site to make sure that the parents were really dead. I covered the woman's body with a rug lying on the ground beside the car. Then I took a camp-bed and covered the man's body. I didn't examine either the inside of the car or the things scattered around it. I went back to my house again, taking the path which leads to the bridge. I crossed this, then turned right without looking at the place where the child lay. I followed and then crossed the railway line and returned to my farm by the lane ending in the courtyard.

It must have been half past two when I went to bed. At four I left with my flock of goats. I didn't see Gustave either when I returned to bed or when I left again. But not having succeeded in falling asleep, I heard Gustave go out three times. I declare that I have told nothing to anyone; neither Gustave nor Clovis know what I have done.

Roger Périès then showed the weapon to Gaston. He recognized it but could not say with certainty how and when he had bought it. He stated that this was the first time he had used it. It was not he who had mended it. He had only noticed that the handshield was missing and that an aluminium ring bound the barrel to the stock.

The magistrate had listened, limiting himself to 'translating' into clearer language whenever Gaston through lack of vocabulary or clumsy turn of phrase failed to express exactly what he had in mind. Spoken language is not the same as written. It is obvious that Gaston did not talk in such consistently formal, articulate sentences. It is a transcription by the magistrate who to some extent dictated the text to the clerk.

Gaston carefully read over the statement and signed it without any hint of dissent. When returning it – three typed pages – he said to the magistrate with a smile, 'I hope you understood me.'

'I think so,' Périès answered prudently.

'It's twenty years since I've got on with my wife. I'm too old to divorce. I've got an opportunity to get out of it. I'm not letting that slip.'

It was a disconcerting remark which the magistrate tried to probe, but without success. Gaston Dominici didn't elaborate. Had he really accused himself of a triple crime to get away from the woman with whom he had lived for forty years, or was it a subterfuge

designed to ridicule a confession which as a result no one would tak
seriously? Roger Périès contented himself with scrupulously record
ing it as an addition to the record.

Back in his office, the magistrate felt troubled. Despite the con
fession – or perhaps because of it – he hesitated to charge Gastor
Dominici. The Grand'Terre farmer had always shown such skill ir
confusing the issues that there was always the fear of his going bacl
on himself and leaving them all stranded again. He sent for Super
intendent Prudhomme and got a full account from him of the cir
cumstances in which Gaston had made his confession the evening
before. Then he decided to confront the old man with his two son
again.

Since their accusation against their father, Clovis and Gustave had
remained at the Palais de Justice waiting to be released. Througl
indiscreet remarks they had learned that Gaston had talked, bu
knew no particulars. When Périés told them what he had in mind
Gustave seemed terrified. Clovis bowed his head, face rumpled.

Gaston gave his sons a look of distant contempt. Elbows on the
arms of his chair, his aim was to intimidate them.

'Do you maintain that you told them nothing?' asked the magis
trate.

'Of course.'

'And you?' the magistrate addressed Clovis and Gustave in turn
Both held to their story of their father's own admissions to them
Gaston angrily called them liars and shit. Moreover, he declared
that he had never mended the rifle. It went on like that, with more
accusation and even more abusive denial. Périés did not interrup
the quarrel between the three. Their use of dialect often preventec
him from catching the exact meaning of the insults and invectives
He hoped that one or the other might let slip a phrase with some
further clue to the truth, for he well knew he was missing a part

'You told me at four in the morning of August 5th that you had
killed the English people,' Gustave yelled at the height of the storm

Gaston inflated his chest, jutted his chin at his son, allowed a
moment to pass in silence, then in a majestic voice responded, 'I
thank you, Monsieur Gustave.'

That was the end of the confrontation, as unproductive as the last
At 7.0 p.m. Clovis and Gustave left the palace. The latter now had
the burden of facing the family gathered at Grand'Terre. Gaston
settled in for the night. The magistrate announced that a reconstruc-

224

tion would take place the next day and only after this visit to the site would he decide whether to charge Gaston.

The magistrate had intended to go there himself in the course of the day, but had been discouraged by the heads of the gendarmerie. Headlines in the newspapers had revived public interest and, it being Sunday, a couple of thousand people were tramping the fields and the banks of the Durance near Grand'Terre. It was hopeless to try getting rid of them.

At 6.0 p.m. M. Harzic, the divisional superintendent, gave an official statement to the press. 'Late last night Gaston Dominici submitted a confession. But his explanations require further investigation.'

Very erect, with slow steps, leaning on his stick, his eyes straight ahead, Gaston Dominici walked to the entrance of his farm. Two gendarmes accompanied him after he had descended from the Citroën unaided. The sky was blue but cold. The area had been isolated since dawn. Route 96 was closed to traffic. Barriers had been set up five kilometres to either side of the place where fifteen months earlier the victims had met their deaths. Only the reporters were allowed inside the perimeter, and even they were kept at a distance. For the second time the Hillman resumed the position it had occupied on the fatal night.

Behind the old man came the group of police officers led by Sébeille and the man in charge of operations, Périès. They followed Gaston, who moved towards the courtyard, then the kitchen entrance. 'No,' Périès intervened, 'there's no use going in there. What interests us is what you did after you left the house.'

One thing that had worried the magistrate since he had received the confession was whether Gaston Dominici at 75 could have caught a child of ten running away in the night. As he had made clear in his day's official directive to the men on the job, that and the hiding-place of the carbine were what he now chiefly wanted to establish.

Gaston looked disappointed. But he continued towards the shed. He entered it, followed by the police officers and the magistrate, together with a photographer from the Identity Section. With raised stick Gaston pointed to the place where the carbine had been hidden – on the shelves. The magistrate ordered photographs to be taken. 'The place was the same as that designated by Clovis and Gustave Dominici,' wrote the magistrate in his report.

When the procession again came in view of the reporters, Gaston walked in front without the least sign of weariness or embarrassment. Périès interfered as little as possible; Dominici's actions must be spontaneous. It was he who knew what had happened and could demonstrate it.

They set off towards the strip of flat ground taking the path nearest to the Route Nationale, which accorded with his statement of the previous day. He passed by the fruit trees, ploughed through the freshly turned earth, hiding his face from the photographers with his hat. Then he proceeded between two rows of vines. On his left Sébeille carried the carbine, on his right walked Périès.

Gaston stopped near the mulberry tree, which stood exactly halfway between the railway bridge and the strip of flat ground. 'It's there I saw the woman,' he said.

'Take it,' said Sébeille, offering him the carbine.

The old man took it. Before him the view he claimed to have seen on the night had been reproduced. Only the victims were missing, and these the inspectors were to impersonate.

Gaston took a few steps forward and the spectators had the terrible impression of reliving the drama. He passed the mulberry tree and lay on the ground, about five metres in front of the car.

'It's here I had the woman,' he said when after a few moments he got up again.

Then he took up the carbine, which he had laid on the ground, and beckoned to Inspector Girolami. 'Take me by the throat,' Dominici ordered.

The inspector obeyed. The old man pointed the rifle at him. 'Take the muzzle,' he went on.

Girolami did so. The two men acted out a struggle, the inspector drawing back to throw a punch, Gaston releasing the weapon, then taking hold of it again. 'That's when the first shot happened,' he said.

Then he motioned Girolami to follow him to the back of the car. He pretended to fire a shot. After that he went to the left rear of the Hillman. 'I fired the third shot, the man was crossing the road.' He turned abruptly and pointed the rifle at the ground where Lady Drummond had lain. 'She went down on the spot,' he stated.

The magistrate noted a contradiction here. During his confession Gaston indicated that he had fired the second shot at Sir Jack from in front at point blank. But he had 'fired' at Inspector Girolami while the officer was fleeing – therefore neither from in front nor point blank. Furthermore he did not mention the Englishman tripping, which left entirely open the mystery of the shred of flesh on the bumper.

'Go on,' he said none the less.

Inspector Amédée had taken up position in the back of the car, awaiting Gaston's signal to rush out like Elizabeth. The old man conscientiously discharged his role as director. Holding the rifle in his left hand, he waved his right as starting signal. Inspector Amédée appeared and leaped to the ground.

He ran past Dominici, who corrected his course so that he grazed the mulberry tree, and reached the path leading to the bridge. Gaston took a few steps, sighted the carbine and pressed the trigger. 'It didn't fire,' he said.

He reloaded the carbine and aimed a second time at the officer, who was then level with the bridge.

'Now run,' Périès ordered.

But Gaston continued at walking pace.

'Weren't you going faster?' asked the magistrate.

'Yes, yes,' the old man snapped, suddenly irritable.

'Well, go at the same pace,' the magistrate urged. The old man's lack of eagerness was an encouraging sign to Périès; Gaston obviously disliked repeating the acts which had led to the most horrible episode of his crime.

'Go on,' the magistrate urged again. To him it was the major experiment; if it failed, the lawyers would have great fun with an examining magistrate who proclaimed an old man with weak legs the winner over a child of ten.

But he was not disappointed. The extraordinary scene that followed so startled its alert, professional witnesses that it left them all momentarily stunned.

With a sudden spurt Gaston darted in pursuit of Inspector Amédée, actually sprinting while holding the gun in one hand and his hat on his head with the other. His coat tails flew out behind him. Périès, like Sébeille, was stupefied by his speed and his lightning acceleration. He outstripped the magistrate and the officers who suddenly, without knowing why, felt a curious disquiet. The old man's wild dash was unnatural.

They caught up with Gaston at the entrance to the bridge and the old farmer put on another turn of speed. However, Sébeille followed close on his heels. 'Go on ahead,' cried Gaston, not the least winded.

He wants me to take the part of Elizabeth, thought the superintendent. He obeyed, passed Gaston and ran on in front of him. It was then that the old man made a swift turn in the direction of the parapet, surprising his pursuers and causing Sébeille to turn round to keep an eye on him.

Was it an involuntary mistake, to avert a stumble? No, since Gaston did not return to the centre of the path. He had swerved purposely. When he came to the parapet his intention became clear: to hurl himself over it and down on to the railway line five or six metres below. It was an attempt at suicide; Gaston Dominici could not face going through the motions he had described the day before of brandishing the gun over the child and bringing it down on her head.

The old man's decision was so unexpected and its execution so sudden that those present seemed paralysed. The first to react was Roger Périès, in the manner of the rugby player he had once been. He leaped on Gaston in a flying tackle and clutched the old man's coat just as he got his right leg over the bridge and was about to do the same with the left. Feeling his grip slowly loosening, the magistrate called for help. Inspector Girolami was the nearest. He ran up and seized Gaston's shoulders – the old man pleading, 'Let me go, that's a good lad.'

The brief moment enabled the others to recover their reflexes. They ran, Sébeille in the lead. Gaston was grasped from all sides. They drew him back to the path, where he stood up. The magistrate beckoned the gendarmes, saying, 'Keep close to him,' and to Gaston, who had resumed the expression he wore on his bad days, 'Don't try it again.'

They had grazed disaster. If Gaston had succumbed on the railway line, it would not only have been checkmate but a snub to justice and a public scandal. Périès at once regarded it as an irrevocable confession. To the magistrate Gaston Dominici had flinched from the test before him.

Slowly now Gaston Dominici walked to the bank. There was no need to make him run – his speed had been demonstrated. Surrounded by gendarmes who barred his way to the Durance, he stopped at the spot where the child had lain. Inspector Amédée took her place, kneeling amid the underbush and stones.

'How did you strike?' Périès asked. Gaston remained motionless, frozen to the spot; the magistrate persisted. 'You don't want to show us?'

The old man came to a decision. As the carbine was broken, he asked for his stick, which was given to him. He corrected the angle of the inspector's head, inclining it more with the pressure of his hand. 'Don't worry,' he said in Provençal, 'I won't strike.'

He raised the stick and brought it down violently in the direction of the police officer's head. He had, he said, struck only one blow. Escorted by the gendarmes, one of whom kept a firm grip on his shoulder, he pointed out where he had thrown the rifle into the river. 'Afterwards,' he said, 'I went to wash my hands in the little irrigation ditch running from my garden into the Durance.'

Returning to the camp site, he took the rug from the bonnet of the car, threw it over the supposed body of Lady Drummond, and crossed the road carrying the camp-bed which he placed on the spot where Sir Jack's body had lain. 'I was drunk,' he said.

Closely surrounded by his attendants, he then followed the path leading to Grand'Terre. 'Did you see Gustave?' asked Périès.

'No, nor at four when I left with the goats.'

As he drew near the farmhouse, he saw Paul Maillet who had been summoned in case he was needed. Wearing a cap with ear-flaps on his head and a canvas jacket, the linesman seemed overjoyed. He confided as he came up to Sébeille, whom he embraced to the officer's great embarrassment, that he had always been afraid of being suspected, but now he could breathe again. When Gaston saw him, he became enraged and tried to attack him. With difficulty, the gendarmes restrained him. 'Swine, murderer,' he shouted.

Sébeille motioned Maillet to leave. The linesman went off, Gaston glaring after him.

'Have you anything to say?' asked the magistrate.

'I acted in a moment of insanity,' Gaston replied.

The time had come for Roger Périès to make a decision. Gaston had repeated his acts and movements, and shown that he had full use of his legs. Moreover, the place where he claimed that he had fired at Sir Jack gave additional substance to his testimony. The Rock-Ola carbine ejects empty cartridges about three metres to the right and the empty case found near the body of Lady Drummond corresponded exactly with the firing point where Gaston Dominici had just stood.

Superintendent Sébeille also called the magistrate's attention to the way in which Gaston had operated the carbine. The gendarmes had twice discovered a cartridge that had been fired near one that had not. Sébeille at the time had deduced that the carbine, which reloaded automatically, had not been functioning well. The murderer must therefore have manipulated the bolt after each shot. Gaston had done that each time, going through the motion of reloading, as if it had been his old Gras shotgun which required the breech to be opened after every shot. This confirmed his statement that he had never used the carbine – or very seldom.

The motive was not yet clear. Neither Périès nor Sébeille believed Gaston's story that he had had sex with Lady Drummond. To Guérino, when he was talking freely, he had given another acceptable explanation – he had been taken for a thief. But obscurities still remained. The doctors had declared that Elizabeth had been killed while lying supine, her head on the ground, and had been struck by the gun-butt several times. Also, Lady Drummond had been hit by three bullets, not merely one. Finally, Sir Jack's position had definitely not been that which Gaston had made Inspector Girolami assume.

In the gendarmes' van which brought Gaston to the prison at Digne, Périès charged him with the three murders. Despite the gaps in the dossier, the magistrate was convinced of the old man's guilt. It should be pointed out here that in France an examining magistrate has sole responsibility for his decisions. He has to account to no one. No appeal is possible against a charge, a sovereign decision left to the discretion of the examining magistrate, considered by French professors of law 'the most powerful man in the country', since no control is exercised over any of his powers. Charged does not mean guilty, however, much less condemned.

Superintendent Sébeille was still not entirely satisfied; he wondered if Gustave's role hadn't been more important; not guilty of the crime itself, but perhaps a witness of it.

'And my dog?' asked Gaston before the van's doors were shut. 'Sébeille promised I could take him with me.'

'Dogs aren't taken to prison,' Périès answered drily.

It was a bitter look that Gaston gave his tormentors before the doors closed. As the vehicle drew away from them, Périés turned to Sébeille and held out his arms. The two embraced. It was 9.45. An hour later the van drew up in front of the Saint-Pierre Prison at Digne. Seventy-six years earlier Gaston Dominici had been born in a furnished room no more than metres away. Some fifty people were now gathered, shrilly demanding his death. The old man didn't seem to hear. He asked that his lawyers be notified, the first of them Maître Charles-Alfred of the Digne bar, who had always looked after his affairs. Then he went through the formalities of committal in silence.

In the Forcalquier cemetery various local officials deposited a wreath on the Drummonds' tomb bearing the inscription: 'The City of Forcalquier.'

On the morning of November 17 Sébeille awoke to fame. His name was in headlines as large as Dominici's. When he learned of Gaston's confession, the Minister of the Interior, M. Martinaud-Deplat, who was presiding at a banquet, rose with the words, 'I propose Sébeille for the next promotion in the Legion of Honour. I shall of course ask for his nomination as chief superintendent.'

More than ever he was the Maigret of Marseilles – even to the British press which hadn't handled him gently. The *Daily Express* offered honourable amends in a short leader: 'When after twelve months of fruitless investigation the inquiry into the Drummond affair was suspended there was lively criticism of the French police in England. For this reason Superintendent Sébeille compels general admiration and should be warmly congratulated.'

The Grand'Terre without Gaston Dominici was Grand'Terre without its soul. For thirty years Gaston had filled the farm with his presence. Even during his long silences his authority was felt. Everybody lived through him and for him, attentive to his wishes, adapting to his humours, respectful of his instructions, bowing their heads before his outbursts. Even Yvette had not been able to shake off the yoke.

A permanent family council remained in session. The Dominicis had never thought of their father as guilty, as a man who could massacre three people. They had never spoken of it because the idea had not occurred to them; besides, if they so much as mentioned the affair, Gaston shut them up. They obeyed, telling themselves that the subject must be painful for the old man, not because he had anything to do with it but because of the trouble it had brought. Now at a single blow they had just learned that the old man was under suspicion and that two members of the family had a hand in it.

It was not exactly a tribunal facing Gustave these evenings, but close to it. Augusta with her seething temper attacked first. 'Saturday morning, when you and Clovis came with the police, you shut yourselves up in the shed. Why?'

Gustave avoided her eyes. 'To show where the gun had been.'

'And did you?'

'Yes,' answered Gustave feebly.

'It wasn't there,' Augusta asserted with vigour.

It was a long time since she had left Grand'Terre. But she was certain that her father was innocent. Therefore the carbine had not been at the farm.

'It's Clovis,' said Gustave.

Under the watchful eyes of his brothers and sisters Gustave tried to justify himself. It was only under pressure from Clovis that he had agreed to reveal where the weapon was kept. They had been together in a room at the Palais de Justice, and Périès's clerk, while talking to them, had made a rapid sketch of the shed and shown it to Clovis. Clovis had put his finger on a spot when passing it to his brother. 'He said to me, "It was there. Say so like me."' And he had done just that, he had no choice. But only after Clovis.

So now it was Clovis who became the 'traitor'. It was not surprising, the family said, he was avenging himself on his father and the old stories surfaced again: the long estrangement because of his going to work on the railway, a bicycle incident, Gaston's refusal to make over a piece of land Clovis wanted.

Marcel Dominici, the farmer from Notre-Dames-des-Anges, decided to go and confront Clovis. He found him at home at Peyruis. Clovis received his brother coldly. He had made the accusation, he still made it, because it was the truth. The two men quarrelled violently. There was no longer any question of who had made the first denunciation; Clovis stood by his, while Gustave didn't; proof enough that the driving force had been Clovis. 'If you knew that Father was guilty,' snapped Marcel, 'why did you allow Gustave to be sentenced?'

'Because I thought the business would end there.'

Only Germaine Perrin, Roger's mother, took Clovis's side. For the others it was an additional reason to see the linesman's accusation as the settling of a score, for Germaine had long been on bad terms with her father. In the eyes of the Dominicis, Clovis was a swine, Germaine a worthless woman and Gustave a weakling, a rabbit, afraid of everything, who said what he was told to.

More than ever Grand'Terre became a citadel, and the Dominicis took turns watching from the battlements. Reporters in particular were kept at bay. They were spoken to only from a distance, although, since there was need of them, they did receive answers, usually belligerently yelled.

'Our father is innocent and Gustave was drugged,' Augusta Caillat shouted at Henri Danjou of *France-Soir*. Yvette backed her up. 'When he came to show where the gun was kept, he walked like a drunk.'

'They were chloroformed,' Clotilde yelled.

Gustave had his own story. If he had accused his father it was because he no longer knew what he was doing. 'Do you know what it means,' he stormed at Henri Danjou, 'to go thirty-six hours without food or drink, to be pushed about for four days and four nights? It drives you out of your mind. It's true that I signed, but they told me, "It's your father or you. He's old, he has no alternative. Do you want to end your life in prison?" '

So he pleaded cowardice. He had broken. But how about Clovis? And his father's confession? Gustave skirted that one. 'Believe me,' he said enigmatically, 'the truth will come out one day. It will surprise you.'

Clovis and his wife were no more forthcoming. They merely shrugged when Gustave's remarks were reported to them. The truth lay in the depositions of November 13. No one could do anything about that. 'I've had enough of it all,' Clovis sighed.

At Digne prison Gaston occupied cell No. 4, four metres by three, with an iron bed, a wooden table, a washstand and latrine bucket, and a dormer window high up which enabled him, if he could reach it, to see the Ganagobie foothills of the Alps.

On the morning of the 17th he received a visit from his lawyers. Maître Charles-Alfred had been joined by Maîtres Pierre Charrier and Emile Pollak. Both had defended Gustave at his trial for failure to render assistance. Pierre Charrier was, at 30, a tall and heavy man with a fleshy face. A militant Communist, he was friendly and outgoing with everyone. Above all, he was an enthusiast who, once he took up a cause, defended it with every ounce of his being. A glutton for work, devoting his nights to reading and re-reading files, seeking desperately between the lines the minutest argument to bolster his own, he found in the Dominici case a kind of technical ideal; almost every phrase could be turned round, interpreted, made to serve either side equally. Coming to the prison with a certain prejudice against his client after reading the newspapers, he listened to him. The old man's face was grey and his moustache drooping. He seemed overwhelmed. 'They've driven me nuts,' he said.

Listening to him, Pierre Charrier was somewhat more encouraged; the situation was not as calamitous as he had believed.

Emile Pollak, at 40, was already one of the luminaries of the Mediterranean bar. Sallow-skinned, with a helmet of thick grey hair tumbling to his neck in a style a decade ahead of its time, with impish grey eyes and a deep, slightly hoarse voice, Emile Pollak was one of those people gifted with a rare natural eloquence. This small, ironic man was a born advocate and had a prodigious talent for comedy. His speeches were dramatizations, he being at once the defendant, of course, the police officer who questioned him, the magistrate, the witness for the prosecution or the defence. Pollak pleading was a compelling figure. In his everyday life he was nonchalant – except at the racetrack. But when he put on his robes, still more when he had the floor, Emile Pollak was transformed, possessed by an inner force which inspired his every word and gesture.

After their first interview with Gaston the three lawyers drew up a letter for the magistrate in which their client asserted his innocence. Although the lawyers displayed extreme discretion, the rumour of Gaston's innocence got to the journalists.

'It's impossible for Gaston Dominici to retract,' Superintendent Harzic maintained.

November 24 brought a fresh sensation: Emile Pollak had suffered severe head injuries when his car collided with a van ten kilometres outside Aix-en-Provence.

Before resuming his inquiry, Périès took a few days' rest on the nearby Côte d'Azur. Then he again plunged into his study of the dossier putting aside the lawyers' letter which hadn't surprised him. A magistrate's examination basically consists of a clear and complete list of the charges, the possible means of defence, the clarification of obscure points, and searching out possible accomplices – in short, an extension of the police investigation, which is merely a prelude to the purely judicial inquiry.

The confessions were not completely satisfactory. Before hearing Gaston again, the magistrate wanted to clear up two things that troubled him – the origin of the weapon and the use made of it in the years preceding the crime, and the exact role of Gustave. It had become evident during scrutiny of the father's confession that the son had still lied. To the magistrate, it was plain that it was Gustave who had created the disorder around the car while looking for the missing cartridges.

Roger Périès first summoned Clovis, who had now become the pivot of the prosecution. Certain things in his deposition had to be ratified. For example, the magistrate was astounded that Clovis, after accusing his father, should deny having recognized the carbine

234

when Sébeille showed it to him. No one dreamed of blaming him for remaining silent for fifteen months, since the matter involved his father. But why deny that he had known the truth as early as August 7 or 8?

'I don't understand it myself,' admitted Clovis. 'I was completely confused after I had denounced my father. We had got into the habit of hiding so many things.'

Périès tried to find out just when Clovis no longer doubted Gaston's guilt: when he saw the weapon or when his father admitted it to him. Clovis could not answer. For a long time he had believed that 'Gustave had something to do with it.' But even after the discovery of the Rock-Ola, even after his father's confession, he could not conceive that an old man, however spry, could have committed such a crime. When Gaston told him that he had done in the English family, he had not dared ask for details of Elizabeth's death; he had a daughter the same age and it all seemed too horrible. He also wondered whether his father had not gone back for the gun after an initial quarrel with Sir Jack. He had first seen the carbine in 1951, when he was messing about Grand'Terre. It was in no way concealed. He did not think to ask where it had come from. It was already patched up. He had remained away from the farm for a good ten years because of a quarrel with his father, which explained why he was unaware of the weapon's presence before then.

Gustave was no more precise when he was questioned at the farm a few days later. In his opinion his father had bought the Rock-Ola from an American soldier, but he himself had been away in the Maquis when the Allied troops came through. He nevertheless confirmed the evidence of the mason Abel Bastide who claimed to have seen Gaston deep in conversation with an American soldier when the first troops went through. He had only discovered the weapon in 1951, Gustave said, but there was nothing surprising in that. Until that time his brother Aimé used the shed to store an old Amilcar he had bought. It was only after his marriage that Gustave had made use of it.

'When you saw it, you never asked your father what so heavy a weapon was for, even though you're a hunter?' asked the magistrate.

'He wouldn't have liked that,' Gustave replied. 'In fact, we never talked except to have a quarrel. He always treated me as a good-for-nothing and told me that if I didn't like it I could leave.'

He had never seen the gun in his father's hands. Did he use it when he went shooting? Gustave couldn't say. Yet as soon as he knew that his father was the murderer he had run to the shed to find out if the Rock-Ola was still there. Why this premonition when his normal reaction would have been concern about the old Gras shotgun, his father's favourite? The answer was vague; Gustave had not recognized the sound of the reports.

Périès's first probe was not a success; the mystery of the Rock-Ola remained unsolved.

Paul Maillet was once more with his 'friend' Superintendent Sébeille. He again gave the impression of reluctant co-operation. But Maillet had always doled out his information piecemeal, like a serial. Since the reconstruction he had dropped more than a hint here and there that he still had some instalments left, surely aware that this would eventually reach the police. Sébeille had got wind of it. Roger Périès commissioned him to find out if Paul Maillet really had anything worthwhile to tell; so far he had been productive, if at his own delayed pace. 'It's about Gustave I want to talk,' he was saying now.

He had only revealed part of the conversation he had had with the young farmer the year before when he went to Grand'Terre to buy potatoes. Gustave had confided to him that he had heard screams, one of the threads the police had subsequently followed up. But Maillet had failed to report the question he had next asked. 'Where were you?'

Gustave had answered, 'Out there in front.' He said it in dialect accompanied by a gesture indicating the lucerne field. The two men were standing under the big tree in the courtyard. The field separated the group of buildings from the orchard. If Paul Maillet was telling the truth, another lie now emerged, and one more illuminating than the others; Gustave had always insisted that at the moment of the crime he was in his room with Yvette, as terrified as she. If he was in the field, he could have witnessed the tragedy. This agreed, moreover, with words he had used to Maillet: 'If you had "seen", if you had heard the screams!'

The linesman declared that this time he had finished – he was squeezed dry, he had nothing more to tell. Mission accomplished, not without difficulty. 'This is the fifth time I've listened to you. You might have said all this earlier,' Sébeille chided.

Before the magistrate, Maillet tried to analyze and justify his behaviour. 'I should have been franker,' he acknowledged, 'but I was very upset. I realized that Gustave knew the murderer. I knew that he had cut across the field to go to the landslide. He told the police that he had followed the Route Nationale. That was strange in itself. Then he told me that the girl had moved. Finally that he had heard screams when he was in the field. So I thought he had seen the murderer but was afraid of denouncing him. I didn't dream of Gaston Dominici, but of someone who might have had something against Gustave.'

'Who?'

'No one in particular. But a man who might have been able to harm him. That's why I didn't say anything. I didn't want to force him into an accusation.'

'And you never suspected Gaston?'

Maillet was categoric. 'Neither him nor Gustave. We were friends. It never entered my mind.'

For Périès, Maillet's disclosure was of immense importance. It was not the first time Gustave had been forced to go back on his word, but this time it looked as if he was cornered.

A few days later Périès therefore had the two of them in at the same time, although he did not bring them together immediately or even let Gustave know that his former friend Maillet was there. The young farmer seemed very edgy, judging by his gaze which the magistrate was never able to meet.

When he heard the shots, he maintained, he had got up only to go to the window. He had seen nothing and gone back to bed. It was only at 4.0 a.m. that he had left his room, having heard his father's footsteps. Périès expressed his surprise; he had heard his father's steps at 4.0 but not at 1.0 after his crime?

'At night,' Gustave explained, 'he went round in slippers, but in the morning he put on heavy boots to go up the mountain.' He added that his father claimed that he often woke up after midnight and could not get to sleep again, so he got up and walked around.

'When you heard the screams,' asked the magistrate, 'you were in your room, not in the courtyard?'

Gustave opened his eyes wide. 'No . . .'

'Paul Maillet claims the opposite.' In a neutral voice the magistrate began to read the statement he had drawn up after hearing Maillet. Gustave reddened. He protested vehemently that it was untrue.

'But you did admit having heard the screams to Maillet.'

'Yes, but from the room.'

The clerk, Barras, went to fetch Paul Maillet, who appeared, leather cap in hand. Gustave pretended not to look at him. The clash between the two men soon became bitter. Paul Maillet stuck to it that Gustave had said the lucerne field.

'You didn't ask me where I was,' Gustave challenged.

'I did, in dialect.'

'You're a liar. I was in my room.'

Maillet shook his head; he remembered very well. Gustave had clearly pointed with his finger at the field. He could even recall thinking at the time that Gustave must have been very frightened. The idea that Gustave might himself be implicated in some way had not crossed his mind.

Périès excused Maillet, who left quickly. His wife was about to give birth.

A long silence followed between the magistrate and Gustave. The magistrate studied the farmer, who feigned an air of indifference without much success. Then Périès patiently went over the case from the beginning, tracing the steps which had led to the father's confession. Each push forward had come from a lie later admitted by Gustave. First where he had been when he had stopped Olivier. Next the movement of the child's arm. Then the bodies he had moved, the screams. He had denied, floundered, got deeper in, then come clean. Périès believed that Gustave was lying as always; he had been up when the shots were fired and not in his room.

Gustave listened, staring at the floor. From time to time he answered with a word, otherwise he remained in his familiar brooding silence. With Gustave it took time for him to submit to the truth, and especially to the idea that others knew it.

He finally made up his mind. 'All right, I'll tell you what happened.'

'I knew that my father was the murderer, not at four o'clock but at two. After the shots we didn't go back to sleep. At one-thirty Yvette gave Alain his bottle. Then we put out the light. Two o'clock had just struck when I heard footsteps in the courtyard. I was surprised because I had not heard my father go down. That's why I got up and went out.'

He had found Gaston standing in the courtyard near the well, watching him approach without moving. He seemed very agitated and Gustave even added that he was like he sometimes was after a dispute with his wife. He could not say how he was dressed but he must have been wearing shoes since he had heard his steps. He didn't have his stick.

'I asked him what he was doing at that hour and whether he had heard the shots. "Of course," he told me. "I fired them." '

Gustave then gave substantially the same account of the scene as when he had set it at 4.0 a.m. There were two variations: he had at once thought of the automatic carbine, but his father had not told him that he had taken it to look for game.

'I went off to the riverbank in a great fright, and it was then I saw the child move. I was appalled and didn't go near her. I went back to the camp site, saw the rug over the body and the camp-bed. I ran back to the house. The kitchen was lit up, I thought my father was there.'

But Gustave's urgent need at the moment was to confide in Yvette because she, despite her youth, was the stronger. 'I told her everything, she was very upset and cried, "We're ruined, what will become of us?" '

They had been unable to go back to sleep. At 5.0 Gustave had got up again and gone back to the camp site; it was then that he removed the rug covering the woman's body. He still said that he hadn't found any cartridges or cartridge cases.

'So your wife knew. How about your mother?'

'She never knew anything until my father's arrest.' He sighed. 'Even now she doesn't believe him guilty. Although I told her he was.'

Was it the whole truth? Périès still wasn't convinced. Who had created the disorder round the car? Why had Gustave moved Lady Drummond's body? Wasn't it to recover the still-missing cartridge cases? But on this point Gustave wouldn't budge. The disorder was not his work, it already existed at 5.0 a.m. He had seen no case or cartridge until after the arrival of the gendarmes.

'And the carbine?' inquired Périès.

'At five I went into the shed. It was no longer there. Nor the clip.'

He had never again spoken of the crime to his father. It was not indifference; he had simply lacked the courage. Oddly, he did not remember that Clovis had questioned him the day Sébeille showed him the rifle. On the other hand, Clovis had confided to him several times his suspicions of Paul Maillet. Périès was intrigued by this attempt at diversion; was Gustave implying that Paul Maillet was not after all in the clear? But Gustave would not be drawn again. Whenever Clovis tried out these hints on him, he said, he just kept his mouth shut, knowing what the true facts were. He still insisted that he had not been outside when he heard the screams.

The magistrate hadn't done too badly. He asked Gustave why he had kept silent until now. His answer afforded an insight into his psychology.

'Having seen my father so soon after the crime, and having gone to the spot at once, I was afraid of being involved. Yvette, especially, feared I might be considered an accomplice.'

Périès immediately decided to examine Yvette. Next morning found him at Grand'Terre, where his appearance caused consternation. Seating himself in the young couple's kitchen, he asked Yvette to remain with him. Gustave was absent, packing beans at the Lurs station with his brother Marcel and a friend. Périès sent a gendarme to get him, in the meantime questioning the young woman. Had Gustave told her what he had admitted the previous day? When she showed signs of hesitation, the magistrate wanted to know whether this meant that she thought Gustave had lied? Yvette gave in. Tearfully she admitted that she had lied from the beginning. But she couldn't have done otherwise. 'It was too hard,' she said.

For a year, she said, she had been living on her nerves, obsessed by her memory of that tragic night. They had heard the screams at the same time as the shots. They were in bed. Like her husband, then, she flatly contradicted Paul Maillet: Gustave was not in the lucerne field. But he got up at once. A quarter of an hour later he was back. 'He was reeling like a drunken man,' she said. 'He told me, "Father has killed the English people." I was overcome, while he kept repeating, "But why did he go down there?"'

He had gone back to bed but Yvette could only doze off for a few minutes, terrified by what had happened. When he finally got up for good, she did as well a moment after, and waited in the courtyard for him with his mother. When he returned this time, he told her that he had seen the little girl, her face all bloody. She could not remember how many times Gustave had gone back to the scene of the crime. She had never repeated to her mother-in-law what her husband had confided to her, had never so much as alluded to it with her father-in-law; altogether she talked to him as little as possible. On the morning of the 5th, Gustave had told her that Gaston had used the American carbine, which she had never seen. She had no interest in firearms.

'Did Gustave know why his father killed the Drummonds?' asked the magistrate.

'I didn't get that impression. We were careful not to talk about it.'

Gustave, brought back by the gendarmes and waiting in the courtyard, was now called into the kitchen. Périès briefly interviewed the couple together. They were in agreement. Gustave admitted that at 2.30 he had not wanted to tell his wife that the child was alive.

Périès left Grand'Terre with his clerk, the dossier enriched by a statement of great importance. Since the night of the crime Yvette, always the first to proclaim the innocence of her kin, had known the old man to be guilty. She could no longer charge the law with committing an offence in arresting him.

Never before had they come so close to the truth. That was why the young magistrate was determined to follow up his offensive, but strictly without publicity – no communiqué to the papers, no information for the correspondents on the spot. But when the journalists are given nothing to bite on they are apt to bite the hand which does not feed them. Criticism began to mount. Why did the magistrate let an accused person rot in prison? The lawyers made their own protest. Dominici had been crushed. To the entire world his name had become synonymous with monster. After Dracula and Frankenstein, Dominici. But his voice had not been allowed to be heard. Were they afraid of it?

Roger Périès refused to be diverted from his goal, although he did agree to talk to the journalists, giving them just enough to ensure their neutrality.

Before an all-out attack on Gaston, he wanted to get as far as he could with Gustave. He therefore limited himself to confronting the old man with Superintendent Prudhomme on the way his confession had been obtained. Gaston burst into laughter. 'It was a joke,' he said.

The magistrate reminded him that he had furnished some disconcerting details. 'I got them from the police,' Gaston declared.

Guérino came, Giraud as well, Sergeant Sabatier; Gaston was delighted. 'I was out of my mind,' he said.

He denied his confession in any shape or form – including the reconstruction. Prepared for this, Périès set out to arm himself to the full, with Gustave's help.

Was it likely, for example, that having seen the child lying on the bank at 2.30 the young farmer had not gone up to her? Was his explanation satisfactory about the moving of Lady Drummond's body? Lastly, was he or was he not in the lucerne field? Paul Maillet hadn't previously lied. Périès was sure he was not lying now, and that Gustave had admitted to him that he had been in the field. But who had seen Gustave? And what was the motive for all his lies? Was it to hide his part in his father's crime?

Périès spent a week re-reading the dossier, undergoing the same torments as Sébeille had previously. The Dominici affair became an obsession to whoever engaged in it. There were so many dead ends. The gun, for instance, which never emerged until the crime, which no one had used and which even Clovis, the most straightforward, knew little about – a gun which was mended even though it lay idle on a shelf. Or Gustave's comings and goings in the night. Or the blows which finished off the child, her last hours, the precise moment at which she stopped breathing. The magistrate caught himself in the night reciting extracts from the statements. Like Sébeille.

The magistrate let Christmas go by before launching his final offensive. In his Digne prison a despondent Gaston bought a litre of wine in the canteen. He paid 64 francs of the period – sheer robbery, he declared. He had always drunk free, his wine costing him only his hours of labour.

At Grand'Terre the holiday was sad. For the first time in twenty years the patriarch was absent. The songs had not been sung, the dinner had been eaten and the wine drunk without gaiety. Visits had been exchanged, but Clovis had not come, nor Germaine Perrin. Gustave was again told that he had been framed. He did not answer. Very soon he retired with Yvette.

On the morning of the 28th the gendarmes came for him. He was now used to it and let himself be taken away without a word. Half an hour later he was in the magistrate's study. 'Do you still maintain that you were in your room when you heard the screams?' the magistrate asked.

'Yes.'

'You heard the shots. We now know that they frightened you. You didn't go to your father to know what he thought?'

'No.'

'But you went out the moment it was all over?'

'Only because I heard my father walking round the courtyard.'

The magistrate then tried to pin him down to exactly what he had seen in the course of his successive visits to the camp site; where were the camp-beds, the rugs, the bodies? It was a difficult task because Gustave was on the defensive, careful to avoid any detail which might lead the magistrate to infer that he had moved anything.

'Listen, Gustave,' the magistrate at last said impatiently, 'let's not play about any more. I'll tell you what I think. You say you didn't go near the child when you heard her death rattle because you were afraid of trouble. But it was two in the morning, the dead of night. Yet at seven, when you might have been surprised at any moment, you cold-bloodedly moved a body. Make up your mind to tell me the truth. Why did you take such a risk?'

But neither this nor any other reasoning could make Gustave face up to the question. He still wondered, he replied with complete serenity, why he moved the body. It certainly was not to look for cartridges or cartridge cases. What had become of the missing ones? Gustave then offered a suggestion which the magistrate registered with a certain satisfaction, for it was additional evidence against the father straight out of the mouth of the son. Gustave had heard his father-in-law, Louis Barth, say that Gaston Dominici had collected four cartridges. It was at a time before the old man was yet under suspicion. The admission must have come from him. A fragment of truth tossed off, most likely, after one glass too many. But for Pérèis it was another piece of the puzzle. The old man had himself done the 'clearing up', then Gustave had taken over.

He swore to the magistrate that he had told the whole truth on December 17. He seemed exhausted. For sixteen months he had been the chief butt, the one exposed to all the shocks, baited by the enemy, told off by his family whenever he showed a sign of weakness, now despised by them for having handed over the keys of the city. Périès did not neglect to turn the knife in this most sensitive spot. 'Did you tell your family that you learned of your father's guilt from Clovis?'

It was while interrogating Aimé Dominici, the brother who worked on a farm in the Bouches-du-Rhône, that Sébeille had come upon this fact. Aimé had stated that Gustave, on his return from Digne on November 17, had justified himself at Clovis's expense.

The magistrate's question embarrassed him terribly. He would have liked to conceal the actual state of affairs at Grand'Terre, the false situation in which he found himself, accusing his father to the magistrate, then joining the family chorus in proclaiming his innocence. 'Yes,' he admitted faintly.

He described the tribunal he found himself before on the evening of November 15. 'All my sisters were there. They bawled me out for hours. They asked me if I was out of my mind.' He had then blamed Clovis for all their ills. Later he had tried to convince his sisters that their father had after all confessed his crime to him. 'But,' he said, discouraged, 'they still didn't want to believe it.'

Périès released Gustave shortly after noon. He had not got much out of him and gave the journalists a gloomy look when Sébeille, returned from a journey through the Basses-Alpes, came to make his report. He had followed up a number of tips that had come in about the weapon; the game hunters might have seen it in the hands of this one or that one, but everything led to a dead end. The magistrate decided to fix the date for the grand confrontation; it was to be on December 30. Afterwards would come another holiday break, the beginning of the New Year. It was no longer possible to turn a deaf ear to the lawyers, among them Emile Pollak who was back, although still suffering from his terrible accident. A whole day was set aside. Measures were taken to put the Palais de Justice under a state of siege.

In his cell, Gaston dictated a letter to Father Lorenzi, the hermit of Ganagobie. 'Write to the magistrate,' he petitioned the monk. 'Testify for me.'

But to a reporter who interviewed him Father Lorenzi said with a sigh that he knew nothing about the case. 'What does he want me to tell the magistrate?'

Dressed in his brown velvet suit and flanked by two gendarmes, Gaston Dominici seemed quite at his ease when, on leaving the Digne prison, he had to face the journalists gathered outside the door. He saluted them with a sweep of his faded hat, greeted the photographers with a playful 'See you tomorrow.' Then he climbed into the van which took him to the Palais de Justice. Meanwhile his two sons made their way independently. Clovis came by train, then on foot from the station, Gustave by a bus which broke down, a photographer from Forcalquier bringing him the rest of the way.

Périès first called in Gaston, who seemed much cheered now that he was surrounded by the three lawyers. The old man immediately repudiated his earlier statements. He had risen only at 4.0 a.m. to take his goats up the mountain. He had only learned of the crime on his return at about 8.0. Impassive, the magistrate made a note of this retraction. 'Still,' he remarked, 'you did confess.'

'Because I was done in.'

'You repeated your confession several times, even after you had rested and eaten.'

Gaston shrugged. 'The police officers dinned into my ears that I wasn't risking much, while Gustave might have his head cut off.'

'And the reconstruction, Gaston Dominici? You repeated your actions. Without constraint, after all.'

With a wave of his hand Gustave dismissed all that. 'I didn't know what I was doing any more,' he said. 'I was so pushed around I wanted to commit suicide.'

'Your sons accuse you,' Périès went on. 'Gustave in the first place.'

The old man's face quivered with rage. 'Bring him along,' he roared. 'I'll make him shiver and sweat.'

Périès ordered Gustave to be brought in. He appeared, pallid and shrivelled, under his father's mocking stare. The magistrate made him sit down. The young farmer was conscious of his father's lawyers stirring behind him; the idea that they were to be witnesses of his 'cowardice' was unbearable. The magistrate began by reading from beginning to end the accusations he had made against his father. 'Do you confirm them?' he asked.

A long silence followed the question, which the magistrate calmly repeated. Gustave shook his head. 'No,' he said.

'You made them six times. Even to me three days ago.'

'I lied to you.'

Périès turned to Gaston. He had in turn accused his son; what would he say today? The old man's face lit up with joy. 'I never said he did the killing,' he returned, and then in a dispassionate tone, 'He's only got to tell the truth.'

Emile Pollak intervened in a honeyed voice. Since Gustave no longer sustained his accusation, it would be interesting to know how he now accounted for his own time. It was a counter-offensive whose object was plain to everyone; if in absolving his father Gustave persisted in saying that he was out of doors at 2.30, what was he doing there? Was he or wasn't he in the lucerne field? Maître Pierre Charrier came to his support; to put these questions was perhaps to solve the Lurs riddle. Roger Périès refused, this was not the time to embark on this particular road. He had never dealt lightly with Gustave, but the present problem did not centre on him. The magistrate had in his hand a dossier containing admissions and accusations. The defendant had retracted and one of the witnesses had done the same. At the moment logic required that they go on to the end and see if the second pillar of the accusation still stood up.

'Allow me, however, to put one question,' Emile Pollak insisted. 'Why did Gustave persist in accusing his father to the examining magistrate?'

'I couldn't do anything else,' answered Gustave. 'I had been too pressed by the police.'

'Why did you retract only today?'

'Because there are witnesses to hear me.'

This could mean either that he was happy to proclaim his father's innocence publicly or that he was intimidated by the lawyers' presence. Gaston in any event was delighted and at once forgave his son. 'They treated him as they did me,' he said. 'He's as innocent as I am.'

The situation was suddenly reversed; it was now the magistrate who faced determined enemies – father and son supported by lawyers of talent and energy. He could look for help only from Clovis. What would the linesman, who had replaced Gustave in the study, say?

Solid, high-coloured, rough-voiced, he did not by so much as a comma alter what he had already said. His father was guilty.

Gaston exploded. 'Dirty swine,' he snarled, 'Judas! If there was a carbine at Grand'Terre it was you who brought it there.'

Clovis exploded as venomously. 'You've tormented us long enough,' he snarled back.

Father and son faced each other furiously. 'You didn't turn your nose up at a murderer's wine,' shouted Gaston.

'I'd planted the vines,' retorted Clovis.

Magistrate and lawyers seized on this outburst, the one to emphasize that Clovis was only telling the truth, the others to argue that it was a desire for revenge which inspired the son's denunciation.

'You'll never make us believe,' one of the lawyers put it to Clovis, 'that you didn't ask Gustave who had used the carbine when you noticed it missing from the shed.'

'I didn't want to know,' murmured Clovis.

He stood up to the lawyers as firmly as his brother had to the magistrate. Périès let him go. To escape the photographers, Clovis left by the palace window. At 2.0 p.m. the deputy prosecutor, M. Pagès, read to the newsmen a memorandum on Gustave's retraction and Clovis's inflexibility. The former was remaining at the palace. He would have been let go if he had maintained his accusation, the lawyers for the defence stressed. Father and son had lunch where they were, Gaston the prison menu, Gustave dishes from a nearby restaurant.

In the afternoon the old man was taken back to his cell. Gustave was visited by Sébeille, who reproached him for his conduct – who was he kidding? A mystery persists about the interview which the lawyers later denounced as inadmissible pressure. Around 6.0 p.m. Périès returned from the prison and sent for Gustave, who had passed long hours in the lawyers' robing room which had been requisitioned for the purpose.

'You retracted this morning,' said the magistrate. 'Do you still?'

'No,' Gustave answered feebly.

'Did your father tell you he had done the killing or didn't he?'

'He told me.'

'Why did you deny it this morning?'

'In front of him I didn't have the courage.' And he added, 'It is painful to accuse one's father. Put yourself in my place.'

Périès cut the interview short. Gustave seemed to him sincere when he spoke like this. The magistrate did attempt, however, to obtain an admission from him that he had been outside when the crime was committed. But Gustave still insisted that he had only learned of it about half an hour afterwards. He begged the magistrate not to confront him with his father again.

The magistrate dismissed him, with the offer of a taxi to take him back to Grand'Terre. The waiting journalists had earned the young magistrate's good wishes as he told them that the examination would not be resumed until after the New Year. A chapter was closed. The special correspondents sent out their last copy of 1953 before leaving by road or rail to rejoin their families for the holiday. At Grand'Terre, Gustave answered in monosyllables his sisters' uneasy questions about what had occurred. At the prison in Digne, Gaston informed a young guard, 'Son, by spring I'll have my farm back.' The guard did not challenge the statement. It was not part of his duties to do so.

The Trial

9

Périès held in his hand a letter written on graph paper. Only a few lines, but with very definite significance for the magistrate. 'Dear Papa,' he read, 'forgive me, I too am suffering terribly. I think of you more than ever and promise you to be strong and tell the truth even in the face of threats. The truth must come to light.' It was signed 'Gustave'. The clumsy writing was almost shaky.

The letter came into Périès's hands quite normally. In French prisons, as in those of most countries, censorship is standard practice, the obvious object being to prevent the smuggling in or out of forbidden material such as escape plans, for instance, or something revealing about the case itself of which the magistrate has the right to be informed.

Having himself spent two months in prison, Gustave was not unaware of this practice. He had nevertheless sent his letter by mail. So he knew that sooner or later it would fall into the magistrate's hands, which could well lead Périès to wonder if it wasn't in fact intended for him. No one could say that Gustave had been influenced by the sight of his father, for they had not seen each other since December 30. The envelope was stamped January 19.

Through the good offices of the prison administration Gaston had just made a journey to Marseilles. Its object was a psychiatric examination, required procedure in such a case. Professors Jean Roger and Henri Alliez, as well as the head of the psychiatric wing of the Timone hospital, Pierre Merlan, had conducted it. They had found no mental defect or illness in the old man. In their opinion Gaston Dominici had attained old age in a remarkable state of psychological health. He was perfectly normal, complete master of himself. Gaston had returned to the Digne prison very satisfied with their certificate, even if one day it might be cited against him.

Gaston was doyen of the prison establishment, but that gave him no special privileges except that it ensured that he was warm and had enough blankets. His appetite was good, his food augmented by parcels of bacon, sausages and sweetmeats from his children. He put on weight. He felt better, the reduction in his daily intake of wine being largely responsible for this improvement. He slept eleven hours a night, emerging from his blankets at eight o'clock when coffee was brought him. He read a good deal. The first book he borrowed from the library was *Robinson Crusoe*.

Périès devoted the first two weeks of January to clearing up the other business in his office, especially the air disaster on which he had also been working. He wanted his mind free to concentrate entirely on the Lurs dossier.

To Anglo-Saxon observers not specialists in French law the examining magistrate is a character with an ambiguous role. In England and the United States he does not exist.

The examining magistrate's function is to take over the police dossier, put it into shape, clear up obscure points, translate charges and presumptions into legal language and, at the end of this, say whether the person brought before him falls within the purview of the law, the exact assessment of his guilt being ultimately a matter for the jury. Representing society and not merely the machinery of justice, the examining magistrate is in principle neither in one camp nor the other. Despite a widespread belief, he is not an extension of the police. He may take up a dossier and dismiss the charges as unsubstantiated. His conclusions may well contradict the report of the investigators from A to Z. In that case he withholds a true bill, a very common occurrence. Frequently police officers complain of not being backed up by such and such a magistrate, so blind he can't see guilt in a man they have brought before him. Conversely, the magistrate is often accused by the lawyers of 'covering up' for the police. Despite his very wide powers, he has little room for manœuvre. Granted absolute independence by the French Code, the magistrate must be watchful both to left and right, concerned with a sole objective – the whole truth.

No criticism, even veiled, has ever been made of Roger Périès's honesty and integrity. He was an upright and sincere man whom lawyers liked to work with, since he never jolted them with unpleasant surprises. He applied the law strictly according to procedure. In his interrogations and confrontations he strove to keep an even balance.

It was for him alone to complete the dossier and put it in order.

An examining magistrate's task is very different from a police officer's. Sébeille worked with a team, assisted by many colleagues, with the material resources and facilities of a criminal investigation service at his disposal. The judiciary in France is much less well treated. In 1954 there were many palaces of justice in which two or three telephones had to serve twenty or thirty magistrates. A typewriter was a rare luxury. If a magistrate didn't own a car, he used whatever police transport might be available. Often it was the nearest superintendent who gave him a lift.

Périès therefore had to count on himself. He worked alone, issuing formal commissions only in matters of detail to Sébeille, who was now engaged in other investigations. The superintendent was also slightly bitter. After his grand triumph in November, he was all but forgotten. Sébeille of course realized that they were waiting for the trial and didn't want to honour him before the verdict, to avoid the lawyers saying that Dominici had been judged even before being brought before a jury. But Sébeille felt that the atmosphere had changed.

At Grand'Terre the silence was greater than ever. Yvette's father, Louis Barth, managed the farm, his authority now similar to that of the prisoner at Digne. The Dominicis rarely showed themselves in public. The clan closed in on itself. There were frequent reunions but nothing of them was divulged. Gustave avoided even his friends. He answered no questions, quickly shook hands and disappeared without a word. The farm had become an enclosure, and strangers were no longer welcome. Those who didn't support their cause, such as Clovis and Germaine, were banished. None of the children would concede even the possibility of their father's guilt. Affection, a primitive sense of honour, desire to save their name, sorrow at seeing so hard-working a father in prison combined to unite them more than all the years of modest prosperity had.

Reading the letter, Périès had no doubt that if Gustave seemed to waver it was because of his family's assaults upon him. He called him in again, this time on February 4. Clovis was also asked to keep himself available.

The magistrate handed Gustave the letter. 'Would you explain clearly,' he said, 'whether you do or don't maintain your accusation.'

'No,' Gustave answered. Even his bearing had changed. He was no longer a man cruelly at a loss, trembling at the sound of his own voice, fearful of questions. 'It's the first time I've written my father,'

253

he went on. 'I wanted him to know that I had lied. As a matter of fact, I don't know anything about the matter.'

The young farmer went back on all his statements. His father had never told him that he had fired the shots. He had not known the carbine and had never seen it in the shed. He had first seen it when Sébeille showed it to him on the morning of August 6. The truth was contained in his first statements, which the magistrate patiently made him repeat in detail, testing Gustave's sincerity. But Gustave had learned his lesson well.

Gustave returned to his version of August 1952, speaking as if nothing had happened since. The confrontation with Olivier which had led to the first admission was forgotten, as well as the testimony of Ricard and the change in the position of the body, Maillet's statement and the screams heard, and Roger Perrin's declarations. All was wiped out.

'You are again contradicting all the other witnesses,' the magistrate said finally.

Gustave didn't deny it. Nor was he impressed by it; behind him, an invisible power which protected and defended him, he felt the presence of the family. He had been duped, but that was in the past.

'You spoke in your letter of threats,' observed the magistrate. 'What threats?'

'The police.'

'Did they strike you?'

'They said, "You'll have your head cut off." '

'And that was enough for you to accuse your father?'

'It lasted two hours.'

'Granted. But later you came before me. Did I threaten you?'

'You always spoke to me properly.' He even added, 'Like a brother.'

'Yet you told me the same as you did the police.'

'I was afraid of going to prison if I said different,' asserted Gustave.

The magistrate persisted. Had he for one moment implied that Gustave, if he retracted, would find himself back in prison? By a word or phrase hinted at any such thing?

'No,' Gustave acknowledged.

Périès rediscovered the former Gustave, clinging to a reply like a handhold he would not let go. It was impossible to dislodge him; he would prefer to let himself be killed on the spot.

'This letter,' said the magistrate, 'you knew I would read it.'

'Yes.'

'In fact, you meant it for me.'

'For my father.'

Word for word, like a record stuck in a groove, he repeated what he had said at the beginning; he wanted his father to know he had lied. Périès held up his hand to stop him. The time had come to bring in Clovis.

When he entered, Gustave changed. His self-assurance weakened, his shoulders drooped, and he turned his face away to avoid meeting his brother's eyes. In contrast, Clovis held himself erect, sturdy, resolute, although his heart was heavy because of what he had heard from his family or through public rumour. Clovis knew what they had said about him, and his resentment burst out as soon as Périès informed him of the conversation he had just had with Gustave.

'Have you anything you'd like to say?' asked the magistrate.

'The whole family's been ganging up on Gustave,' Clovis complained.

He wasn't surprised by the about face. He drew a letter from his pocket, sent to him by his brother Gaston, the level-crossing-keeper, who insisted that he stop accusing their father.

'Where do you stand now?' asked the magistrate.

'Where I did,' replied Clovis. 'My father is guilty.'

His face suddenly darkened. He would have preferred not to utter the sentence again. But he wasn't prolonging the agony. It was the obstinacy of his brothers and sisters that forced him to these harrowing repetitions.

'When you first noticed the disappearance of the carbine, did you in fact have a conversation with your brother?'

'Yes.'

'Well, Gustave?' Périès queried.

Gustave slowly raised his head. Encountering the combined gaze of his brother and the magistrate, he said nothing.

'Is Clovis lying?' pressed the magistrate.

Gustave shook his head. 'No.'

'Then why did you say a little while ago that you had never seen the carbine?'

'I was lying,' came the mumbled answer.

'Then you had seen that carbine?'

'Once, after my brother Aimé's marriage.'

With Clovis's help, Périès began again.

'Your brother then asked you if you were the murderer. You said no. Did you have the impression that his suspicions no longer existed?'

Gustave gave a surprising answer. 'I never thought that Clovis suspected me.'

'But you think he was the murderer?' the magistrate asked Clovis.

The linesman shook his head, his reply astonishing the magistrate even more. 'There's one thing comes back to me,' he said, 'which I never mentioned until now.'

It was this, he went on: on August 7 or 8 Gustave had told him that their father had done the killing. But he didn't take what he said seriously. It seemed to him impossible that an old man should commit such an act. So Clovis had continued to suspect Gustave. He hadn't pressed the matter; he didn't know what to say, didn't dare discuss it with Gustave, fearing that the shameful and terrifying truth would blow up in his face. The lawyers were to tear into this unexpected revival of memory. Imagine Clovis discovering that his father was the killer and conveniently forgetting it for eighteen months! Gustave had been bitterly reproached for his lapses of memory. Didn't Clovis deserve the same treatment?

Périès raised the objection at once. Why had Clovis delayed so long?

'Because,' he answered, 'I didn't think of my father's guilt until he confessed it to me.'

'Clovis is right,' Gustave corroborated. 'It must have been that day that I told him Father had done the killing.'

For the magistrate it was quite a victory, since Gustave, who on entering his study totally denied everything, now went farther than ever. Almost from the first hour he had shared the secret with Clovis. Having come in intending to wipe out his entire testimony, he had not only confirmed it but had added to it.

It was 7.0 p.m., and Roger Périès, having no further need of Clovis, dismissed him, remaining alone with Gustave, who looked more wretched than ever. The magistrate wasn't yet finished with him, and when he released Gustave, another torment awaited him; how to justify such an utter defeat to his brothers and sisters. Acquitted by the improvised tribunal at Grand'Terre, he had relapsed. Gustave was simultaneously answerable to two systems of justice with conflicting demands – a difficult position if ever there was one.

Roger Périès did not deal gently with his witness. 'Your behaviour is absolutely inconceivable,' he began. 'One could to some extent understand your contradictions before November 15th.

But since your father's confession they're unacceptable.'

The magistrate carefully listed Gustave's admissions and denials, according to whether he was in his father's presence or his brother's. 'I just wish I understood you,' the magistrate sighed.

His words overcame Gustave's last resistance. He was almost pitiable, close to tears. 'They pestered me so,' he said. Then, like a lament, 'No one will believe me. I don't know any more where I am.'

'Was it your brothers and sisters who made you write the letter?'

'No,' said Gustave. 'It was my idea.'

Since his father's arrest, he went on, he thought of him constantly. Despite rebuffs, outbursts of anger, and the contempt lavished on him, Gustave had retained an affection for the old man. Gaston's power of work still aroused admiration in Gustave, who recognized that Gaston had exerted himself entirely for his family. This was why he hated accusing him, it was beyond his strength. In any event, he would never have the courage to repeat in his presence what he had heard on the morning of August 5. It would be perfectly useless for Périès to subject him to that ordeal again. Périès could easily promise not to; the result of such a confrontation was obvious.

Gustave left the magistrate's office distinctly cowed. Not only had he failed to discharge the mission with which he had been entrusted, but he had left new weapons with the enemy. He would not return to a hero's welcome at Grand'Terre. He was in no doubt about that.

Gustave found no difficulty in saying in the street the exact opposite of what he had stated in Périès's office. It was the magistrate who suffered later from the air pockets in which the truth suddenly plunged. When the magistrate learned from a press agency report that Gustave, meeting a journalist, had assured him that his father was innocent and that he had been forced to accuse him, only following his brother Clovis in this, Périès had had enough. He sent some gendarmes to bring in the Grand'Terre farmer. It hadn't been two weeks since Gustave had confirmed his accusations.

The magistrate did not waste time on cordiality. 'Gustave, you're talking without rhyme or reason and it's got to stop. Is it true that you told your brothers and sisters that you had only accused your father after Clovis had?'

'Yes.'

'You know very well it's a lie.'

Gustave shook his head. And the explanation he now gave for the first time surprised the magistrate. It was a fairly skilful attempt to justify his zigzag course. It is unlikely that Gustave thought it up himself.

'I told the family that I had accused my father only because Clovis had told me of his conversation with him while I was in prison.'

Périès reflected a moment, halted by this unexpected reply. Quickly, however, he pounced on the improbability: Gustave had admitted to him that he had told his immediate family of his father's confession on August 5. Therefore he could not have told his brothers and sisters that he had not known of Gaston's guilt before his conversation with Clovis. 'Once again,' the magistrate pronounced, 'your answer is worthless.'

Gustave knitted his brows and his face assumed the mulish look which Périès now knew well. He went on to ask if Gustave had indeed said this to his family.

'Yes,' he finally admitted, 'but no one believed me.'

'So,' said Périès ironically, 'since no one believed you, you ended up not even believing yourself.'

He was not altogether joking. His thrust provided quite a good picture of Gustave oscillating between one side and the other. Gustave immediately adopted it, apparently delighted to be so well understood. 'My sisters kept saying I must not accuse our father,' he said. 'In their eyes he is innocent.'

'And in yours?'

Gustave looked thoroughly perplexed. 'Mine?' he asked at length. Then he suddenly made up his mind. 'I've been wondering whether he's guilty or not.'

'He told you he was,' said the magistrate irritably.

'Maybe he was drunk.'

'Had he been drinking?'

'I don't know. But he acted like he did when he'd had a glass too many.' Without leaving time for interruption, Gustave added, 'In all his letters he writes that he's innocent. How can you expect me to accuse him?'

Summoning all his patience, the magistrate tried to show Gustave how his new attitude could rapidly become untenable. Had he not told his family that he had seen the carbine, thus confirming the rest of his statement?

'That's so,' said Gustave. 'But I still wonder how it got into the shed.'

'Wasn't it your father's?'

'I don't know, I never spoke to him about it.' He added that the others thought he was mad; none of them had seen the weapon. Another question from Périès: had he or had he not heard the shots and what had he done? Gustave shamelessly answered that he had gone to bed and not left it. Was it going to be necessary to recall Olivier, Ricard, Maillet – all those who had overcome Gustave's obstinacy, start again, pick up one by one the everlastingly dropped stitches? Périès chose another method: to record this retraction as scrupulously as the others, adding another play of light to the distorting mirror Gustave used to blind the enemy.

When Périès had read and signed the draft, he passed the statement over to Gustave for him to initial. It was the last time he saw him before the trial.

'The troubles always come from the same quarter . . .

The magistrate read and re-read the sentence, written with a practised pen, on a sheet of graph paper. At the top was the name Gaston Dominici and his address – the Digne prison, stamped to certify its origin. The prisoner hadn't written it. He had dictated it to a guard, and signed with clumsy letters. It was addressed to his daughter Clotilde Araman, his most passionate defender after Augusta Caillat. But he, like Gustave, was well aware that Périès would read the letter before she did. So he was writing the letter to the magistrate as well. 'Tell the truth without hesitation,' it ended.

Périès accepted the obvious invitation. Whatever truth he obtained from Clotilde would be interesting when compared with the others.

Clotilde was a woman of 42, strongly built, with a determined face. She didn't hesitate in explaining to the magistrate the 'bad side' of the family. 'It's Germaine,' she said at once. 'She has never loved us, neither us nor our father.'

'How could the trouble come from her, at least on this occasion?' Périès asked.

Clotilde's answer lacked clarity. Certainly her father was alluding to past quarrels, to the fallings out which Germaine tried to blame on him but which she was responsible for. Périès remarked that these conflicts interested him only in so far as they were connected with the crime and Gaston's arrest. Clotilde dodged; she didn't know anything about that except that Germaine's son Roger was a 'half-wit'. Did he have anything to do with the killings? Clotilde refused to commit herself.

Périès remembered a letter she had sent to her father in the early days of his imprisonment. She had written him that 'he had arrested one murderer and was about to arrest another.' Was she urging him to denounce some guilty person?

Clotilde's reply was no clearer than the first. She had been misunderstood or had expressed herself badly. She merely meant that if her father could have brought about the arrest of a second murderer, he would certainly have done so – an allusion to Gaston's hour of glory when he had once intercepted a murderer.

'So he can't accuse anybody?' the magistrate concluded.

'Ask him,' answered Clotilde.

Which is what Périès did a few days later, having ordered Gaston to be brought before him. The old man seemed in excellent form, cheerful, unshakable, sure of himself, repeating firmly that he had nothing to do with the affair.

'Gustave has again accused you,' said the magistrate.

Gaston shrugged. 'Bring him here, I'll make him shake in his shoes.'

The same old questions were asked by Périès, who had the sensation of going round in circles. To whom had the carbine belonged? 'Why not to Clovis?' the old man returned. And when the magistrate pressed him to say on what he based this, Gaston replied that it was not up to him to cast light on the subject.

The magistrate came to the letter, asking what he meant by 'The troubles always come from the same quarter . . .' Gaston seemed pleased that the subject had been raised. Leaning towards the magistrate, he said in a low voice, 'I've thought about it. I've got the impression that my grandson Roger Perrin could be the killer,' and he added, 'He's a good-for-nothing.'

This was the first time he had made this accusation, and it echoed the sentence about his grandchildren in his confession. 'If you know something,' Périès said, 'now is the time to tell it.'

The old man fell silent and the magistrate pressed him. One didn't make such accusations without some proof or at least evidence. Tomorrow would be too late to supply them. The whole investigation had been bedevilled by belated revelations which, if they had been made in time, might have allowed the veils to be stripped away. If Gaston was wrongly imprisoned it was because of the lies piled up by the family. He should therefore speak at once.

But Gaston repeated what he had just said without going into any detail. Why did he accuse Roger Perrin? Was it simply to turn aside suspicion by taking refuge behind the boy's incomprehensible lies? For by now Gaston knew the whole of the dossier. He knew that the interrogation of his grandson had left both Superintendent Sébeille and the magistrate perplexed. He was obviously playing on it. Otherwise why wouldn't he give reasons for his suspicions?.

Périès, however, refused to let it go at that. He took Roger Perrin's file and studied it at length, enough to convince him that he couldn't finish the inquiry without putting the adolescent through a long interrogation.

So Périès made the acquaintance of the boy who, in the face of stiff competition, carried off all the gold medals for lying. For what remained unexplained in the young roundsman's lies was their gratuitousness. That he lied about how he spent his time on the evening of August 4 was understandable; he didn't want to be suspected of having spent the night at Grand'Terre. But why should he contradict all the other witnesses about the day of August 4 which was of no interest to anyone?

Before Périès, he modified his previous statements only when it was obvious they would no longer stand up. 'Everything I said to the police officers was true,' he declared with fine audacity.

'Except the milk from M. Puissant, who's been dead a long time.'

'The gendarmes misunderstood me.'

'And Galizzi?'

This was the farm boy whom Roger had summoned to his rescue, declaring that he had asked him to call for his milk the morning of August 5. Galizzi at first lied, then admitted to the gendarmes that he had yielded to his friend's pleas.

'Why did you require a false witness if you weren't involved?' asked Périès.

'I was beginning to realize that the gendarmes suspected me.'

'That was the time to tell the whole truth.'

This was evidently not Roger Perrin's logic. His answer was bewildering. It was a fact that he had lied but he no longer knew why.

'It's too much to believe that you tried to set up an alibi only to prove to the investigators that you got up at five instead of seven,' Périès remarked.

For in the end, after a compilation of Roger Perrin's lies, it was obvious that the structure put together with Galizzi's help had no other purpose. But the harder the magistrate tried to demonstrate to the boy that he wasn't believed, the more Roger Perrin insisted that he had only learned of the crime from Faustin Roure after 7.0 a.m. And if he induced Galizzi to lie, it was to persuade the gendarmes that his behaviour that morning had been the same as on other days.

With Perrin, questions attracted lies as steel rods attract lightning. However, he did bring to the inquiry one indisputable fact: the visit of the English mother and daughter to the farmhouse. Périès asked if he stood by it. The boy said he did. Why had he waited months to reveal it? 'Because my Aunt Yvette told me never to speak of it,' he said.

This was the magistrate's sole benefit from Roger Perrin's appearance before him. The boy was one of the main planks of the prosecution's case. It was too bad it was so shaky. But like Sébeille, Périès didn't know whether to attribute Roger Perrin's lies to some share in the crime or merely to his presence at Grand'Terre on the evening of August 4. The magistrate realized that he was saddled with a heavy burden.

The Dominicis did not go in much for writing. If the exchange of correspondence with the prisoner passed routinely through the magistrate's hands, there was a risk, run willingly or not, that correspondence between members of the family would also reach his office. So it was with a letter apparently written by Clovis to Gustave's father-in-law, Louis Barth. M. Barth more or less ran Grand'Terre now. He was one of the most intransigent instigators of the campaign in the prisoner's favour. It was he who passed Clovis's letter to the magistrate; it seemed to him right to expose Clovis's motives for accusation, as well as the pressures he was bringing to bear on his brother.

'See that Gustave does not retract,' Clovis advised Louis Barth. 'So many things weigh on him, though he is quite innocent, since it's that old bandit who committed the crime. He knows he has to consider his wife and babies. He is acting badly, letting himself be influenced by his brothers, brothers-in-law and sisters. Above all, advise Gustave to think what he's doing . . .'

To Louis Barth this represented blackmail and explained clearly why Gustave had caved in: he had yielded to the joint pressure of the police and Clovis; Périès sent for the latter.

Clovis had not changed. Rugged and solid, distressed and angry at this development which once again required him to play the part of traitor, he declared that the letter had been written by his wife. But he had known about it and had not dissuaded her from sending it. He therefore accepted responsibility for it. 'There are plots going on around Gustave,' he said.

262

'Who is behind them?'

'Everybody. If he's backed down, it's their fault.'

They aroused his pity and anger. They shut their eyes to reality, not realizing that in acquitting their father they were opening the door to a new inquiry and Gustave would be the victim. But Gustave was guilty of nothing. It was because of this threat that Clovis had wanted to warn a man he judged to be reasonable, Louis Barth. He now recognized that he had mistaken his man. His face sad, he confessed his sorrow to the magistrate in a hollow voice. 'Gustave can't deny what he said to me.'

Again Périès expressed his surprise; Clovis now declared that Gustave had confided their father's guilt to him on August 7 or 8. Why had he concealed it in November when it mattered little whether the confidence had been made to him or not?

'Because I forgot that detail,' Clovis replied.

'You call it detail, that your father was a murderer?'

'I didn't believe it.'

Clovis was a Dominici and Périès realized it after hearing this unsatisfactory excuse. 'Detail' - to Clovis this signified, as he explained, that he feared his brother was guilty. Consequently, he hadn't paid attention to the accusation against their father which only confirmed his suspicions. He had not wanted to ask anything more precise; the truth frightened him. A disconcerting analysis, but Périès had to be satisfied with it; Clovis offered no other. He had to be accepted as he was.

'Your father now claims,' the magistrate resumed, 'that the carbine belonged to you and that you had perhaps lent it to your nephew, Roger Perrin.'

Clovis didn't get angry. But there was nothing euphemistic about his reply. 'My father is a liar, he knows perfectly well that the carbine was never mine.'

'Why did he say so?'

'To get out of trouble,' came the short, sharp answer.

Through a skylight half-obscured by a plank placed diagonally across it, Gaston Dominici saw spring, then summer come and blossom. But during his daily walk in the courtyard his companions saw him look at the crests of the nearby mountains, sniff the wind, and breathe in the air as if trying to smell the oak plantations where he had spent his best times. It was that solitude he now missed. For long hours he could remain silent, his arms crossed on his chest, holding his pipe, his gaze vacant, his lips moving in a perpetual monologue with himself. The other prisoners, most of them young, called him Dad and he accepted the name, giving them advice on eating, to chew very slowly and take their time, to eat only natural foods, never preserved ones which poisoned the body. He commented freely and ironically on the soup served to the prisoners which bore only the most distant resemblance to the soup the Sardine prepared for him, heavy with the odours of all the vegetables she simmered in it. Garbage sauce he called the prison soup when dipping his spoon into his mess tin. But he swallowed it, and his stomach never balked.

Wednesdays and Saturdays were visiting days. Gustave had never received a permit. Nor had he made any great effort to obtain one. He wasn't eager to come face to face with his father in the narrow visitors' room where one talked under the observation of an attentive guard who never took his eyes off the prisoners or their visitors. Gaston had invented a name for his sons – the Bazaines.[1] He freely indulged in historical analogies; for him the Digne prison was the Island of Elba, meaning the place from which one returned in triumph. He had no doubt that he would be acquitted. For this reason he pressed his lawyers each time he saw them to push on with the trial. He was in a hurry to rejoin Dick, his goats and, incidentally, the Sardine.

He hadn't yet decided on his future arrangements. Sometimes he planned to return to Grand'Terre as if nothing had happened and Gustave would have to tread softly. He would again be the master and set everybody to work. Or else he would throw out Gustave and Yvette and make do with labourers. Or else he would sell his lands and live according to his taste as an independent shepherd and hermit. But in any event the affair would have served to show that he was surrounded by incompetents and bloodsuckers. He would take charge in his own house.

Augusta Caillat was the most loyal. It was she who informed him that Gustave had retracted and would not accuse him again.

'None too soon,' growled Gaston.

He devoured books from the library and periodicals from which the pages referring to his case had been removed. 'They're quite right not to make me read that bloody nonsense,' he jeered.

A councillor, M. Borelli, visited the prison which was under the

[1] After Achille Bazaine, the French general imprisoned after the Franco-Prussian War for surrendering at Metz. (*Tr. note*)

authority of his department. 'Are you sleeping well?' he asked the old man.

'Like a man with a clear conscience.'

He was uneasy about who was drinking his wine. Not Clovis, at least? The family pressured him; the traitor had not shown himself at the farm. Only the loyal were tapping the barrels, and any surplus was sold. He could count on Louis Barth, a scrupulous and upright administrator. Gaston agreed; he had every confidence in his son's father-in-law. Life had not changed at Grand'Terre except that the young couple again shared the kitchen with Marie Dominici. As for his room, it was shut up and no one entered it except now and then for cleaning. Every article was in place. When Gaston returned he would find it as if he had left it the day before.

But the old man's most steadfast daughter hid the disagreeable aspects from him – such as the Italian mason Gustave had asked to do a small repair who spat as he refused, the faces at Lurs and Peyruis that looked the other way, the hateful and despicable anonymous letters. Opinion in the country was divided. Some held that Gaston had been sacrificed to England because a culprit had to be found, some were persuaded of his guilt but did not extend it to the whole family; some were stern judges who condemned all the Dominicis.

It will never be known whether the prisoner was told of a truly pathetic scene that took place a few metres from Grand'Terre. Clovis was passing on his bicycle just as Marie Dominici was walking along the road towards the field. He braked and wanted to go to her. But the mother turned her head away as if she had not seen her son. Clovis pedalled off quickly. There were tears in his eyes.

During the whole of 1954, at least until November, the Dominici affair had little prominence in the press. In truth the inquiry conducted by the magistrate was beginning to run down, although Périès himself pushed to the limit. He called in all the members of the Dominici family one by one to pose the question, 'Did you see the weapon?' Nor did he rest content with their answers; he probed into their taste for, or lack of interest in, shooting, took a census of their armoury, made a detailed inventory of their guns and the use they put them to. No interesting results emerged from this long and painstaking work.

He had also ordered an expert study from which he expected a great deal: that of the oil used on the Rock-Ola. He had confiscated Gustave's guns and Gaston's old Gras, as well as those of Clovis and the Perrin family. By comparing the oils it should be possible to deduce the owners or users of the carbine.

But the experts reached some surprising conclusions. 'The lubricants used on the Rock-Ola present similar physical characteristics to those found on the gun 6844 and the Simplex, thus indicating their belonging to the same structural group. On the other hand, there is no connection with any of the other weapons, including those from Grand'Terre.'

The Simplex and the 6844 belonged to Clovis. The magistrate did not evade the question – it was too serious. If the oil on the Rock-Ola was the same as that used by Clovis, didn't it mean that he had handled the rifle, for boar for instance, and, like a careful sportsman, had oiled it before returning it?

Clovis was questioned. 'I never use mineral oil,' he said, 'but always my own olive oil.'

'Impossible,' returned Périès, himself an amateur of firearms. 'You know very well that the acidity of olive oil would ruin the metal parts.'

But Clovis stuck to his story. He had had his guns repaired and it was the gunsmith who had used the oil the expert had detected.

Périès referred back to the experts – could one establish similarity between the oils?

'No,' they answered. 'They are homologous, that's as far as you can go.'

Another dead end for the magistrate.

In June, Périès decided to close the inquiry. According to the rules of procedure, he undertook a final interrogation of Gaston Dominici, a formality whose purpose was to establish irrevocably the definitive attitude of the accused. There were no surprises; the old man formally denied being the murderer. Sitting before the magistrate, his expression tranquil, at times ironic, he heard the magistrate go over the investigation, read the record of his confession, the accusations repeated by Gustave and Clovis. Nothing troubled him. He reiterated that they were traitors and that he would confound them at the trial.

'If I am convicted,' he said grandiloquently, 'I don't want to be guillotined, I want to be burned like Joan of Arc, exiled like Napoleon, or crucified like Christ.'

Roger Périès signed the writ for the dossier to be sent to the prosecutor's office.

*

The judicial mill, a picturesque expression, is in a sense quite correct. But it shouldn't be given too derogatory a meaning. If before sending a defendant to the assizes the French Code requires a review of the dossier by the prosecutor's office, it is to give the accused an additional guarantee. Three jurists of the court of appeal preside at a hearing in camera where prosecution and defence are allowed to present their arguments. Only after this private debate is it decided whether to bring a defendant before a jury. It can well result in a dismissal from which there is no appeal.

It was to Aix-en-Provence that the Dominici dossier was referred. Counsel for the defence, led by Maître Emile Pollak, had few illusions. If they were to win, it would have to be at the assizes before public opinion. The combat was therefore purely a matter of form. The prosecutor's office, as foreseen, sent Gaston Dominici for trial before the Assize Court of the Basses-Alpes sitting at Digne. The trial was expected to take place at the beginning of autumn.

However, the lawyers immediately carried the struggle to the Supreme Court of Appeal, pleading that the law had been violated, notably at the reconstruction of the crime. The Dominici affair posed a serious problem. It constituted a test case, in that jurists consider it an indispensable precedent each time the powers of examining magistrates are called in question, and the name of Dominici is therefore inscribed in all handbooks on penal procedure.

The problem posed by the defence was this: Gaston Dominici had been indicted after a delay which had but one purpose: to prevent his being helped by lawyers and to leave him alone in face of the judicial machinery until he was confused by proofs which were in reality without foundation.

'The law of December 8, 1897, is specific,' maintained the lawyers, 'regarding the guarantees accorded to the defence. A suspect must be indicted as soon as the charges assembled against him are sufficient. From that moment he has the right to communicate with counsel of his choice. The latter should from then on be present at all proceedings, giving his client the benefit of his knowledge and experience. Of course he may be a nuisance and considered so. His role is to frustrate intrigues as well as warning the accused of the risk he runs by taking part in a reconstruction. It was to prevent our being present at the scene on November 16 that the magistrate Périès did not charge Gaston Dominici until after that operation.'

The debate began with the report of a counsellor, on this occasion

M. Maurice Patin, a noted expert in penal law known for his integrity and the passion with which he invariably denounced any infringement of the rights of the defence. A jurist of the old school, a genuine scholar in penal science, M. Patin's presence was an assurance to the defending counsel. They themselves were present only as spectators, since no one could plead before the Supreme Court except a handful of specialist lawyers, to whom all appeals must be directed. The one chosen was among the most renowned, Maître André Mayer.

Maurice Patin, however, caused some surprise. Despite his liberalism, he did not adopt the lawyers' thesis. According to him, the magistrate certainly went to the extreme limit. He would have exceeded it if he hadn't charged Gaston on the site itself when the reconstruction was concluded. But the way in which the confession had emerged, the wild run down the child's attempted escape route – incredible in an old man – and Gustave's oscillations could leave room for doubt. Therefore caution rather than trickiness explained the behaviour of the Digne magistrate, which the counsellor approved. On the other hand, he gave his support to two small criticisms – purely matters of form – made by the defence. Gaston Dominici had been interrogated for the last time without mention being made that the dossier had been communicated to his lawyers. In addition, there was no trace of the fact that the clerk had notified the lawyers of the writ of committal. These formalities had been neglected.

Maître André Mayer then launched his attack on the principal question. The essence of his speech consisted of demonstrating that the reconstruction had added nothing new. Périès had no more grounds to indict Gaston Dominici afterwards than he had before. Simple logic demanded the conclusion that the magistrate feared the lawyers being interposed between him and Gaston Dominici.

The judgment of the Court of Appeals was practically identical to M. Patin's. It was a vindication of Périès; he had violated the law of 1897, but not by much. If he had delayed in charging the Grand'Terre farmer it was due to scruple. The Supreme Court judges recalled the circumstances of the confession, the contradictory statements of Gustave and Gaston. 'It was in the competence of the magistrate,' they concluded, 'to charge Gaston Dominici only after satisfying himself that he had participated in the crime in question in circumstances of such a kind as to involve him in criminal responsibility, and, having done this, while not introducing documentary evidence or other procedural elements to avoid the disposition of the law of December 8, 1897, the magistrate has in no way infringed the rights of the defence . . .'

On the other hand, the court recognized that Périès had committed two errors of form; it set aside both Gaston Dominici's last confession and the writ of committal. It appointed the court at Grenoble to revise these two instruments. This only resulted in a brief postponement of the trial.

To conform to the requirements of the Court of Appeal, the errors it had pointed out had to be corrected. The dossier was sent to Grenoble and Gaston Dominici made a journey to the Dauphiné capital at the expense of the prison administration. He was pleased, distractions being rare in prison. He in no way modified his position: he was innocent and would say so until his dying day. The scattered chorus in the Lurs countryside echoed him. Apart from Clovis and Germaine Perrin, the family missed no opportunity to repeat the words of its patriarch: an unfortunate man was being persecuted because a guilty one had to be found at all costs.

10

His index finger following the typed lines, Gaston Dominici slowly read the two blue sheets, nodding his head as if finding the confirmation of what he had been saying for months. The notice had just been passed to him by the governor of the prison; it informed him that on November 17 next he would be brought before the assize court at Digne for judgment.

Gaston carefully folded the summons and put it in his pocket. Then he raised his head to the guard standing near by. Since it had turned cold he had again established himself in the little room called 'the oven'. There he passed his days, devouring all the books the library could supply him.

'I shan't grow mouldy here,' he said. 'This is October. In a month at most I'll be acquitted and leave you.' A nostalgic shadow crossed his face. 'I'll be at Grand'Terre again with my dog and goats.'

'And your children and your wife,' the guard murmured, not without a trace of sarcasm; he had heard Gaston say often enough what he thought of his family.

'Them!' sighed the old man.

Neither Yvette, Gustave nor the Sardine had ever come to see him. But he knew that his companion of fifty years had started going to church again on his behalf. She could be seen once a week lighting a candle before the statue of St Anthony, patron of lost causes. Gaston would often smile about it. He did not think God cared much what happened in men's tribunals. He placed greater confidence in his lawyers – and in the good impression he would make on the jurors, men like himself, folk from his own country who would understand him better than Marseilles police officers or magistrates from heaven knows where. 'They'll easily see that I'm innocent,' he said with assurance.

The news soon became public property, putting Digne on the

map again. Within two or three days the hotels in Digne and the surrounding neighbourhood received more requests for bookings than they had rooms. The president of the court was badgered by telephone calls from the European press; one of his problems was how to fit over a hundred working reporters into a room barely more than ten metres by ten.

The lawyers gathered. One afternoon in November they assembled at the scene of the crime armed with metal tape-measures and surveyors' instruments. For three hours they took measurements, comparing their observations with the dossier they had brought with them. 'Since we were not at the reconstruction,' they said, 'we'll have to make our own.'

As the trial date neared, long articles appeared in the papers reviewing the whole affair. In general, Gaston's guilt was not disputed. Sébeille still wore his laurels. Nevertheless, a good deal of space was given to the lawyers' criticisms. The possibility of a sensational development which would throw altogether new light on the case was not dismissed.

Several days before the trial Digne was packed, down to the last available rooms being let by the local inhabitants. The Department of Posts and Telegraphs (PTT) had made every effort to cope with the telephone communications which would link Haute Provence with the rest of Europe. Seventy extra lines had been laid. The presidential police car, a perfectly equipped mobile post office which accompanies the President of the Republic on all his journeys and renders the same service on other important public occasions, made its appearance in the city.

Fierce arguments raged about seating. The journalists alone practically filled the courtroom. The British journalists complained bitterly: their French colleagues had cornered all the best places – unfair considering that they, after all, had furnished 'the raw material'; another tricky problem that the president had to resolve.

It was like the climax of a serialized whodunnit. Would the trial be as sensational? Only one man said nothing and refused to receive the reporters – Clovis, holed up in his own house. 'Let him alone,' his wife, Marie-Rose, kept repeating. 'Do you think it's funny having to accuse your own father?'

At 6.30 a.m. on November 17, while it was still dark, the curious, the photographers and the journalists were assembled under the walls of the prison. Twenty armed gendarmes kept them away from the door. Suddenly it opened wide and Gaston Dominici appeared, directing a faint smile at those gathered waiting. He was at once escorted to the Black Maria, which was preceded by three policemen on motor-cycles and followed by a van with ten gendarmes. At the Palais de Justice he was conducted to a room he knew well since it was there he had confessed to the triple crime. The armchair was the same, the red velvet a little more torn.

A sky of matchless purity such as only Provence can produce, a blazing sun and a sharp north wind – this was the climate in Digne on that morning of November 17, 1954. By 8.0 a.m. a compact throng was pressing against the gates of the Palais de Justice. Some had been there for three or four hours.

When the order was given to open the gates there was a stampede. In the end space had virtually been measured out in centimetres. Once seated, the journalists dared not get up; they could not have squeezed back into place. The photographers – still admitted into courtrooms before a law later prohibited them – had installed themselves in several ranks on the improvised, dangerously fragile stands. The gendarmes had to clear the entrance for the lawyers, who could not get through the crowd.

At 9.0 a.m. the court entered. Its president was Counsellor Marcel Bousquet, 51 years old, tall, strong, authoritative. A Niçois by origin, and a practising Catholic, M. Bousquet had since the Liberation presided over the Tribunal of the Armed Forces at Marseilles, where he had directed all the great trials of collaborators, and of the Gestapo. At his side sat the first assessor, M. Roger Combas, a counsellor of the court at Aix-en-Provence, a short man with an asymmetrical, extremely intelligent face, a former Mâcon lawyer who had entered the magistracy after the Liberation.

Two magistrates represented the prosecution: the Digne prosecutor, M. Sabatier, who had watched the investigation from the start, and an advocate-general attached to the court at Aix, M. Calixte Rozan, a 45-year-old pure-blooded Provençal, with a sing-song accent which added a flavour to the trial, and an incisive manner and gift for racy retort which were useful assets when faced by men like Emile Pollak and Paul Charrier on the defence bench. In addition there was Maître Claude Delorme, a future deputy, whose great extra-curricular absorption at the moment was with the construction of the Serre-Ponçon dam to make the wayward Durance navigable.

At 9.5 President Bousquet ordered the accused to be brought in.

A complete hush came over the room. Through a small door at the back of the dock Gaston Dominici made his entrance. He seemed to falter momentarily before the barrage of cameras, but he recovered quickly and held himself straight as a yew. He wore a dark suit, a white shirt, and had a knotted scarf round his neck. His face looked older, worn, but his eyes were alert. They surveyed the room, showing neither fear nor disquiet. His mouth was in constant movement as if he were endlessly chewing gum.

When asked to stand he did so in one quick and supple movement. 'Gaston Dominici,' he answered the president, 'aged seventy-seven, married, nine children, proprietor of Grand'Terre, Basses-Alpes.'

His voice was strong and clear. He had asked that he might have a little white wine during the trial, an excellent fortifier of the vocal cords.

His whole family was there but he did not seem to notice it. The clan was divided in two; on the one side Yvette in a dark coat, Gustave, Marie the mother dressed in mourning, the loyal brothers and sisters; on the other Clovis, bundled up in a heavy jacket, his expression vacant.

The jury was drawn by lot. The lawyers objected to a woman, natural enough in 1954 in a case where a child had suffered a horrible death. In the end five farmers took their seats, together with one butcher and one retired butcher. Since the proceedings promised to be long, M. Bousquet had two substitutes named.

The indictment was read. Gaston listened, his head high, his expression one of mockery at the passages describing him as high-handed, violent, a drinker, uncommunicative.

The witnesses were summoned and shepherded into the rooms where they were to wait until called. Orders had been given that Clovis, Roger Perrin and his mother were to be kept separate from the rest of the Dominicis. During a short recess Gaston Dominici joked with the photographers, clapped his hands, stuck out his tongue, dived into the dock to hide his face from their lenses, and came up again to thumb his nose at them.

At the resumption of the hearing the defence opened its first attack: could the Hillman be made available for a possible reconstruction? But the Hillman was now in England. Have it brought back, suggested M. Pollak. It was not to be found, answered the advocate-general. An English paper revealed the next day that it had been bought by a showman to be exhibited at travelling fairs. The defence settled for a similar car.

The interrogation of Gaston Dominici now began. As usual President Bousquet first inquired into the defendant's life. A pungent dialogue began between the judge and the old man. It was in a way Gaston's first victory. Lively and at times juicy answers revealed an engaging character to those who could discern it, a mixture of peasant guile, good sense and good humour, always with the right word to excuse or explain his weaknesses, displaying cunning and sometimes subtlety. One feature, however, struck observers: the difference in language between judge and defendant. The writer Jean Giono, who was present, later noted that the old man had a very limited vocabulary, while the judge and advocate-general could call on thousands. The estimate may not have been exact, but it was true that Gaston at times had no answer, because he had not understood the terms in which the question was put to him.

'I don't even know who the justice of the peace is,' he said proudly. One curious phrase he kept repeating at every opportunity did puzzle for a while until it was realized that each time he said '*Je suis franc-z et loyal,*' he was not constantly calling all to witness that he was a loyal Frenchman, but was trying to emphasize in his incorrectly slurred French that he was frank (*franc*) and honest. He even added with a certain ill-humour, although the fact had not yet been raised, 'It wasn't me who committed the crime, I'm innocent.'

He was moved only once, when the president referred to his grandchildren, 'Ah, yes, I've got nineteen and I love them all the same.' He took a large checked handkerchief from his pocket and wiped his eyes. It was on this note that the morning's hearing ended.

In the afternoon President Bousquet took up the examination of the dossier. He began by recalling who Sir Jack Drummond was, referred to his career, described his journey across France until the evening of August 4. Then he called on Gaston Dominici to say what he had done that night.

At this another character emerged, the unpredictable one Sébeille and Périès had known so well, in turn ironical and hot-tempered, smiling when his aim was to convince by his demonstrable serenity, as well as his words, but becoming flustered and indignant when the president reminded him of his confession. How long was he to be bored with this nonsense? From time to time he would appeal to the spectators: couldn't they see he was sincere? Often he angrily jerked up his trousers as though getting ready for a brawl.

In fact he returned quite simply to his first version. He had not got up, he had heard the shots, thought it was a poacher, risen at about 3.30 a.m., had learned of the drama from his daughter-in-law only on his return at 8.0. If 'parables' had been introduced into this story, it was not by him.

The president recalled the scene in which Clovis fell on his knees at the sight of the carbine. Gaston asked triumphantly, 'Why didn't Sébeille arrest him, since he knew the carbine?'

M. Bousquet was astonished: was Gaston accusing his son? The defendant seemed to hesitate and the courtroom held its breath: was the old man going to denounce the son who had denounced him? 'I don't know if he did it,' he finally said, 'but it wasn't me.'

'You're sacrificing yourself for somebody else?' the judge pressed.

Gaston shrugged his shoulders. 'If I have to pay for somebody else it'll just be my misfortune. Send for the family, send for Clovis.'

'They're coming.'

'Good.'

So, faced with what looked like a critical moment, the old man settled for evasion; if he was wrongly accused and knew the truth, he wasn't going to set justice straight, content once again to deny and disavow his confession. He had not admitted his crime to Gustave, still less to Clovis. As to his confession to the gendarme Guérino, then to Superintendent Prudhomme, he didn't remember; he was too worn out after his day with Sébeille and his men. 'They were so on top of me that I felt their spit on my face. They kept repeating that they would cut off Gustave's head while I risked nothing.'

The president then asked if it was to save Gustave that he had accused himself. But Gaston again refused a direct answer, falling back on the way he had been 'worn down' by the police.

'They drove me out of my mind. To me, an old farmer of seventy-seven, they bawled right in my face, "You're a murderer." I couldn't take any more. I talked rubbish to Prudhomme because I was out of my mind.'

He summed it all up in a sentence: 'What I said, I said, but I didn't do it.'

The president started on an examination of the confession. It contained certain elements which accorded with the established facts, but it threw no light on the motive. The president unhesitatingly ruled out the scene in which Sir Jack found Gaston in Lady Drummond's bed. It was not credible. He recalled Gaston's remark, 'I have committed a crime of passion.' It was a joke, wasn't it?

'Exactly,' exclaimed the defendant triumphantly. 'What does it mean?'

'It means,' returned the president severely, 'that you made a vile attempt on this woman.'

Explosion on the defence benches: their client could never have uttered those words, which proved that his entire confession was nothing but a fabrication. Cries, invective, banging on tables. Gaston joined in the uproar, hammering with his stick on the edge of the dock and almost laughing at having caused such a din in a courtroom. It was only with great difficulty that the president restored order.

It was nearly 6.0 p.m. Gaston had been standing much of the time since the morning. He had held himself like a rock, tireless it seemed. But by now his face was drawn, his shoulders bowed and his voice strained. He hunted for words, stammered, answered only with delay. 'I'd like to stop,' he said at last.

The president, looking at him, could see that this was no stratagem; the old man was tired. 'My client is tired of talking,' said M. Pollak, and added, 'As I am of listening . . .'

The hearing was suspended until next morning. In the witnesses' room the Dominicis had been waiting all day. During a recess Marie Dominici saw her son Clovis. Coming abreast of him, she slowed down and made as if to spit on the floor. Augusta, who followed her, stopped, inspected her brother with a sort of pity, and muttered 'Wretch!' Gustave avoided looking at him altogether.

With a firm, easy step and a relaxed expression Gaston Dominici entered the dock, brought his hand to his forehead and gave the jurors a superb military salute. Then he sat down, obviously pleased with this dramatic gesture.

The president took up the interrogation where he had left off the evening before. He wanted the defendant to state his present position explicitly so that there would be no misunderstanding. Innocent? Dominici repeated it. Then who was guilty? Clovis?

'No, no,' protested Gaston.

'Roger Perrin, then? You accused him during the inquiry.'

'No, no,' the defendant said again.

'I'm sorry, but you did say it was he.'

The defendant looked embarrassed. 'I accuse neither Clovis nor Gustave. At times I thought Roger because he's a good-for-nothing. But it was only a suspicion.'

Suddenly he challenged the judge: 'You already think I'm guilty.'
'Not at all.'

'You act as if you did.' Hands on hips, his gaze shifting from the court to the spectators and back again, he boomed, 'I tell you in front of the assembled people, I am innocent.'

'He made this solemn proclamation with splendid simplicity, like a Roman tribune before the Senate,' wrote Pierre Scize in *Le Figaro*. And there were certainly those who were shaken enough by the old man's self-mastery to begin to have doubts. How could this bucolic patriarch, an illiterate who could nevertheless command such verbal resources, have changed at a stroke into a murderous monster?

Gaston Dominici was then turned over to the prosecution, Maître Claude Delorme and advocate-general Rozan. Towards them the defendant showed himself considerably less tractable. He declared that he understood nothing of what M. Delorme asked him about his actions during the reconstruction. The prosecuting attorney did not press him and M. Pollak was called upon.

At this point M. Pollak was less concerned with interrogation than with making some pointed observations about the confession and the reconstruction. He noted, for instance, that the number of shots heard by the defendant did not correspond to the number of cartridges and wounds, particularly Lady Drummond's. He recalled that Superintendent Prudhomme had stated that it was he who had steered Gaston towards the subject of lewdness. He emphasized that the carbine – a prohibited weapon – was in a shed anyone could enter; Gaston Dominici was too wary to commit such an imprudence. Moreover, if he was the murderer, why had he thrown the Rock-Ola into a still reach of the Durance when he knew that a few metres farther on there was a current which would have carried the exhibit far away? He was indignant at the president's statement the day before that Gaston had confessed nine times. 'He confessed five times and retracted five times.' Then, after a pause, in a sarcastic voice: 'I don't think these things are decided by majorities.'

He sat down. More had been expected. But a trial builds up, and this was only the second day. It was now the turn of the first witnesses, the psychiatrists. Their conclusions were emphatic: Gaston Dominici was a man remarkably well-balanced for his age, despite a slight softening of the brain disclosed by the encephalogram.

Drs Merlan and Alliez, who followed on the stand, were each submitted to the same penetrating cross-examination by the defence. Was Gaston Dominici a man capable of being influenced? Could false admissions be extracted from him under pressure? In short, had his confession been suggested to him or not? Could exhaustion bring him to the point of admitting to a fiendish crime?

The experts gave guarded answers. 'It is evident,' said Dr Merlan, 'that after long questioning a man of seventy-seven would naturally be tired. But I do not see Gaston Dominici capable of altogether inventing a story.'

'Dominici,' said Dr Alliez, 'has perfect control of himself. His physical and moral resistance is considerable.'

'Even after twenty-four hours of interrogation?' M. Pollak challenged.

'No doubt a little less. But it would survive.'

Dr Dragon was an important early witness since the elderly practitioner from Oraison had been the first medical man to examine the bodies, a little after 8.0 a.m. on August 5. His evidence led to some vigorous exchanges because it bore on one of the more baffling riddles of the case: when and how Elizabeth had been killed.

Dr Dragon had been surprised that the child's feet bore no sign of bruises, for it seemed obvious that she had run away to escape her murderer. 'I confided my surprise to Superintendent Sébeille,' he said, 'during Gustave Dominici's trial for failure to render help. The superintendent told me that an experiment had been made with a girl of the same age, and that he had not found any bruises. But that didn't convince me; you can't compare the blind dash in the night by a frightened little girl with that of a child asked to run sedately in the daytime.'

The doctor was sure that the English girl had died at once; she had received two or three blows from the gun-butt delivered with incredible violence. The wounds were such that in his opinion Elizabeth had been struck while lying on the ground. Triumphantly, Pollak exclaimed, 'That's directly opposed to what Gaston Dominici did at the reconstruction. According to him, the child was kneeling.'

The advocate-general, Rozan, intervened. Dr Dragon was putting forward a hypothesis, nothing more. Personally he thought it wrong. But the doctor supplied the defence with another argument: the parents' *rigor mortis* was not the same as the child's. He even added a supporting detail – namely, that he had been able to move Elizabeth's limbs whereas it had been impossible to open out Sir Jack's arm. Therefore the child could well have died two or three hours after her father and mother.

M. Pollak seized his opportunity. He summed up Dr Dragon's

testimony. According to the doctor, Elizabeth died from the blow but two or three hours after her parents. Therefore it may have been that she had been killed in two stages, stunned by a first blow, then finished off when the murderer found that she was still alive. It was also conceivable that she had been carried to the shelter of the bank where the murder could be done without being seen. The advocate-general once again protested; one could not speak of the path as it now was, trampled for two years by thousands of sightseers. At the time it was covered with grass, which explained the absence of injury to the child's feet.

The defence had nevertheless scored some points with Dr Dragon's evidence. The prosecution immediately responded by bringing forward two other doctors, Jouve and Nalin.

The first was a surgeon, a specialist in cranial injuries. He had not examined Elizabeth's body. He could, however, state that death was not necessarily immediate even with the skull horribly smashed in. 'I once operated on a child,' he went on, 'who had fallen from a second floor and had his head shattered. He survived eight hours.'

Dr Nalin had performed the autopsy together with Dr Girard, but the latter had died in September 1954, so that Dr Nalin had to report their findings alone. He did not agree with Dr Dragon.

About the parents' death he was categorical: it had been immediate. But in the case of Elizabeth he drew a distinction: the first blow had been delivered while she was on her knees, the second after she had sunk to the ground. But it was not impossible that the murder of the child had occurred at the same time as that of the parents. *Rigor mortis* overtakes the body of a young person more slowly than that of an adult. Two or three hours might elapse before a child's limbs reached the same state as a grown person's deceased at the same instant. Consequently Dr Nalin saw no reason to deny that the tragedy occurred within a few seconds.

It was a draw between the defence and prosecution with a slight advantage to the latter, for Dr Nalin supplied an explanation for the pool of blood found near the cesspool. Until now it had not been accounted for either in the confessions or the reconstruction. But Dr Nalin thought that it had been left by Sir Jack when fleeing; he had been shot in the liver and such wounds bleed freely.

M. Pollak counter-attacked on a matter still obscure: the gash in Sir Jack's hand. According to Gaston Dominici's confession, it had been caused by a bullet discharged while Sir Jack was holding the weapon by the barrel to turn it aside. Was this possible?

279

'No,' admitted Dr Nalin frankly, 'because the hand would have been mangled.'

'So on this point too the reconstruction is false,' M. Pollak reasoned.

According to the lawyer, Sir Jack was injured when stumbling against the car's bumper, an incident which did not figure in the defendant's confession. Moreover, a shred of flesh had been found there. What had become of it? Nobody knew. It was, said Dr Nalin, the late Dr Girard who had analysed it. Since then it had disappeared – a disappearance which would outrage the British journalists, already shaken by a procedure a little too concerned with psychology and not enough with clues and material evidence.

From the dock Gaston Dominici had followed this scientific debate attentively. Now and then he would lean over to ask his lawyers to explain a detail he had not understood. He had seemed excited by M. Pollak's theory about the death of Elizabeth. His elbows on the edge of the dock, his face thrust forward, his moustache quivering, he nodded in approval at each fresh step in his counsel's argument. He kept notably quiet, as if too absorbed in registering every last word of valuable information.

The hearing continued with the testimony of the Marrians, the friends the deceased had come to stay with at Villefranche-sur-Mer a few days before the crime. It was merely formal evidence but it triggered off an incident with Gaston, enraged by a remark of Mr Marrian.

'The day of the burial,' he said, 'I went with my wife to the place where my friends had died. I saw an old man: Gaston Dominici. He showed me where Elizabeth had fallen, then her parents. I am sorry to say he looked like a guide expecting a tip.'

Gaston reared up in the dock, tensed like a fighting cock. Fixing Mr Marrian balefully, accent heavy and laden with spite, he ground out, 'A peasant of the Basses-Alpes doesn't ask tips from anybody when he gives information!'

Dressed in black, white-haired, extremely dignified, Mrs Marrian followed her husband. Like him, she had the impression that Gaston expected a tip. 'He even made a gesture like this,' she said, rubbing thumb against forefinger. This time Gaston was beside himself with anger. Before his lawyers could stop him he was up in the dock again, shaking his forefinger at the witness. 'You're lying,' he shouted.

It was the prosecuting counsel who restored silence. Erect, almost face to face, M. Delorme ordered him to be quiet.

Gaston glared at him for a moment, seemed about to stick his tongue out at him, then sat down without a word.

The hearing ended with the evidence of the gendarmes who made the survey on the morning of August 5, and the truck drivers who had passed along the road that night. The lawyers were interested in the route the drivers took, and especially in the notorious Lereboulet, the phantom tramp. He was a useful suspect; everybody had seen him, if at different places and different times. In addition, Emile Pollak and Pierre Charrier had the gendarmes relate the ready lies told by Roger Perrin. At each mention of his grandson Gaston pricked up his ears.

November 19 is marked on the French calendar as St Elizabeth's day. As the trial entered its third day a moving ceremony was taking place at the Forcalquier cemetery. Before the grave of the Drummonds a couple in black bent their heads in prayer: Mr and Mrs Marrian had come to lay a wreath in memory of the dead child.

In the courtroom an odd character was called on to 'perform', the only suitable word for that morning's first witness, Aristide Panayotou, the man who towards the end of August 1952 had caused a lively sensation by claiming to have seen the murder. He later admitted that he had lied. Then why call him as a witness, demanded Emile Pollak, instead of prosecuting him for false evidence? 'Because,' the advocate-general Rozan retorted, 'if we hadn't called him you would have blamed us even more.'

Another motive had doubtless determined the magistrates' decision. In a criminal case false witness is not punishable unless it is repeated at the assizes, the reasoning being that a witness can repent up to the last moment. If after having made an accusation during the inquiry he retracts before the jury, he is considered to have made amends and cleared himself. Otherwise he risks the same penalty as the accused whom he has helped to convict; if the accusation is one of murder, he can be condemned to death like the one he has put in the dock.

Not that Aristide Panayotou accused Gaston Dominici, since the person he described bore no resemblance to him. He stoutly maintained that he had seen 'a man in his forties wearing leggings shoot another who was staggering across the road.' He was soon under fire from the president and advocate-general, both of them reminding him of his contradictions and lies. Aristide Panayotou remained unperturbed. He showed great firmness and a fine indifference in face of the magistrates' grim warnings. He even made a remark that delighted the lawyers: 'I have always been useful to the police same as I have to anybody.' He left the box under dark threats of prosecution, which never came to anything.

Then came the turn of the real witnesses, the very early ones, beginning with the motor-cyclist Olivier who had tripped up Gustave Dominici. His testimony had decreased in importance because it was Gaston and not Gustave in the dock. He was heard with something less than interest.

Faustin Roure, the railway foreman, came to give evidence about the landslide. Gustave had notified him of it but he, Roure, had had no instructions to give. He had discovered the bodies in the morning and described a scene which greatly pleased the defence. He was at Grand'Terre when Gaston returned with his goats. He had heard Yvette say to her father-in-law, 'There's been some fine goings-on in the night and murder at the end of the field.' To the defence this was proof that Gaston was innocent and that Gustave had never told his wife during the night that 'my father did it'. Otherwise how was this remark of Yvette's to be explained? Unless – and the defence did not rule this out – the young woman and the old man were putting on a pre-arranged act before the outsider Faustin Roure.

Gaston rose to assert that he had not seen Faustin Roure because he had been hidden by the wall; he thought he was alone with his daughter-in-law. Tempers rose and the defence pestered Faustin Roure, much to the manifest irritation of some of the jury, which the lawyers noted grimly. But with an eventual appeal in mind, they entered no formal objection.

With Captain Albert came a return to more factual evidence. He gave a detailed report of the investigation he had conducted, making, of course, no reference to the divergence of opinion between himself and Superintendent Sébeille, nor to the bad feeling that at times existed between them. He admitted that despite precautions the prints of crêpe-soled shoes found on the path were no longer visible when the scene-of-crime van arrived at Lurs. They posed a problem since the feet seemed to be going in opposite directions, and for no accountable reason. As to the path followed by Elizabeth, Captain Albert, who saw it as it was before the invasion of the crowd, described it as all but unformed, with scattered tufts of grass.

The hearing suddenly came alive when he repeated a conversation he had had with Gaston Dominici. It was about August 8 and Captain Albert had come to Grand'Terre. There he ran into Gaston who came up to him to ask how the investigation was going. The officer gave a vague answer, asking in turn what the Grand'Terre farmer thought of the affair.

'What he then told me,' reported the captain, 'closely resembled what one could read in any newspaper at the time. But when he spoke of Elizabeth he said, "When they shot at the little girl . . ." I cut him short which was wrong of me, since I had in fact noticed the slight wound on the child's ear. Besides, no paper had mentioned it. My interruption spoiled everything, for he turned red and stammered . . .'

'I can find no trace of this incident in your report,' snapped M. Pollak. 'Why wait till now to mention it?'

The captain was embarrassed. He had not, he declared, attached much importance to the words. He told himself that after all the old man, having seen the body, could have noticed the graze on the ear and made the same deduction as he did. In that case, the lawyer replied drily, if it was something to be dismissed so casually at the time, it seemed needless to introduce it now, blown up into an additional charge.

Objective and impartial, Captain Albert later somewhat restored himself in the eyes of the lawyers when Pierre Charrier and Emile Pollak questioned him on another of the puzzles of the case: young Roger Perrin's lies, brought to light in the course of the officer's inquiry regarding the bicycle leaning against the mulberry tree on the morning of August 5. False alibis, inconsistent statements, lies and trumped-up testimony, why all these acrobatics, demanded the defence.

'It's true that his behaviour was peculiar,' Captain Albert acknowledged. 'He would talk freely and suddenly stop, blushing. Sometimes he anticipated my questions. "There were no firearms in the shed," he told me, for instance, when we were talking of something quite different. He told me voluntarily that it was his Uncle Clovis who had taught him how to poach and that he used to set snares at the place where the child was found. We pressed him to see how far he would go with his lies. We led him to contradict himself in the same sentence.'

What credence, then, could be placed in this spinner of yarns? And above all, was this travesty of the truth due to a congenital habit or to the need to fake an alibi? Captain Albert had his own very definite opinion about this and he gave it, to the distinct gratification of the defence. 'In my opinion,' he said, 'Roger Perrin slept at Grand'Terre and he and his whole family wanted to hide the fact.'

'Pure supposition,' retorted the advocate-general, who put the boy's contradictions down to fear of a scolding from his father if it was discovered that he had left La Serre that night. He said, M. Rozan recalled, that he was afraid of a 'roasting'.

A semantic argument began on the meaning of the word. Had Roger Perrin been afraid of a beating? Or simply of being bawled out by his father? The advocate-general argued that in Provençal the term did not imply violence, merely a tongue-lashing. 'When I was a boy my father, who was a justice of the peace, might "roast" me, but I assure you he never struck me.'

'To roast someone in Marseilles,' replied M. Pollak, 'is to knock him about.'

Gaston Dominici had followed the argument intently, apparently not wanting to miss anything said about his grandson. Roger Perrin plainly did not share in the affection which he gave the other eighteen. But what did he actually know about him? Had he slept at Grand' Terre or not? The moment had come to face Gaston with the question, a fundamental one since on the first day he had stated that, if he had any suspicions, they could only be of the boy.

The old man got up, looking puzzled. 'Whether Roger slept at our house or not, I can't say.'

The president said that surprised him. 'I go to bed and get up early,' was Gaston's easy explanation.

The advocate-general said, equally surprised, 'If he was there the night of the crime you would have known it. In any event you spoke of that night during the next few days?'

'If anyone had mentioned Roger's presence,' returned Gaston shortly, 'I'd have said so.'

Was it conceivable that in the atmosphere of Grand'Terre in August 1952 Roger Perrin's presence had been concealed from the despotic old man? Is it even possible that he, the absolute ruler, did not know that the boy had slept at the farm? President Bousquet tried to find out if at times the grandson who had passed part of his childhood at Grand'Terre came back to spend the night there. And if so, in which room he slept. Gaston did not answer. Another case of his making an accusation without offering the smallest shred of proof. The hearing ended on a bad note for him. If he knew the truth or even only a part of it, he had let an opportunity to say so slip away.

*

It was Saturday, November 20, and in the witness box at the beginning of the fourth session stood that strange lad Roger Perrin. Now 18, he was broad, round-shouldered, his face dull and stolid, his ears enormous. He was wearing dark blue trousers and an ill-fitting jacket. His large hands rested on the rail before him and he looked ill at ease. Since he was the grandson of the defendant, it was not necessary for him to take the oath.

From the first it was evident that the youth was out to break his past records and say anything that came into his head. Either Roger Perrin was feeble-minded, or he was a cunning rogue who knew how to mislead everyone.

In the witness box his account of how he had spent his time was not even the version he had given the gendarmes. He had not slept at Grand'Terre. He had not arrived there until 7.0 a.m. and had helped his grandfather cover the body of the little girl. Why had he lied to the gendarmes?

'My Aunt Yvette told me not to say anything.'

But to Sébeille and afterwards to Périès he had not reported this instruction from the young woman except as it related to the English visitors to the farmhouse. Why extend it now to his own alibi? The president pointed out to him that the two facts had no connection. Roger Perrin stared at him, uncomprehending, not uttering a word. He behaved the same way when the judge asked him if he had not helped to turn Lady Drummond's body. He said no, without the least sign of either disquiet or indignation at this incriminating suggestion.

President Bousquet turned the youth over to the advocate-general and the defence, wishing them better luck. The advocate-general and M. Pollak tried their hand, the latter especially. He adjured, implored, lost his temper, exhorted, pleaded, almost went down on his knees to the witness, who looked and listened, intrigued by this new game. The result: nil. Roger Perrin gave not one satisfactory explanation of his lies.

'In my opinion,' repeated the advocate-general, 'Roger Perrin was chiefly afraid that his father would scold him for loafing in bed. Notice one thing: all his lies relate to what he did from five o'clock, the time when he ought to have got up to water the horses, to seven, the probable time of his getting up.'

'Then let him tell us so himself,' M. Pollak responded. 'After two years he hasn't much to fear from his father.'

But Roger Perrin merely gave them a smile as enigmatic as his silence.

'At what time did you see your grandson?' the president asked Gaston Dominici.

The defendant got up again, one hand on the edge of the dock, the other on his hip. He confirmed that it was on his return, that is at about 8.0. No discrepancy here with his grandson who had recalled that it was after 7.0, and that he had just now named an hour at random. At this point, why quibble over a trifle?

The president then tried confronting grandfather and grandson. 'You have before you this boy whom you have accused,' he said. 'You said of him, "I have my suspicions because he's a good-for-nothing." Well?'

Calmly, without haste or raising his voice, Gaston answered, 'Well, it's quite possible that he's the murderer.'

In the box Roger laughed as if at a good joke.

'Why does Clovis accuse me?' Gaston demanded.

What connection was there between the two facts, the president asked in surprise. Was the defendant implying that he was being sacrificed to save Roger Perrin?

'Or someone in the house. Otherwise why should a son accuse his father? Clovis loved me and he says that I am guilty.'

'But the guilty one could also be Gustave,' the president objected.

'Him too,' said Gaston calmly.

Quite as baffling as this dialogue was the atmosphere in which it unfolded. A grandfather accuses his grandson, with his son as an accessory – a situation tragic, melodramatic, bewildering. Yet Gaston spoke with the same unconcern as if he were telling a good story. Roger Perrin was enjoying himself as if recalling a moonlit night when he had set a snare and caught a fine hare.

'Yes or no,' the president asked impatiently. 'Did Roger Perrin sleep at Grand'Terre?'

'I've no idea,' Gaston answered.

M. Pollak undertook a final attack. When he arrived on the scene had he seen Sir Jack's pyjamas? The boy said he had, only to be pulled up by the lawyer: the Englishman was hidden under a camp-bed and it was impossible to see what he was wearing. He therefore must have seen the body before the camp-bed was placed over it, and therefore must have been at Grand'Terre.

The advocate-general drew some photographs from the files. In his view the pyjamas protruded a little. M. Pollak replied that the gendarmes had noted otherwise. A prolonged controversy followed which was a perfect illustration of the whole business: the most commonplace fact became a source of fruitless argument.

Like the English family's canvas bucket. They had it when they came to the farmhouse for water, but it had never been found. Yet Roger Perrin declared that they had one. Yvette had denied the whole visit of Lady Drummond and her daughter. But according to M. Pollak, if Róger Perrin was telling the truth he had not invented the canvas bucket. Consequently he had seen it and therefore he had been at Grand'Terre. Either that or else he was lying from A to Z. M. Pollak made a great deal of this canvas bucket in his cross-examination.

But the experiment fell flat. Perhaps it would have had a chance with someone else, but Roger Perrin remained silent, utterly bewildered by such complicated intellectual machinery. 'I was at home,' he reiterated. Over his head a discussion began which put magistrates and lawyers in an unusual position. M. Pollak was indignant at the indulgence shown a demonstrable liar, but the judge pleaded extenuating circumstances in favour of a boy clearly mentally unstable.

At the lawyers' request Mr and Mrs Marrian, who were in the room, were recalled. Did they know of the canvas bucket's existence? Vaguely, they answered. They knew it existed among the camping equipment, but they had never seen it. Each side drew support from this: the prosecution to stress that it was an additional reason for supposing that the English mother and daughter had come to the farmhouse, the defence to denounce Roger Perrin's lie about his alibi.

Germaine Perrin was called. Her testimony aroused the same reactions as her son's. Roger's mother steered through contradictions with perfect ease. Thirty-eight years old, thin, with chestnut hair, hollow cheeks and suspicious eyes, she maintained that Roger had slept alone at La Serre. 'He didn't go to Grand'Terre any more after I quarrelled with my father.'

'But,' exclaimed the president, 'you yourself have stated that if Gustave passed your way that evening he would have taken your son with him so as not to leave him alone. They were good friends in spite of your estrangement. They went poaching together.'

Germaine Perrin denied that she had made any such statement. Nevertheless such a statement existed. Who had invented it?

Sébeille, Périès? In the best Dominici tradition, the young woman met these questions with silence.

'Do you know that your son has lied continuously?' asked M. Pollak.

'I scolded him for it,' she admitted.

'Did you ask him why he lied?' the president wondered.

'He told me he was afraid.'

'Of what?'

Stubborn silence from Germaine Perrin. Questions rained on her. The downpour left her unmoved.

'It's hard to resign oneself to the Perrin family's lies,' sighed M. Pollak.

'Hard indeed,' the president agreed, 'but what can we do?'

M. Delorme intervened to ask Germaine the reason for the break between herself and the defendant.

'He said nasty things about me,' she replied.

Until now Gaston had listened with no more than casual interest. But suddenly he came to life, a smile on his lips. He got up and with obvious relish filled in the details. 'Her husband came to tell me that he had surprised his wife with men. I told him, "Don't ferment your wine if you don't want to drink it afterwards."'

He looked over at his renegade daughter without the slightest hint of tenderness. This denunciation 'before the assembled people' was his revenge. He gloated over it and, sitting down, added a new formula to his protestations of innocence. 'I've never even killed a grasshopper.'

The afternoon was devoted to another star witness, Paul Maillet. This tall, thin, long-faced man clutched the rail eagerly. There was no need to press him, he got off to a quick start, launched into his recital without omitting the minutest detail, scarcely paused for breath as if fearful that someone might slip in an interruption, gave quotations in dialect, swore at every turn that he was sincere, digressed, started again at the beginning, and came out with expressions which delighted the whole room. 'The dishonour overhung my honour,' he declaimed dramatically when alluding to the suspicions which had once attached to him.

He had heard of the tragedy from a fellow worker who told him there had been 'butchery' at Grand'Terre. His first thought was – he did not say why – that old Dominici had massacred his goats. Then he went to the farm and took a pastis with the mayor of Lurs, who was there. He had even seen the magistrate Périès. Then he had received Gustave's confidences, about the screams, the lucerne field, and the rest. He swore that he had invented nothing. 'May my children die if it isn't true,' he ended ringingly.

M. Pollak went for him gently. He had liked Paul Maillet's evidence. He would have liked it even better if the linesman had spoken up earlier. Why had he for months concealed what had been revealed to him, even when being questioned under oath? He switched to irony. What benevolence on the part of the law towards those who refused to help it, who deceived it, lied by omission! Wasn't this because after the discovery of the sub-machine-guns in his house it had a hold on him?

Paul Maillet defended himself by saying that if he had not spoken before it was because the Dominicis were his best friends. He was in an impossible situation, caught between two fires. 'I hoped that Gustave would decide to speak.'

In the dock Gaston Dominici shifted and rumbled. It was plain that Paul Maillet was in for some home truths. The defendant was suddenly on his feet ready to speak his mind. 'I want to answer him on that,' he began.

He was furious, another person, malignant and pitiless. 'He's had time to plot with Clovis,' he shouted. 'He's a liar and a crook . . .'

The president tried to calm him. 'He's talking bloody nonsense,' snarled Gaston.

The judge's call to order didn't pacify the old man. 'I tell you, Paul – ' he turned to the witness – 'I am innocent in spite of your plots.' And thrusting a finger at him: 'Paul, look me in the face.'

Maillet did so. The two stared at each other, Gaston's face quivering with rage, the linesman wide-eyed, tense. The public was silent, waiting. But all that Gaston had to say was that Maillet had plotted against him with Clovis while he was hanging about the house, being served with fresh pastis and even at times having two eggs cooked for him to help him digest the drink. The voicing of this ingratitude appeared to fill the old man with as much pleasure as the airing of his daughter Germaine's morals had earlier.

'Is that all you have to say, Dominici?' asked the president.

'Yes,' the defendant replied, sitting down.

It was another anticlimax. The hearing ended with the evidence of Superintendent Constant, who described his investigation. In passing he made a telling remark about Gustave's behaviour. 'All the lies in the world do not constitute proof. Believe me, if we had wanted to frame someone, as we have been accused of doing, we had only to choose Gustave. It would have been child's play. But that is not a police officer's mentality.'

The following morning the sun disappeared from the Digne sky. Heavy clouds enveloped the neighbouring mountains, dissipating in a mist which made the spectators waiting for the doors to open shiver with cold.

M. Pollak took the offensive from the start. He asked the president that the members of the family should be required to take the oath. The example of Roger Perrin had been enlightening. Everybody had recognized that he was a liar. Yet he risked nothing, since he had not been sworn to tell the truth. Now the other members of the clan were to come. Why should they be allowed to get away with the same thing? The French Code does not forbid the swearing of an oath by the defendant's relatives. It is customary to let them off it in order not to place them in too painful a position. But in this case the trial depended on their honesty. It was impossible to give way to sentiment when the life of an old man hung on the words of his kin. The Dominicis must be made aware that should they lie when in the witness box they might incur the same penalties as the defendant.

'I agree,' replied advocate-general Rozan. 'All the Dominicis have lied at one time or another.'

Gaston, when the president asked him what he thought about it, answered with a smile, 'It would rather please me if they took the oath.'

The court, however, rejected M. Pollak's application. After deliberation, it ruled that in its interpretation the Code purely and simply forbade enforcement of the oath on the defendant's relatives.

'All right,' M. Pollak said bitterly, 'the witnesses know they can lie as they please.'

The president reprimanded him, reminding him that a lawyer had no right to comment on a ruling which had the immediate authority of a decision. And without further ado he called the next witness on the list, Superintendent Sébeille.

The man called the Maigret of Marseilles, and the pillar of the prosecution, came into the box haloed with a glory which was still bright. For the jurors, ordinary citizens attached to order, the word of a superintendent was worth its weight in gold. If he designated a person guilty, especially after a year's investigation in which he had had time to ponder, there could not be much doubt. For the defence, it was essential to diminish the credit he enjoyed.

For more than two hours he retraced the course of his inquiries. Soberly dressed, his hair sleek, straightforward in word and bearing, he made an excellent impression on the journalists studying him. His sequence of events sounded totally logical. He did not hide his doubts. It had soon become apparent to him that Gaston Dominici was open to suspicion, but he had not rejected two possibilities: Gustave's participation at some stage of the crime and Roger Perrin's presence at Grand'Terre. The objections now raised against him were not novel to Sébeille because he had thought of them himself. He recounted in detail the way in which he had obtained the admissions, insisting on the chronology which today seemed to him basic: it was Gustave and not Clovis who had first accused their father. There could thus be no question of pressure exerted by Clovis on his brother, since he had not been there when Gustave broke down weeping on the police officer's shoulder. 'The truth in my view,' he said, 'is contained in Gaston Dominici's sentence to the gendarme Guérino: "They took me for a prowler. I fired."'

After several questions from the president, M. Pollak rose slowly, remaining silent for a moment while he consulted his notes, husbanding his surprises, alert to the tension which suddenly gripped the room. The outcome of the trial perhaps hung on that moment. Sébeille had won the first round; he had been credible. It was now for Pollak and his colleagues, Pierre Charrier and Charles-Alfred, to undermine the jurors' and the courtroom's confidence.

'What does a police officer do when he receives from a witness a statement that is manifestly false?' the lawyer attacked.

'He tries to find out why he lied,' the superintendent replied tranquilly. 'But if he refuses to say, you can't make him.'

'So when Dominici said he had had Lady Drummond, didn't you react?'

Edmond Sébeille answered that he wanted to keep 'the authentic character' of the statement. 'If I had wanted to make the confessions agree with the material findings it would have been easy.'

'And you, the lawyers, would have been the first to blame him,' remarked the president.

The observation let loose thunderbolts. The other lawyers joined M. Pollak in accusing the president of aiding and even anticipating the prosecution. President Bousquet flushed with anger. He had had enough, he said, of being accused by the press, especially the British press, of a lack of impartiality. British justice was one thing, French another, and the procedures were not the same. And from counsel he took criticism even less readily.

Calm returned and Emile Pollak went on with his questions. He expressed surprise that Superintendent Sébeille could without batting an eye record a confession unrelated to fact. After all, a police officer had the right to say to a suspect, 'Your confession is inconceivable.' In reality, hadn't Sébeille quite simply feared that Dominici would retract? 'If this man had told you that he had killed with a crossbow, would you have noted it down in all seriousness?'

'Well, no,' Sébeille conceded, smiling.

And Clovis's and Gustave's lies which went on even after they had 'freed their consciences', had these not surprised the superintendent?

'Of course. But you have to take these people as they are. They utter a particle of truth, then start lying again.'

The lawyer listed a series of facts which gave him reason to think that the police had 'set up' the affair: oddly, Gaston Dominici gave as his motive for the crime one that Sébeille had suggested in his first report; Paul Maillet talked after the sub-machine-guns had been found in his house; Roger Perrin was looked upon as a mythomaniac but had been used as if he possessed the truth. 'You had only liars before you,' he concluded, 'yet you believed them. How many liars does it take to compose a truth?'

Sébeille answered that he hadn't had to wait for M. Pollak in order to learn that honesty was at a premium in Lurs. But even with liars it was possible, by pitting them against one another and comparing what they said, to arrive at some positive reality.

M. Pollak had finished. Had he turned the tide? Very little, it seemed. Journalists and spectators exchanged puzzled glances. Perhaps they had expected too much of the clash between the police officer and the lawyer. The general feeling was conveyed by Jean-Bernard Derosne in L'Aurore: 'To convince us henceforth of the defendant's innocence it will have to be demonstrated that Superintendent Sébeille is raving mad and that we are all mad to believe a word he says.' And Pierre Scize in Le Figaro: 'The calibre of the defence's guns was too small and their ammunition insufficient.'

Following his colleague, M. Charles-Alfred told Sébeille that he had interpreted the unfired cartridges near the bodies incorrectly. The superintendent had deduced from them that the murderer – the lawyer did not of course say Gaston Dominici – not knowing how to use the semi-automatic carbine, believed that it had to be reloaded after each shot, which involved the ejection of the cartridge introduced into the loading chamber by the expulsion of the previous one. But he pointed out that in the gunsmith's report the undischarged cartridges had been 'lightly percuted'. The gunsmith explained this by the fact that these cartridges were not made for the weapon. Had the superintendent paid attention to the expert's conclusion and altered his view? Sébeille admitted that the point had not occurred to him, which shocked the British journalists; they were again astonished that the law and the police concentrated so much on psychology and were so often negligent when it came to exploiting the more material clues.

As the law requires, the president gave the last word to the defendant. Gaston had listened watchfully, attentive to his old enemy's evidence, his fist supporting his head on the edge of his wooden enclosure. He looked tired, his cheeks hollow, pouches under his eyes; but this hadn't hindered him from intermittent side-line refereeing. He became indignant when the police officer repeated their conversations as weapons against him, calling on his lawyers to note the animosity of a man he had welcomed like a son, smiling with an air of exasperation when the witness described the circum-stances of his confessions. Then during M. Pollak's counter-attack he straightened up, exultant, inviting the president with a motion of his hand to follow his defender's luminous reasoning, gesturing pro-vocatively at the advocate-general, nodding his head vigorously to mark his approval of M. Pollak.

The courtroom fell silent as Gaston Dominici launched into a long and laborious soliloquy made up largely of jerky, often dis-connected sentences. 'You remember, Monsieur Sébeille, the terrible night you made me go through. You didn't even ask me if I had had anything to eat. I had nothing in my stomach. You made me turn somersaults. When they took me away it never stopped. You told me exactly what I must do there. You put your fist under my nose. You kept saying, "It was you, wasn't it, say it was you." And the things you did to me, what you did to me! I didn't sleep. You didn't hit me, it's true, but I had a very bad night. I was in a sort of delirium. I am sincere and honest. You will see that from Gustave and all the family. It's like the dog, I beat him, he's a good dog, he's greedy, you have to correct him, he herded the goats.'

He might have been talking to himself, as if reviving old memories. His voice was low and the words were hard to catch. Then he again turned his eyes on the superintendent, who stood in the witness box. 'In the morning,' the defendant went on, 'you gave me a little coffee. What you did to me! Since the day before I had not eaten. You made me say what you wanted me to. That's what you did to the father of a family. I assure you, Monsieur Sébeille, that I am sincere and honest. Yes, I am sincere and honest. I've done harm to nobody. We'll see when Clovis and Gustave are here. Clovis was trembling all over, so that the magistrate was obliged to get down on his knees and put his ear to his mouth to hear that he was accusing me. And the police officers tried to talk to me in dialect. But they didn't know it. You remember, Monsieur Sébeille. In the morning you said to get up. I couldn't stand. You had coffee brought me, but not out of pity, Monsieur Sébeille. You said, "It's good, the coffee is good." I drank it, and what was in the coffee? What did you put into it, eh, that I went off my head? It made me dizzy. I was out of my mind and didn't know any more what I was saying.'

He broke off for a moment and regained his breath, his Adam's apple moving up and down in an obsessive rhythm.

'The guards, good lads, saved my life. They took care of me day after day. At Marseilles, at Saint-Charles, I was even better off. The head guard looked after me as if I had been his father . . .'

The words tailed slowly away into silence and the president waited a moment. But Gaston Dominici did not resume. He had finished. Resting on his arms on the edge of the dock, he contemplated the superintendent, who smiled faintly.

'In short,' said the president, 'you claim to have been drugged. You never said so until now.'

Gaston protested, 'I told the magistrate the first day. It hurt me very much.'

'And it was in the coffee that they put this drug?'

The judge's scepticism irritated the old man. 'If they hadn't given me the coffee, would I have made such a fool of myself? It had to be a drug for me to act the fool like that.'

The president turned to M. Pollak. Did he mean to plead that his client had been drugged with some truth serum?

The lawyer looked embarrassed. 'You have to understand the defendant,' he began.

'We understand,' the advocate-general chaffed him. 'Confessions can be most disconcerting.'

'We'll explain them,' the lawyer promised, 'even without drugs. But Gaston Dominici simply means that after drinking the coffee he lost control. Baffled, he came up with this explanation. I have another one which I shall give you.'

The president asked Gaston if he had anything else to say. Now was the time; afterwards it would be too late. But Gaston shook his head. 'I've said it all,' he declared, 'thank you, Monsieur le Président.'

He sat back again, looking very tired, no longer listening and mechanically submitting to being led out when the court rose.

11

Tuesday, November 23. The sun had reappeared at Digne but Dominici had not recovered his zest or his rebellious spirit. He sat bowed in the dock, inattentive, listless, washed out. Several times he yawned openly.

The policemen who had first received his confessions followed each other in the box, from the gendarme Guérino to Superintendent Prudhomme. In minute detail they recounted what they had seen and heard. At the time he let himself go with Guérino, Gaston was no longer subjected to any pressure. It was he who volunteered, 'They took me for a prowler.' And the policeman emphasized that he had said nothing, overawed by the instructions he had been given to listen and remain silent. Moreover, Guérino knew little about the affair. He would have been incapable of breathing so much as a hint about it to the defendant.

The lawyers wrangled over the slight differences they discerned between his original statements and his evidence in the dock. He had just said, for instance, that Dominici had prefaced his confession with a groan of, 'The little one, the little one.' Until now, Guérino had never reported these words.

'It's true,' he admitted. 'They've come back to me since.'

Dominici, when questioned, declared that he remembered absolutely nothing of what he might have said to Guérino. 'I was out of my mind,' he asserted. It was the line he would take consistently throughout the morning as the gendarme Bocca, the concierge Giraud, and Superintendent Prudhomme were called successively to testify. Prudhomme had a few nasty minutes with the defence. Pierre Charrier found it more than surprising that the superintendent had felt it necessary to telephone his colleague Sébeille to check various points in Gaston's confession and notably the existence of the mulberry tree. Didn't Superintendent Prudhomme know about it? Hadn't he ever been to the place? The officer answered, 'Only once.' Defence counsel expressed ironical surprise over this lack of interest on the part of a man who operated in the region. It seemed to them that Prudhomme and Sébeille had set this up between them, and Prudhomme's lofty ignorance was intended to mislead; for example, how could he have made any suggestion to Dominici when he didn't even know of the mulberry tree?

A little before noon President Bousquet requested the court usher to bring in Marie Dominici, the Sardine. The trial was entering a new phase: it was finally the family's turn for the limelight. For five days brothers and sisters had been awaiting this moment. They had been seen each day leaving the palace in two groups, the faithful on one side, the deserters on the other. The former went at lunch-time to a modest restaurant in old Digne whose owner was a friend. A table was reserved for them and they ate separated from the rest of the world by an invisible barrier, refusing to answer questions, driving away the photographers who soon stopped following them. In the evening they returned to Grand'Terre, where mattresses had been placed in every corner.

Only Clovis, who could not return home every evening, slept at Digne in a hotel room. Sometimes he lunched with Germaine, but mostly he was alone. He suffered and would speak to no one. He fled the journalists and even his friends. He received insulting letters and believed that most of them were inspired by his brothers and sisters. One of them contained a newspaper photograph of him; the anonymous sender had pierced the eyes with a pin. It was a form of curse. Clovis's throat tightened.

A black scarf on her head, wrapped in a dark robe which outlined her long, frail figure, Marie Dominici went into the box. Gaston looked at her, then sank down in the dock leaning against the wall. The only life in the old woman's thin, wrinkled face was in her eyes, which retained their alertness and depth. But at no time did she glance towards her husband.

What she said dovetailed at all points with the official family line; she had seen nothing, heard nothing except the shots which for her had no significance. She had learned of the crime in the morning. The English mother and daughter had not come to the house in the evening and she had not thought of going to verify if the child was beyond help. She had never seen the carbine, although she went to the shed practically every day.

M. Pollak asked her about her married life. 'I've never wanted for anything,' she answered. 'I have nothing to reproach him with.'

Gaston Dominici rose. He was prey to a powerful emotion which reduced the courtroom to dead silence. His trembling hands grasped the edge of the dock. His chin moved convulsively. Several times he passed his fingers over his lips as if to loosen them. Long seconds elapsed before he could speak. Perhaps he would utter some words of love. Had the Sardine waited fifty years to hear her husband express affection for her in a court? 'Marie,' he finally said, 'when I got back in the morning were my trousers wet, stained with blood?'

The public was flabbergasted. There was even some laughter, the result of the preceding tension. Only Marie Dominici did not seem surprised. She calmly replied that her husband's trousers had been dry, without stains. It was a reply meant for the prosecution, since according to several witnesses, notably Inspector Girolami, trousers were drying on a line in the courtyard of Grand'Terre on the afternoon of August 5.

When the court adjourned for lunch, Marie Dominici was swallowed up in the crowd flowing out. To catch a glimpse of her husband whom the gendarmes were taking away, she got up on a chair and made signs to him with her hand. He did not see them. Marie Dominici suddenly broke into sobs, still standing on the chair, a statue of despair that tore at the heart. It was Gustave, coming from the witnesses' room, who took her by the arm and helped her down. 'What did you say?' he asked.

When the hearing was resumed at about three, Yvette Dominici was brought in, wearing a striped blue suit over a red and green pullover with a gold cross suspended from her neck by a chain. She seemed neither intimidated nor worried.

But her evidence was delayed because M. Pollak again demanded that all the Dominicis should take the oath, beginning with Yvette. The court took an hour to deliberate before the claim was dismissed as being 'inopportune at the present stage of the trial'. Yvette was therefore heard without being sworn.

Her testimony was a compromise of her various statements. The young woman fell back on her original position, although she had to modify it by the addition of some awkward details. Certainly, she repeated in accord with her husband, they had not got up at the sound of the shots and had only learned of the tragedy in the morning. But she was forced to admit that her husband had told her 'the child was still alive.' She had not put herself out to see if she could do anything for the child.

'What indifference!' murmured the president with a sigh.

Yvette said nothing.

'On December 18th, 1953,' the president went on, 'you made quite another statement.'

On that day, in fact, the young woman had acknowledged that Gustave had got up immediately after the shots and seen his father reeling about the courtyard. He had gone down and the old man had confessed to the crime. How could she have made such a statement if it were not true? She had even added details; her father-in-law seemed dazed, like a man drunk. One does not invent such things.

'The magistrate told me,' Yvette asserted, 'that if I did not say the same as Gustave it would go badly for him. My father-in-law is innocent, but so is my husband. I was afraid they would arrest them both.'

The president read out sentence by sentence the statement of December 18. Yvette impugned it all with a shake of her head, repeating that they had not got up before 5.0. M. Delorme intervened. Did she know that it was her husband and not Clovis, as she seemed to think, who had first accused his father?

'They hit him,' she said. 'He told me so.'

This revelation, of which she seemed to expect much, excited no reaction whatever. She affirmed that Gustave had sworn to her that he had spoken only because Clovis made him do so. But M. Delorme pointed out that it was impossible that she could believe this since she knew that Clovis had left the Palais de Justice on November 13, 1953, before Gustave broke down in tears on Sébeille's shoulder. Yvette hesitated a little, but never lost her head, returning always to her original and unshakable version: they had not got up. She stood up to both the counsel for the prosecution and to the advocate-general, unmoved by reminders of what she had said on other occasions, determined in support of what she said now. Although not a blood member of the family, she would not betray it by so much as a word.

It was time for Clovis Dominici to testify, but as it was late the defence wanted it put off until the next day. A compromise was reached: Clovis would make his statement and the cross-examination would be held over until the morning. So the faithless son arrived in the witness box, carefully shaved, his square face strained, features drawn, dressed like his father in velvet trousers and grey jacket. His voice choked at first, and the words came with difficulty. He was visibly mortified at having to accuse his father 'before the assembled people'. Gaston Dominici's face displayed not so much hatred as a kind of sardonic malice.

Clovis described his torment since Superintendent Sébeille had shown him the carbine on the railway line. He recognized it clearly, having seen it on the shelf in the shed. For a long while he suspected Gustave, even after his father had admitted to the crime one evening in the kitchen. He wondered if his father was not simply drunk at the time.

As Clovis's testimony proceeded, Gaston Dominici became restless in the dock. Sweat broke out on his forehead. The movement of his Adam's apple quickened.

'Are you aware of the charges you are making?' the president asked Clovis when he had finished.

'Perfectly,' answered Clovis, passing a hand wearily over his forehead.

'It is a shocking tragedy,' the judge pursued. 'But it would be even more shocking if a son were wrongfully to hold his father responsible.'

Clovis nodded. 'I know.'

The judge studied him for a moment, then spacing his words to emphasize their solemnity, he said, 'Clovis Dominici, this is a serious moment. Do you maintain what you have just said? If you have lied, there is still time to admit it.'

Clovis breathed a despairing sigh. Then in a broken voice he answered, 'It's terrible, but I can only stand by what I have said. It is the truth.'

The emotion in the courtroom was intense. In the dock, Gaston listened with his mouth open. His expression was frozen, his look stony. Then suddenly his muscles relaxed, and he looked a very, very old man.

The hearing was adjourned. It was a necessary respite, the tension had become unbearable. Followed by the hostile gaze of his brothers and sisters, Clovis left.

'It'll kill me,' he murmured to the journalists who accompanied him. 'Why does my father go on denying it? He's an old man, he's to be pitied . . .'

Wednesday, November 24, the seventh session. At 9.0 a.m. Clovis resumed his place in the box. His face looked tired and his shoulders were bowed. In the dock Gaston was on edge and restless, his face quivering like that of a hunted animal.

After a few questions from the prosecutor Sabatier, Emile Pollak was called upon. He first remarked that Clovis had a strange reputation: he passed for an honest man. Yet he continued to lie, even after having accused his father – and on a matter of major importance, the carbine. He had claimed that he didn't know it. Why disguise the truth once the main accusation had been made? Clovis's answer was confused; he had recognized the weapon but hadn't known to whom it belonged. Emile Pollak shrugged his shoulders; Clovis was joking, since on his own admission he had seen it in the shed at Grand'Terre though the magistrate Périès had had to fight like a lion to get even this much out of him. Why? Was it because at some time or another Clovis had handled the weapon? Or because other members of the Dominici family had used it and he wanted to shield them? Clovis answered these questions in monosyllables.

Why was he the only one to have seen the carbine, and not the other members of the family? Where was it exactly? Clovis repeated that it was on a shelf and you had to get on a chair to see it. That was how he had found it when he was looking for some twine.

It was Gaston Dominici's turn. Getting slowly to his feet, he tapped his forehead to imply that Clovis was not all there, 'And what's more,' he said, 'he's always lied.'

The example he chose spat from his mouth. Clovis had said during the inquiry that in December 1952 he had gone to Grand'Terre for Christmas but that he could not eat, he was so sickened by the behaviour of his father who got drunk and started a row.

'It's true he didn't eat,' said Gaston, 'but that was because he had been celebrating disgustingly on the way. Well, you swine – ' he glared directly at the detested Clovis – 'what about it?'

Clovis gave a start but did not answer.

'He always plotted against me,' Gaston charged.

'I've told the truth!'

'Liar!'

'In front of all these people, I swear . . .'

The altercation went on between the two without getting anywhere. Gaston accused Clovis of being a poacher, and the son defended himself as if it were the most heinous of crimes.

'What are you doing to the family honour?' Gaston flung at him.

'The family honour – that's good after what you've done,' Clovis flung back.

Gaston admitted that while Clovis was at Grand'Terre during Gustave's imprisonment he had quarrelled with his wife and that his son had become involved. But it had had nothing to do with the English people and their death. Gaston spoke of the subsidence. In the confusion it was difficult to understand what he was getting at when he apparently stated that he 'had gone out because of the landslide.' Disorder reigned, and the president cut it short by dismissing Clovis.

It was only at nightfall that the trial resumed its normal course. At 4.45 after the president had questioned a few interim witnesses on points of detail, Gustave Dominici was called. The courtroom quickened.

The farmer entered in a jacket a little too tight for him, a white shirt and dark tie. Full-faced, high-coloured, cheekbones prominent, mouth tight, the immediate impression was of an iron-hard man. But as soon as he got under way, the mask slipped. He reverted to the real Gustave of the early days, a man with a mind incapable of grasping and holding a truth, yet not in the least dismayed at being caught out, his defeats and admissions forgotten. Whatever words he uttered became in that moment the only reality, blotting out all those he had spoken previously. His evidence was incoherent, but no reproof or insult touched him. He was made of marble.

Like Yvette, he returned to his first statements. He had not risen until 5.0 a.m. and it was then that he discovered the child's body. He even went back on the testimony that had brought about his conviction in December 1952: that he had seen the child's arm move. Then in November 1953 the police officers had come for him. 'When they saw that I wouldn't talk they struck me,' he declared.

He maintained that they had forced him to accuse his father, that Gaston was innocent. He had said so to the magistrate Périès, who had laughed in his face. He had understood that Clovis was at the bottom of it all: 'He wanted to make Father out a murderer.' That was why he had wept on Sébeille's shoulder. Later he had indicated the carbine's position because Clovis had shown him a sketch.

'They kept repeating, "Choose, you or the old man! At his age it's better it should be him." That's why I accused him. But it was the worst moment in my life. I can state plainly: "My father is innocent. The whole family as well. We knew nothing, we had no part in it." '

The president heard him out. Had Gustave finished? 'Yes,' he answered.

'Then,' said the judge, 'we can begin.'

An extraordinary judicial duel ensued. The president attempted by sheer perseverance to seize a truth which had just fallen to pieces. With tireless obstinacy Gustave kept tearing the reconstituted fabric apart. He brought a remarkable self-control to the task. Not a drop of sweat showed on his brow, not a sign of worry on his stolid face.

The judge remarked with surprise that Gustave had never before alleged that he had been struck. The witness replied that he had told the magistrate Périès, whereupon the president took an exceptional step. Roger Périès, who was present as a spectator, was ordered to come forward.

He grimly took his place beside Gustave. 'Gustave Dominici told me,' he said, 'that he had been roughly handled. I therefore asked him if he had been struck. He answered no. Otherwise I would have called in a doctor.'

'I was punched in the stomach.'

'You're a liar,' snapped Périès. 'You never told me that.'

The president decided to run through the whole dossier with Gustave. The result was surprising. Gustave now claimed that he had let himself be convicted at Digne on his own confession by falsely declaring that he had seen the child move when she was actually quite dead. Moreover, he had given way to the motor-cyclist Olivier when the latter lied for no perceptible reason.

'Listen,' the judge admonished, 'you can't have it both ways. Either you are lying now or you lied to Superintendent Sébeille. And you have done a terrible thing in accusing your father. I have conducted many trials, but I have never seen a witness like you.'

Gustave was in no way embarrassed. 'It was Clovis who did the accusing.'

'You know that's not true.'

'It is true,' maintained Gustave, unruffled.

Three times Périès was called. Patiently, almost resignedly, he flatly contradicted the witness. For instance, Gustave had asserted that it was on the magistrate's advice that he had admitted in December 1953 to going out at 2.0 a.m.: if he said he had seen the little girl at 4.0 he would have been accused of killing her. Where was the sense in all that, Roger Périès indignantly demanded. Then Gustave once more repeated that it was Clovis who made the first accusation, asserting that he had had this from Périès. The latter only declared, somewhat discouraged, that 'Gustave is lying again.' Finally, under further questioning, Gustave said he had 'spoken because the police had forced him to.' This time Périès became angry. 'I state flatly that Gustave Dominici never complained to me of any

303

constraint whatsoever. He even said to me once that I had always treated him like a brother.'

President Bousquet tirelessly pressed home his attack. He listed the details Gustave had given, the shots, the screams, his father reeling round the courtyard as if demented, the old man's admission, and the desperate conversation Gustave had had with his wife: they had felt it was all over for them. Had all that been invented, inflated by the police? 'They never tried to find out the truth,' Gustave sighed.

At this the courtroom broke into cries, murmurs, even catcalls. Little by little the hostile atmosphere broke down Gustave's self-control. His face began to twitch, his jaw to contract, and his hands clenched on the box.

'You have done nothing but lie,' the president flung at him.

'I have never told any lies.'

The public let out a spontaneous 'Oh!' of amazement, at which Gustave very nearly lost his temper. He turned glowering to the spectators. 'I've always told the truth,' he insisted.

Suddenly Gaston rose in the dock. 'It was Gustave who first accused me,' he said.

'There,' remarked the president. 'It's decided.'

Gustave was in no way put out. 'I've lied all along,' he said.

During the short recess that followed, Gustave strolled in the corridor with Yvette on his arm. He appeared unperturbed by the curious stares he encountered.

After the recess the defence took over. Gustave continued to offer two alternative explanations: either the police had dictated everything or else he had followed Clovis. He seemed to have understood nothing, retained nothing of what he had said previously. For these people past and present had no meaning, as witness a curious remark of Gaston's: 'I'd like to know why Gustave accuses me like that.'

Gustave had long since ceased to do so, but for Gaston time had crystallized at the moment when his son had denounced him. He had neither forgiven nor forgotten. He was happy to see Gustave on the rack, it was his punishment. The pleasure the old man took obliterated the rest.

The remark brought a heartfelt response from the president. 'We should also very much like to know,' he said. He turned to Gustave. 'What did you say to M. Périès on November 13, 1953, when you stated that it was your father who had done the deed?'

Silence from Gustave.

'I will remind you. You said, "I'd rather you had it come from somewhere farther off. I wouldn't want my father to know that it was me who accused him." And, "Don't confront me with my father, I could never repeat the accusation I made against him."'

Gustave still said nothing, while the old man watched him from the dock with a hard and implacable eye.

'Did you in fact say that?' asked the president.

The witness had turned very pale. 'I don't remember,' he muttered.

The president shook his head, discouraged. 'It's you, Gustave, who made your father out to be a triple murderer. The most elementary courage requires you to accept responsibility for your accusation. You have refused to do it. Is that right?'

'No, it's not right,' Gustave admitted, scarcely audible.

'And is that all?'

Another long silence. 'Yes, that's all,' said Gustave.

The hearing was adjourned amid general surprise. Why wasn't Gustave handed over to the prosecution and the defence for questioning? At that moment he seemed helpless; his powers of resistance were perhaps exhausted.

By interrupting the proceedings the president allowed Gustave an unhoped-for respite. By returning to his family he could draw fresh strength from them. But if the president was strongly criticized by some for the adjournment, it should be pointed out that it was already nearly 7.0 p.m. The proceedings had been going on since morning. They had been absorbing, tense, exhausting. The jury had shown signs of impatience. Furthermore, no one objected, not even the lawyers, who were themselves beginning to feel the effects of fatigue.

In any event, the examination of Gustave marked a decisive turning-point in the trial. Doubt had crept in. Until now observers had praised Sébeille and Périès. Now they began asking whether they hadn't stopped short of the whole truth.

'If by chance,' wrote Pierre Scize in *Le Figaro*, 'the court convicts Gaston, the aged defendant, we shall be confronted with a strange judicial error in reverse, singular not in that it will have condemned an innocent man but that it will have allowed a guilty one to go free.'

'This trial is frightening,' wrote Jean-Bernard Derosne in *L'Aurore*. 'It is heading straight for a judicial error, the error being that only one will be convicted where several are guilty.'

Thursday, November 25, the eighth session. Gustave was called immediately. In the dock Gaston's face looked thinner as he regarded those present with a dispirited gaze. Nevertheless it was he who lit the fuse by interrupting the prosecutor, Sabatier, when he was putting questions to Gustave, who had regained the self-mastery which had deserted him the evening before.

'He's accusing me!' the old man snapped.

'Not any longer,' observed the prosecutor.

'He did accuse me.' And he turned to address his son, unexpectedly moving, again assuming the character he had played in the early days.

'I loved you, Gustave,' he said. 'We didn't see much of each other, I went to bed and got up early, but I did everything for you. And you've brought me to this! You denied your mother. You denied your brothers, you denied me. Because of you they shut me up like a sheep in a fold. You have committed a mortal sin. You know that I am innocent.'

He turned to the president. 'He knows perfectly well where the carbine was. It did not come from far away.'

Instantly the atmosphere of the day before was recreated, highly charged, the courtroom suddenly still: had the moment of truth at last arrived?

'When Gustave was in the lucerne field with someone,' the defendant went on, 'he knew who had that carbine.' Leaning over the dock, he fixed his son with a gaze as if lying in wait for him with a secret he intended to use like a weapon.

President Bousquet turned to Gustave. 'Your father has just made a grave assertion.'

Gustave shook his head. He seemed embarrassed. 'I wasn't in the field.'

'You must tell the truth,' Gaston continued authoritatively. 'The carbine was at La Serre [the Perrin farm]. Think of the honour of the family!'

'I am thinking of it, Father.'

Gaston raised his voice. He stood tall in the dock, arm outstretched, expression dramatic. 'The dishonour you are sowing in the family is shameful. Have you thought of the grandchildren? Would you rather I was in prison?'

'I have said it,' Gustave protested. 'You are innocent.'

But Gaston, levelling an avenging arm at him, said, 'That's not what you ought to say. You ought to proclaim, "I know the truth and here it is"; you saw it!'

306

Gustave rebelled. 'No, I didn't see it.'

But Gaston kept on: Gustave knew, he had seen, he should speak. Gustave stubbornly insisted that he knew nothing.

'Gustave,' pleaded M. Pollak, 'everybody begs you to tell the truth. Save us from this appalling doubt.'

'My father is innocent,' was all Gustave answered.

'Say it, say it,' Gaston urged.

'I've told the truth.'

The room rumbled like a wave about to break. How long was this scene, at once so harrowing and frustrating, to go on?

'You see,' the president finally brought it home to Gaston, 'there's nothing to be got out of him.'

'No, nothing,' the old man said, and sat down again.

Gustave left the box without a glance at his father, and the hearing continued, although with no reduction in tension. Five or six times the proceedings seemed about to take a definitive turn as the Dominici family settled its accounts. Brothers and sisters followed each other in the dock, united in defence of their father and hatred of the traitors. But the quarrel remained on the level of insult and invective.

It was of course Clovis who was the chief target. He had been assailed by his sister Augusta, a plump, excitable woman who almost at once insisted on a confrontation with him. She was convinced that it was he who had first accused their father, and did not believe the president when he pointed out to her that on the contrary the initiative had come from Gustave alone.

Clovis was recalled and Augusta at once demanded why he had accused their father. Clovis told her that he had only revealed what he had heard, and especially the sentence in dialect: 'I'm the one who killed the three of them. If I have to kill one more, I will.' Through Augusta, the Dominici clan voiced its own interpretation of this false confession. Gaston had not said, '*I* killed . . .' but '*He* killed . . .', meaning Paul Maillet, whom Clovis, like everybody else, had suspected. Glaring at him, Augusta declared that if Clovis had seen the carbine, it was elsewhere than in the shed. But Clovis didn't give an inch; he had seen the Rock-Ola in the shed and nowhere else.

Next in line came Augusta's husband, quite ready to land Clovis one for having said that he had seen the carbine whereas he had admitted in front of him that he didn't know it and that in his opinion it belonged to Paul Maillet. 'Are we all liars then?' Clément Caillat asked truculently.

He was standing very near Clovis, his fists clenched, ready to strike. The president called him to order, and Caillat contented himself with a volley of abuse which Clovis didn't seem to hear, although a slight quivering of his face indicated his distress. Each of Clément's insults ended in the refrain that it was Clovis who had accused his father. Eventually M. Delorme asked that Gustave be recalled; it was necessary that he publicly acknowledge that he had been first to accuse, and perhaps then the Dominicis would concede that they were mistaken or had been deceived.

It was an uncomfortable moment for Gustave. He found himself incapable of maintaining before Clovis that he had followed and not preceded him. He therefore put all the blame on the police; they had only wanted lies, he said.

Gaston rose to his feet. 'That's true,' he said. 'And the big one over there is the biggest liar of all.' He pointed a finger at Clovis and added a sentence which passed almost unnoticed in the hubbub. 'He's the one who put the disc on the gun.' Then he remembered that until now he had not known of the existence of the American weapon. 'At least I suppose so,' he corrected himself.

He launched another broadside of curses which took in Clovis as well as the other members of the family. The hearing was suspended. Clovis remained alone in the box. 'It's terrible, terrible,' he kept repeating.

There was an interlude which gave time for tempers to calm down. A Hillman car was shown to the jurors in the courtyard of the palace. Around the vehicle a lively discussion went on as to whether Sir Jack could have caught his hand on the bumper.

Little time was needed for the atmosphere to heat up again when the trial was resumed. The president began by confronting another man who had come forward months earlier, Joseph Chauve, who sold rings and identity discs – probably including that on the rifle – with all those who might be suspected of possessing and patching it up: Gustave, Roger Perrin, Clovis, Paul Maillet. Chauve did not recognize any of them. The judge had no more success with the truck driver Duc, who in the night had seen a man at the scene of the crime.

But with daughter-in-law Marie Dominici, wife of son Gaston, there was another incident. She affirmed that shortly after her father-in-law's arrest she had sought out Clovis at the Lurs station to rebuke him for his conduct. 'He answered me, "Forget it, it's better that an old man should go to prison than a young one."'

Clovis denied saying any such thing and his sister-in-law, after flinging a contemptuous insult at him, was ordered from the box by the president. The swirl of hatred surrounding Clovis did not shake him. Solid, rough-hewn, his brothers' and sisters' outbursts of anger broke over his head with no visible effect.

But this was only in appearance. In fact, the succession of vicious attacks, these waves of assault unceasingly renewed, were wearing him down. The clan was staking its all. They had only this one day left in which to reclimb a slope down which they had daily slipped a little farther. Clovis was the scapegoat. It was plain that he was holding on only by a superhuman effort.

The height of the struggle came when Clotilde Araman was called. Like the others, she declared that Clovis had accused his father while harbouring the most serious doubts about Paul Maillet. The president had the two brothers put in the witness box. Clovis denied having seriously suspected Paul Maillet.

This so infuriated the usually placid Gustave that he seized Clovis by the arm and all but shook him, while his brother tried to hold him off. 'You betrayed me,' cried Gustave.

'You know that isn't so,' said Clovis more calmly. 'You were convicted out of your own mouth.'

But Gustave – who had doubtless been blamed for being too soft – was beyond hearing. He shouted, 'Clovis has betrayed everybody, his father and his brother.'

'You know very well that's not true,' said the president.

Maillet was recalled, risky in the circumstances, for the atmosphere between the three men, Gustave on the one hand, Paul Maillet and Clovis on the other, soon developed into that of a street brawl. Paul Maillet, gripped by Gustave, confirmed that Clovis had had nothing to do with what Gustave had confided to him: the child had moved. Gustave was by now in a paroxysm of rage; he brandished his fist in front of Clovis and Maillet, glaring at both of them. The president let it go on for a moment; some light might emerge from the collision.

Gaston intervened. He distributed blame and praise in a way completely removed from logic but that satisfied his grudges. Gustave had indeed been in the lucerne field and in this respect Paul Maillet was to be believed. But the carbine had not been at Grand'Terre; it belonged to Clovis. 'Ask him to whom he lent it.'

Clovis's mouth tightened involuntarily, which incensed the

lawyers; this was no laughing matter. Gustave seized the opportunity to go for him again but Clovis roughly repelled him.

'It's Maillet and Clovis who dreamed up all this nonsense,' Gaston concluded.

Gustave echoed his father, with an addition of his own. Why had Clovis denounced him?

'Don't take on the task of justice, Gustave,' the president reprimanded him sharply. 'You hardly have the right.'

The hearing ended with a very quiet statement from a Dominici: Léon, a nephew who had been brought up by the defendant along with his own children. Léon was beyond question a more cultivated man than his cousins. He described in a few emotional sentences what his life had been like at Grand'Terre. He was surprised that his uncle should have been spoken of as a bully. 'I've seen him called the boar of Grand'Terre, the tyrant, the despot. Nonsense! He was like a father to me. I have never seen him raise his hand to a child. He thought only of working to keep us.'

Léon had settled in the Jura and knew nothing of the case. But certain facts surprised him. He had never, for instance, seen the carbine, but if it had been at Grand'Terre it would have been shown to him as useful for shooting boar. Moreover, he remembered the harsh grass of his childhood; he did not see how Elizabeth's feet could have remained unmarked.

After the day's storms he brought a breath of fresh air. Léon Dominici was the last of the witnesses to be heard. The trial had come to its fateful closing stages.

Friday, November 26. The time for the final summing-up had arrived. One after another counsel for the prosecution and the defence would seek to impose their own conviction on the seven jurors who in this trial had been the most unobtrusive of participants; throughout the entire eight days they had asked not a single question. As obliged by the law, the president had asked them after each witness's testimony whether they wanted any point clarified. None of the seven ever did, as if everything said had been admirably self-explanatory.

Frost and sleet in Digne. Gaston Dominici reflected the weather, his complexion grey, his movements slow, his expression dazed. His fatigue was such that the lawyers thought of asking for a day's adjournment to allow him some rest. But he flatly refused.

M. Claude Delorme spoke first.[1] He was a thin, dark, severe-looking man. He was a civil practitioner with little criminal experience. As a result he strained too hard at times. But his recital of the facts had the virtue of clarity. He opened by recalling the life and career of Sir Jack Drummond. Then he moved on to his thesis. 'If Gaston Dominici is innocent, it must be allowed that he wanted to sacrifice himself for his family.' Was this possible?

'It's a puerile notion,' M. Delorme declared. 'You have seen the members of this family. Have you observed any nobility in them, and especially in this old man who is ready to accuse his sons and even his grandson to save himself? The background to this case is the tissue of Dominici lies; they can only be accounted for by the need to conceal from justice an obvious guilt.'

For M. Delorme there was no need to look much farther; the truth resided in the *spontaneous* statement – he emphasized this point – made by Gaston Dominici to the gendarme Guérino. The whole Dominici affair, a news story and a trial that had excited the whole world, came down to a stupid row between an English scientist who took the neighbouring farmer for a prowler, and the farmer offended at being driven off his own land.

M. Delorme's speech retraced step by minute step the details of the investigation and the indictment. He acknowledged the absence of material proof, but there was no disregarding the incriminating testimony, corresponding demonstrably with the facts established in November 1953. That month had brought the moment of simple truth: that Gaston was guilty. The speaker could envisage only one penalty: death.

The afternoon should have been devoted to addresses by the prosecutor, Sabatier, and the advocate-general, Rozan. But the comings and goings between an overheated room and the frozen streets had been too much for the advocate-general's health. The hearing was cut short; the jury would hear only the prosecutor that day.

[1] It is necessary to explain here M. Delorme's place among counsel for the prosecution, since it has no equivalent in English or American practice. He was *la partie civile*, roughly the plaintiff, a role filled in England and America exclusively by the Crown or the State. He nominally represents the injured individual or individuals at a criminal trial, and puts forward their claim for damages against the defendant. At the Dominici trial there was no such individual, but as will be seen, M. Delorme obtained a verdict for one franc's damages, less than a farthing or a cent at the time. (*Tr. note*)

Sabatier's speech was a stern marshalling of the facts, touching here and there on points designed to anticipate the defence. The leads offered to the police, for instance, had all been followed up, and he was surprised that anyone should say in the course of the trial that they had not been thoroughly explored. Gustave's complaint of violence he repudiated with indignation. He himself had worked closely with Sébeille and his colleagues, and could testify that no witness had been maltreated. He had seen to it that they received food and drink. Like M. Delorme, he was convinced that this was a crime committed in anger and that therefore Gaston had acted alone. Sabatier ended without calling for a specific sentence, leaving that to the advocate-general.

Saturday, November 27. When the spectators filed into the Palais de Justice they found the technicians busy equipping it with a loud-speaker system. The advocate-general's loss of voice was the reason for this procedure, normally prohibited in French judicial proceedings. By some error, perhaps deliberate, loud-speakers were placed outside the palace as well so that part of the advocate-general's speech would be broadcast beyond its precincts, a shocking form of publicity in the eyes of some. In any event microphones appeared in a hall of justice for the first time.

Calixte Rozan was a man of fine presence with a plump face and a Provençal accent. He had mentally composed his speech weeks before and had moulded it into something of an ode. The British journalists listened to it astounded. 'Is a man brought to trial,' they asked their French colleagues, 'to enable an advocate to display his literary gifts?'

The advocate-general spoke sitting down. He had asked the president's permission. The microphone was perched on two fat law books at mouth level, and he leaned towards it like a crooner. He at once announced his theme: Gaston Dominici alone was guilty and neither Roger Perrin nor Gustave could have had any part in the crime.

He began by brushing aside the 'fables'. The Intelligence Service? A joke. Sir Jack had never been a member of it. Then he made short work of Aristide Panayotou. The Marseilles grub, he called him, and if the police had no other helpers, then he had no confidence in them.

He then came to the tragedy. 'In the majestic landscape where the Drummonds had elected to camp everything changes at night. When the moon illuminates the mountains, the shadows lengthen and stir; every shrub takes on a human form. The child is afraid. They put her in the car. Lady Drummond lies down under a rug. Her husband, more sensitive to the dramatic, endeavours to reason with himself, tells himself he has no fear of ghosts, tries to sleep, dozes off.

'Then suddenly Sir Jack is aware of a human presence near him. He awakes with a start and sees a "monster", because he does not know this man with his patched jacket, his broad-brimmed hat, his Gallic moustache. This unknown figure of frightening aspect is carrying a gun. For us Provençals he would be a poacher. For Sir Jack he is the very image of a Calabrian bandit.'

Who was this man? The advocate-general answered, 'He could only be Gaston Dominici.' Why not Gustave? 'Because the young farmer had been at work all day threshing and would hardly think of walking about in the night, tired as he was.' Roger Perrin? It was impossible he should have slept at Grand'Terre, he was at La Serre to look after the horses. He was too scared of his father; what a box on the ear he would have got if a horse had strangled in his own halter! Therefore only one name was possible, that of Gaston Dominici, who had rested all afternoon and was uneasy that evening because of the landslide.

'He took the carbine in case he found a target, since the night was exceptionally bright. Where did the carbine come from? I am convinced that, as is common practice, it had been used by the whole family, that they lent it among themselves, and so everybody had handled it, even Clovis. And whoever used it oiled it. This is the explanation of the olive oil and the similarity of the oils to Clovis's.

'But Gaston was not used to such weapons, only to guns which are reloaded after every shot. That is why he ejected a cartridge every time. During the reconstruction he did exactly that.

'Why did he go to the camp site? I have a theory. When he was young Gaston dreamed of having a roof of his own. The only people who slept out of doors were vagrants – "gipsies". And now respectable people often had a little trailer attached to their car. But the Drummonds did not even have a trailer. They slept in the open. That was what he wanted to see. It wasn't to see the English lady undress that Gaston went there. She had already gone to bed. He said that because he thought people would believe it had been a crime of passion, and view it less seriously. In reality curiosity drew him on. And a fatal misunderstanding ensued.

'Sir Jack was afraid and Gaston Dominici did not understand that one could be afraid of him. Both were in good faith. The English scientist wanted to protect his family and Gaston was furious at being attacked on his own property. He fired. Lady Drummond cried out. She had to be silenced . . . The child ran away. How many shots were fired? I don't know and I'm not sure that Gaston himself knew in his panic.'

The advocate-general then pictured the death of the child. 'If you had killed only the parents,' he exclaimed, 'the good God might have offered you a helping hand. You had no more cartridges, you might have ended this massacre. It would have been an accident, since you had shown pity on a child of ten. But you caught her. She had run through the Provençal grass, and if surprise has been expressed that her feet were unmarked, well, I've never heard that our local girls get their calves scratched when lying with their lovers in that grass!

'Elizabeth fell on her knees, trembling with terror. You had before you the face of the child lit up by the moon, you the grandfather of nineteen grandchildren. But you struck like a brute, as they used to strike down in the slaughter-houses.'

He then answered the criticisms directed at President Bousquet for suspending the interrogation of Gustave just when he might have been on the point of breaking down. 'Of course Gustave lied. Without doubt he collected cartridge cases on the site. He was convicted of failure to render assistance. But I am sure of his innocence. I was afraid the other day, yes, I was truly afraid that an error was about to be committed. I feared that a man so weak might confess himself guilty. When the old man called out to his son, "Tell the truth," I trembled lest this man who was faltering, at the end of his resources, should declare, "Yes, I did it." Then a frightful miscarriage of justice would have resulted. I should never have succeeded in convincing anyone that the guilt lay with Gaston who alone is guilty. And the next day the press, public opinion, would have acclaimed the abominable notion that justice had been done when in sober truth it had not been.'

The prosecution had finished. Without explicitly demanding the death penalty, the advocate-general indicated that the jury should answer yes to questions regarding guilt without extenuating circumstances. 'You will have no pity for this man,' he adjured, 'since – ' and he echoed the words he had already used – 'he had no pity on a child of ten.'

The defendant had at first listened to the hostile speech with an expression of amusement, even pleasure, when his family life and his attitude to his wife were described, laughing every time that M. Rozan referred to the latter as 'the Sardine'. Then his face darkened. He looked angry when he understood that the supreme penalty was being asked for. He turned his face away with contempt and pretended not to hear words that mightily offended him.

Three speeches for the defence followed, those of M. Charles-Alfred and his son Bernard, then that of M. Pierre Charrier. The style was very different. The two former were attorneys at the Digne bar. Charles-Alfred, born in Martinique, was a shrewd pleader, an ironic critic of the advocate-general, whose exaggerations he exposed. His son recounted his conversations with Gaston in prison. Pierre Charrier then exploited his powerful talent as a polemicist. Their task was to prepare the way for Emile Pollak who would plead on Sunday morning, to clear the ground of irrelevancies.

'If it were a question of awarding you the Prix Goncourt,[1] M. l'Avocat-General,' ended Charles-Alfred, 'I should give it to you at once. But the head of this old man, never!'

Sunday, November 28, the last session. Emile Pollak was in his place well before time. The Marseilles lawyer was unnaturally nervous and tense. In order to relax, he had taken part in a big bélote[2] tournament in Digne the previous evening which he had won brilliantly; it seemed to him a good sign. When Dominici entered the dock he touched his lawyer encouragingly on the shoulder; he had confidence. In the room, the corridors and the adjacent square the crowd was packed to suffocation.

Emile Pollak spoke for three hours. In matter as in form it was an answer to the prose poem of Calixte Rozan. He did not deliver his speech, he lived it, acted it; the Dominici affair became a dramatic work in which he assumed in turn the role of all the characters – Sébeille, the Dominicis, Maillet, Périès – at times whipping himself into near-delirium, beating his breast, passing from a whisper to a roar, from the sober to the shrill, as he reconstructed the entire drama for the jury. No verbal transcription can recapture the spectacle which the courtroom witnessed that Sunday morning.

Emile Pollak grappled, for instance, with the confessions, the cornerstone of the prosecution. 'They did not strike him, it is true, but he is an old man now of seventy-seven. And for how long did they question him? Twenty-three hours! Do you think that's a

[1] A major French literary award.　　[2] A popular French card game.

triviality with no ill-effects? Yet he was fresh as a daisy, say the police, he took up his stick and made a show of leaving. Really! For twenty-three hours they had talked to him of the crime. They had said, "It's you or Gustave. They'll cut his head off. To you they won't do anything. They'll put you in prison, let you have your dog, your wine and even your goats while you're there." For twenty-three hours they drummed it into him. And they repeated like a catch phrase, "You're the murderer, you're the murderer." He was utterly out of his depth; he cast about for what to do, became afraid for his grandchildren. It's Clovis, no it's Gustave, no it's Roger Perrin. What should he do, what should he say? For twenty-three hours! He was desperate. It's understandable, isn't it?

'Then calm returned. He was alone with Guérino. They had a friendly chat, no more shouts, no more raised fists. They talked in dialect. Gaston kept asking himself, "Who?" And a soft voice whispered in his ear, "What if it were an accident?" Suddenly he saw daylight. That's what he would say! Yes, of course it was an accident. Victory! He had confessed.

'Hardly had he done so than he retracted. No, it wasn't he. He had accused himself to save his grandchildren. They haggled and he confessed again. "It was for the woman," they suggested to him. For the woman? All right, it was for her. And then before the examining magistrate a strange thing happened: he at first said he was innocent. We know this thanks to M. Périès's honesty. So, to sum up: yes to Guérino, no to Bocca, yes and no to Prudhomme, yes and no to the magistrate. These are the confessions on which they want to condemn a man to death. Does it take a psychiatrist to know what they are worth?

'The magistrate had so little trust in what he had just heard that he ordered a reconstruction – unfortunately without summoning the lawyers. On the spot, Gaston Dominici went through motions which only distantly corresponded with the dossier. So much the worse. He was charged. Everything in that confession is false: motive, chronology, number of shots fired. Superintendent Sébeille recognized as much himself, and it borders on the fantastic: everything in the confessions was untrue, nevertheless they were true. They are so true that Gaston Dominici is under threat of the death penalty because of them and of them alone.'

To offset the defendant's confession, Emile Pollak pointed out the lies of others. 'The road to truth is often through mire and dirt. In the Dominici affair we have had to pass through some revolting

316

stretches. They bear the names of Paul Maillet, Roger Perrin, Clovis, Gustave. And who is foremost in this unbridled competition in lying? Roger Perrin beyond a doubt. He was believed when he said he had not slept at Grand'Terre. He was believed again when he declared that the English mother and daughter had come to the house. Why was he not considered a possible suspect? Because, it was said, this was not a "juvenile crime". I make no accusation. I recall only that a few years ago two defendants were condemned to death in this very court; they were less than twenty years old.

'As for Clovis, he is the ringleader of the conspiracy. It was he who advised Gustave not to say that he had seen the child's arm move. "Don't say anything," he urged him. Can you then swear that these two men did not reach an understanding to let their father be accused? They talked as much as they liked, as much as they were able. I have always found the return of the police in November 1953 odd when there was nothing new to justify it. It is my belief that someone tipped them off: the plot was sufficiently ripe. It's only a supposition, you don't have to accept it from me. But it explains the marvellous linking up of the confessions. And Clovis would lie even after his accusation simply because he had at once recognized the carbine: it was his! That explains his agitation.

'As for Gustave, he turned accuser when he had become too trapped in his own lies. But why did he lie? Here is the core of the Dominici mystery. Why did he conceal the collection of the cartridges, the covering of the bodies? Because he was harbouring a secret, because he could not say what he was doing in the lucerne field.'

Emile Pollak turned to Gustave, who was silent, unheeding, his look unfathomable, his body tense. 'Gustave, Yvette, understand that you are bringing disgrace on yourselves. Understand, Gustave, that if the blade one day falls on your father's head, the blood will spurt out over you. If you have anything to say, say it now. The man there is he who fed you, brought you up, led you by the hand. Gustave, for pity's sake!'

But Gustave remained on his bench, as if the words had stopped halfway. A profound silence reigned, which the lawyer purposely prolonged. Regretfully, it seemed, he resumed his speech, which was nearing its close. There was no proof in the dossier sufficiently convincing to send a man to his death. It was noon. The angelus rang out from a neighbouring belfry.

'Gaston Dominici, have you anything to add?'

The defendant rose painfully to his feet. He hesitated. 'I can only tell you,' he said, 'that I'm here and that I don't want to take the place of anyone else. I am frank and honest. I'm not a murderer as has been said.'

The president read out the seven questions which the jury had to answer and which divided the triple crime into component parts. The court and the jurors retired amid a great commotion. A long wait began. The faithful of the Dominici clan withdrew, Marcel, the Notre-Dame-des-Anges farmer being delegated to be present with Léon at the verdict.

2.25 p.m. A bell interrupted conversation. It was the signal that the deliberations were ended and the verdict about to be given. This is always an agonizing moment to which no one, not even the most hardened frequenters of courtrooms, is insensitive, especially when the life of an old man is at stake.

Led by President Bousquet, the court entered, then the jurors. The room was invaded by a mob. Eighteen-year-old Marie-Claude Caillat, who had always shown an unfailing tenderness for her grandfather, had remained along with Léon Dominici. At the last moment Marcel had said he couldn't face being in the courtroom, he would wait outside. Clovis and his wife, Roger Perrin and his mother sat among the public, impassive.

The president ordered the defendant to be brought in. Gaston entered, looking tired, worn, dejected. Erect in the dock, he was ready to hear the verdict.

'The jury's answer and that of the court to all the questions has been "yes". The majority has found no extenuating circumstances,' the president announced. The sentence followed automatically from the jury's answer: the supreme penalty. After reading the articles from the Code, the president pronounced the fateful words, 'By virtue of this judgment, Gaston Dominici is condemned to death.'

The defendant did not flinch. He bowed slightly as if in greeting when the judge advised him that he had 'five clear days in which to appeal.' An indescribable tumult filled the room as the reporters made a frantic dash for the telephones. Clovis and those with him seemed unmoved. Only Marie-Claude wept in silent distress.

The trial was over save for a few moments to wind up its civil aspect: M. Claude Delorme obtained without argument the one franc damages he asked for. Gaston Dominici seemed stunned. When the president ordered him to be returned to prison he leaned over towards his lawyers. 'But I'm innocent,' he said. Then before

318

leaving the dock he turned towards the courtroom and cried out, 'Oh, the swine!'

The almost universal comment of the press was: 'It is not an error of justice, but full justice has not been done.'

Léon Dominici quickly disengaged himself from the crowd in the corridors. In the courtyard he found Marcel. 'The death sentence,' he called brokenly. Marcel plunged into the squall of rain now falling on Digne and ran to the nearby hotel where the family had taken refuge. They were gathered in the kitchen whose shutters had been closed. When he appeared his distraught expression left the Dominicis in no doubt.

'They've condemned him?' Gustave quavered.

'Yes.'

Yvette collapsed weeping in her husband's arms.

'The guillotine?' asked Augusta Caillat.

Marcel did not answer but everybody had understood. The old lady waiting at Grand'Terre had now to be told. They found her by the fire, poking at the embers. She already knew. People had passed along the road and called out to her, 'Poor Gaston . . .'

They fastened the shutters and closeted themselves in the kitchen, cut off from the world. It was only at 6.0 p.m. that Augusta emerged. To the reporters surrounding the farm she cried, 'Fine justice! They'll hurry up and kill him. It stinks, all of it!'

Clovis returned home with his wife. It was she who received the reporters. 'They shouldn't have condemned him to death,' she said, 'but believe me, he did it all by himself. He is too arrogant to sacrifice himself. If he had had an accomplice he would have denounced him.'

Before returning Gaston to prison the gendarmes allowed him a respite in the small room with peeling walls where defendants waited during recesses. The crowd had to be given time to disperse. Charles-Alfred and his son had followed him; he was sitting on a wicker chair. 'I'm paying for somebody else,' he contended yet again; he seemed on the verge of exhaustion.

'For whom?' asked Charles-Alfred anxiously.

But the old man remained silent. The lawyer pressed him. Gaston had let slip several opportunities to speak. This was without doubt the last. Gaston raised his clouded eyes to his defender. 'Speak,' Charles-Alfred said.

Gaston nodded a weary head. 'Yes,' he said slowly, 'I think I will.'

The Second Inquiry

12

Their ears strained to catch every syllable, the four lawyers listened to Gaston Dominici. Since morning they had been in the condemned man's cell. Seated on the bed, he faced Charrier and young Bernard Charles-Alfred, who were standing against the wall, while Emile Pollak and Charles-Alfred sat on two stools. The old man regarded them in turn. He spoke in halting sentences, some of which were unintelligible. What he said followed no logical pattern, it seemed dictated by a mind overcome with confusion, stupefied, still stunned by the shock of the previous day.

Gaston repeated that he did not want to pay for another. The other? Gustave, of course.

'Have you proof?' asked Emile Pollak in a soft voice which didn't conceal his impatience and irritation.

The days following an unsuccessful defence are always bitter. During the trial he and his colleagues had pleaded with their client to reveal anything he might know. Now it was probably too late. From experience Pollak knew the force of a verdict; to get the law to reverse itself would require a mammoth effort.

'He told Yvette,' said Gaston Dominici.

'How do you know?'

But Gaston did not answer. His mind wandered in all directions, unable to distinguish present from past, material from immaterial. He groaned, cursed, never raising his voice, talking to himself as much as to his lawyers, reliving his own tale in his own befogged way. His visitors let him run on, knowing that it was hopeless to contradict the whims of a mind teetering at times on the very edge.

'Luckily, I needed my lighter,' he said suddenly.

'Why?' asked Pollak as if the remark were the most natural in the world.

'I shouldn't have heard what they said.'

Scrap by scrap, patched with digressions and irrelevancies, the lawyers fitted together the scene to which the old man was referring. It had occurred one afternoon several days after the crime. Gaston wanted to have his siesta, as he did every day, either out of doors or in the kitchen. But he had forgotten his lighter. So he went up to his room, only to fall asleep there. He stretched out on his bed, where he slept for two hours. Then he got up, and through the half-open door of Gustave and Yvette's room heard them talking in low voices.

'She was talking about jewels,' he said, 'and I even thought she wanted her husband to give her some. He had just collected a hundred thousand francs for the apricots. But afterwards she said, "And the child?" Gustave answered, "She fainted." "Who carried her?" Yvette wanted to know. "Roger," Gustave told her.'

Then some question of a handkerchief came up between the couple. But the lawyers did not understand what it had been used for and nor, it seemed, did Gaston. 'It was then I found out that young Roger was mixed up in it,' he went on. 'I thought the jewels Yvette was talking about could have belonged to the English people.'

He did not stop there. The carbine had, so to speak, weighed on his heart. And sharing his favours – or disfavours – impartially now between both his sons, he declared that Clovis often used this weapon to kill a boar at 150 or 200 metres. In his opinion the Rock-Ola had been kept at the Perrins', whose farm was the nearest to the usual hunting ground.

That seemed to be the sum of it for now. Gaston said no more, peering at his lawyers; it was up to them now to transform this murky gleam into a blaze. He was surprised at their silence.

'Why didn't you tell all this at the trial?' Pollak asked. He recalled the occasions missed, the confrontations, Gustave's agitation, the condemned man's denials when the president asked him if he was acquainted with the weapon. He had been mute when he was being pressed from all sides to tell what he knew.

'Did you expect to be acquitted?' asked the lawyer.

'I thought you were going to make Gustave talk.'

Certainly an illusion, as Pollak pointed out to Gaston. When the hearings had ended and the chance was given him to speak, he could still have seized it. Undoubtedly the trial would have been adjourned.

'It is not for a father to accuse his son,' the prisoner replied proudly.

That put an end to the interview. None of the four lawyers was exactly happy. As always when dealing with a Dominici, the truth –

or what passed for truth – appeared in the form of a halting compromise which took no account of improbabilities and inconsistencies. Why, for instance, have reminded Gustave several times that he had been in the lucerne field and said nothing of the conversation with Yvette? Had Gaston naïvely thought it was enough to cast a doubt without going so far as a real accusation?

After a conference in Charles-Alfred's chambers the defenders decided to draw up a memorandum for the Lord Chancellor. They reported their conversation with the old man they had been unable to save, adding their observations on the trial itself. In conclusion they asked for an additional inquiry into the disclosures just made.

The climate was favourable. A press campaign was already under way, its theme the same as that which marked the final hearings: Gaston Dominici's conviction had not been a judicial error, but others guilty were still at large. It was of course not the position taken by the lawyers; for them their client was absolutely innocent. But they were supported by public opinion on the inquiry issue at least, since this might bring the rest of the guilty to book.

Justice itself came under a barrage of fire once more. Sébeille, of course, was foremost among the sufferers. His hour of glory was over, and would never return. The Maigret of Marseilles was now only the muddler who had neglected the most elementary verifications and had not known how to use the opportunities offered him.

President Bousquet was accused of wanting to defend a bad dossier at all costs, and by extension, all those police officers and magistrates in various investigating capacities who contribute to and are in the final instance responsible for its preparation.

The public is not privy to the compiling of the dossier, but it is more than privy to the trial which results. And the Dominici trial, marked by so many confused sessions, so many incongruous lies on both sides, left it with an overall sense of profound disquiet. Having ranged a family against itself, the Dominici affair now ranged public opinion against the workings of justice.

The Ministry of Justice was headed at the time by a liberal man, M. Guérin de Beaumont, a former diplomat who had moved from the Quai d'Orsay into politics and had himself been disturbed by the account he read of the hearings. The English press had made an impression on him. The British journalists were the first to assert that less than justice had been done at Digne. The Lord Chancellor decided to hear Gaston Dominici's case through a surrogate.

*

Silence and solitude invaded Grand'Terre under the pale sun of winter. Apart from members of the family, no visitor was admitted. The stupor which had fallen on the Dominicis after the verdict had not lessened with the days. In the evening there were always one or two couples, brothers and sisters, engaged in bitter discussions. Curses were lavished not only on the jurors but on Clovis, young Perrin, his mother, Paul Maillet, all who had contributed to their misfortune. Gustave was one of the first to join in the denunciations.

Gaston had written. His letter was addressed to the Sardine. It consisted of a few words only, implicit with emotion. 'Goodbye, we shan't see each other again. I am condemned to death. It's all over. Leave Grand'Terre and go and live with one of your daughters, Augusta or Clotilde, because the farm will have to be sold to pay the cost of the trial.'

On this point he was mistaken and would perhaps be annoyed when he learned of it. For one of his secret gratifications was to tell himself that Gustave would not remain on the property. He would become a 'vagabond' – something Gaston's own diligence had spared him – a man who had to hire himself out to others and put up with a boss. It would be a just revenge for his faults, a punishment for his weakness in pouring it all out on Sébeille's shoulder.

But Gustave knew from the lawyers that the trial would not cost the wild sum that had been predicted. It was Yvette who asked for the total. At a rough estimate it would amount to 500,000 francs. They could borrow and the harvests would make up the rest. They would have to economize a little, but the land was safe.

Gaston also wrote to the one who had defended him most ardently, his daughter Augusta. He bequeathed her several objects at Grand' Terre, among them the sideboard which he valued. 'You will no longer be allowed to see me. Write often, it will give me pleasure.'

Little by little, however, the Dominicis learned about the revelations made by the condemned man. They could not ignore them, the press featured them too prominently. But they treated them in their own way, selecting typically only what suited them – chiefly of course their father's insistence on his innocence. They rejected anything that cast so much as a suspicion on any of themselves, even including Roger Perrin, for all their ceaseless grumblings about him.

Their attitude became even more astonishing when they had a letter from the prisoner himself in which he confirmed his new statements. It was addressed to the whole family, and a year later was published in a weekly paper.

I can state that it was Gustave and Roger Perrin who did this fearful thing and are the murderers of the Drummond family. I can assure you I am innocent, as I always said and will maintain to my last breath. I write in this sad prison. I write of all the torments I have suffered, since Gustave . . . Alas, my life has been a very cruel one. But I never laid a hand on Gustave. I wanted to make a man of him, but he never listened to me. He wasted all the money he laid his hands on and all that he earned . . .

Of course Gustave was indignant. But his standing in the family was in no way diminished by this new complication. The family wanted to rescue the prisoner but in no circumstances to deliver another of their own in his place. Gaston's accusations were put down to mental disorder resulting from the fate decreed for him, not to mention the pressures put upon him and the possibility of blackmail: 'Speak and there will be a new trial.' What couldn't those jailers extort from a man who had spent his life in the open air and was now suffocating between four walls? They shut their eyes and ears to everything except the rumours that their father's innocence would be established, thanks to the reopening of the case.

Gustave nevertheless got in touch with a Marseilles lawyer, rejecting those who had previously defended him and later helped his father. On the principle that 'his interests were no longer the same' as his father's, he chose M. Bottaï, a familiar figure at the Bouches-du-Rhône assizes, a jovial fat man regarded as extremely shrewd. Gustave also wrote to the President of the Republic: 'They have made the mistake of attacking only the residents of Grand' Terre . . .'

But Gustave supplied the head of state with nothing but a valueless argument, reviving the outdated story of the second Hillman which might have followed the Drummonds after their arrival in France.

Les Baumettes is a prison almost as famous as the Santé or Sing-Sing. The names of some of the biggest criminals are inscribed in its registers. Marseilles and its violent quarters provide the establishment with an unending supply of inmates. On visiting days the queue of women waiting for the gates to open always contains a number of well-dressed, well-made-up ones come to cheer up their men inside. There is not a criminal in Marseilles who has not at some time or another made the acquaintance of one of the cells of this prison, at one time considered a model one. It is a detention centre, welcoming all those under arrest and awaiting trial.

Consisting of tall white buildings in a hollow of the mountains which overlook Marseilles and the sea, Les Baumettes resembles a large suburban complex. Gaston Dominici had been confined there when undergoing psychiatric examination. He was taken there again some days after his conviction, Digne prison not being suited to a condemned man's regime. Nevertheless certain exceptions were made because of his age. He was not put in irons, and the light was reduced at night as much as possible. But he had to discard the velvet jacket and trousers which had been his costume for years and wear a coarse greyish woollen uniform. It was in this outfit that he received the Lord Chancellor's surrogate, Joseph Oddou, delegated to receive his statement. He was in a very bad humour.

But he willingly repeated the statement that his lawyers had already heard, adding only a few unimportant details.

'Do you formally accuse your son and grandson?' asked the magistrate.

'They've certainly something to do with it,' the prisoner answered guardedly. 'But I don't know who committed the crime.'

The magistrate drew up a statement which he had the prisoner sign. This he sent to the Marseilles prosecutor, who forwarded it to the Lord Chancellor. Without delay the latter asked the Minister of the Interior to designate some police officials to carry out an investigation. François Mitterand, head of the ministry, chose the assistant director for criminal affairs, Charles Chenevier, and one of his principal colleagues, Chief Superintendent Gillard.

Chenevier was then a great name in the French police, a small, sturdy, square-faced man, giving a powerful impression of physical strength. He was the man who after the war, in the troubled era of the Liberation, had broken up the gangs then flourishing. He was a police officer in the best tradition of his profession, upright, respectful of the rules of the Code even if they impeded him, universally respected. The Dominici affair had fascinated him both professionally and personally. He had even sent Gillard to Digne to follow the trial. He was therefore not on unknown ground.

The orders given by the Lord Chancellor to the prosecutors at Aix-en-Provence were explicit: the investigation would be conducted by Chenevier alone, to the exclusion of all local functionaries. If a judicial inquiry was called for, it was to be submitted directly to the Ministry. Extraordinary directives; they were accepted reluctantly.

On December 18, 1955, Chenevier and Gillard arrived in the

office of M. Orsatelli, the attorney-general. They were received with a certain condescension. Charles Chenevier has described the scene in his memoirs.[1] It left him both amused and irritated.

'What do they want in Paris?' the prosecutor asked scornfully. 'It's not the first time a condemned man has promised revelations. They are usually uninteresting.' And M. Orsatelli gave his own forthright directive which was flatly contradicted by the Lord Chancellor's: Chenevier and Gillard should limit their errand to interviewing Gustave and Yvette. 'I will ask the justice of the peace at Forcalquier to arrange it,' he added.

Chenevier was left with no illusions; he would get anything but enthusiastic support from the magistrates, who regarded his coming to the South as useless, if not insulting.

'According to the instructions I received,' he observed, 'I should also hear Gaston Dominici.'

'A surrogate has done so. Do you think you will learn more?'

Chenevier conceded that he might not be any luckier than M. Oddou. But he thought he remembered, he added gently, that among the instructions issued by the Minister was one that he receive permission to communicate with anyone he wished to see.

'You shall have it,' M. Orsatelli said sourly, unable to disregard altogether the orders from Place Vendôme.

The officials from the Sûreté then proceeded to Digne, where they were received by the prosecutor, M. Sabatier. His affability did not conceal either his scepticism or his hostility. In his view there was only one guilty party; the condemned man. And this yielding to the pressure of public opinion was regrettable, considering that the investigation had been conducted with all due severity by scrupulous and able people.

'I've no intention of reflecting upon them,' protested Chenevier. He belonged to no clique, he added. Paris was not setting up in opposition to the province. And besides, should there be rivalry between police departments? The prosecutor allowed himself to be persuaded. He supplied the two officials with a warrant to check Gaston's statements and to go into any necessary detail.

So they were given the green light. Or did it only appear so? In an article in *France-Soir*, Jacques Chapus reported on an inquiry he had conducted in judicial circles. Opinion there was that Chenevier and Gillard were heading straight for failure. 'It appears that nothing obliges the persons recently laid under suspicion by Gaston Dominici

[1] *De la Combe aux Fées à Lurs*, Flammarion, 1962.

to answer the Paris police officers. The two are only appointed to Lurs to acquire information. They have no formed commission and the witnesses they interview can refuse to answer their questions. These witnesses can even refuse to admit them. They will have to hear them in a police headquarters or station or town hall, where they can be detained only twenty-four hours at most.'

After reading the article, Chenevier commented, 'Only a miracle will get a witness to talk.'

Sitting on the edge of his bed in the narrow, yellow-painted cell, Gaston Dominici acknowledged the entrance of the 'Parisians' with a nod of the head. His moustache carefully brushed, his expression relaxed, his eyes at once calm and distrustful, he seemed content. Chenevier and Gillard's visit was a pledge; he was not forgotten, the verdict at Digne had not settled the matter. Chenevier sat down on a stool. After an interchange of greetings he said abruptly, 'Do you believe in God, Grandad?'

'Yes,' replied Gaston, surprised. 'A little less than before, but all the same I do.'

'And in Paradise?'

'Yes.'

'Well, you've done well.'

Gaston's face creased in astonishment. Out of the corner of an eye he looked at this police officer who came to the prison to talk to him of God and heaven. Did he think he was the chaplain? Chenevier drew a file from his briefcase. 'I am going to read you what you stated to the magistrate Périès: "I am innocent but I am sacrificing myself for my grandchildren." Well, that's that. Why are you rebelling now? You've won, you're going to procure your salvation, your grandchildren are saved. Why this sudden change?'

The line of attack somewhat disconcerted Gaston.

'Paradise, paradise,' he growled, 'I'm in no hurry to get there.' And added, 'Not for somebody else at any rate.'

'In short, you sacrificed yourself on condition that it came out all right.'

Turned cautious, Gaston said nothing, refusing to follow Chenevier on what seemed slippery ground. 'All I know,' he said finally, 'is that I didn't do it.'

'Who did then?'

'I told the magistrate.'

For two hours he kept repeating in different forms what he had already told the surrogate Oddou, but added nothing new. Nor did Chenevier insist. He studied his man, watched his gestures, his postures, listened to his voice, his inflections, his silences. He brought out certain details. As a result Gaston fixed the date on which he had heard the conversation between Yvette and Gustave. It was the day on which Dr Nalin had given Gustave a certificate to get him out of being questioned by Sébeille: August 8, 1952. Chenevier told the condemned man of the surprise he had felt on reading Oddou's transcript. Had Gaston never asked his son about the conversation he had overheard which was of such crucial importance? Had the tragedy which had just occurred left him so indifferent? Even if he had no intention of denouncing his son as a murderer, had he felt no desire to know?

'We talked so little,' Gaston mumbled.

'Granted. But at the trial you could have told all that.'

Gaston sighed. 'I thought I would be acquitted.'

He next explained about the carbine. He knew that Clovis had one because one day his son mentioned a boar hunt, regretting not having had it with him as a boar had passed at 150 metres, too far off for an ordinary shotgun. The carbine had never been at Grand'Terre.

'Yet you pointed out the shelves where it had been stored.'

'Because the police told me so. They believed Gustave and Clovis. I lost my head.'

He insisted tenaciously that his confessions had been extorted through fatigue; he was exhausted and that was why he thought he should offer himself as a sacrifice. The moment of aberration quickly passed. When he came to himself it was too late: the magistrate's hearing was already over. The truth was determined at the moment of confession. 'And it was all nonsense,' he declared.

It was 6.0 p.m., the prison hour for the evening meal. Chenevier did not pursue his interrogation; moreover, Gaston looked tired.

The next afternoon the police officers saw Gaston Dominici in the visiting room. They questioned him for two hours but he still wouldn't go beyond his story to the surrogate. He knew no more and neither the exhortations nor the pessimistic remarks of Chenevier and Gillard could budge him. He couldn't invent what he didn't know.

But towards 5.30 Emile Pollak and Charrier arrived at the prison. Chenevier received them and told them flatly that his interviews with Gaston had been disappointing. They did not warrant the reopening of the case. No Minister of Justice, however open-minded, would order another formal inquiry on the strength of such meagre scraps.

Together Pollak, Charrier and the two officers went in to Gaston. Pollak did the talking in his everyday unemphatic voice. 'Gaston,' he said, 'I beg you to speak. Have no illusions, this is your last chance and we have given it to you. We pleaded with you during the trial to tell the truth. You didn't listen to us and were condemned. If you don't speak up today your fate is settled. Never, never will anyone believe you again.'

Chenevier and Gillard listened to the lawyer in silence. Gaston's gaze was fixed, unmoving, on Pollak.

'Speak!' Pollak ordered.

So Gaston spoke, embarking on another of his rambling mono-logues, this time with occasional interruption from Chenevier. His narrative was interrupted also by reflections, reminiscences, com-plaints and curses, which the police and the lawyers tried to grasp as best they could, with Chenevier holding on to the thread, fearful that at any moment it would snap and Gaston would stop.

'There was Roger,' Gaston began, 'Gustave brought him on his motor-cycle. They went out during the night, it was ten minutes after one. I was in bed, I heard the shots, I got up, went down to the courtyard, I saw Gustave with the boy, they were crossing the lucerne field, they were coming from up there . . .'

'Up there' was the camp site where the Drummonds were sleeping. So if he was to be believed, Gaston had been present at a part of the murder. Chenevier pressed him to go on. Pollak and Charrier ached to tell their client to stop beating about the bush once and for all and get on with it; Gaston's twists and turns made the lawyers uncomfortable.

'No,' Gaston said suddenly at one such turn, 'I can't lie like this, I didn't get up.' And a little later, 'If I die I die, but I won't lie.'

Patiently Chenevier put him back on course. Gaston had told how he had seen Roger Perrin carrying the child. Was that true or false?

'I saw them,' said Gaston.

There was a sigh of relief from the lawyers. But almost at once came the retraction. 'I was woken by the shots, I turned on the light but fell asleep again until morning.'

'Then you didn't see anything in the lucerne field?'

'I can't say things I don't know.'

Chenevier had a suggestion for Gaston which might perhaps extricate him and loosen his tongue: Gaston could have been only a

332

witness of the tragedy. If that was it, why not say so and do away with all the half-truths which had brought so much harm to the whole family? But Gaston shook his head; he had heard a sound but that was all, not even the voice of Gustave or Roger. 'Damnation!' he exclaimed. 'How I'd like to know!'

According to him, the 'plot' had been hatched by Gustave and Clovis. They had had eight months to prepare it. He ended by producing a fact he had not previously revealed: when he got up at 3.30 a.m. the door of the kitchen giving on to the courtyard was half-open. He thought that his son had already got up, the implication being that he had returned to the scene of the crime.

With the agreement of the lawyers, the interview went on until 11.0. Once Pollak and Charrier were outside the prison with Chenevier and Gillard, all four went over what they had just heard. For the defence lawyers Gaston's sincerity was, of course, undeniable. Chenevier was more guarded; certain intangibles had undoubtedly bothered him. But in general, how to explain the complete reversals, the sudden retreats, the balking at truth, this singular inability of all the Dominicis to commit themselves to a coherent set of facts and tell a story that wasn't full of holes?

'We're no wiser than you,' the lawyers confessed.

For two whole days Chenevier and his colleagues went round the Basses-Alpes, questioning the members of the family, in particular Augusta Caillat, Clotilde Araman, Marcel and Léon Dominici. Their questions bore especially on the carbine: had any of them seen it at Grand'Terre or in the hands of Clovis, Gustave or Roger Perrin? Not one of them had. But each did his best to convince Chenevier that if it were not for Clovis, Gaston would never have been arrested. Gustave? A 'mannikin', said Marcel, the farmer from Notre-Dame-des-Anges, he did what Clovis told him to. And Clovis was a 'first-class swine'. He had never loved his father. He was only interested in his inheritance. He was having his revenge.

Armed with his dossier, Chenevier returned to Paris. He had an appointment with the Lord Chancellor.

A police officer placing the result of an inquiry before the Lord Chancellor is no ordinary event. Exceptional circumstances are required to bring it about. On that afternoon of December 27, 1954, the fate of an old Provençal goatherd, whose allotted destiny had been to live and die at the foot of his mountains, was being weighed in the vast, magnificent office of the Lord Chancellor. With all the clarity of which he was capable, the superintendent related his findings and his views on them. The interview with Gaston Dominici had certainly been disappointing. Nevertheless it remained true that the dossier contained many obscurities.

M. Guérin de Beaumont listened with absorbed attention. Like every Frenchman, he asked himself the agonizing question: had justice been done at Digne on November 29? In every part of the country discussion was intense. The Dominici affair had become a real-life detective story, and every armchair sleuth had his own solution.

Chenevier went over the case from the beginning. For the information of the Minister, who was flanked by two high officials of the Chancellery, he drew a critical picture of the whole investigation, first Sébeille's, then Périès's, then of the trial itself at Digne. His conclusions were severe: everything had been ordered to lead to the confessions. But these meant nothing. Chenevier gave examples, dissecting counsels' speeches and the reports in the press. He was surprised that no one had seriously challenged the *passionel* motive in which no one believed. He compared Gaston's successive stories to the gendarme Guérino, to Superintendent Prudhomme, Sébeille, Périès; no two of them were alike. Chenevier was ruthless about the reconstruction and ironical about the word used by the examining magistrate Périès: convincing. 'It was so far from being so that Gaston Dominici's actions differed from those he had described the day before. When he acted out the killing of Lady Drummond and Elizabeth he totally contradicted himself. The magistrate charged him nevertheless. It was a mistake.'

He did not disguise his opinion that Gaston's disclosures didn't warrant his conviction. But they could provide a starting-point. He had sensed an edge of tension among the Dominicis. It should be taken advantage of as quickly as possible.

The Minister took a few days to think it over. On January 4 his office circulated a communiqué: 'Without waiting for the result of the appeal lodged with the Court of Cassation,[1] the Minister of Justice recommends the Prosecutor's Office at Aix-en-Provence to institute an investigation against X for complicity in the triple crime at Lurs.'

This was to be one of M. Guérin de Beaumont's last acts; a sick man, he was succeeded in office by M. Emmanuel Temple. Trained as a jurist, a lawyer who had gone into politics, deputy for the

[1] The supreme court of appeal in France.

Aveyron, the new Minister summoned Chenevier and Gillard to his office. His decision, after hearing a recapitulation of their views, was slightly different from his predecessor's. Through a juridical scruple he deferred the opening of the inquiry until after the Court of Cassation had rendered judgment. If the latter overruled the verdict the problem would be resolved at once since there would be a second trial. The high court was instructed not to delay its consideration of the case.

For the second time the judges of the court had before them the Dominici dossier, amplified now by the clerks' minutes of the trial in the Assize Court at Digne. Assembled in the same room, the solemn Criminal Chamber, the eleven counsellors, presided over by M. Nicolas Battestini, had three speakers before them, the *rapporteur*,[1] M. Maurice Patin, who had already discharged the same role in June of the previous year and achieved a partial revision of the dossier, the counsel for the appellant, M. André Mayer, and the advocate-general, M. Jean Dupuiche.

According to the rules of procedure, the *rapporteur* opened the hearing. A petition in an appeal is founded upon a memorandum in which the counsel for the appellant has listed the errors in law which according to him have invalidated the conduct of the trial. M. André Mayer had enumerated four: three in the trial itself, the fourth from the period before the trial. The first held that the indictment had been signed by the chief prosecutor at Aix-en-Provence when the Court of Cassation on the earlier appeal had directed that it be done by the chief prosecutor at Grenoble. The second objected that the advocate-general's speech had been transmitted out of doors by loud-speakers, without the authority of the president, the resulting uproar being to the detriment of the accused. The third claimed that the witnesses related to the defendant should have been put on oath so as to be subject to prosecution for perjury if they lied. The fourth pointed to the lack of an essential date, that of the last session, which hindered counsel from seeing the clerk's dossier, a delay which might have prejudiced the appellant.

From the *rapporteur*'s first words in reply to the memorandum it was clear that he was in favour of the total rejection of the appeal. To him, none of M. Mayer's arguments seemed valid. The broadcasting of the prosecutor's speech outside was only a technical accident, the men who installed the apparatus having plugged in to

[2] 'Court reporter' in loose translation, there being no equivalent official in British courts. (*Tr. note*)

335

the control centre which was in their truck. As soon as they knew about it, President Bousquet stopped it . . . As to the oath not being required of the Dominicis, the president had full power not to require it of relatives, without need to justify himself to anybody . . . An indictment must be drawn up by the court to whose authority the assize court is subject. In this case the Court of Cassation had appointed Digne; hence the chief prosecutor at Aix-en-Provence was competent to prepare it . . . If the last session was dated late, all the others bore their proper date, hence there could be no confusion.

M. Mayer then answered M. Patin, retracing the content of his appeal, amplifying it with precedents and leading cases. But he had no illusions, M. Patin was an experienced criminal jurist and would be followed by his colleagues. The advocate-general spoke last, forcibly hammering home the *rapporteur*'s conclusions. He even engaged in polemics with the journalists, whom he accused of having 'tried to dictate their view to the high court judges who had no need of lessons from anybody' – a sentence showing the atmosphere prevailing in the magistracy since the Digne verdict and Chenevier's inquiry. The attack by the press had shocked most jurists; the authority of the *res adjudicata* is a sacrosanct principle.

After two hours of deliberation President Battestini read out a decision based entirely on Patin's statement of the case. The appeal was rejected on every count; no further appeal was possible. The Digne verdict could now be overruled only by a presidential decree should a 'new fact' which might cast doubt on Gaston's guilt be discovered – by Chenevier, for instance.

That morning Gaston had received a letter at Les Baumettes prison signed by several of his children. 'Whatever happens, Father, be brave, as we all are . . .'

It didn't please the old man. 'It's me, not them, who'll have his head under the blade,' he growled. 'They don't give a damn about me.'

Of all the members of the family Léon Dominici devoted himself with the most practical enthusiasm to saving the condemned man. This nephew, raised at Grand'Terre and settling later in Franche-Comté, had given touching evidence about his childhood, and the affection he retained for his uncle dedicated him to his vindication. On his own initiative he retraced the investigation, compiled a dossier, went to see the journalists more or less favourable to his cause, carefully studied the circumstances of Elizabeth's death, and ceaselessly stoked up the clan's energies, aided in this by the two women most fiercely pledged to their father's rehabilitation, Augusta and Clotilde.

He very soon realized that all his efforts ran into the same obstacle. The family's unanimity, which might impress public opinion and the investigation, lost much of its strength because of Clovis's defection. The good reputation he enjoyed, the sturdiness he had given proof of at the assizes, the impression he gave of living out a tragedy, meant that however much admiration the solidarity round the condemned man might evoke, it was Clovis who was believed. Léon decided therefore to go to see his cousin. Until now their relations had not been close. Léon was a good deal younger than Clovis and, as often happens when generations overlap, Clovis called Léon his 'nephew'. By the time Léon had come to Grand'Terre Clovis had already left.

Léon sought out Clovis one Sunday morning in his vineyard where with his wife he was tying back the vines. The two men shook hands, embarrassed to find themselves face to face, looking at each other like strangers. There was misunderstanding right from the start; Léon wanted to ask Clovis to forget the past and act as if it had never existed. For Clovis it had stopped definitively at November 13, 1953. But Léon was determined to convince him.

Clovis put his hands on his hips and his wife drew nearer. 'I wanted to ask you,' said Léon, 'if you would come to Grand' Terre.'

Clovis slowly shook his head. 'Never.'

'They'd like to talk to you,' persisted the young man.

'After all they've said!' Rancour thickened the linesman's voice.

'Exactly. Why stay on bad terms?'

'I won't go.'

Léon thought it useless to insist. When Clovis said no he meant it. Grand'Terre was not only the place where they assembled to curse him, it was the scene of his childhood, the centre of memories he had had to betray, the house where he had found out about his father. Too many painful associations now clung to those walls.

'Then can they come to you?'

'I've never yet thrown anybody out,' said Clovis.

'This afternoon?'

'If you like.'

At 4.0 p.m. two cars stopped at Clovis's little house in Peyruis and out got Léon, then Gustave, Augusta, Clotilde Araman and her husband Aimé, the younger Gaston and Marie Dominici, Marcel and his wife Victoria – all those fighting for their father. M. Bottaï brought up the rear. Clovis frowned when he saw him. 'I said the family only.'

Léon spoke up on the lawyer's behalf; he had taken the dossier in hand, his presence would be helpful. But Clovis stood firm. 'We're among ourselves, we'll stay among ourselves, he shan't come in.'

M. Bottaï yielded at once; Clovis's position, he said, was logical. He withdrew and Clovis led his relatives into the kitchen. In an uncomfortable silence each found a place in the narrow room.

'Clovis,' said Léon, 'we must save Father.'

Clovis shrugged. 'I'd very much like to . . .'

'You know an inquiry is about to begin?'

'So I've read.'

One by one he regarded his relatives, distrustful, remembering the insults he had endured in silence.

'If you are questioned, what will you answer?'

'What I always have,' he said, stiffly and unhappily.

'You're not thinking of retracting?'

'Not at all.'

All their eyes were on him, the initial discomfort growing by the second. There was no doubt what all those looks said.

'If Father has his head cut off it will be your fault,' a voice cried.

'It wasn't me who accused him.'

Gustave stared at the floor.

'You're the only one who's doing it now,' Gaston challenged.

'I'm doing it because it's the truth and you know it.' Little by little Clovis was giving way to anger. 'You can do what you like, I'm not budging.'

'You're a coward,' said another voice.

Clovis turned livid. 'What would be cowardly would be to retract.'

Until now each had restrained himself in the hope that the meeting would achieve its purpose, that Clovis would yield and after apologizing rejoin the family circle. He had shown himself intractable; it was therefore useless to deal gently with him. All the grievances rose to the surface and the family conference turned into a squaring of accounts.

'And your gun?' demanded Gaston. 'The one with which you boasted you could shoot rabbits at 150 metres?'

338

'You know very well I never had one,' retorted Clovis.

'You're lying.'

'You know perfectly well I'm not. When I spoke of shooting rabbits at 150 metres it was with the Russian sub-machine-gun at the Perrins'.'

The weapon was one of those seized after the beginning of the investigation during the police raid of August 1952. But as far as the Dominicis were concerned, Clovis was merely trying to confuse the issue between the sub-machine-gun and the Rock-Ola. And when one of them still accused him of denouncing his father in order to shield himself, he burst out, grabbing Gustave by the jacket, 'Tell them it was you, damn it!'

Gustave protested, then gave up. 'I was beaten,' he said.

'It's not true and you're lying,' cried Clovis.

Léon separated the two and tried what he could do in his own quieter way. 'You made a mistake in reporting your father's words. He said, "They've killed the three of them," and not "I killed the three of them."'

It was one of the points raised at the trial, one the family intended to raise again during the second inquiry, and it was essential that Clovis should back them up.

'It's not true,' he returned. 'He said, "I killed them."'

Shouts, insults, threats followed. Clovis was accused of having been paid the reward by the police. 'Sébeille gave you a million,' Gustave snarled.

This time Clovis wouldn't be held. Snatching up a chair he hurled it violently across the room. Gaston barely dodged it. The incident put an end to the family reunion, which would be the last.

Save necessarily during the second inquiry, Clovis would never again see his brothers and sisters, except for Germaine Perrin who suffered the same ostracism. The last thread that bound him to the family had just been broken. For him it was a lacerating subversion of his whole life, a divorce from the memories dearest to a man's heart, those of childhood; isolation, the sacrifice of a love, and of a mother who henceforth refused to see a son who had turned his back on them. Later Clovis would speak with nostalgia of the old woman as if she were no longer alive. 'She was very good,' he was to tell Chenevier, 'I loved her very much.'

The second inquiry was to be a torture to him: the confrontation with his brothers, Gustave especially, the pretext for fresh quarrels which could only reawaken his grief. It would have been easy to be reunited with those close to him. One word was all it would have taken. Who would have blamed him if he had spoken it?

A new examining magistrate had been appointed since the reopening of the case. Roger Périès having been promoted to magistrate at Marseilles, a young magistrate from Digne took over: 30-year-old Pierre Carrias, a sportsman, strong-minded, aware of his duties, and determined to hold the reins of the investigation. As the law required, Chenevier and Gillard were only his auxiliaries.

With the dossier in his hands for the first time, Carrias decided as his first step to have Gaston Dominici interviewed again by a colleague in Marseilles, one of the most noted examining magistrates of the time who already had a number of celebrated cases to his credit. Jacques Batigne was a former lawyer who had joined the magistracy after the Liberation. He was a man of wide curiosity, unconventional, forever looking for the deeper motivations of those who came under his examining eye, endowed with both subtlety and human warmth. He accepted his commission with enthusiasm, the Dominici case having fascinated him. However, he limited himself for the moment to two undertakings: hearing the condemned man and recording his words, and summoning Gustave and making him repeat his statement in his father's presence.

The divergence between father and son was total, as might have been expected. Gustave did not admit having had the conversation with Yvette which his father attributed to him. He stuck to the version he had offered at the assizes: he had known nothing before 5.0 a.m. Jacques Batigne left it at that for the time being, his only aim now was to establish initial contact. Before proceeding, however, he had to wait until Chenevier and Gillard had begun their researches.

It was on March 16 that Pierre Carrias saw the two officers and heard the account they had already given to two successive Lord Chancellors.

'We are not at all sure that Gaston Dominici learned the circumstances of the murders through the conversation he overheard,' Chenevier told him. 'But his statement does have an interesting facet; Gustave was outside at the time the crime was committed – something which he asserted several times during the trial. Put that against Gustave's, Yvette's and Roger Perrin's lies. They are explicable only if they were perfectly aware of what happened during the night.'

The officers added a small piece of information they had just acquired. Despite the pause in the investigation while the matter was before the Court of Cassation, they had already made some routine checks. One had taken them to Dr Morin at Nice. It had been quite productive.

Dr Morin was the out-of-doors hunter who had early on turned up at the Nice police headquarters, prompted by a feeling for justice; he had resented it being said that the Dominicis were hostile to campers near their land. He had camped there in 1951, and Gustave had seen him one day and even invited him to join a shoot. Reading over this statement, Chenevier had an idea; sportsmen liked to talk about the weapons they owned. Perhaps Gustave had mentioned the existence at the farm of a carbine.

The doctor's answer had been more explicit than Chenevier had expected. 'I think I've even seen it,' he said. 'It was in a shed near the house.'

For Chenevier it was something to go on. Neither the indictment nor the trial had cleared up the mystery of the Rock-Ola, an object seen only by Clovis and – momentarily – by Gustave. The fact that Dr Morin had seen it could call everything into question once more. No one wanted to admit that he had ever owned it, even and especially Clovis. The doctor's evidence was a stone flung into the pond. If the Dominicis had shown him the weapon in 1951 it was because they were not on their guard, contrary to what had been said by their lawyers whose principal argument had been that anyone owning a military rifle doesn't keep it in a shed accessible to all.

At the same time the officer made the magistrate a promise that he would take up his quarters in Digne and work under his constant supervision. Every evening the magistrate would receive his notes, thereby being in a position to judge the right moment for his intervention. The aim would be to entangle the liars in such a web of contradictions that they would one day be obliged to tell the whole truth.

'I'll think about it,' Carrias replied.

On June 16 – two months later – he again summoned Chenevier and Gillard. 'I'm ready to give you a formal commission,' he said.

Chenevier had prepared the list of questions he intended to put to the witnesses; they numbered 450.

'I'd like to question Gustave and Roger Perrin myself,' Carrias said. He explained that he was afraid of what the lawyers would say to his delegating such wide powers to the police. Gustave and Roger

Perrin were the chief targets of this inquiry. It was useless to give the lawyers a juridicial pretext for hampering it.

'They will only be witnesses like the others,' replied Chenevier.

But the magistrate didn't give way. He asked time to study the officers' dossier and an appointment was made for the next day.

When Chenevier and Gillard next saw the magistrate, they found that he had changed his mind. His study of the questionnaire made him realize that the police officers were planning a virtually new inquiry. According to him, their commission was less extensive. It was limited to precise details and notably to Gaston's new statements. Chenevier and Gillard, on the other hand, were reopening the whole case, going over arguments which had consumed hours at the trial.

'A verdict exists,' Carrias summed up. 'It can only be disputed on the basis of new elements resulting from facts previously unknown or discovered only after the jury's verdict.' In other words, it was not for Chenevier to call in question Sébeille's investigation or the indictment, still less the trial itself. He must restrict himself to the 'revelations' of the condemned man and to what he could discover using them as his starting-point.

Chenevier protested: the job couldn't be done piecemeal. The old man's statements cast doubt on everything that had been said – and especially on the lies of his relatives. The discussion grew heated but Pierre Carrias could not be moved; in these circumstances he would not issue the formal commission. Chenevier and Gillard left for Paris.

So, having already stirred up and divided so many, the Dominici affair now stirred up and divided the whole judicial body. It struck at the roots of the entire judicial system. Criticism already made of the handling of other cases was powerfully reinforced by the handling of this emotive issue. The public was going much farther than those pleading for the reopening of the inquiry in search of accomplices. That an old man of seventy-seven was wrongly condemned to death was openly denounced as a scandal, and the magistrates were roundly accused of wanting at all costs to protect an appallingly inadequate dossier.

For any jurist, still more to those called on to give judgments, the safeguarding of the law involves the unconditional acceptance of verdicts rendered. To obtain the annulment of a verdict, a 'new fact' must be produced which offers overwhelming proof that the jury made a mistake; a fact as irrefutable, say, as a confession by the real criminal.

In the Dominici affair the majority of magistrates felt that the Lord Chancellor, pressed by public opinion, had 'fallen in step' too obligingly. Nothing really contradicted what had been heard at the trial. The accusations of the old man were too vague to be taken seriously. The credit they were given seemed exaggerated, insulting to the first investigators and especially to Périès. A man under sentence of death was believed and honest judges suspected. The controversy grew heated; the whole magistracy ranged itself solidly on the side of their repudiated young colleague.

The jurors who had pronounced the verdict were less categorical. They had not put a single question during the trial, but now they spoke. Interviewed by Marcel Montarron, a journalist known as a historian of notorious crimes, they expressed themselves in general favourable to the fresh inquiry. 'We have been criticized,' said Marcel-Jean Bernard, for instance, a farmer at Saumane, 'but what else could we do? We aren't learned, we're ordinary enough. They asked us to answer yes or no. We could see we were dealing with a pack of liars, all of whom knew what had happened on the night of the crime. We judged by their attitudes. No one, including the old man, was disposed to tell the truth. Our conviction has not changed: the old man was the real culprit . . . It is possible that he did not kill the child Elizabeth. We hoped up to the last that he would change his attitude . . . Our conviction was formed and the speeches could not change anything. We hope that the new inquiry will tell us the whole truth.'

Patiently Léon Dominici set about building up the strength of the vanquished side, sustaining the morale of his own, pressing the witnesses, fostering opinion, dedicating himself to his uncle's cause. It was he who had the idea of appealing to one of the highest moral authorities of the French bar, the Paris *bâtonnier*,[1] the former deputy for the Seine, Marcel Héraud. It was he who also found a lawyer already considered a leading criminal expert, René Floriot. Héraud also retained the original defence counsel.

In July a shock offensive opened. It took the form of a press conference by Marcel Héraud. He did not mince words. He had just come from a visit to an important magistrate in Aix-en-Provence

[1] For this there is no English or American equivalent. The title is given to the president of a body of lawyers attached to a particular court, hence the leader of the bar. (*Tr. note*)

whom he did not name but whom many took to be the chief prosecutor himself, and he felt that the magistrate's remarks should be publicized. M. Héraud had expressed surprise at such long delay in giving Chenevier and Gillard a formal commission.

'I encountered,' he said, 'a reaction which seemed to me beneath criticism. The magistrate considered that for the Minister of Justice to send two police superintendents, MM. Chenevier and Gillard, to institute an inquiry, implied a distrust on the part of the higher authorities of the court's verdict. The presence of these superintendents, the investigation they conducted, and the fact that at the end of it an examining magistrate had been named to seek out complicity in the crime had created unrest in the prosecutor's office, the magistracy and the court.

'Of course I want to make no charges against anyone,' M. Héraud assured his audience, 'and I don't want what I say to be taken as showing my disapproval of the machinery of justice. But the first answer I received was "Ah, Chenevier and Gillard, we don't want them. Give us the names of two other officers, no matter who, we will use them but not these." I tried to make this magistrate understand that if I suggested the names of other officers and if MM. Chenevier and Gillard were set aside it would appear that they had been impugned because they knew things which it would be preferable to ignore.'

It was another stone in the pond. Such a declaration by a *bâtonnier*, the abandonment of traditional reserve, the transfer to the public forum of conversations always regarded as confidential was cause for more scandal. But a few days later Chenevier and Gillard were granted a formal commission. It disappointed them, certainly, for it was confined to one single angle: how Gustave and Roger Perrin had spent their time on August 4 and 5. But it was better than nothing and the two officers left at once for Digne, loaded with a mountain of files.

A statement to the press by a deputy prosecutor, Louis Pagès, greeted them. It was ambiguous. It announced that 'an important step forward has been taken,' which was perhaps a slight word of welcome to the police officers. But it was primarily intended as a tribute to Sébeille and Périès, 'without whose toil, perseverance and fairness nothing that we have done and shall do could have been accomplished.'

The most revealing passage was to come: 'After having received the lawyers' suggestions it seemed to us of interest, before entering upon the second part of our inquiries, to hear the first investigators because we are anxious to neglect no elucidation on any point whatsoever. They have supplied us with useful information on the behaviour of certain persons, which once more proves with what conscientiousness they have studied the tragedy and its protagonists.'

In plainer language, this meant that Pagès had had a long talk with Sébeille and Périès and that all three had discussed Gustave and the others. The superintendent and the magistrate had renewed their efforts to unveil the lies and reduce the contradictions. They had been no more satisfied than Chenevier had been at Gustave's zigzag course.

Chenevier and Gillard set to work. Their first visit, they decided, would be to the condemned man.

13

Gaston now lived in a room rather like that in a modern hospital. He had reverted to his familiar costume, the trousers and jacket – and even the black hat which he put on when he expected a visit. This was how Jacques Batigne found him, sitting on his bed, when he came to see him in preparation for the interview with Chenevier and Gillard. The niceties called for the police officers to question Gaston Dominici with a magistrate as intermediary. Jacques Batigne was chosen because he had already interrogated the prisoner in March.

'Well, Grandad,' said the magistrate, 'seems to me you're doing better and better.'

Gaston shook his head, his expression surly. 'You're wrong, my good sir.'

'You were in bed last time I saw you. Now you're up and about like a young man. You can even look at the countryside.'

The prisoner's eyes turned towards the barred window. 'I don't much like this countryside.' The magistrate sat on a stool while Gaston, taking up his stick, walked back and forth between the bed and table.

'What I don't much like,' said Batigne, 'is Gustave's character.'

'Nor me!' returned Gaston.

In a relaxed, conversational tone the magistrate began his interrogation. Did Gaston confirm his statements of December, particularly about the dialogue he had overheard between his son and daughter-in-law?

'I told the truth,' Gaston maintained.

'There is, however, one odd fact,' the magistrate said. 'My colleague at Digne didn't want to leave anything to chance. He went to Grand'Terre and saw the layout of the rooms. He even carried out an experiment with Gustave and Yvette to find out if you could hear them. His conclusion was that you couldn't.'

Gaston didn't seem at all put out. 'Of course! They knew the magistrate was there, but they didn't know I was listening. That makes quite a difference, doesn't it?' He was almost indignant: were the magistrates really so simple-minded as to place any value on such an experiment?

'Tell me what Gustave and Roger Perrin did that night.'

'But I don't know anything, my good sir. If I knew I'd tell you, and I wouldn't be here.'

Jacques Batigne expressed his surprise; by his statements after the verdict Gaston had sent the law into a spin. Two successive Lord Chancellors had been upset, two of the best police officers in France had been mobilized. Now the author of all this upheaval coolly declared that he had nothing more to say. Who was he kidding?

'I am frank and honest.' The condemned man tranquilly trotted out one of his favourite expressions.

Had he seen Gustave and Roger in the lucerne field or not? Was Roger carrying the child?

'Not at all,' Gaston replied, as if the very mention of such a circumstance were new.

'You said so several times.'

Gaston shook his head without getting angry, looking the magistrate serenely in the face. Jacques Batigne admired the impressive candour the old man seemed to radiate. He couldn't have handled the matter better. 'I couldn't have said that because I hadn't got up.'

'Your logic is crushing,' the magistrate commented ironically.

Jacques Batigne discovered, like others before him, how true it was that with the Dominicis words took flight. It was incontestable that Gaston had said before lawyers and police officers the words recorded in various reports. He had forgotten them and they had left no impression on him. He had dismissed them, therefore they did not exist, had never existed.

'After getting to know him better,' Batigne wrote in his memoirs, 'I can affirm that he expressed himself very well when he wanted to and that his lucidity left nothing to be desired . . . At what point he told the truth is not for me to judge, but when he did not tell it, it was because he did not want to and not out of any verbal or mental confusion.'

Next day Chenevier and Gillard revisited the inmate of Les

Baumettes in Jacques Batigne's company. The magistrate spoke first. He reminded Gaston that if the police officers were in the room, it was as the result of his statements. But he had withdrawn them. What was one to think?

'Simply that I'm innocent,' the prisoner answered.

Chenevier was not discouraged. He didn't launch a frontal attack, which would have been useless with a customer quite capable of repeating for hours in front of a white horse that it was a superb chestnut. Instead he fell back on the questions he had prepared: at what time had Roger Perrin arrived if he had slept at the house? Had Gaston heard Gustave speak to anyone when he arrived on his motor-cycle after going to see Faustin Roure? Who had gone to inspect the landslide, Gustave alone or with someone? Was Gustave in the habit, when Roger Perrin was alone, of going to fetch him so that he might sleep at Grand'Terre? Chenevier's tactics were plain: skirt the lies and contradictions, accept them provisionally, while drawing his own inferences until the final moment when even a Dominici would be obliged to recognize the improbability of his position. Whether that moment would ever come was another question. Chenevier was an optimist who believed in reason and its presence, even if imperceptible, in all men's minds. With patience he hoped to awaken it in Gustave and the others.

So far as Gaston was concerned, the victory was not immediate. His refrain was, 'I don't know, I didn't see anything, I can't say anything.' Why this sudden change? Who had made him withdraw his accusations? Chenevier put off examining this problem. 'That's all for today, Grandad,' he said, 'but we'll meet again.'

'I count on it,' responded Gaston as the officers and the magistrates left.

Neither Chenevier nor Gillard lost any time. Their days began at 8.0 a.m. and seldom ended until late at night. The first witness on their list was Faustin Roure, now retired. Had he instructed Gustave to survey the landslide from close up? Had he passed by the Perrin farm the morning of the 5th for a litre of wine, as Roger claimed? Chenevier strove to keep within the limits of his commission: how the two suspects had spent their time. But at times he was obliged to overlap this boundary.

One can hardly blame him for this, for with a dossier of this scope it was now impossible to isolate any one event since each involved a thousand built-in details. With Clovis, for instance, Chenevier openly tackled the question of whether he had suspected his father or his brother, when and why.

'I repeat,' Clovis said, 'that as soon as I saw the gun, I realized that it was someone at Grand'Terre. I thought of Gustave because I could not see my father running after a child. I was not convinced until my father accused himself one evening.'

Nor did Paul Maillet retract. He put one hand on his heart and raised the other as if swearing an oath. 'I'm the father of a family,' he said. 'Do you think I'd accuse Gustave of lying if it wasn't true? He has two children, after all.'

Chenevier proceeded with the encirclement of his prey. His greatest hope lay in Gustave.

In the course of his career he had interrogated vicious and resourceful crooks capable of the most bare-faced lies. In his opinion Gustave wasn't in the same class with them; he wouldn't hold out. The one thing he left out of his calculations was that there was an essential difference between Gustave and gang leaders: in their clashes with the police the gangsters remained prisoners of a system in which they participated, so to speak, like other auxiliaries of justice. Words had the same meaning for them as for their questioners. Gustave and his kin, on the contrary, were a law unto themselves; they abided by no rules but their own when it came to words. Chenevier didn't know what was ahead of him.

On August 10 the major offensive began. Yvette and Gustave were brought to police headquarters at Digne. Gillard took charge of Yvette, Chenevier of Gustave. Yvette repeated with her usual vivacity the statement she had made at the trial.

'One thing worries me,' said Gillard. 'Your statement to the magistrate Périès on December 18th, 1953. That day you said that Gustave got up after hearing the shots and that he had seen his father who admitted to the crime. And you cried out, you, Yvette Dominici, "We're ruined. What will become of us?" '

Yvette straightened up, her face already flushed with anger. 'It's a lie!' she said. 'The magistrate made me say it.'

Gillard expressed his scepticism: magistrates are not in the habit of forcing witnesses to lie. But Yvette stood by her accusation. 'He had Gustave sent for,' she asserted, 'and my husband told me to say the same as he did. When we were alone the magistrate warned me that if I said anything else it would go hard with Gustave. I was afraid . . .'

Gillard interrupted impatiently. 'I don't believe a word you're saying. No power on earth can make anyone lie so terribly. If the Dominici family had nothing to do with this affair you had only to tell the truth. That's what the magistrate wanted.'

The answer came pat. 'My father-in-law has been condemned to death and yet he's innocent.'

'He even accuses you!'

Voices hard, faces strained, the officer and the young woman stonily confronted each other. 'He'll say anything,' she retorted.

Yvette of course denied that the Englishwoman and child had come to the house, and especially that Roger Perrin had been ordered to lie about it. Moreover, the boy was not at the house that night. In short, everything that had been said or suggested since the trial was false; Yvette knew nothing about it.

'I know,' Gillard said cuttingly. 'You didn't even think of going to see whether anything could be done for the child – you, the mother of a family. You counted on her being dead.'

Yvette turned pale, but the moment of shame was soon past. She repeated that they had acted very badly towards Gustave and that his admission had been extorted from him. 'The police told him it was him or his father, but it was better it should be his father. They kept harping on his father's drinking, his tattoo marks, his loose life. For his father it would mean an old people's home; for him, having his head cut off and the children made public charges because they would put me in prison too.'

Meanwhile Chenevier was tackling Gustave, starting with a brusque warning: he did not intend to let go until he had the whole truth. The crime originated at Grand'Terre, that was obvious to everyone. The conspiracy of silence had existed since August 5; Gustave's own statements acknowledged that he and Yvette had decided between them never to say that they had heard the screams.

'Because it was a detail of no importance,' Gustave replied.

The answer set the tone for what Chenevier might expect from him. Gustave was being himself. It needed a furious assault, like that of November 1953, to make him abandon his own comfortable ground. Chenevier didn't intimidate him.

It did not take the officer long to realize this. Gustave this time surpassed himself. Chenevier had heard some pretty tough liars in the course of his long career, but Gustave beat the lot. The superintendent was particularly struck by the superb ease with which he proffered the most staggering enormities.

It was when Chenevier brought up the arrival of the Englishwoman

350

and child at the house that Gustave really got going. He had admitted the fact on November 12, 1953, in the presence of Roger Perrin. But when the superintendent reminded him of this, Gustave assumed an air of astonishment. 'Are you sure of what you're saying?' he asked.

'There is a record.'

'I told the boy off, I called him a liar, so I can't say the same as he did.'

'Are you saying that Superintendent Sébeille faked it?'

Gustave nodded emphatically. 'Probably,' he said. With absolute serenity he recounted what, according to him, had happened; Sébeille had faked a confession to obtain Yvette's, then he had done the same with Gustave.

'Do you want that statement recorded?' asked Chenevier in an attempt to warn Gustave of the possible consequences of being prosecuted for contempt of court.

'I'm telling the truth,' Gustave said.

His interrogation lasted the whole day. Chenevier took him out to lunch at a restaurant with the promise that they would not discuss the affair while eating. At the end of the afternoon Gustave was well back into his stride again and casting doubt on the magistrate Périès. Had he or had he not admitted to Périès that he had risen at 4.0 a.m.? 'You told the magistrate so on November 13th,' Chenevier pointed out.

Gustave seemed to make a great effort at recall. 'November 13th, did you say? I don't believe the magistrate questioned me that day.'

Without a word Chenevier held out the record. The farmer glanced at it absently. 'It's possible,' he admitted.

'You confirm what you told him?' the superintendent asked with no great hope.

'Not at all. I told the magistrate that I'd had enough of being knocked about. I asked him to accept the truth. He took a pencil and began to write, then he laughed and said, "No, no," and handed me back to the police.'

Chenevier didn't pursue the matter and went on from there. Without meaning to, Gustave betrayed himself, revealing unwittingly why he 'forgot' the interrogation of November 13, and did not remember that Sébeille had then drawn up the report of his accusations against his father. The only thing he recalled was his confession to the magistrate the next day – after Clovis had talked. It was a desperate, childish attempt to prove that he had not been the first to crack. Another thing on his mind was the moving of Lady Drummond's body. He had not touched it, he said, pressing Chenevier hard to write down what he was saying. If he had admitted it, it was due to being beaten. 'I said what they said.'

'Then they might have made you say that you were guilty.'

'They kept repeating it wasn't me.'

'One guilty or another, what did it matter to them?'

Gustave found no answer to that except that 'it was they who had written the deposition,' though granting that they were justified in basing themselves on what Clovis had said to him. Similarly, if in the course of the preliminary examination he had repeated that his father was guilty after having retracted, it was because Roger Périès had threatened him; there had to be a guilty person among the Dominicis, and if it wasn't Gaston it would be Gustave.

It was 2.0 a.m. when Chenevier decided that he had no more questions to put to Gustave. The whole dossier had been gone over: the report of the interview filled fifty closely written pages. 'What strikes me most,' he said, 'is that you seem to be reciting a lesson. The same words are to be found in all the Dominici family's depositions. As for your accusations against the magistrate, I confess that it is the first time in my life that I have heard them in this form. I am used to hearing police officers insulted, but not a magistrate.'

Chenevier pleaded with Gustave, 'Tell the truth. Is your father innocent or are you lying – which I should understand – to save him from the guillotine?'

'We had nothing to do with the crime,' Gustave repeated.

During the night the superintendent had him conducted back to Grand'Terre. Gustave's statements created a new situation. In challenging the records the farmer cast doubt on the whole dossier. Since he refused to engage in any discussion taking these documents as a point of departure, he blocked the entire inquiry. Chenevier came to his own definite conclusion; the abscess had to be drained, Gustave must be confronted with Sébeille and Périès.

Next day the superintendent reported the situation to Pierre Carrias. Carrias asked for time to think it over. While awaiting his decision, Chenevier and Gillard returned to Paris. The first round had ended in a draw.

After weighing the matter for a whole month, Pierre Carrias opted for a limited confrontation: to question Gustave, and confront him with Sébeille but not disturb Roger Périès, now magistrate at the civil tribunal at Marseilles. The dialogue between the farmer and the magistrate had taken place in circumstances no one could challenge; in public at the Basses-Alpes assizes. Périès had given short shrift to Gustave's complaints of violence and the farmer had remained silent, declaring only that he had been well treated by the magistrate. If there was a time when he might have lodged accusations it was then. They would have had vast repercussions. Gustave had taken great care not to. Pierre Carrias considered that Gustave's silence at the tribunal justified the present operation.

He summoned Gustave to his office; it was September 19, 1955. The farmer sat down lumpishly on the chair the magistrate indicated, showing no disposition to co-operate. Carrias had his dossier at his fingertips.

The magistrate remarked that they had failed to appreciate the significance of Gustave's admission that the motor-cyclist Olivier had been right.

'I don't understand this transcript you're showing me,' Gustave protested.

Carrias handed over one after the other the interrogations Gustave had undergone. 'I signed a lot of things that did me harm,' he observed without the slightest irony.

Leafing through the records, Gustave came to the remarkable days of November 1953. 'I still don't understand how I came to sign all that,' he mused.

'Then all the details you gave are false?'

'Absolutely.'

'You said to the magistrate Périès that he had been like a brother to you.'

'That didn't stop him from putting pressure on me,' Gustave maintained.

The next day he found himself facing Superintendent Sébeille, whom the magistrate had sent for. The superintendent was now a bitter man who had resumed routine duties, overlooked and forgotten. All important tasks passed him by. The Legion of Honour was far off, like the promotion he had not received. He had been deeply hurt by the behaviour of Chenevier and Gillard, who had not even tried to see him.

Gustave refrained from putting on airs with the superintendent. He hardly dared look at him, smiling to give himself countenance.

'Well, Gustave,' said Sébeille, 'it seems I've been guilty of faking.'

'What I mean to say is . . .'

The magistrate interrupted. 'Gustave Dominici, did you accuse your father to Superintendent Sébeille? Yes or no?'

The farmer considered a moment. 'I don't think so,' he said finally.

Sébeille remained calm; he had seen so much of this. 'Look, Gustave, you don't remember. You wept and put your head on my shoulder.'

Gustave put his hand to his forehead as if the memory had suddenly come back to him. 'Maybe so,' he conceded.

Carrias seized his opportunity. Did Gustave withdraw his accusation which Sébeille hadn't invented? The magistrate picked up the statements of November 12. He re-read the details and Gustave confirmed them; he had really spoken such words. He had repeated them to the magistrate.

'Then why did you say the contrary to Superintendent Chenevier?' demanded Sébeille indignantly.

'With that sharp accent of his I didn't understand a word he said.'

Sébeille hadn't done any faking, Gustave acknowledged, he had reproduced his exact words, but they had been uttered when he was at the end of his strength. Exhaustion alone and the wish to have done with the interrogation had been responsible for them. He had never known if his father was guilty or not because he had not got up. In short, the records were correct but they contained only lies. Sébeille's honour was safe but not his dossier. They were back to square one. Like a hunted animal, Gustave had gone to ground in the nearest cover. Sébeille left Digne wishing good luck to those who still nursed the illusory hope of extracting a shred of truth from this man.

Chenevier had received the formal commission he had been asking for since January. Nine months had gone by. They had certainly reduced the police officer's chances. But Chenevier did not lose heart. The Dominici mystery fascinated all who dreamed of solving it. Like Sébeille before him, Chenevier read and re-read the dossier in an attempt to discover some truth he had missed. After receiving the formal commission authorizing him to re-examine the matter from top to bottom, he packed his bags and left by train with his colleagues, Charles Gillard, two senior police officers, Leclerc and Goguillot, another officer, Gaumery, and Inspector Mouillefarine. He had a plan of attack based on the weapon, a new angle stemming from the deposition of Dr Morin of Nice.

354

The doctor stood by his deposition unreservedly. He had been invited to Grand'Terre, and over a drink had enjoyed discussing with the Dominicis the mutual passion of hunting. A young lad was present who might have been Roger Perrin. They had talked about guns and Gustave had taken him to a shed to show him the carbine with which he shot boar; it resembled the one used in the crime. Dr Morin left the farm with the promise that a hunt for big game would be arranged for him the following year.

Gustave again appeared before Chenevier. The witnesses, whether members of the family or not, stood no chance with him; he was in agreement with none of them. He had certainly met Dr Morin when he was camping near Grand'Terre. But the doctor had never come to the house. He could therefore not have seen a firearm kept in the shed.

'Then how did he know there is a reproduction of Millet's *Angelus* in your father's kitchen?'

It was among the questions set as traps by Chenevier, who had asked Dr Morin to describe the place. Gustave was nonplussed for a moment, annoyed at being teased with unforeseen details.

'I can't explain it,' he said.

'Nor I,' commented Chenevier ironically.

Gustave was confronted with Dr Morin. 'Why should I hide the truth?' asked the doctor. 'In the early days of the investigation I came forward on the side of the Dominicis because they were said to have acted rudely to campers.'

For Gustave the position was simple. Sincere thanks to the doctor for defending the family, but otherwise he belonged with the other falsifiers who had done him so much harm. He ended on a despondent note: 'They always want to make me out a liar and I'm only telling the truth.'

Chenevier then turned to Clovis. The investigators from Paris worked at police headquarters at Digne, not in the Palais de Justice like their predecessors. The correspondents returned; most of them had covered the first inquiries. They were sceptical of Chenevier's getting results. Many of them stood up vehemently for Sébeille, to whom they still felt friendly.

The scene of the interrogations was a narrow office. It was permanently lighted by a lamp, for in order to prevent photographs by telescopic lens Chenevier had lowered a rice-straw blind. Resigned but suffering, wondering if his purgatory on earth was to consist of repeating until his last breath the statements he had made in November 1953, Clovis faced the superintendent. For two whole days he answered questions covering practically the whole case. Adhering to the tactics he had adopted, Chenevier used the carbine as a lightning conductor. He was in fact following Sébeille, who from the beginning had declared to all that 'the weapon would speak', though unfortunately not knowing how to apply the formula when the occasion arose. This similarity of approach, deliberate or not, seemed to demonstrate that it was the key to the riddle. But it may have been too late now.

Clovis repeated that he had recognized the weapon in Sébeille's hands on August 8, but had not wanted to believe in his father's guilt. Then why, Chenevier queried, had he first stated on November 13, 1953, at the time he admitted to Sébeille that he knew the murderer, that he had never seen the carbine? What was the point of this useless lie? Clovis shrugged his shoulders. It was one of the rare distortions of the truth he had committed. Why?

'I'm still wondering,' was all he said.

'Nor do I understand,' Chenevier went on, 'why your father was carrying the rifle in the middle of the night. He hadn't gone shooting for a long time.'

'That's true,' Clovis acknowledged. 'He might have gone back for it,' the implication being, after he had quarrelled with the Drummonds. But he had asked for details neither from Gustave nor from his father, horrified by the brutal crime. Moreover, he had never dared ask questions about the origin of the weapon when he had seen it one day, a year before the crime. He told himself that it had come from the Maquis and let it go at that. 'Luckily I never took it,' he said resentfully. 'I've been harassed enough as it is.'

Had he accused his father because he was angry with him for obscure reasons to do with the inheritance, having never borne him any great affection? Clovis protested energetically. That's what his brothers and sisters said, Chenevier reminded him. 'Bring them along, I'll make mincemeat of them,' Clovis snarled.

Had he told his brother Marcel that he would 'never retract nor retreat an inch'?

'Certainly,' answered Clovis sharply.

'To sum up,' said Chenevier, 'you stick to your accusation. You refuse to admit that you may have been mistaken when your father said in dialect, "I'm the one who killed the three of them." You're infallible, in short.'

'If I denounce my father it is because it is the truth,' Clovis said vehemently. 'I sometimes thought it was Gustave. If I knew it was, I'd say it as well. I realize now that some things are anything but clear in this case, seeing all he denies.'

'Which things?'

'I tell you I don't know anything, otherwise I'd speak up.'

Chenevier badgered Clovis. How had he been able to keep it to himself after his father blurted it out at the very time Gustave was in prison? Why hadn't he ever mentioned it to any other member of the family?

'Because my father asked me not to.'

Then there *had* been a conspiracy! Hadn't it subsequently been turned round, Chenevier suggested pointedly, uniting Gustave and Clovis in accusing their father and sending the police on a false trail? Clovis stood up to the attack well. From the day he had first spoken he had never varied. Did they think it was an easy thing to have condemned his father?

But his trials were not yet over; the next day Chenevier arranged to confront him with his brothers and sisters one by one. It was the grand scouring, the ultimate clash, and Chenevier and Gillard would referee, hoping always for some revealing flash of light out of the pitiless family battle.

Augusta: 'I am ready to forgive all the harm he has done us. But let him say why he kept the secret after Father spoke to him, if it's true.'

Clovis: 'It was up to Father, not me. It was his secret, not mine.'

Chenevier pointed out to Augusta that her father accused Gustave. Why believe him when he proclaimed his innocence and refuse to listen when he named someone else?

'Because he offered no proof,' she was quick to return.

Marie was the one to whom Clovis might have said after his father's arrest that 'it was better that an old man should go to prison rather than a young one.'

'I never said that,' Clovis protested.

'So I invented it?' Marie retorted.

Marie affirmed that no inmate of Grand'Terre was involved. On what did she base this conviction?

'On plain speaking,' she asserted without batting an eyelid.

And the condemned man's accusations?

'He's old,' she replied. 'You can make him say anything you like.'

With Gaston, the lock-keeper at Saint-Auban, things really deteriorated. It was regarding the visit in a body which Léon

Dominici, the nephew, had organized in March 1955 to bring Clovis back into the bosom of the family – a disastrous visit. Clovis recalled with bitterness that Gaston had accused him of receiving a million francs from Sébeille.

'I never said that,' declared Gaston. 'I said that since the beginning of the business I had run through 200,000 francs and you answered that I was a damn fool, because you had gained from it.'

Out burst the insults, and before Chenevier or Inspector Goguillot, who was at the typewriter, could stop them, the two were at each other's throats. A general scuffle followed in which the police took part, Clovis coming out of it with a black eye.

Now it was Yvette's turn to answer Chenevier's questions. She pretended not to look at her brother-in-law, ignoring him completely. Yvette declared that in the car which had taken them from Grand'Terre to Digne after the visit to the shed on November 14, Clovis had said that he had learned of his father's guilt from his own confession to him and not on August 8 from Gustave. It was always the young couple's concern to place Gustave second in the sequence of denunciations. Clovis retorted that it was a lie; that day he had revealed to Yvette that Gustave had shared his secret with him from the beginning. Otherwise this particular exchange passed off without incident, Yvette remaining cold and contemptuous to the end.

And at last Gustave. Chenevier took some precautions when facing him with Clovis. An inspector stood behind each man ready to intervene – a wise measure because several times it looked as if the brothers would come to blows.

The quarrel obviously related to the carbine which Gustave claimed he had never seen. How, then, had he pointed out to Sébeille the place where it used to be kept? Gustave reverted to the explanation he had given at the trial: Clovis had made him do so with the help of a sketch. Clovis was swift in denial. There was a dredging up of all the stale recriminations: the New Year's party at which Clovis had been present, saying nothing, the apéritif he had gladly taken with their father, knowing him to be a murderer, the inheritance he coveted. Doggedly, as if everything really revolved around this, Gustave maintained that he had never confided to Clovis that their father had killed the English family.

'It's all due to him,' he declared. 'While we were still in the car going to Grand'Terre he said, "Don't be a damn fool, say that the old man went out to shoot badger, otherwise we'll be there for a week."'

Clovis reddened with anger. 'Swine!' he exploded. 'I never said that. But there were others who egged you on.'

'If anyone egged me on it was you,' Gustave retorted. 'And we're in a fine mess through listening to you.'

Chenevier returned to the very start of the affair. He tried to find out if on the morning of August 5 there had been an understanding between the brothers. But he ran into a brick wall. Gustave even challenged the testimony of the motor-cyclist Olivier and then came up with a new line. 'It is up to you to prove that I lied,' he said insolently.

It was nearly midnight. Chenevier had no more to gain from the confrontation, but he had still some questions to ask Gustave. 'You will come back tomorrow,' he directed. 'Yvette as well.'

As October 1955 drew to its close, Yvette and Gustave were to endure for the last time the harassment of interrogation they had now undergone for over three years. But they no longer suffered, or at least there was no outward sign of it. They knew as well as the police the weakness of their position. Their answers were ready. They knew they would have some bad moments but these would not last for ever. All they had to do was to wait patiently for the others to tire. If they were branded as liars, the name had become familiar to them. One got used to everything.

Yvette repeated that the magistrate Périès had 'forced me to speak' on December 17, 1953. Chenevier went hard for Gustave. 'One thing is plain,' he told him. 'If your father was condemned it's your fault and not Clovis's. I won't go into that again. So we can go over the whole dossier taking that for granted. You've been a coward, since you asked the magistrate never to say that you had accused your father. You then convinced your family that the traitor was Clovis. But with the police you never tried to hide behind him.'

Gustave's reactions were always unforeseeable. 'It's true,' he said. 'I still wonder why, when I accused my father, I didn't mention Clovis.'

Chenevier listed Gustave's lies. He had plenty to choose from. Gustave listened impassively. He had only discovered the murder at 5.0 a.m. and they would never again budge him from that. If there had been a plot it was between the police and Clovis, whom they paid to confirm Gustave's admissions.

'You're the one,' Gustave confided, 'that I'm telling the truth to for the first time. I heard my father's guilt spoken of only after I came out of prison when Clovis was cutting wood with me and repeated what my father had told him.'

'And was it then you decided to protect yourselves if necessary by accusing your father?'

'Certainly not. But there'd have had to be a family council,' Gustave retorted.

'Every time you've been suspected, you've accused your father,' Chenevier observed.

'I've never been suspected,' replied Gustave indignantly.

He was caught in the trap of his own contradictions, and Chenevier pulled him up unceremoniously. 'You *were* suspected; that was how you explained away your wife's statement in December 1953, the one where the magistrate said to her, "It will go badly for you."'

'That's true,' Gustave allowed. 'That day I was suspected.'

It was no more than a transient victory for Chenevier; Gustave was done with concessions. But the superintendent was not letting him go without a warning. 'Your answers are absurd,' he said crisply. 'They can only strengthen my doubts about you. Our present job is finished, but I tell you outright that I believe in your complicity.'

It didn't bother Gustave. 'My father and I are innocent.'

'Yet you yourself condemned him,' murmured Chenevier.

'I've told you the truth . . .'

These were Gustave's final words. The last serious effort to entangle him in his own inconsistencies, begun in August 1952, all but ended with this interview. When Gustave left police headquarters at Digne at about 8.0 p.m. on October 25, 1955, to return to Grand'Terre, Chenevier may still have had hopes that he might one day catch him. But he may also have realized that he had an expiring dossier on his desk. As a police matter, the Dominici affair was nearing its end.

At Les Baumettes prison Gaston had organized his life. His routine at the infirmary much resembled that of an old people's home, outings excluded, where the inmates are closely supervised. A very young nurse, blonde and gentle, looked after him. It was she who in the morning brought him the hot drink that passed for coffee.

He read, smoked his pipe, mused by the barred window from which he could see the chalky hills of the Marseilles landscape. He did not get used to it. His eyes were used to the green of the oak-planted slopes of Provence; this was too white, colourless, decomposed, like death. He disliked it.

Chenevier and Gillard visited him, accompanied by the magistrate Batigne. They added the last pages to their dossier. Where did Gaston now stand with regard to his revelations? Dressed in his invariable jacket, pipe in mouth, trusting in himself and the weight of his words even if they totally contradicted yesterday's, he denied having told Chenevier that he had seen Roger Perrin and Gustave during the night in the lucerne field, coming from the camp site.

'I heard you say so myself,' snapped Chenevier, finger pointed to ear to emphasize that he had not dreamed it.

'Then I must have been out of my mind,' said Gaston.

'Your fate is at stake, don't forget.'

'I didn't go out, I didn't see anything.'

'And the conversation between Gustave and Yvette?'

'Yes, I heard that.'

'They deny it.'

'Well, they're wrong.'

What was he getting at now? Yielding to family pressures in one instance and protecting himself in the other? Had he decided it was better to have seen nothing, thereby proving that he had been snugly in bed? Another maze for Chenevier to struggle through. He brought Gustave and his father together again, but he could have spared the effort, the two men jogging round in circles insisting monotonously, the one that he had heard the conversation, the other that it had never taken place.

Clovis saw his father for the first time since he had been sentenced and was deeply moved. Gaston seemed touched to see the man to whom he owed the verdict at Digne, but he quickly recovered and the two exchanged steely looks as Clovis repeated that his father had one evening confessed to being the murderer.

'You ought to be ashamed,' growled the prisoner.

'I've always told the truth,' Clovis maintained, his face as if ravaged by his own words. And turning to Chenevier, 'For months and months I had to go over and over what I knew. I wish I'd never heard or known that it was my father who killed the English people, but he told me so and I can't say otherwise.'

'You want to save somebody else.'

'Who?' asked Chenevier.

'If only I knew!' answered Gaston.

The most pathetic scene occurred when the statements were

signed and Clovis was about to leave. He turned to his father, who was sitting on the edge of his bed, and in a low, controlled voice urged him in words recorded by the magistrate Batigne: 'Listen, Papa, I tell you once more, for the last time, that what I did was not done to harm you. If I had wanted to do that I would have spoken the first time I saw the carbine and I didn't. You told me that it was you who killed the English people. I wish it wasn't true. So tell M. Batigne it isn't true, that you lied to me, tell him you didn't kill anybody, but don't say that you didn't tell me because you did.'

Gaston Dominici seemed not to hear. Clovis and he would never see each other again.

The interview with Roger Perrin degenerated into farce. The grandfather and grandson agreed on nothing, not even the most insignificant detail, as if even a fleeting corroboration would be a wound to their self-esteem. They exchanged the vilest abuse on whether they had been together when Gaston first saw the child's body. Why, when it didn't matter? For good measure Roger Perrin threw in that on that morning his grandfather had turned his back on the gravel patch when going off with his goats, while on other mornings his way led in that direction.

'You little swine!' shouted Gaston.

Bursting into laughter, in excellent humour, sure of himself, Roger Perrin teased the old man. 'Well, go ahead, Grandpa, if you've got anything against me, now's the time to tell it.'

The youth asserted that he had not been at Grand'Terre. It was therefore impossible that Gustave had spoken of him with Yvette. The old man insisted that he had heard everything, it was the very day Gustave had been ill after the first interrogation. Roger guffawed, 'Maybe he had good reason to be ill. They questioned me too, but that didn't stop me from eating and sleeping.'

The last to be brought face to face with her father was Augusta, the loyal one. Like those who had preceded her into the prison infirmary, she was to find herself at odds with the prisoner. And despite herself, Augusta furnished an argument to those who believed there was only one guilty party.

She was being questioned about the conversations she had had with him at Les Baumettes. Had he repeated to his children the words of the conversation he might have overheard and what had they thought of them? In the course of several rejoinders the tone grew bitter. Gaston declared with rancour that 'you all wanted me to pay for others'. Augusta pulled him up sharply. 'I have always defended you, but what you are saying isn't true.'

'It is!'

'Then why didn't you say so at the trial?'

'Because I thought I'd be acquitted.'

'It's not true,' Augusta erupted. 'A few days before the assizes I went to see you. You said, "They're going to be nasty."'

'I never said that,' he stormed back, outraged at being crossed by one of the womenfolk in whom he had put confidence.

Wanting to press the argument further, Chenevier was in the same dilemma that had plagued all the investigators from the start; with the Dominicis one had either to accept that they had a different truth for every day in the year or else tirelessly reconstruct the sequence of events by filling in the holes. Neither method ever seemed to get anywhere.

At the end of November Chenevier and his team returned to Paris. They now had to mull over what they had collected. They arrived in the capital with a heavy load of documents, impressions, hypotheses and deductions, but also with a few new concrete facts. The most important without doubt was the disappearance of the Drummonds' camera. Chenevier was the first to express surprise that the inquiry had overlooked this curious circumstance. While ticking off the list of articles found with their belongings, he had stopped on coming to a roll of film. A film surely implied a camera. Where was the Drummonds'? The Marrians, asked about it, replied that there had been none in the suitcase left by their friends at Villefranche-sur-Mer. Therefore it must have been stolen after the murder. But by whom? The murderer? His accomplices? Chenevier's immediate thought was that someone had wanted to remove a snapshot of Grand'Terre which would prove that Lady Drummond and Elizabeth had visited the farmhouse. He associated this disappearance with that of the canvas bucket, still unexplained. Certainly there was not enough new in the way of hard facts to warrant a retrial, but there was enough to seek further information. On this basis Chenevier began composing his report.

At the end of February 1956, Superintendent Chenevier submitted his report to his superior, head of the Criminal Investigation Department. His conclusion was that the investigation undertaken against X should be pursued. He indicated what lines to follow, the search for possible accomplices. He emphasized that in his opinion nothing could be accomplished unless a confrontation were first arranged between Gustave and the magistrate Périès. It had to be determined whether the farmer would persist in denouncing as false the record of an interrogation vouched for by as reputable an authority as an examining magistrate.

Pierre Carrias's answer came nine months later. He had done some checking of his own meanwhile; for example, he had demonstrated that from the courtyard Gaston could not have seen Gustave and Roger Perrin in the lucerne field. But in November 1956 he signed the document which definitely closed the dossier as then established. It had the force of a final judgment. From then on, only the confession of a guilty person could contradict it. The decision was received with general indifference; for a long time now no one had believed that the affair would ever be revived.

The overall grounds for the magistrate's decision were that the second inquiry had not produced sufficient new evidence to justify a reopening of the case. The most important element in Gaston's revelations had been retracted, namely, the presence of Gustave and Roger Perrin in the lucerne field. 'Disconnected', 'incoherent', topographically improbable, the revelations were altogether too vague to serve as a basis for the incrimination of anyone.

Gustave's lies were real enough, but nothing new, 'and in no way established his connection with the crime,' Carrias concluded.

In passing, the magistrate was more than a little rough on the Paris police officers. He accused them of having conducted a biased investigation. They believed they had deduced from a badly taken photograph that in November 1953 Gaston Dominici had not designated the same shelf as his sons for the position of the carbine; in fact the prints in the dossier did indeed show the sons pointing to the lower shelf and Gaston to the upper. But Sébeille explained the difference; it had been necessary to take several pictures and with a gesture of impatience Gaston had raised his stick a little too high.

Did the bloodstains near the cesspool point to Elizabeth having been wounded there first and then finished off on the bank? Carrias said no. Sir Jack had been mortally wounded in the liver, which bled copiously. The stains gradually diminished between the spot where the bullet had struck him and the place where he collapsed.

'On the contrary,' the magistrate considered, 'our present information, taking into account some fresh details about the trousers drying in the courtyard, serves to confirm Gaston Dominici's guilt;

it serves to exclude the complicity of Roger Perrin, whose attitude towards his grandfather and his Uncle Gustave, at times insolent, seems to establish that he did not fear any compromising revelation on their part; it offers no new element affecting Gustave, whose suspicious conduct and obvious desire to hinder the inquiry are only explicable by assumptions not necessarily implying his personal responsibility and not in any case sufficient to support a charge . . . '

The Dominicis learned of the result through the press. They scarcely reacted. At Les Baumettes, Gaston now only awaited the decision of President René Coty. On him alone his life now depended. But here too no one had any doubt; the oldest person ever condemned to death would not be executed. The reprieve came at the beginning of 1957, the sentence being commuted to life imprisonment. It aroused no comment. Forgetfulness had already set in.

It may seem foolhardy to try to put any order into a dossier like this. Forty months of investigation, examination and supplementary inquiry had swelled it to mammoth proportions and subjected it to considerable strain. Filled with sound and fury, containing unexplained and perhaps unexplainable passages, some of which defied even the most elementary laws of logic, it has with time become a sort of sacred monster of judicial history. These thousands of pages offer the archetype of the injuries truth may undergo when stretched on the rack of justice. In the Dominici affair every single level of the legal apparatus was at some point involved, and at each stage the critical observer could point to its defects and weaknesses. In this sense the case of the old Lurs farmer constituted a testing-bench for the engine on which all men may one day or another depend.

Which brings us to the essential question. Does the dossier reveal the basic secret of the drama? Does a sifting through the accumulated layers bring us anywhere close to what really happened that night of August 5, 1952? What, in fact, remains of the Dominici mystery?

Lacking any last-minute sensational development, a bona fide confession of guilt, the long and tortuous path ended in the decision of the magistrate Carrias. The one recourse left is to retrace it in an attempt to see clearly. The choice is limited to three hypotheses: that Gaston was innocent; that he alone was guilty; that he was guilty together with accomplices who went unpunished.

First the certainties. The murderer came from Grand'Terre, the weapon also. On the first point no doubt exists. The fiercest upholders of the old man's innocence do not dispute it. There is no lack of argument for it; the child's flight in the opposite direction from the farm, the conduct of its inhabitants, their lies, especially those of the first day, all point the same way. Only the family still maintains against all probability that the murderer came from somewhere else.

Only one member dissented, Clovis, but he told only what he knew, each time adding that one must have pity on an old man. He suffered torment, but in opposing him his brothers and sisters were not contemptible, rather the contrary. It would have been easy for them to bow to public opinion, to abandon their father when he was found guilty. But they never did. Such behaviour deserves respect, even if it implies a wilful blindness.

So far as the weapon is concerned, some, like Superintendent Chenevier, were less sure that it came from Grand'Terre. But it seems impossible that it could have come from anywhere else. The way the crime occurred – whoever committed it – shows decisively that the murderer must have had it immediately available. Moreover, what did Clovis do when Sébeille showed it to him on August 8? He hurried to the shed where he had seen it one day to verify that it was in fact the same carbine. Another testimony, Dr Morin's, though given late, spoke of a military weapon he had seen in the shed.

Another unassailable point: Gaston Dominici's admissions had value, less for their content than for the circumstances in which they were made and the support they received from the joint accusations of Clovis and Gustave. The chain of events by which the police succeeded in November 1953 in confounding the old man ends in a logically unimpeachable conclusion: Gustave's accusation; Clovis's resigned confirmation; Gaston's breaking down not when being harassed with questions but when quietly alone with the gendarme Guérino.

Even the course pursued by Clovis provides something of a clue. He began by saying that he had heard from his father's own lips his confession of guilt. He later admitted that he knew of it on August 8 from his brother. In his reticences, half-truths, Clovis was certainly no exception to the general Dominici rule. But why did he act like that? Quite simply because, like his brother, he was embarrassed at having known the truth from the beginning and stubbornly concealed it from the police.

One of the keys to an understanding of Clovis's conduct is his saying to his brother, on the night of November 14, 'It had to come to this.' For months he had hidden what he knew. That is why the accusations hurled at him – revenge, settlement of old scores with his father – are ridiculous. Having stayed grimly silent, Clovis spoke up only after Gustave. If he had wanted to take revenge on his father, it had long been open to him to harm him. He refrained; but once he had confessed, he never went back on it, still embarrassed by his long silence. It is in this light that Clovis must be understood.

Was there a conspiracy between the two brothers? A reading of the records indicates the contrary. If Clovis and Gustave plotted for a year and a half to send their father to prison, they had time to make up a consistent story free of discrepancies. They didn't. Basically they didn't know much about the tragedy itself, Clovis at any rate. They had, for instance, no explanation for the fact that their father had gone out armed during the night. If they had put their heads together, would they have left this circumstance unexplained? The sketch drawn by the clerk to indicate the weapon's location itself invalidates the idea of conspiracy; Clovis and Gustave would have had no need of it if they had previously reached an understanding.

On this basis, and with an eye on the dossier, some attempt can be made to reconstruct the events of the night of August 5. That evening Gaston, like all the inhabitants of Grand'Terre, was uneasy about the landslide. He did not have unbounded confidence in his son Gustave, who had, moreover, worked all day harvesting at a friend's whose help he was reciprocating and was therefore very tired. Gaston decided to have a look at the condition of the embankment; if the railway company had to be indemnified he would have to pay his share like anyone else. While he was out, he saw the English campers. Sir Jack had just got up; medical evidence showed that his bladder was quite empty, which proves that at 1.0 a.m., the time he was killed, he had just urinated. The two men quarrelled and Gaston, who was probably drunk – the joint statement of Gustave and Yvette on December 17 and 18, 1953 – went to get his gun. This was the tragedy.

Gustave was awakened by shots. Alarmed, he went downstairs. It was then, in the courtyard or the lucerne field, that he encountered his father, who told him briefly what had happened. For the next few hours Gustave continually went back and forth between the scene of the crime and the house. When he saw the child on the bank she was still alive. It was 1.30 a.m. at the latest, which coincides with the medical findings of the doctors who conducted the autopsy. The lawyers for the defence doubtless preferred the conclusion of

Dr Dragon, who did not take part in the autopsy but simply examined the bodies superficially. But the opinion of the forensic experts has a higher value.

What did Gustave actually do? It was undoubtedly he who searched the car and moved the bodies, but there was no sordid motive in this. Gustave was not a thief. What he was looking for might well have been the camera; it is very possible that the evening before Lady Drummond and Elizabeth had taken photographs of the farm they had visited. To the little girl, camping in the French countryside and seeing the peasants at home was a novel experience. Her instinctive response was to preserve a memento of it on film. But for Gustave it was a connection to sever. He had already decided that the only tactic was to appear to know nothing, not only of the tragedy but of its victims, to have merely glimpsed them and taken little notice. There was no need to be a specialist in criminal investigation to guess that the police would turn first to Grand'Terre. Gustave expected to be suspected, interrogated, harassed. He looked for the cartridges, his father having told him that he had picked up only four. He was afraid. They were, as Yvette was to say, 'unlucky'. The day of the 5th could bring only ruin and disgrace.

Gustave's whole future attitude stemmed from the help he gave to a murderer, who was his own father. He lied and was compelled to lie in order to save his family; he could never shake loose from his original commitment. Constantly forced to give way under the pressure of other testimony – that of Olivier, Maillet, Ricard, Roger Perrin – he became confused, contradicted himself, stumbled, until the day when he coldly decided to deny even what he had signed, to dispute even that he had been questioned on a date on which he divulged the truth. But his moment of truth did indeed fall, like Yvette's, on December 17, 1953. The proof is that subsequently the couple struggled to explain their statements by the pressure the magistrate Périès put upon them, a contention even their lawyers disregarded; it assumed a dishonesty on the magistrate's part nothing short of preposterous. For if certain oversights by the magistrate might be criticized, his integrity certainly could not be. Roger Périès was, by unanimous consent, a man of the highest professional scruples. Perhaps too much so; to an extent this accounts for the defects in his preparation of the evidence. From an examination of the dossier it appears that on December 17 and 18 he came very near the essential truth of the Lurs tragedy.

Are Clovis's lies, or rather silences, to be explained in the same way, particularly with regard to the weapon? The experts' report on the oils established a possible connection between Clovis's guns and the carbine used in the murder. It seems almost certain that all the members of the family had at times used the Rock-Ola, which was an attractive firearm for hunting boar and gave its user the prestige to which all sportsmen are sensitive. This is why Clovis stubbornly denied throughout the proceedings that he had ever fired the weapon. Caught in his own lie, he could not later withdraw it for fear of arousing suspicion. Yet if there is one point on which there is unanimous agreement, it is Clovis's innocence. No one accused him, not even his father. But during the examination the linesman had everything to fear if he admitted that he had used the Rock-Ola to hunt boar after having declared that he had seen it only in the shed.

As for Roger Perrin, it is not impossible that he had slept at Grand'Terre. Captain Albert always thought so because of Gustave's bicycle found leaning against a tree. But did Roger Perrin's presence imply his participation in the crime? And were his lies explicable by any complicity whatever? Gustave, learning of the crime and its perpetrator, would surely hasten to rouse the boy, give him the bicycle and send him home to prevent his being involved in the affair. The bicycle's presence next day would be accounted for by Roger's returning with it, which in turn would account for his thousand and one inventive lies. As for treating him as an accomplice, if it is granted that he spent the night at Grand'Terre, no material or psychological factor justifies this hypothesis.

Now to come to Gaston Dominici's own admissions and submissions, which to some extent contradict this reconstruction. What are they worth, and how much of them can be accepted?

First there is an important observation to make, insufficiently emphasized in the polemics that followed the trial. The minutes of the proceedings of November 13, 14 and 15 show plainly that neither Sébeille nor Périès dictated or even suggested his statements to Gaston. Paradoxically, the magistrate and the superintendent have been reproached both with telling the old man what he should say and with accepting from him utterly improbable affirmations. But such reproaches are mutually exclusive. Either the officer and the magistrate substituted themselves for the suspect and edited the minutes as they went along, making them correspond with the material evidences they possessed, or they listened in silence and recorded whatever came into Gaston's head. This is probably what happened.

The complaint that can be made against Périès is that on this occasion he paid too much attention to the old man's words. He wanted to keep their 'spontaneous' character, not point out their enormities – the sexual encounter with Lady Drummond, for instance. By accepting this improbable motive, the magistrate effectively inhibited himself from later establishing what was indubitably the real motive, the one that came out while Gaston was talking to Guérino: a sudden stupid row, a misunderstanding in the night. It would perhaps have been better to try to bring him back to this more acceptable explanation, which is without doubt the true one.

During the preliminary examination and the trial the lawyers stressed that Gaston's story in no way corresponded with the circumstances of the murder as revealed by the inquiries. They therefore refused to allow the confession any corroborative value. But two observations must be made. The first is that the admissions of a criminal never or hardly ever coincide exactly with reality, even in a case where his guilt is established. A murderer is the witness of his own crime; why should he be immune to those lapses of memory or of the senses which affect anyone reporting what he has seen or heard? The Lurs affair took place within a few moments. It was the result of emotion, panic and perhaps alcohol. Is it surprising that Gaston Dominici should have retained only an approximate recollection of the events?

There was also an element of calculation. Why should he have gone for the motive of 'lechery', responding to the suggestion of Superintendent Prudhomme, except to prepare the way, if not for a justification, at least for the motive most likely to win sympathy, a crime of passion? Gaston Dominici had a cunning mind, and it was not necessary to be a dialectical genius to perceive that, even if one confessed, it was better to mingle truth and falsehood; one could always plead doubt, or at least ambiguity. When Gaston Dominici declared that he had fired only once at Lady Drummond and felled the child with one blow, it is obvious that he was trying to lessen the fury which had actually been unleashed. On the other hand, if he was innocent, how could he state that one bullet only had been fired at the fleeing Elizabeth? Gaston's admissions thus represent part of the truth. They cannot be wholly disregarded.

They are all the more valid in that they cannot really be replaced by any other solid fact. It is curious that the same commentators who hold these admissions to be invention are ready to credit the old farmer with telling the truth in his disclosures of December 1954, after the verdict. For if his confessions can be disputed, what value can be placed on the later disclosures unconfirmed by anything in the dossier? In the event they contain only one new item: the conversation between Gustave and Yvette about the 'jewels'. But no jewels belonging to the Drummonds had disappeared, apart from a watch of no value. There had been no robbery and the dialogue attributed by the condemned man to his son and daughter-in-law is unsubstantiated. As for Gustave and Roger Perrin's presence at the site of the crime and the scene Gaston claimed to have witnessed, he had retracted, even declaring that Chenevier had been dreaming. When the superintendent took him up on it, he answered that he 'didn't remember anything about it'. It is interesting to speculate how Gaston came to bring Gustave and Roger Perrin into it in the first place.

The starting-point is a premise which has been put forward from time to time. During the preliminary examination and then at the trial, when his sons were in the box, Gaston indicated Gustave and Roger Perrin as the murderers, but without adducing any evidence; he accused without accusing, claimed to know no more. It was hardly a tenable position considering that for years he had been the despotic master of Grand'Terre, that Gustave and even Clovis were cowed by him, and that he had always jealously insisted on respect for his authority. If he was innocent and Gustave or Roger Perrin guilty, is it credible that he would not have demanded to know what had happened? Is it possible that they would – could – have refused to tell him? The inescapable answer is that if he himself was innocent, he was perfectly aware of the truth.

Did he sacrifice himself as has sometimes been suggested? He hinted at it often enough. But this generous interpretation is belied by his actual conduct; from the beginning he accused. Not only did he deny his own guilt; he implicated Gustave while refusing to say why and how he knew him to be guilty. Does this indicate that he could not elaborate because he would thereby incriminate himself? Did he remain vague because anything more explicit would implicate him along with his son and grandson? Was he the prisoner of a truth which would crush him in crushing others?

Such an analysis is absurd. If it was so, why did Gaston risk accusing not only Gustave but Roger Perrin? Of course he had nothing more to lose, having been condemned to death. But from the moment he could foresee that his tactics were doomed to fail, why use them? They fell short and the only result was that Roger defied him to his face: if he had something specific to say against the boy, let him say it. He didn't, and the argument turned against him. Again, the explanation is simple: he had no means of pinning any part of the guilt on Gustave or Roger.

But it is striking how his accusations made use of the substance as well as the chronology of the inquiry and the indictment. Gaston cunningly exploited what he read in the dossier and heard at the trial. Gustave in the field? Paul Maillet had just said so. Roger Perrin at Grand'Terre? It was what the lawyers maintained in the course of the hearings. The carbine patched up by Clovis? There was the similarity between the oils. The child carried to the bank? It was the chief dispute at the trial. He did not begin to accuse Roger Perrin until the end of the preliminary examination when stress was laid on the youth's lies. Attentive and alert, Gaston Dominici made up his story little by little from material supplied by the dossier and the events of the hearings.

In all probability, then, Gaston alone was guilty. How does it happen that controversy still continues and many still proclaim themselves unconvinced? Should one applaud unreservedly those who helped lay the foundations for the eventual verdict? Are Superintendent Sébeille and the magistrate Périès beyond reproach, and did the former in particular pay with unmerited disgrace for what was in reality a victory? He brought the guilty one to punishment. He thus discharged his task and succeeded brilliantly in a case which roused public opinion to fever pitch, yet his career was broken by what should have been its culmination. Was Sébeille the victim of a judicial error when he in fact prevented one?

'A crime clumsily committed, an inquiry clumsily pursued, a trial clumsily conducted, a defendant clumsily judged,' wrote an English journalist.

A severe verdict. It is easy to refight lost battles and consign to perdition not only beaten generals but those who missed a decisive victory. This was doubtless the case with Sébeille and Périès. Their mistake was to pass up certain opportunities which might have allowed them to deliver a knock-out blow instead of winning on points. The author of this book was among those who at the end of the trial were not satisfied. Like many of his colleagues, he had doubts. Having rechecked the inquiry, re-read the dossier, he has changed his opinion.

The tragedy of the police officer and the magistrate was not to have grasped the opportunities that were offered. There were on the first day the trousers neglected by Sébeille. In his memoirs the superintendent expresses a doubt of their existence. But Inspector Girolami surely did not invent them. An expert examination of the freshly washed garment might have supplied the material element the investigators lacked. Among other objects which escaped the superintendent's attention was the camera, whose disappearance would have explained the search of the car.

Then Clovis falling to his knees on the railway line at sight of the carbine and Sébeille not immediately realizing and pursuing the implications, although he had declared that 'the weapon would speak.' From this distance it is possible to say that on that day the investigation foundered; the fifteen-month delay it suffered began at that moment. At the beginning of September Sébeille was robbed of another chance when, having cornered Gustave thanks to Olivier, the interrogation was broken off by order of the chief prosecutor.

British journalists have often claimed that in England the Dominici case could not have suffered the same delays and uncertainties. They maintain that detectives from Scotland Yard would have got on with the police work and skipped the psychology. Their criticisms are not altogether unjustified.

For instance, the famous shred of flesh found on the bumper whose origin was so vehemently argued at the trial. Did it come from Sir Jack's hand, torn off by the gunsight he had clutched? It was impossible to say because it had been lost. Yet in his memoirs Sébeille coolly reveals that he had kept it as a souvenir, not including it in the dossier because he did not think it could provide any information.

The same applies to the Rock-Ola; no one thought of finding out why the murderer had ejected unexpended one cartridge in two. Sébeille and Périès had deduced that Gaston Dominici, ignorant of its operation, had reloaded it each time though it functioned automatically. In his book *Judicial Errors*, René Floriot strongly criticized this deduction, stressing that an expert had detected on the unexploded cartridges faint traces of percussion. There had therefore been some other complication, but of what sort? The answer is not in the dossier because the question was never put to a firearms expert. It would seem that the murderer had used cartridges whose calibre did not exactly correspond to that of the weapon, thereby blocking the automatic functioning. But in the absence of an expert check this is only hypothesis.

Finally, in November 1953, shouldn't Sébeille have taken advantage of Gustave's breakdown when he collapsed on his shoulder? It was 2.45 p.m. Only at 4.30 did Périès record the statement. Gustave had had time to reflect. Similarly, on November 14, Gaston went back on his confession and accused his son. Why were the two not at once brought face to face? In the atmosphere of that moment it might have been possible to achieve some positive result.

It is necessary to recall these lost opportunities not to reproach two men who otherwise gave proof of unstinting dedication, but to make clear why public opinion could be so shaken. Justice arrived at the truth by doubtful means. In war the only thing that counts is the last battle, but it is sometimes hard to forget those lost before then. Whether through honesty, whether because they were misled by the family's incredible lies, Sébeille and Périès left huge holes in the dossier. Yet despite everything, they probably arrived at the truth. Convinced they were right, they imagined that their conviction was transmissible. The jurors were persuaded but public opinion was not. That is the lesson of a strange and terrible story.

Epilogue

In the courtyard of Les Baumettes, between the high pale walls, there are gardens belonging to the guards. In the garden was a prisoner. From their barred windows his companions could see him in the evening watering the vegetables and flowers, removing a weed, reviving a plant. Gaston Dominici had found his career; he had become the prison gardener. As time went on he had acquired a title, that of the oldest convict in France.

He was not unhappy. At any rate he seldom complained. He had only one grievance against prison regime, and that he repeated to all his visitors whether lawyers, doctors or magistrates: the cooking was done with ground-nut oil, margarine or other vegetable fat, whereas there was only one good way and that was with olive oil. So at times he was given a treat: as thanks for looking after the vegetables so well, the guards would slip him a ratatouille, aubergines and courgettes exuding the delicious smell of the olive press.

Gaston should really have been at Cognac, the institution set aside for elderly convicts. There had been some question of sending him there. 'Is it far?' he asked.

'Quite far.'

'In the Bouches-du-Rhône?'

'In Charente.'

'Then I won't go.'

It was not for a prisoner to determine his place of residence, but Gaston, perhaps because he was a good gardener, had his way. He stayed on at Les Baumettes, where he had the impression that the wind sometimes brought him the scents of his Haute-Provence.

At times his mind clouded. For days he remained silent or uttered only incoherent remarks, mingling the events of his youth and his trial, introducing into his case people long dead to whom he assigned a mysterious role. Then he came to as if he had just woken up. He

375

plunged into reading, devoured Victor Hugo ('A bit old-fashioned'), made a stab at Gide ('It's deep'), was disappointed by Jean Giono ('He doesn't understand anything about the Basses-Alpes').

In 1960 a television programme obtained permission to bring its cameras into Les Baumettes for a long interview with the prisoner. Gaston agreed with complacency. He resumed his personality of the simple patriarch whose wisdom had been refined by tribulation. He was innocent; he was frank and honest; he was the victim of a dark conspiracy. One of the viewers was a VIP. Moreover, Gaston's fate depended on him; he was General de Gaulle, President of the Republic.

Was there any connection between the broadcast and the decision shortly afterwards taken by the head of state? Did the sight of the old man move the General? Clemency being a royal prerogative, and as such requiring no explanation, no one can give an answer and the President was not a man given to publicizing his innermost thoughts. The fact remains that on July 13, 1960, he signed the decree which remitted Gaston Dominici's sentence and set him free.

The news created a sensation. Nor was it greeted with unanimous enthusiasm. A deputy for the Basses-Alpes, Gabriel Domenech, who had also followed the case as a journalist, put a question to the Minister of Justice who answered that no criticism could be addressed to the head of state who exercised a sovereign right. The mayor of Manosque, vice-president of the General Council of the Basses-Alpes, wrote: 'Nevertheless there is in the Forcalquier cemetery the body of a little girl. She has just been killed a second time.'

Gaston Dominici returned to Lurs in triumph. It had rained all morning, but when he got out of Gustave's 4 HP, driven by Yvette, the sun shone and the Durance sparkled. The whole family was assembled, grandchildren included, three of whom the old man did not know. But there were some absent ones: Clovis had died the year before of cancer of the liver and in any event would not have come. Germaine Perrin had never been reconciled with the others; Roger stayed away.

Amid a crush of photographers Gaston performed his first acts as a free man, kissing the Sardine who, like him, had aged considerably. They were dried out, bowed, the skin of Gaston's face was drawn tight over the bones, his colour had disappeared leaving in its place an ivory tint, his cheekbones protruded and his chin was a mere scrawny hook.

With his stick he thumped the old chestnut tree in front of the house, stroked the fig leaves, plucked a fruit, smelt it, went to sit down on the low wall where he had formerly liked to daydream, lit a pipe, smiled at Gustave's youngest son who was nearing seven and whom he was seeing for the first time.

'Are you going to live here?' asked the journalists.

He made no answer, but the next day he left Grand'Terre. He didn't want to remain there. Gustave and especially Yvette had saved the property, paying the expenses of the trial – 690,000 francs in all – by borrowing. But he no longer felt at home. Gustave had never come to see him in prison. Only the Sardine had come to pay him two or three visits. Between father and son still loomed the memory of November 1953. Neither Yvette nor Gustave made any effort to keep him. He went first to his daughter, Augusta Caillat, at Sainte-Tulle. Then he lived for a while with Clotilde at Montfort. In 1962, his health having deteriorated, he was admitted to the old people's home at Digne where he could receive the necessary care. A little later the Sardine, who was in little better shape, joined him. A few yards separated the male and female wards, but when they met they no longer recognized each other. The past was dead for both. For Gaston his companion of fifty-five years was only a dark silhouette he did not distinguish from the other old women.

In April 1965, as the signs of spring appeared in the mountains, Gaston fell ill of congestion of the lungs. 'I've had it,' he told the doctor.

He asked to confess. It was the almoner, Father Audibert, who heard him and gave him extreme unction. On Sunday the 4th at 3.30 p.m. he died. Contrary to what he had promised, he left no will with one of his lawyers, or if he did, it has remained secret.

The whole family was present at the funeral. He was buried in the cemetery at Peyruis in the same alley as Clovis. The two graves are almost opposite.

Gustave and Yvette with their children sat in the front row. In the past year a great change had taken place in their lives; they no longer lived at Grand'Terre, which had been sold in 1964 to a young cabinet-maker from Marseilles for 45,000 new francs. Gaston Dominici had signed the deed of sale, being still the owner of the property. A variety of reasons had led to the young couple's decision, among them the steady decline in agricultural income. Gustave had preferred to become a mason, and moved into a little flat in Peyruis.

It was impossible to know what Gaston Dominici had felt on seeing the fruit of his life's work passing into other hands. He no longer loved Grand'Terre, perhaps because of the memories it held, but in refusing to live there any more, which ones was he fleeing? Those of a night of sudden folly or the bitter battle lost after fifteen months of resistance? Remorse or pride? Regret at having in a few instants destroyed fifty years of effort, or anger at not having had the better of his enemy?

Twenty years have passed, and life has resumed for all who appeared in this long-drawn-out drama. What has become of them?

Sébeille, after his testimony at the Digne trial, all but vanished into the shadows. For two or three years he continued as a member of the Marseilles mobile force, but he was no longer entrusted with anything but minor matters, having in his own words 'bungled the Lurs affair'. In 1958 he was relegated to a local police station where he dealt with domestic quarrels, petty thefts and drunken rows. He retired in 1962 after thirty-two years of service, and lives quietly between Marseilles and his country house in the Aveyron.

His colleague Constant did not stay long in active police work. Very soon he succeeded in procuring an appointment to a judicial commission, a post which installed him in the Palais de Justice at Marseilles, where he helped the magistrates with rapid investigations and the executions of various writs, acting as a link between the police and the judiciary. He often met Roger Périès, who through normal promotion became in about 1965 president of a superior court at Marseilles. Constant maintained his connection with Forcalquier and kept an eye from a distance on the destinies of the participants in the tragedy.

It was Gustave whose life underwent the greatest upheaval. In 1967 Yvette sued for and obtained a divorce. The news aroused some curiosity when it became known. Had the pair separated because they were incapable of sharing indefinitely a guilty secret? 'Not in the least,' Yvette answered shortly. 'But with age Gustave has become as domineering as his father. I couldn't stand it . . .'

She married a gendarme and at first lived in the region, but she soon moved away – the only one of all who played a part in the affair to do so. Gustave stayed on at Peyruis. He has never remarried. Nor does he ever answer questions about the drama that changed his destiny. He works as a mason, and is doubtless the only one now who could tell the whole story from A to Z. Probably he never will. For him and his brothers and sisters the death of the English family was to become a family matter which concerned no one else.

The Sardine long survived her husband. She was finally taken in by the Caillats, the most loyal of the family. Her memory failed rapidly, and she died at the beginning of 1974 aged ninety-five. She was buried beside the husband from whom she had been separated so long. The whole family attended her funeral, including Yvette, who made a final appearance at her former husband's side.

Roger Perrin has never married and is a butcher's roundsman at Peyruis. His mother Germaine, gravely ill for years, spends long periods in Digne hospital. She has never been reconciled to her family.

Faustin Roure, the railway foreman, has been dead for several years. But Paul Maillet is still hale and hearty. He is the only one who is willing to talk of the affair. He has no doubts. 'The old man killed the English people,' he keeps repeating. Any scepticism makes him indignant. Over the years he has acquired an up-to-date vocabulary and calls Gaston a 'Black Panther'. He and Gustave do not speak when they meet.

Grand'Terre did not become a service station as its purchaser, Pierre Bline, intended. It is now an inn bearing the signpost La Montagnière. Bline and his wife are very bitter at the suggestion that they tried to get publicity out of an affair that so stirred public interest. In fact, they kept nothing that might be regarded as a relic; for them, too, the past must be obliterated. Pierre Bline has built himself a workroom in which he practises his original trade of cabinet-maker. The corner where Gaston used to like to sit smoking his pipe is now a terrace where customers can lunch in fine weather.

A hundred and fifty yards away the mulberry tree, somewhat thickened by the years, throws its shadow over a patch of gravel which remains the same as when the Drummond family chanced upon it on the evening of August 4, 1952. Nothing has changed. The path leading to the bridge is perhaps a little stonier from being trampled by the curious on Sundays. For twenty years it has not been uncommon for cars to stop and passengers to get out and pace the few square yards in quest of sensation. A cross still stands where Elizabeth fell; it is often strewn with flowers. The grave of the Drummonds is carefully tended. The dead scientist, Lady Drummond and the child are not forgotten, either by the Marrians or the local people.

A few yards away the Durance flows with a force and colour which change according to the seasons. A wide sky is reflected in it. When night was falling twenty years ago an English tourist was tempted by the landscape for lack of any more attractive camp site. Enter an old man rightly proud of a laborious and upright life. Each believed that he saw in the other an enemy, a threat, a peril. It was a drama of mingled fear, anger and perhaps drunkenness. In its horror it resembled many another, but it started a chain reaction: a family met its death; another was shaken to its foundations; the judicial system was challenged at every level; doubt cast on all caught up in the resulting whirlwind. An old man strolling at night with a patched-up rifle released the fearful energy of which he was the final victim.

FOR THE BEST IN PAPERBACKS, LOOK FOR THE

In every corner of the world, on every subject under the sun, Penguin represents quality and variety – the very best in publishing today.

For complete information about books available from Penguin – including Pelicans, Puffins, Peregrines and Penguin Classics – and how to order them, write to us at the appropriate address below. Please note that for copyright reasons the selection of books varies from country to country.

In the United Kingdom: Please write to *Dept E.P., Penguin Books Ltd, Harmondsworth, Middlesex, UB7 0DA*

In the United States: Please write to *Dept BA, Penguin, 299 Murray Hill Parkway, East Rutherford, New Jersey 07073*

In Canada: Please write to *Penguin Books Canada Ltd, 2801 John Street, Markham, Ontario L3R 1B4*

In Australia: Please write to the *Marketing Department, Penguin Books Australia Ltd, P.O. Box 257, Ringwood, Victoria 3134*

In New Zealand: Please write to the *Marketing Department, Penguin Books (NZ) Ltd, Private Bag, Takapuna, Auckland 9*

In India: Please write to *Penguin Overseas Ltd, 706 Eros Apartments, 56 Nehru Place, New Delhi, 110019*

In Holland: Please write to *Penguin Books Nederland B.V., Postbus 195, NL–1380AD Weesp, Netherlands*

In Germany: Please write to *Penguin Books Ltd, Friedrichstrasse 10–12, D–6000 Frankfurt Main 1, Federal Republic of Germany*

In Spain: Please write to *Longman Penguin España, Calle San Nicolas 15, E–28013 Madrid, Spain*

In France: Please write to *Penguin Books Ltd, 39 Rue de Montmorency, F-75003, Paris, France*

In Japan: Please write to *Longman Penguin Japan Co Ltd, Yamaguchi Building, 2–12–9 Kanda Jimbocho, Chiyoda-Ku, Tokyo 101, Japan*

CRIME AND MYSTERY IN PENGUINS

Deep Water Patricia Highsmith

Her chilling portrait of a psychopath, from the first faint outline to the full horrors of schizophrenia. 'If you read crime stories at all, or perhaps especially if you don't, you should read *Deep Water*' – Julian Symons in the *Sunday Times*

Farewell, My Lovely Raymond Chandler

Moose Malloy was a big man but not more than six feet five inches tall and not wider than a beer truck. He looked about as inconspicuous as a tarantula on a slice of angel food. Marlowe's greatest case. Chandler's greatest book.

God Save the Child Robert B. Parker

When young Kevin Bartlett disappears, everyone assumes he's run away . . . until the comic strip ransom note arrives . . . 'In classic wisecracking and handfighting tradition, Spenser sorts out the case and wins the love of a fine-boned Jewish Lady . . . who even shares his taste for iced red wine' – Francis Goff in the *Sunday Telegraph*

The Daughter of Time Josephine Tey

Josephine Tey again delves into history to reconstruct a crime. This time it is a crime committed in the tumultuous fifteenth century. 'Most people will find *The Daughter of Time* as interesting and enjoyable a book as they will meet in a month of Sundays' – Marghanita Laski in the *Observer*

The Michael Innes Omnibus

Three tensely exhilarating novels. 'A master – he constructs a plot that twists and turns like an electric eel: it gives you shock upon shock and you cannot let go' – *The Times Literary Supplement*

Killer's Choice Ed McBain

Who killed Annie Boone? Employer, lover, ex-husband, girlfriend? This is a tense, terrifying and tautly written novel from the author of *The Mugger*, *The Pusher*, *Lady Killer* and a dozen other first class thrillers.

FOR THE BEST IN PAPERBACKS, LOOK FOR THE 🐧

CRIME AND MYSTERY IN PENGUINS

Call for the Dead John Le Carré

The classic work of espionage which introduced the world to George Smiley. 'Brilliant . . . highly intelligent, realistic. Constant suspense. Excellent writing' – *Observer*

Swag Elmore Leonard

From the bestselling author of *Stick* and *La Brava* comes this wallbanger of a book in which 100,000 dollars' worth of nicely spendable swag sets off a slick, fast-moving chain of events. 'Brilliant' – *The New York Times*

Beast in View Margaret Millar

'On one level, *Beast in View* is a dazzling conjuring trick. On another it offers a glimpse of bright-eyed madness as disquieting as a shriek in the night. In the whole of Crime Fiction's distinguished sisterhood there is no one quite like Margaret Millar' – *Guardian*

The Julian Symons Omnibus

The Man Who Killed Himself, The Man Whose Dreams Came True, The Man Who Lost His Wife: three novels of cynical humour and cliff-hanging suspense from a master of his craft. 'Exciting and compulsively readable' – *Observer*

Love in Amsterdam Nicolas Freeling

Inspector Van der Valk's first case involves him in an elaborate cat-and-mouse game with a very wily suspect. 'Has the sinister, spellbinding perfection of a cobra uncoiling. It is a masterpiece of the genre' – Stanley Ellis

Maigret's Pipe Georges Simenon

Eighteen intriguing cases of mystery and murder to which the pipe-smoking Maigret applies his wit and intuition, his genius for detection and a certain *je ne sais quoi* . . .

PENGUIN TRUE CRIME

A series of brilliant investigations into some of the most mysterious and baffling crimes ever committed.

Titles published and forthcoming:

Crippen: The Mild Murderer   Tom Cullen

The famous story of the doctor who poisoned his wife and buried her in the cellar.

Who Killed Hanratty?   Paul Foot

An investigation into the notorious A6 murder.

Norman Birkett   H. Montgomery Hyde

The biography of one of Britain's most humane and respected judges.

The Complete Jack the Ripper   Donald Rumbelow

An investigation into the identity of one of the most elusive murderers of all time.

The Riddle of Birdhurst Rise   R. Whittington-Egan

The Croydon Poisoning Mystery of 1928–9.

Suddenly at the Priory   John Williams

Who poisoned the Victorian barrister Charles Bravo?

Stinie: Murder on the Common   Andrew Rose

The truth behind the Clapham Common murder.

The Poisoned Life of Mrs Maybrick   Bernard Ryan

Mrs Maybrick died of arsenic poisoning – how?

The Gatton Mystery   J. and D. Gibney

The great unsolved Australian triple murder.

Earth to Earth   John Cornwell

Who killed the Luxtons in their remote mid-Devon farmhouse?

The Ordeal of Philip Yale Drew   R. Whittington-Egan

A real-life murder melodrama in three acts.